FREEDOM IN AMERICA

WITHDRAWN

William Ker Muir Jr.
University of California, Berkeley

Los Angeles | London | New Delhi
Singapore | Washington DC

CQ Press
2300 N Street, NW, Suite 800
Washington, DC 20037

Phone: 202-729-1900; toll-free, 1-866-4CQ-PRESS (1-866-427-7737)

Web: www.cqpress.com

Cover design: Stefan Killen Design
Composition: C&M Digitals (P) Ltd.

♾ The paper used in this publication exceeds the requirements of the American National Standard for Information Sciences—Permanence of Paper for Printed Library Materials, ANSI Z39.48-1992.

Printed and bound in the United States of America

15   14   13   12   11   1   2   3   4   5

Library of Congress Cataloging-in-Publication Data

Muir, William Ker.
    Freedom in America / William Ker Muir., Jr.
      p. cm.
    Includes bibliographical references and index.
    ISBN 978-1-60871-844-3 (alk. paper) 1. United States—Politics and government. 2. Democracy—United States. 3. Power (Social sciences)—United States. 4. Liberty. I. Title.
    JK275.M85 2011
    320.473—dc22

                                                              2011006950

I pray that you will grow up
to be a brave person
in a brave world. I pray
you will grow up to be useful.
Marilynne Robinson, *Gilead* (2004)

I'm full of optimistic expectations
of freedom coming to China in the
future, because no force can block
the human desire for freedom.
Liu Xiaobo, in his final statement
upon receiving the Nobel Peace
Prize, December 10, 2010, before
going to serve his 11-year prison
sentence for sedition

This book is dedicated to my wife,
Pauli Wauters Muir, whose counsel,
support, and love I treasure.

ABOUT THE AUTHOR

William Ker Muir Jr. was born in Detroit, Michigan, and earned his Ph.D. in political science at Yale University. He has taught at the University of Michigan Law School, Yale, and (for three decades) the University of California, Berkeley, where he served as Department Chair. He has also worked as an attorney, consultant to the Oakland, California Police Department, committee staff member in the California State Assembly, speechwriter for Vice President George H.W. Bush, writer in Governor Pete Wilson's gubernatorial reelection campaign, and weekly columnist for the Oakland *Tribune*. In 1996 he won the Republican nomination for his State Legislative District and proceeded to lose—handily—to his Democratic opponent. He has gained several awards for teaching, including the Berkeley campus Distinguished Teaching Award and the Northern California Phi Beta Kappa Association's Excellence in Teaching Award. He and his wife have two daughters and three grandchildren.

Other books by William Ker Muir Jr.:
Law and Attitude Change: Prayer in the Public Schools
Police: Streetcorner Politicians
Legislature: California's School for Politics
The Bully Pulpit: The Presidential Leadership of Ronald Reagan

CONTENTS

Part II. Institutions of Freedom   **135**

PREFACE

The spur to write this book was a phone call in 1989 from a faculty colleague, Andrew Janos, who had been born in Hungary. The Berlin Wall had just fallen, and so had the Iron Curtain, behind which for four decades the Soviet Union had barricaded the nations of Central Europe. Hungary at last was free of communist rule and was beginning its transition to democracy.

Professor Janos called to ask, "What books can I send my friends in the Old Country to explain how America works?" I struggled for an answer. My first thoughts turned to Alexis de Tocqueville's *Democracy in America*, so full of brilliant and prescient insights into American society in the 1830s. I also mentioned *The Federalist Papers*, the eighty-five essays composed by Alexander Hamilton, James Madison, and John Jay during the campaign for ratification of the American Constitution in 1788. I doubted, however, that *my* personal favorites were suited to *his* needs. While both those classics were uniquely insightful regarding the principles and tendencies of America's free society, I felt certain that they were dreadfully out of date and hardly descriptive of the workings of the contemporary United States.

Other, more current works on what made America tick came to mind, but all seemed too specialized for foreign readers. That was especially so for anyone whose experience had been confined to the kind of closed societies characteristic of the Soviet Union and its former satellites. Fine as these books were, they depicted particular institutions and events, but not the contexts that nurtured them.

I was surprised at the small number of accessible studies that surveyed America's wider political and social landscape. Moreover, those authors who had attempted to depict American society as a whole tended to examine it through what I thought was an excessively narrow prism of material equality. What Professor Janos's friends needed, I believed, was a book describing the personal freedom we in America enjoyed. And so I set out to write such a book.

I soon discovered that my notion of personal freedom was inadequate. Freedom was not simply being left alone; nor was it merely the freedom of thought and "individuality" that John Stuart Mill celebrated in his 1859 essay *On Liberty*. The opposite of freedom was not slavery, but *impotence*. Humans are social animals and need the assistance of others to achieve their every undertaking. *Personal freedom was power.* Unless individuals had the means to enlist others' collaboration in the pursuit of their goals, they were not free. Power and its distribution were the keys to freedom in America.

My focus became clear. The pivotal question to answer was how Americans—whatever their pursuits—exercised power. Both *Democracy in America* and *The Federalist Papers* spoke to that question. Suddenly, these books appeared as timely and relevant as the day they were written.

Of course, every kindergartner learns the basics of power and how to get one's way with others—by threatening (*coercion*), by give and take (*reciprocity*), by changing others' minds (*moral power*), or some combination of these three techniques. It takes considerable skill, however, to employ these techniques in the adult world, for power is a paradoxical thing. Untutored attempts to enlist collaboration frequently result in unexpected, unintended, and *unwanted* consequences for oneself as well as for others. To exert power adeptly—that is, to achieve desired results and minimize bad surprises—may require acting counterintuitively, in defiance of common sense. Therefore, to be truly free to pursue their happiness, Americans had to understand and negotiate *the eleven paradoxes of power.* Those who didn't, more often than not, would find themselves shackled to frustration and failure.

With that perspective, I returned to Professor Janos's question. What makes America work is the availability of political and economic institutions that facilitate the ordinary person's exercise of power. The nation's political system of checks and balances, its array of central and local authorities, its political parties that organize the opinions of the people, its independent media that inform and enable individuals to team up with one another, and its free markets that are secured by the rule of law—all these institutions make it easier for individuals to be free to choose their goals, gain assistance, and earn success.

Two centuries have passed since *The Federalist Papers* and *Democracy in America* were published—centuries in which the nation experienced a murderous Civil War, complex foreign entanglements, great waves of immigration, and astonishing technological developments. Remarkably, America's institutions still stand, extending personal freedom to its ever-growing population. The object of this book is to explain why they have "worked."

Acknowledgments

There are more people than I can name who have influenced this book—family and relatives, former teachers, faculty colleagues, public servants of every persuasion, clerics, and friends in the business and legal world. And I haven't mentioned those who over the years and centuries have taken the time and care to preserve their humane insights in books, articles, and poems. Thank you all.

There are, however, four particular acknowledgments that I want to make. First are the students I have had over a half-century of teaching at numerous universities, but especially the young men and women at the University of California, Berkeley, many of whom were first-generation Americans and who, by their stimulating questions, their embrace of life, and their commitment to becoming useful to others affected me more than they can ever know.

Next, I need to thank the reviewers of my manuscript, whose generous remarks persuaded CQ Press to assume the risk of publishing it: John DiIulio, University of Pennsylvania; Joel Lieske, Cleveland State University; Kenneth Miller, Claremont McKenna College; William Parente, Scranton University; Paul Quirk, University of British Columbia; and Kathy Uradnik, St. Cloud State University.

Then, I am deeply indebted to a truly gifted teacher and perceptive scholar, Robert A. Kagan, who laced gentle reminders of facts overlooked and ideas undeveloped with a wonderfully whimsical sense of humor.

Finally, like so many others, I was lucky to know and learn from the late Aaron Wildavsky, an extraordinary colleague, a generous friend, and a proud patriot.

William Ker Muir Jr.
Berkeley, California
March 2011

INTRODUCTION

I am aware that many of my contemporaries maintain that nations are never their own masters here below, and that they necessarily obey some insurmountable and unintelligent power, arising from anterior events, from their race, or from the soil and climate of their country. Such principles are false and cowardly; such principles can never produce aught but feeble men and pusillanimous nations. Providence has not created mankind entirely independent or entirely free. It is true that around each man a fatal circle is traced beyond which he cannot pass; but within the wide verge of that circle he is powerful and free; as it is with man, so with communities. The nations of our time cannot prevent the conditions of men from becoming equal, but it depends upon themselves whether the principle of equality is to lead them to servitude or freedom, to knowledge or barbarism, to prosperity or wretchedness.

Alexis de Tocqueville, *Democracy in America* (1840)

What is personal freedom? Under what circumstances does it flourish? What dangers inhere in a free society? Most importantly, is American civilization, founded as it is on the value of personal freedom, worth fighting for?

These four questions have confronted Americans throughout the nation's history, but in the twenty-first century a considerable number of its people have become uncertain in their answers. Many leaders in politics, business, and the professions, as well as journalists and academics, appear hesitant to sound a certain trumpet. That is a perilous development, because ambivalent minds can take erratic and self-defeating actions.

They are not simple questions, but they are fundamental ones, and they often underlie America's most contentious political issues. Search through your newspaper on any normal day, and you will discover just how basic these questions are. Recently I did just that, and here is a sample of what I found:[1]

- In the "Letters to the Editor" section, a physician wrote about the confusion of a patient with metastasized cancer who sought an unconventional but expensive medical therapy that was backed by little evidence. He wrote, "Patients are told that medical care is a right. Familiar rights such as freedom of speech or the right to vote have no budgetary constraints and certainly need not successfully pass any scientific test. In practice, the right to medical care seems similar to these other rights, with the drunk, helmetless motorcyclist greeted in the emergency room with an open checkbook. Yet when [my patient] concludes that Avastin is life-saving and cost is irrelevant, she is confronted with scientific and economic evaluations that have the potential to override her 'empowerment' and deny her treatment."

Query: Does personal freedom simply mean the right to be left alone, or something more, like freedom from want—from hunger, homelessness, illiteracy, unemployment, and illness?

- In an article describing a 2011 case before the Supreme Court (*Snyder v. Phelps*, involving an unlikable extremist group engaging in despicable speech outside the funeral of a U.S. Marine killed fighting in Iraq), I read that forty-eight state attorneys general and forty-two U.S. senators were urging the Court to permit suppression of such speech.

Query: Does a society, in order to be free and flourish, need to suppress some freedoms?

- In another article, this one about Cuba's recent reforms freeing up its economy, an anxious twenty-one-year-old university student in Havana is quoted, "It's like we're being left alone to fend for ourselves."

Query: Does a society that is free abandon persons to "fend for" themselves?

Moreover, each of these three incidents—the patient's confusion, the despicable protest, and the Cuban's lament—reminds us of the important role of government in enabling us to live free; officials in America secure our safety, enforce our legal rights, and facilitate cooperation. Explaining why they do so is one aim of this book.

But while we will examine how and why the American government uses its power benignly (or at least tries to), we will also explore how individual Americans possess and exercise power to "fend for" themselves and enlist the assistance of others. That they have such power is key to their living free.

This book is divided into three parts. Part I explores the nature of power and the three elemental techniques by which government and individuals alike get their way—*coercion* ("the power of the sword"), *reciprocity* ("the power of the purse"), and *moral power* ("the power of the pen"). The exercise of these different techniques is complex and full of paradox, and Part I elaborates on eleven of these paradoxes. Understanding them and how they impinge on and enhance personal freedom is crucial to understanding the way America's institutions function (and have succeeded for over two centuries).

Part II examines eight public institutions central to America's free society—its presidency, national legislature, legal system, political parties, media, system of free markets, means of taxation, and federalist structure, whereby the citizenry has recourse to alternative governments.

And Part III concludes by examining the kind of people Americans have become from living in a free society. They are diverse, anxious, commercial, prosperous, hard-working, self-reliant, entrepreneurial, pragmatic, cooperative, proud, generous, idealistic, religious, convinced of their moral equality, jealous of their freedom, and committed to a national mission of extending that freedom to other peoples. They are by no means perfect, but as Britain's greatest prime minister, Winston Churchill, is alleged to have said, "Americans always do the right thing—after they've tried everything else" (with an emphasis on the word *tried*).

Machiavelli and the Notion of Personal Freedom

But before we begin to look at contemporary America, let us take a moment to tip our hats to the man who brought the classical notion of personal freedom into our modern world. His name was Niccolò Machiavelli (1469–1527). Readers may find it curious that personal freedom's first modern advocate could be a man whose name has become synonymous with deceit and cruelty, and who declared, "[A]ny one compelled to choose will find greater security in being feared than loved."[2] Consequently, it is useful to say a few words to explain Machiavelli's importance.

A bit of background: With the diminution of Roman imperial domination in the fourth and fifth centuries, Western Europe reverted to a kind of savage and unenlightened barbarism. Not that there wasn't some civilization: the Catholic Church played a key role in preserving the learning—the science and the literature—of Roman times. But at least relative to the peaceful stability, the rule of law, the widespread commerce, and the personal freedom that the Roman Empire had brought to its dominions, things European were dark, impoverished, lawless, dangerous, plague-ridden, and anarchic.

In the fifteenth century, however, the darkness lifted, and Europe came alive with invention and creativity. Ironically, it was a defeat—the fall of Constantinople to the armies of the Muslim Caliphate in 1453—that stimulated Europe, for the Muslim conquest in Turkey caused many eastern scholars to flee to Italy, bringing with them books, manuscripts, and traditions of Greek and Roman scholarship. They prompted a cultural awakening, a rebirth of learning and art that we call the Italian Renaissance.[3]

The Spirit of the Italian Renaissance

These treasures of the past gave birth to a century of significant invention. Paper, printing, the mariner's compass, and gunpowder were but a few of them. In addition to such technical achievements, the Renaissance embraced important scientific revolutions (including the substitution of the Copernican system of astronomy in place of the Ptolemaic one), breakthroughs in architecture and perspective, geographic explorations of vast new continents, and dazzling commercial innovations in banking and investment. Most importantly, a wholly new ideal supplanted the medieval ideal of a life of penance and salvation in an afterlife as the highest and noblest form of human activity. The truly good life came to be defined in terms of using one's powers of imagination, creativity, discovery, and wisdom. Mastery of nature, not resignation to its thrall, became the animating idea of fifteenth-century Europe.

In the artistic achievements of Italy, with their images of God and man's position in the universe, one can witness the humanist spirit of the Renaissance transforming medieval penitential Christianity into the life-affirming theology of modern times—in Michelangelo's depiction of God transferring His creative energies to man in the vast fresco of "Genesis" on the ceiling of the Vatican's Sistine Chapel; in Raphael's representation of human-kind's reasoning powers in his fresco, "The School of Athens," picturing Platonic and Aristotelian scholars conversing; and in the architect Donato Bramante's design for the new Vatican, with its gigantic St. Peter's, which is less a monument to God than a tribute to God's greatest creation, humanity.[4]

The Consolidation of Great States

The fifteenth century was not only a time of artistic and philosophical rebirth, but also of political renaissance. Old feudal structures broke up. Established in their place were national monarchies, reigning over exten-sive nation-states, with their national languages and national armies.

In 1452 the House of Habsburg united Germany and Austria under its dominion. In 1453 the Hundred Years' War between England and France ended with the expulsion of the English from French soil, enabling a nationalist monarchy to consolidate its authority throughout France. And most important of all, in 1479 the marriage of Ferdinand and Isabella united Castile in western Spain with Aragon to its east. The two monarchs joined their armies and over the next decade conquered the rest of Spain. Their campaign of unification climaxed in 1492 with the expulsion of the Muslims from the last Islamic foothold in Western Europe, Granada. Spain, even more than France and the Habsburgs, went looking for new territories to acquire, not only in the "West Indies" across the Atlantic, but also wherever regimes of Western Europe and Mediterranean Africa were vulnerable.

The Italian peninsula was especially open to conquest because it was disunited, shattered into tiny and weak city-states. The impotence and vulnerability of these Italian principalities invited the three new nation-states—Habsburgs, France, and Spain—to lay claim to parts of the Italian peninsula. The Habsburgs coveted the seaport of Genoa and the rich valleys of Lombardy and its principal city of Milan. In the boot of Italy, south of Rome, the Kingdom of Naples (including Sicily) became the object of Spanish ambition. In Rome, the Vatican, now under the control of its first Spanish pope, the wily, deeply corrupt, profoundly ambitious Alexander VI, laid claim to the former papal states along Italy's Adriatic coast. In the northeast the island republic of Venice—wealthy, secure from invasion by virtue of its insularity—sought to seize territories on the Italian mainland, especially parts of Lombardy.[5]

Florence and the Medici Family

On Italy's west coast, north of Rome, lay the most inviting prize of all, the city of Florence and its surrounding region of Tuscany.

Florence was Italy's crown jewel, flourishing beyond imagining, largely because of the competency of its civic leadership. Since the beginning of the fifteenth century, a group of wealthy businessmen had governed Florence's public affairs. First among these leaders of commerce and finance was the Medici family. Thanks to their cloth and silk manufacturing and their inventive banking operations throughout Europe, the Medicis were the most prosperous members of the Florentine business community. They were the foremost financial supporters of the construction and decoration of palaces, churches, and monasteries. They were more than mere financiers of large and elegant building projects, however; they themselves possessed an enlightened artistic eye. Without doubt, the Medicis were the most munificent and astute patrons of the arts that the West had ever seen.

Not being soldiers, the Medicis resisted their foreign adversaries with diplomacy and bribes rather than with armed battalions. Moreover, in the civic life of Florence itself, they courted favor with the middle and poorer classes, and their determination to be *popolani* ("democratic" in the language of today) led them to develop a new and distinctive kind of leadership. They mingled with ordinary people, wearing no distinctive garments and establishing a rule of law that treated all Florentines equally and provided them the freedom to pursue their private interests.

Of the various Medicis, the most celebrated was Lorenzo the Magnificent (born 1449), who embodied the cultural ascendancy of Florence. For fourteen years, from 1478 to 1492, as chairman of the City Council, he presided over a flourishing and independent city. Then in 1492—the year the Muslims were expelled from Spain and Christopher Columbus arrived in the New World—he died, at age forty-three. Two years later, France invaded the Italian peninsula and seized Florence. France's aggression sparked half a century of ceaseless violence and international intrigue throughout the Italian peninsula.

Machiavelli was a citizen of Florence. Born in 1469 into a once wealthy family that had fallen into bankruptcy, he was twenty-three when Lorenzo died. He had observed Lorenzo's political methods: establishing order, lowering taxes, relaxing regulations, stimulating the economy, identifying with the people, retaining his status as an ordinary citizen, and constantly searching for talented persons to run the Medici businesses.

When the French invaded and briefly occupied Florence in 1494, the Medicis went into exile, and without their presence, things fell apart. Anarchy, followed by a theocratic tyranny, reigned; for four years, Florence's freedoms were crushed, until the business community, backed by the citizenry, asserted itself and regained control. It established a republic with executive powers conferred on a city council.

Machiavelli, now twenty-nine, applied for an appointment as secretary to the chairman of the council (today the position would be called chief of staff to the mayor). He got the job and over the next decade and a half won the respect and trust of his city's leaders while gradually expanding his own responsibilities. Machiavelli was a gifted politician, with an instinct for power; a skill for overcoming opposition to his and his bosses' initiatives; a memory of the wastefulness of civic disorder; and a vision of an Italian people once again united, free, prosperous, and strong enough to repel "the barbarians" (i.e., the French, the Spanish, and the Habsburgs).

His versatility was astonishing. He organized the city's security force and was its commanding general. He wrote speeches for his boss, established public policy agendas, and managed undertakings assigned him by the council. He led diplomatic missions to France and Germany, where he observed the growing geostrategic strength of these new nations, as their monarchs consolidated their once-divided domains. In his time, Florence flourished, expanding its boundaries and extending its authority throughout the Tuscany countryside.

Then, abruptly in 1512, Machiavelli's political career came to an end. A new generation of Medicis, now backed by the papacy, returned to Florence. They sacked him and sent him into exile in a small subsistence farm outside the city. Machiavelli was forty-three and at the peak of his intellectual and physical powers. For the next fifteen years, until his death, he would seek political appointment from a variety of leaders, but in vain.

Imagine Machiavelli's frustration, standing idle, unable to use his immense talents and rich experience, all the while watching Italy, once home of the greatest empire in the Western world, become the plaything of foreign aggressors. Machiavelli tells us what he did. In a letter to his best friend, Francesco Vittori, in 1513, he wrote:

What my life is I will tell you. I get up at sunrise and go to a grove of mine which I am having chopped down. I spend a couple of hours there, checking up on the work of the previous days and passing the time with the woodcutters, who are never without some trouble or other, either among themselves or with the neighbors. . . .

When I leave the grove, I go to a spring and from there to my bird snares. I carry a book under my arm—Dante or Petrarch, or one of the minor poets like Tibullus, Ovid, or the like. I read about their amorous passions, and their loves call my own to mind, so I delight in these thoughts. Then I betake myself to the inn on the highway. I chat with the people going by, ask for news from their hometowns, learn a few things, and note the various tastes and curious notions of men. Meanwhile lunchtime arrives and, together with my family, I eat whatever food my poor house and scanty patrimony afford. Having lunched, I return to the inn. There I generally find the innkeeper, a butcher, a miller, and two kiln-tenders. In their company I idle the rest of the day away playing at *cricca* and *tricchetrach*—games that give rise to a host of quarrels, cutting remarks, and insults. Often we fight over a penny and are heard yelling as far off as San Casciano. Set down among these lice, this is how I keep the mold from my brain and find release from Fortune's malice. I am content to have her beat me down this way to see if she won't become ashamed.

At nightfall I return home and enter my study. There on the threshold I remove my dirty, mud-spattered clothes, slip on my regal and courtly robes, and thus fittingly attired, I enter the ancient courts of bygone men where, having received a friendly welcome, I feed on the food that is mine alone and that I was born for. I am not ashamed to speak with them and inquire into the reasons for their actions; and they answer me in kindly fashion. And so for four hours I feel no annoyance; I forget all troubles; poverty holds no fears, and death loses its terrors. I become entirely one of them. And since Dante says that there can be no knowledge without retention, I have set down what I have gained from their conversations and composed a little book, *De Principatibus*, in which I probe as deeply as I can . . . into the subject, discussing what a principality is, what kinds there are, how they are won, how they are maintained, and why they are lost.[6]

By reading that "little book," *The Prince*, we know what lessons Machiavelli learned from his conversations with Dante, Petrarch, the ancient world's greatest lawyer Cicero, and Rome's foremost historian Livy. No doubt, he wrote *The Prince* to advertise his availability as a political consultant. But the book was more than that; it was also a statement of his own socially democratic vision, that the enduring strength of a nation stemmed from freeing all its citizens (no matter how ordinary) to put their talents to work to improve and prosper *themselves* and their families. In short, the people should freely pursue their own happiness, and the prince should assist them in their personal efforts; his job was to "*encourage* his citizens peaceably to pursue their affairs, whether in trade, agriculture, or any other human activity, so that no one will hesitate to improve his possessions *for fear that they will be taken from him*, and no one will hesitate to open a new avenue of trade *for fear of taxes*. Instead, the prince ought to be ready to *reward* those who do these things and those who seek out ways of enriching their city or state."[7] (Emphasis added.)

Machiavelli emphasized two lessons. One was an economics precept so far ahead of its time that it would be another 250 years before Adam Smith would repeat it—the doctrine of the 'invisible hand."[8] When individuals prosper, their community prospers as a consequence.

The second lesson was political: a revolutionary doctrine that the purpose of government was to *assist* the people ("encourage," "reward"), not to prey on them ("take," "tax"). Governments, in other words, were established to secure the people's liberties against wrongdoing and help them pursue their goals, their self-interest, their "happiness."

In understanding Machiavelli, it is vital to imagine him observing Lorenzo de Medici and writing *The Prince* in order to express Lorenzo's notion of a good society, a "commercial republic" where the government is the servant of a free people. That vision, that practical ideal, was what made Machiavelli's contribution to political thought so distinctive.

Think how radically different such a vision is from some of today's competing alternatives: a "dictatorship of the proletariat," or a fascist dictatorship where individuals serve a Führer by virtue of his monopoly of force and a secret police, or a technocratic elite benignly "spreading" the wealth of others. Quite to the contrary, Machiavelli's prince emboldened his people to have dreams, to be entrepreneurial, and to act on their own initiative, undertaking improvements of their own invention. His vision of a free, democratic society is not what Machiavelli is remembered for, but it is why he deserves our respect today, five centuries later.

Law and Order

Machiavelli was convinced of one reality: that freedom could only survive on a foundation of law and order. While his experience had taught him that most citizens desired to engage in their own commercial affairs, to do so they needed to feel personally safe. Lacking security from predators abroad and thieves at home, they had to divert their energies to self-protection. It was also plain to him that the people, when occupied as farmers, merchants, financiers, engineers, scientists, educators, poets, builders, and health care providers, were happy to delegate responsibility for foreign and homeland security to specialists practiced in applying force. Thus, sociologically (as he saw it), any free community naturally stratified into, on the one hand, a large commercial class and, on the other, a small political one, specialized in policing disorder and aggression. The commercial stratum collaborated through exchange and disdained politics; in turn, it paid the political class to master the skills of war and threat as means of protection.

Machiavelli understood that only a relatively few persons would want to be in the political class, with its burdensome protective responsibilities. Sometimes circumstances would attract to this governing endeavor the best and brightest, persons with sufficient vision, political skill, emotional intelligence, and organizational abilities to be effective leaders. But too often, lamented Machiavelli, it was the case that an individual who aspired to take up politics would lack the integrity, competence, or fortitude to protect the people and provide civil order. They would be out of their depth, dreamy-eyed idealists, or cowards. And there would be others who merely wanted to be in charge of the government's monopoly of force—its police, armies, and lawyers—in order to enrich themselves and dominate others. The question, then, was how to weed out the craven and corrupt?

Even those who happened to possess both skills and integrity differed over visions and the means to realize them. Machiavelli knew from first-hand experience that constant conflict, disagreement, and hostile rivalries made life in the political stratum bitter and full of suspicion.

He also understood the consequences of defective procedures for selecting a boss: a vicious cycle of violence and resistance. Because some of the aspirants to the government's police powers would be treacherous and remorseless, even the competent and virtuous politician would be "compelled" to resort to intimidation if he were to prevail, and the struggle to survive thereafter would tend to corrupt character, weaken self-restraint, sow suspicion, extend ignorance, and provide a pretext to turn barbarous. Under such primitive circumstances, political power would corrupt.

In short, Machiavelli was acutely aware of politicians' tendencies toward moral and intellectual degeneration if left unchecked in a badly ordered politics. The underdevelopment of Italy's political system—its primitive rules for regulating political rivalries—deeply concerned him. He sought answers to how the process of selection might be reformed so that the unacceptable aspirants could be turned away. How could the outcome of the rivalries be decided by laws rather than by force? How else could the game of politics be decided?

In the concluding chapters of *The Prince*, Machiavelli challenged future generations to devise better ways of picking political leaders. "Nothing so much honors a man newly come to power," he wrote, "as the new laws and new ordinances he brings into being. Such things, when they are well based and impressive in scope, win reverence and admiration; and in Italy there is no lack of matter awaiting the impress of new forms."[9]

He had no illusions that effecting new procedures for selecting political leaders would be easy. He warned,

> It must be realized that there is nothing more difficult to plan, more uncertain of success, or more dangerous to manage than the establishment of a new order of government; for he who introduces it makes enemies of all those who derived advantage from the old order and finds but lukewarm defenders among those who stand to gain from the new one. Such a lukewarm attitude grows partly out of fear of the adversaries, who have the law on their side, and partly from the incredulity of men in general, who actually have no faith in new things until they have been proved by experience. Hence, it happens that whenever those in the enemy camp have a chance to attack, they do so with partisan fervor, while the others defend themselves rather passively, so that both they and the prince are endangered.[10]

But if he was aware of the dangers and difficulties of managing "the establishment of a new order of government," he rejected hopelessness, and he was right to do so. Nearly three centuries after his death, and in a country far removed from Italy, a "new form" was originated. I speak of electoral democracy—general elections with a broad electorate—what we today call "popular sovereignty."[11]

The Consequences of New Forms

Democratic forms gave people outside the political stratum the power of the vote—a club with which they could threaten virtual assassination of any incompetent, self-serving, or corrupted political aspirant. Democracy transferred the power of removal from the hands of the few princely aspirants and gave it to ordinary people, thereby cutting the vicious and counterproductive cycle of threat and counterthreat of Machiavelli's time.

With political democracy the tool of victory would become ideas, beliefs, and public persuasion. Political battles would be regulated and in the open, and compromise and coalition-building would become the essential political skills. That "new form"—those democratic procedures for deciding who would be "prince"—was America's invention, but it owed its inspiration to Machiavelli and to the Florentine Republic he so loved.

Tocqueville and Machiavelli

Machiavelli concluded *The Prince* with this eloquent testament to humankind's potential for civilizing itself:[12]

> I am not unaware that many men have believed and still believe that the affairs of the world are controlled by fortune and by God in such a way that the prudence of men cannot manage them, and indeed cannot improve them at all. For this reason they are inclined to think that there is no point in sweating much over these matters and that they should submit to chance instead. . . . Nevertheless, since our free will must not be denied, I estimate that even if fortune is the arbiter of half our actions, she still allows us to control the other half, or thereabouts. I compare fortune to one of those torrential rivers which, when enraged, inundates the lowlands, tears down trees and buildings, and washes out the land on one bank to deposit it on the other. Everyone flees before it; everyone yields to its assaults without being able to offer it any resistance. Even though it behaves this way, however, it does not mean that men cannot make provision during periods of calm by erecting levees and dikes to channel the rising waters when they come, or at least restrain their fury and reduce the danger.

Compare this eloquent ending of *The Prince* with the inspirational words of Alexis de Tocqueville's epigraph[13] at the head of this Introduction, and you will find a remarkable similarity. The likeness of the two passages is no coincidence. Tocqueville's imitation of Machiavelli was his way of thanking the latter for pointing the way to a free society by means of checking and distributing power.

But what is power, and what is its relationship to freedom? With this pair of questions in mind, we begin our exploration of personal freedom in America.

NOTES

1. *Wall Street Journal,* October 6, 2010, A20, A17.
2. Niccolò Machiavelli, *The Prince,* trans. Daniel Donno (New York: Bantam Dell, 1996 [1513]), chap. 17.
3. Scholars living in the fifteenth century were quite conscious of the changes Western Europe underwent in their time. They coined the term *Middle Ages* to describe the stagnant interval between the downfall of the Roman world and their rediscovery of the achievements of the classical world.
4. This humanistic understanding soon spread throughout Europe. Leave it to Shakespeare to give it perhaps its finest expression: "What a piece of work is a man, how noble in reason, how infinite in faculty, in form and moving how express and admirable, in action how like an angel, in apprehension how like a god!" *Hamlet,* Act II, Scene 2.
5. In one of his few allusions to these times in Italy, Alexander Hamilton, in *Federalist* No. 6, noted that Venice, despite being "a commercial republic," undertook wars of choice against its neighboring states.
6. As quoted in Daniel Donno's introduction to his translation of Machiavelli's *The Prince,* 4–5.
7. Ibid., chap. 21. I like to imagine Machiavelli were he an American living near my home in California today. There he'd be in the morning, on his meager farm in Castro Valley, cleaning out pig stalls, digging holes, and building miles of fences. Then, as 4 o'clock rolled around, he would go into Oakland and drop in at his favorite bar to watch the end of the baseball game and throw some craps with the guys hanging out there. Then he would drive home, take a shower, put on his slippers and blazer, have dinner and an hour with his family, and then, finally, retreat to his library to read the works of his political heroes—James Madison, Alexander Hamilton, George Washington, Alexis de Tocqueville, Abraham Lincoln, and Woodrow Wilson. There he would "converse" with them about the practical and theoretical aspects of America's current problems and write down the lessons he would have drawn from his conversations.

8. Adam Smith, *The Wealth of Nations* (1776), book 4, chap. 2:

> As every individual . . . endeavours . . . both to employ his capital in the support of domestic industry, and also to direct that industry so that its produce may be of the greatest value[,] every individual necessarily labours to render the annual revenue of the society as great as he can. He generally, indeed, neither intends to promote the public interest, nor knows how much he is promoting it. [H]e intends . . . only his own gain, and he is in this as in many other cases led by an invisible hand to promote an end which was no part of his intention. Nor is it always the worse for the society that it was not part of it. By pursuing his own interest he frequently promotes that of the society more effectually than when he really intends to promote it.

9. Machiavelli, *The Prince,* chap. 26.
10. Ibid., chap. 6.
11. Machiavelli's acknowledgment of the obstacles to political reform has an uncanny timeliness in these times when America seeks to introduce democratic ways into the nations of the Middle East, used as they are to the unruly methods of fifteenth-century Italy.
12. Machiavelli, *The Prince,* chap. 25.
13. Alexis de Tocqueville, *Democracy in America,* trans. Henry Reeve (New York: Bantam, 2000 [1840]), vol. II, book 4, chap. 8.

PART I

FREEDOM AND POWER

1

ANARCHY

[I]n such condition there is no place for industry, because the fruit thereof is uncertain; and consequently no culture of the earth; no navigation, nor use of the commodities that may be imported by sea; no commodious building; no instruments of moving and removing such things as require much force; no knowledge of the face of the earth; no account of time; no arts; no letters; no society; and which is worst of all, continual fear, and danger of violent death; and the life of man, solitary, poor, nasty, brutish, and short.

Thomas Hobbes, *Leviathan* (1651)

Chaos in Marysville

Consider Marysville, California, as it existed mid-January of the year 1850, a year after the discovery of gold in the Sierras. Marysville sat at the confluence of the Feather and Yuba Rivers in northern California. Located on a navigable river and only a few overland miles from the Sierra gold fields, Marysville was the closest river port available to the prospectors. It promised to become a prosperous commercial hub, functioning as the outfitter and banking center for the gold country. Countless newcomers, from every walk of life and virtually every region of the country, came to Marysville, hoping for riches and personal fulfillment.

17

But in January 1850, there was no law in Marysville. There was only chaos. When Mexico ceded California to the United States in 1848 as a result of its defeat in the Mexican-American War, its jurisdiction ceased. In theory, the U.S. War Department was to establish civil order throughout California until a constitution for the state could be ratified and a government established. But Marysville, more than a hundred miles from San Francisco, was too remote for the military to extend its presence there. In Marysville there were no police, no jails, no courthouses, no government.

Even in this legal vacuum, many of the newcomers behaved well, conducting themselves according to neighborly habits they brought from the civilization back east. But there were others around Marysville who acted unscrupulously, once they found there was no punishment to fear. Speculators sold land they did not own. Squatters sat on properties they had no claim to and cut down timber that wasn't theirs. Thieves stole the cattle of ranchers and the gold of prospectors. Anarchy—the rule of thugs—reigned.

And so, in this land of seeming promise, anyone who sought to create wealth became the easy prey of scoundrels. As a result, it was foolish to build a decent house, cultivate a farm, or lay out a road. There were no stores, no financial institutions, no schools, no hospitals, no churches—not even embankments to keep the rivers from flooding the town in spring. Worst of all, disputes were left unsettled and grew into deadly vendettas, and lawless criminality led to lawless self-defense and a general erosion of self-restraint among the settlers.

Into this no man's land came a young lawyer from New England named Stephen J. Field. A son of a minister, raised in peaceful and orderly Connecticut, Field arrived in Marysville hoping to establish a practice there and was dismayed by the thuggish state of things. Determined to bring order out of the chaos, he convinced the townsfolk to establish a rule of law and a government to enforce it—and, further, that in order to secure their personal safety, they should elect him the *alcalde,* an office that combined the powers of judge, mayor, tax collector, registrar of deeds, and police chief.

In the ensuing weeks, he created a rudimentary legal system. Reminiscing some years later about the actions he took to create a system of criminal justice in Marysville, Field wrote, "As a judicial officer, I tried many cases. . . . In civil cases, I always called a jury, if the parties desired one; and in criminal cases, when the offence was of a high grade, I went through the form of calling a grand jury, and having an indictment found; and in all cases I appointed an attorney to represent the people, and also the accused, when necessary."[1]

At first, his decisive actions had widespread support from the citizenry. According to his reminiscences, "The Americans in the country had a general notion of what was required for the preservation of order and the due administration of justice; and as I endeavored to administer justice promptly, but upon a due consideration of the rights of every one, and not rashly, I was sustained with great unanimity by the community."

Because Field had no jail in which to incarcerate the worst offenders, he resorted to punishments that he hoped would put an end to the vicious cycle of threat and retaliation. For example, without a jail in which to secure one defendant who had been convicted of robbery, he decided, "There was but one course to pursue, and, however repugnant it was to my feelings to adopt it, I believed it was the only thing that saved the man's life. I ordered him to be publicly whipped with fifty lashes, and added that if he were found, within the next two years, in the vicinity of Marysville, he should be again whipped."

In other words, knowing that the townspeople were ready to turn into a mob and lynch the robber, he acted without any legal authority, partially satisfying the cry for vengeance by conducting a public whipping. Then he ordered the defendant to get out of Marysville forever, before the crowd changed its mind.

The Effect of Judge Turner

But despite Field's initial success in bringing order to Marysville, the town was so remote that, even after a state legislature was established and began to pass legislation, the official law was of little consequence, for there were no police to enforce it. In fact, the new state government made things worse by sending to Marysville a judge named William R. Turner, who was a violent scoundrel himself. Turner walked the streets, cowing peaceful folks with threats to do them harm.

Turner particularly reviled Field and tried to run him out of town. Field recalled that Turner "frequented the gambling saloons, associated with disreputable characters, and was addicted to habits of the most disgusting intoxication. Besides being abusive in his language, he threatened violence, and gave out that he intended to insult me publicly the first time we met, and that, if I resented his conduct, he would shoot me down on the spot."

Fearful for his life, Field traveled to San Francisco to get the advice of Judge Nathaniel Bennett, a man used to western ways and esteemed for his wisdom. "Judge Bennett asked if I were certain that he had made such a threat," Field wrote. "I replied I was. 'Well,' said the Judge, 'I will not give you any advice; but if it were my case, I think I should get a shot-gun and stand on the street, and see that I had the first shot.' I replied that 'I could not do that; that I would act only in self-defence.' He replied, 'That would be acting in self-defence.'"

Judge Bennett's counsel alarmed Field, but caused him to reflect on the difference in the courteous, forgiving behavior appropriate in an orderly civilization and the brutish vindictiveness required to survive anarchy. "When I came to California," he later remembered, "I came with all those notions, in respect to acts of violence, which are instilled into New England youth; if a man were rude, I would turn away from him. But I soon found that men in California were likely to take very great liberties with a person who acted in such a manner, and that the only way to get along was to hold every man responsible, and resent every trespass upon one's rights."

From San Francisco he returned to Marysville and, in his words, "purchase[d] a pair of revolvers and had a sack-coat made with pockets in which the barrels could lie, and be discharged; and I began to practice firing the pistols from the pockets. In time I acquired considerable skill, and was able to hit a small object across the street. An object so large as a man I could have hit without difficulty."

Field committed himself to confront Turner: "I had come to the conclusion that if I had to give up my independence; if I had to avoid a man because I was afraid he would attack me; if I had to cross the street every time I saw him coming, life itself was not worth having."

He devised a strategy to cow Turner and his drunken cronies. He publicly announced that he would take preemptive action if Turner continued to make violent threats:

Having determined neither to seek him nor to shun him, I asked a friend to carry a message to him, and to make sure that it would reach him, I told different parties what I had sent, and I was confident that they would repeat it to him. "Tell him from me," I said, "that I do not want any collision with him; that I desire to avoid all personal difficulties; but that I shall not attempt to avoid him; that I shall not cross the street on his account, nor go a step out of my way for him; that I have heard of his threats, and that if he attacks me or comes at me in a threatening manner I will kill him." I acted on my plan. I often met him in the streets and in saloons, and whenever I drew near him I dropped my hand into my pocket and cocked my pistols to be ready for any emergency. People warned me to look out for him; to beware of being taken at a disadvantage; and I was constantly on my guard. I felt that I was in great danger; but after awhile this sense of danger had a sort of fascination, and I often went to places where he was, to which I would not otherwise have gone. Whenever I met him I kept my eye on him, and whenever I passed him on the street I turned around and narrowly watched him until he had gone some distance.

The plan worked, and Field was convinced that no other form of resistance would have succeeded. "I am persuaded," he wrote, "if I had taken any other course, I should have been killed. I do not say Turner would have deliberately shot me down, or that he would have attempted anything against me in his sober moments; but when excited with drink, and particularly in the presence of the lawless crowds who heard his threats, it would have taken but little to urge him on. As it turned out, however, he never interfered with me, perhaps because he knew I was armed and believed that, if I were attacked, somebody, and perhaps more than one, would be badly hurt."

The point is that a "reasonable," conciliatory response would have emboldened Turner to even greater insolence. It was the convincing use of coercive counterthreats that put an end to Turner's bullying. Or, at least, that was the way observers at the time saw it. "I have been often assured by citizens of Marysville," Field related, "that it was only the seeming recklessness of my conduct, and the determination I showed not to avoid him or go out of his way, that saved me."

No doubt, Field took pride in vanquishing anarchy in Marysville, but his account of how he brought order and safety there concluded on this rueful note: "But at the same time my business was ruined. I lost nearly all I had acquired and became involved in debt." Even one as skillful at coping with bullies as Field had become ultimately was "ruined" by the effort. (By way of epilogue to this story, when law and order eventually did come to California, Stephen Field prospered as a lawyer, and twelve years after his arrival in Marysville, President Abraham Lincoln appointed him to the U.S. Supreme Court, where he served for the next thirty-four years.)

Disorder in Today's Inner Cities

Marysville's kind of intimidating, miserable disorder is not some quirk of a remote past. Today, in some of America's most notorious urban neighborhoods, there exist conditions resembling the anarchy of Field's day. Law is absent, police stay clear, and too many lives are wasted as a consequence.

Alex Kotlowitz, a *Wall Street Journal* reporter, hung out in one of Chicago's most notorious public housing projects for two years. He befriended two youngsters, aged eleven and thirteen. In the time he observed them, thugs killed nine of their schoolmates and acquaintances. The only business done in the neighborhood was lawless drug dealing, and terror was the instrument of the drug dealers.

In his book *There Are No Children Here*, Kotlowitz described the effects of the anarchy present in what we now euphemistically call our "inner cities":

> [T]he neighborhood had become a black hole. [One] could more easily recite what wasn't there than what was. There were no banks, only currency exchanges, which charged customers up to $8.00 for every welfare check cashed. There were no public libraries, movie theaters, skating rinks, or bowling alleys to entertain the neighborhood's children. For the infirm, there were two neighborhood clinics, the Mary Thompson Hospital and the Miles Square Health Center, both of which teetered on the edge of bankruptcy and would close by the end of 1989. Yet the death rate of newborn babies exceeded infancy mortality rates in a number of Third World countries, including Chile, Costa Rica, Cuba, and Turkey. And there was no rehabilitation center, though drug use was rampant.[2]

The feelings of aloneness that haunted the neighborhood—and the despair of individuals resulting from their isolation—overwhelmed Kotlowitz: "[N]early half of the families in [the public housing project] had no telephone. Residents also felt disconnected from one another; there was little sense of community . . . and there was even less trust. Some who didn't have a phone, for instance, didn't know any others in their building who would let them use theirs. Some neighbors wouldn't allow their children to go outside to play. One mother moved aside her living room furniture to make an open and safe place where her children could frolic."

Those who dwelled in the housing project were not free to do what they wanted to do—to walk outdoors, talk with their neighbors, rely on strangers, or get assistance when they needed it. The irony, of course, was that this anarchy—this terrifying, intimidating presence of unsuppressed coercion—went on in so-called "public housing": *government housing*. Government was too weak to repel this tyranny of thugs.

NOTES

1. Stephen J. Field, *California Alcalde* (Oakland, Calif.: Biobooks, 1950), 28. Field's papers are held by the Bancroft Library, University of California, Berkeley. Further quotes in this chapter, unless otherwise attributed, come from this source.
2. Alex Kotlowitz, *There Are No Children Here* (New York: Doubleday/Talese, 1991).

2

COERCIVE POWER

All things fall apart; the center cannot hold.
Mere anarchy is loosed upon the world.
The blood-dimmed tide is loosed,
And everywhere the ceremony of innocence is drowning.
The best lack all conviction,
While the worst are full of passionate intensity.

William Butler Yeats, "The Second Coming" (1919)

Of all the political tasks a government of free people must perform, the most important is civilizing coercive power.[1] Neglect taming humankind's bullying instinct, and there will be no society. Where there is no police power, the worst of us soon start threatening others into submission. As the poet Yeats knew, when intimidation comes to dominate every important relationship, "all things fall apart," "innocence" dies, and existence becomes "pitiless."

The presence of unregulated coercion renders freedom impossible, brings misery to its practitioners and victims alike, and (most importantly) turns morality topsy-turvy. What is it about coercion that perverts a civilized morality—those behavior-governing values like honesty, kindness, empathy, curiosity, dutifulness, and loyalty—into their antitheses—deceit, brutality, detachment, dogmatism, irresponsibility, and betrayal?

To understand the insidious moral effects of unregulated threat, we need to examine the nature of coercive power and four important paradoxes incident to it.[2]

The Paradox of Dispossession

Coercion is not force, but the *threat* of force. To use threat effectively, a predator needs victims who possess two things—a hostage and a ransom. Anything a victim values greatly can serve as a hostage—a child, a reputation, a business, a precious object, even life itself. A ransom is something the victim values less dearly and therefore will surrender in order to preserve the hostage from harm—his bag of gold dust, his cattle, his land, the commodities in his store, or his freedom.

The key thing to keep in mind about coercion is that, while a predator manifests a willingness to destroy his victim's hostage, his real object is to *preserve* it so that he can extort a ransom. If a potential victim can dispossess himself, he can escape having to submit to coercion. If he has no children, for example, a kidnapper has no kids to take hostage. The farm labor leader César Chávez used to instruct his followers, "You cannot picket barren ground." Like the childless adult, the farmer in winter offers no hostages, in contrast to his vulnerability in summer, when his fields are abundant with crops.

Moreover, if someone is a pauper and not a prince, he has no ransom to pay. Lawyers speak of the dispossessed as "judgment-proof"; why sue someone who has no assets to give up? The threat of a lawsuit against the destitute is an empty threat.

Let us call this curious freedom from coercion the **paradox of dispossession:** *the fewer assets one has, the less vulnerable one is to another's threats; the more assets, the more vulnerable.* The dispossessed—the tramp, the bankrupt, the life prisoner in solitary confinement, and the visionary whose life is worth less than his martyrdom—all are impervious to coercive power.

If an individual is in possession of valuables he cannot protect, his only recourse may be to discard them and dwarf himself as a target of coercion. Should he choose otherwise—should he want to have children, maintain a business, create a work of art, or build a good reputation—then he must place his possessions in a safe haven, a sanctuary, out of easy reach.

A sanctuary may be based on custom, law, or force. Once upon a time, aristocrats were honor-bound not to expose the dirty linen of their peers to public view. Their discretion provided a custom-based sanctuary that protected aristocratic reputations. Likewise, in the contemporary under-world of the Mafia, the wife and children of a gang member are customar-ily deemed "outside the business" and hence not subject to injurious threats. But custom can erode, and customary sanctuaries cease to be safe. It once was taboo among American politicians to defile the reputation of colleagues by publicizing "private" faults. No longer does this seem to be the case.

A more reliable sanctuary is the law. We designate our possessions "legal property," entitling us to call on the lawmakers to protect all we care about with a fortress of police, prosecutors, and prison guards.

But when the lawmakers are too weak to enforce the law, as was the case in Marysville in 1850 and in the public housing project that Alex Kotlowitz described, victims have no legal recourse and, hence, are compelled to pro-tect their valuables with their own threats of force. As Niccolò Machiavelli admonished, under anarchic circumstances potential victims must fortify well.[3] Even if they succeed in their own self-defense, however, the cost is ruinous: like Stephen Field in Marysville, they must divert virtually all their energies to the wasteful task of fortification.

Marysville highlights one more point. Coercion is the classic vicious circle, in which both parties end up dwarfing themselves. Every coercive relationship has the potential of exposing victimizers (like Judge Turner) to retaliation. Once victims begin resisting, predators have to dispossess themselves of valuables they cannot protect. The paradox of dispossession dooms prey and predator alike to a violent and eventually barren existence.

The Paradox of Detachment

Three other paradoxes complicate the practice of coercion. Let's call the first of these the **paradox of detachment.** Consider the frustration of the extortionist who takes a hostage but finds that the victim doesn't care about its loss. For example, the kidnapper of the daughter whose parents are glad to be rid of her ends up with an unwanted child on his hands—and no ransom. Had the parents been able to convince the kidnapper of their indifference before he snatched their daughter, he would not have abducted her in the first place. Demonstrating detachment may sound difficult, but consider a familiar example: the invulnerability of a democratically elected politician who early in his term declares he doesn't care to run for reelec-tion, thereby removing the voters' threat to defeat him.

The point is that if we can make it clear to anyone who would threaten us that we are indifferent to our daughter or our public office, or whatever other possessions we can't safeguard, then our unconcern renders those valuables useless hostages. Paradoxically, the key to removing things we love from harm's way is to demonstrate we don't love them. To put this irony another way, *the less the victim cares about preserving something, the less the victimizer cares about taking it hostage.* The prison rule—that guards must shoot at escaping prisoners even though it means they may incidentally kill any fellow guards who have been taken hostage—makes sense because it may convince prisoners that society is indifferent to the lives of prison guards. By reducing the utility of kidnapping them, we reduce the frequency of their being kidnapped. As contradictory as it sounds, we willingly kill prison guards in order to save them.

Of course, detaching ourselves from friends, like fellow prison guards, is far more difficult than pretending an indifference to things, like public office. Human detachment must be continually dramatized. Convincing predators that we lack normal human sympathies may require abnormal action. We may have to "make an example" of our heartlessness, and then we have to live with the results. Think of Shakespeare's Prince Hamlet. Intending to save his beloved Ophelia from being used as a pawn in "castle politics," he broke off his engagement to her. He even publicly rebuked her to make his detachment obvious, but his seeming pitilessness drove her insane.

The Paradox of Face

A third paradox of coercion is the **paradox of face:** *the more ruthless your reputation, the less ruthless you have to be.*[4] It is key to understanding the truly ruinous consequences of coercion.

We say persons have "saved face" if they have gained a reputation for being mean and meaning it. Just as having "good will"—a reputation for fair dealing—is an invaluable asset in the marketplace, having "ill will"—a reputation for being vicious—is necessary in coercive relationships. Notoriously brutal extortionists rarely need to be brutal; their reputation for vindictiveness persuades each victim to submit without calling their bluff.

Recall Stephen Field reflecting on the fact that it was "the seeming recklessness of [his] conduct" that convinced the bullying Judge Turner that he meant what he threatened ("If [Turner] attacks me . . . I'll kill him"). Field's threat enjoyed "credibility" partly because Field cultivated a reputation for deadly accuracy with the pistols he carried in his pockets. More importantly, however, Field publicly displayed how much he would enjoy the chance to gun Turner down; as he put it, the prospect had "a sort of fascination" for him, and he let everybody in town know it.

The theory of the balance of power is that adversaries with reputations for implacability, who genuinely mean what they threaten, will coerce one another not to coerce. Here's an important instance where a notoriety for doing evil may be the only means for accomplishing good.

In exercising coercion, threats work on their victims psychologically, not physically. Effective use of coercive power gets the victim to anticipate the loss of the hostage and submit to avoid its destruction. A successful labor strike, for example, is the one not called, but which induces the employer to capitulate upon the union's threat of one. A union has failed if it actually has to call its members out on strike. Their pay ceases; their bills can't be paid; their feet ache from walking the picket line; and, most disastrous of all, their employer may go out of business, leaving them without jobs.

Confronted by these disincentives to strike, how does a union leader convince an employer that he means to put the firm out of business unless the workers get a few cents more per hour? The answer: By seeming as if the union membership will enjoy bankrupting their employer, no matter the cost! By pounding his fist fiercely on the bargaining table! By speaking class warfare! By demonstrating that he will be voted out of office if he backs down from his union's initial demands!

It pays to look nasty if it frightens your victim so much as to refrain from calling your bluff.

The toughest problem facing practitioners of coercion is what to do after their bluff is called. To save face—that is, to maintain their cruel reputation—they have to behave with malevolence.[5] The pressures are relentless to carry out threats once uttered. Being forgiving after making a threat risks inviting resistance. Then, it's either surrender or fight to the death.

The Paradox of Irrationality

Key to practicing coercion successfully is a reputation for severity—sometimes even cruelty. Recall what Machiavelli counseled the prince who would attempt to bring peace to Italy and save it from the ravages of anarchy: "[A]ny one compelled to choose will find greater security in being feared than loved."[6]

Yet there are occasions when even the most brutal reputation will prove inadequate to make the victim submit to an extortionate threat. Sometimes only ignorance will suffice to convince the victim that the threat is real. To be stupid, unaware, or even crazy—or at least seeming so—is useful in two ways. For the aggressor, it enlarges the seriousness of his threat. If a man says, "Stay away, or I'll kill us both," he is likely to get his way if he looks crazy enough to kill himself. If executing a threat is so self-destructive that no sane person would execute it, only an insane person can utter the threat credibly.[7]

There is a second reason not to have all one's senses. Irrationality often can ward off threats. If the victim is incapable of understanding that he is being intimidated, he can't be deterred by threats. For example, it is impossible to blackmail a deaf person over the telephone. Once the victim's condition becomes apparent to the extortionist, there is no reason to go on threatening. In coercive relationships, a fool often can go where angels fear to tread, because the *obvious* fool really has less to fear. Being sensible increases exposure to coercion, while not knowing enough to know better (or seeming so—"studied ignorance," it's called) serves as a defense.

The tendency to insanity and stupidity in coercive relationships is called the **paradox of irrationality.** In a nutshell, it recognizes that *the more delirious the threatener, the more serious the threat; the more delirious the victim, the less serious the threat.*

Much like the practical resolution of the other paradoxes of coercion, making a dramatic example—in this instance, of one's irrationality—is essential, but difficult. The difficulty stems from the strong presumption that most members of humankind are *homo sapiens*. Hence, the burden of proving one's craziness is a heavy one, and if it is impossible to feign madness, it may be necessary to become truly mad and truly believe what is otherwise illogical—to become, in a word, ideological, so that adversaries see how irrational one has become. The demagogue breathing fire and brimstone, the Ku Klux Klansman with his devout belief in apartheid, the American Civil Liberties Union zealot with her convictions about moral absolutes—all in their own way overcome their opponents' assumption that they are reasonable. The risk of the paradox, of course, is that if it is rational for each party to become irrational, the result may be the ultimate illogic—mutual suicide.

The Role of Politicians

The stark fact about exercising power by threat is this: it compels individuals to transform their personalities. To survive (much less succeed) they must cultivate cynicism, insensitivity, cruelty, and stupidity. Anarchy creates a morally monstrous world, where everyone, victim and victimizer, is plagued by the four paradoxes of coercive power.

During much of the seventeenth century, the Englishman Thomas Hobbes (1588–1679) watched his beloved nation dissolve into anarchy. Hobbes was an adviser to kings—and he survived regicide and two brutal revolutions. He was a canny man, and the more he reflected on politics, the more he likened it to a then-popular card game called whist, the ancestor of our modern game of contract bridge. "Politics," Hobbes declared, "is like a game of cards in which any suit may be trumps, but in the absence of agreement, clubs are trumps."

The essence of the political vocation in a free society is keeping coercion under control, to prevent human society from spiraling into anarchy. It is left to politicians to negotiate agreement so that some other suit than "clubs" becomes "trumps." To politicians falls the task of establishing justice so that people habitually resort to some other kinds of power to get their way (i.e., commerce, or diamonds; ideas, or hearts; and honor, or spades). If the political class fails and unregulated coercion becomes the primary means by which people gain the cooperation of others, then, as Hobbes would write in his masterpiece, *Leviathan,* "the life of man [becomes] solitary, poor, nasty, brutish, and short."[8]

Summary

Let me highlight four important points. First, where there is no law, there is a tyranny of thugs. Anarchy invites bullies to dominate by threat and permits them to get away with it. In fact, one brute left free to run amok may be enough to terrify an entire community. Recall the effect of the oppressive Judge Turner, who transformed Stephen Field's Marysville into a horror.

Second, unregulated coercion makes the strong weak and the weak strong; the seemingly powerful, prosperous, well-endowed, creative, and resourceful are rendered vulnerable by their assets, while those that have nothing or think nihilistically ascend to dominance. Experts in international affairs speak of "asymmetrical relationships," by which they mean that the very destitution of some nations advantages them in any confrontation with a major nation that has a seemingly overwhelming abundance of economic, intellectual, cultural, and military resources (like the United States).

Third, anarchy corrupts personal morality. The paradoxes of coercion rout out civilized behavior; to survive in a society where everyone is either victim or victimizer requires qualities of destructiveness, detachment, vendetta, and madness. In the lawless chaos of Marysville, ordinary people could protect themselves from thugs only by becoming thugs themselves. As a consequence, notions of virtue and vice were turned upside down, with the good man demeaned for his goodness and the wicked man admired for his ruthlessness. To "the disreputable characters" hanging out in the Marysville saloon, a hand held out in peace signified cowardice; a willingness to forgive was evidence of a weak will; a show of mercy meant one's bluff could be called with impunity; and cruelty earned their respect.

Fourth, the creation of sanctuaries—safe havens where people can escape threats—is key to a creative civilization. With respite from danger, individuals become free to put their talents and energies to good use. The first essential of a free society, therefore, is to establish reliably safe places. Then art, enterprise, invention, and love can thrive.

NOTES

1. Throughout this book, the word *power* means "getting others to do what one wishes them to do." Or, to put it another way, getting persons to "cooperate" with you, whether by means of threat (coercive power), exchange (reciprocal power), or shaping the way they think (moral power), is power.

2. The following analysis of coercion is largely derived from economics Nobel laureate Thomas C. Schelling's *The Strategy of Conflict* (Cambridge, Mass.: Harvard University Press, 1960). Particularly apt and insightful are Chapter 2 ("An Essay on Bargaining") and Chapter 3 ("Bargaining, Communication, and Limited War").

3. Niccolò Machiavelli, in *The Prince*, trans. Daniel Donno (New York: Dell, 1996 [1513]), chap. 17, cites approvingly the great Roman historian Tacitus's warning, "[Q]uod nihil sit tam infirmum aut instabile quam fama potentiae non sua vi nixae" ("[T]hat nothing is so weak and unstable as a reputation for power which is not based on one's own strength"). Tacitus, *Annals* XIII, 19.

4. The fourth-century Roman general Vegetius expressed a version of the paradox of face this way: "Qui desiderat pacem, praeparet bellum" ("Who desires peace, should prepare for war").

5. George Shultz, U.S. secretary of state from 1982 to 1989 and one of the twentieth century's most successful diplomats, emphasized that "the most useful lessons for dealing with a hostile world didn't emerge from his long years in diplomacy, but in labor, in the experience of collective bargaining: 'You show me a union that will never strike, and I'll show you a union that isn't going to get anywhere. You show me a management that will never take a strike, and I'll show you a management that's going to get pushed around.'" Daniel Henninger, "The Weekend Interview with George Shultz," *Wall Street Journal,* April 29, 2006, A8.

6. Machiavelli, *The Prince,* chap. 17.

7. See Ralph Peters, "The Counterrevolution in Military Affairs," *Weekly Standard* 11, no. 20 (February 6, 2006): 19, where Peters remarks on the credibility of the threat posed by the fundamentalist religious zealot:

> Not a single item in our trillion-dollar arsenal can compare with the genius of the suicide bomber—the breakthrough weapon of our time. Our intelligence systems cannot locate him, our arsenal cannot deter him, and, all too often, our soldiers cannot stop him before it is too late. A man of invincible conviction— call it delusion, if you will—armed with explosives stolen or purchased for a handful of soiled bills can have a strategic impact that staggers governments. Abetted by the global media, the suicide bomber is the wonder weapon of the age.
>
> The suicide bomber's willingness to discard civilization's cherished rules for warfare gives him enormous strength. In the Cain-and-Abel conflicts of the 21st century, ruthlessness trumps technology. We refuse to comprehend the suicide bomber's soul—even though today's wars are contests of souls, and belief is our enemy's ultimate order of battle. We write off the suicide bomber as a criminal, a wanton butcher, a terrorist. Yet, within his spiritual universe, he's more heroic than the American soldier who throws himself atop a grenade to spare his comrades: He isn't merely protecting other men, but defending his god. The suicide bomber can justify any level of carnage because he's doing his god's will.

8. Thomas Hobbes, *Leviathan, or the Matter, Form, and Power of a Commonwealth, Ecclesiastical and Civil* (1651), chap. 13.

3

TYRANNY

A nation, despicable by its weakness, forfeits even the privilege of neutrality.

Alexander Hamilton, *Federalist* No. 11 (1787)

The only effective way to restrain those who abuse coercive power is to intimidate them. Just as Judge Bennett advised Stephen Field to frighten the bully of Marysville into a standoff, Abraham Lincoln, in the midst of the American Civil War, would explain to a Quaker practitioner of nonviolence, "[While] on principle and faith, [each of us is] opposed to both war and oppression, [we] can only practically oppose oppression by war."[1]

That is such an important reality that it bears repeating: coercion is the *only* practical way to check abusive coercion. Meeting threat with counterthreat is the indispensable key to a just peace—real peace, not the peace of the graveyard. Unless a community has the strength and determination to extort civility from would-be extortionists, thugs will dominate. It is an idea ages old and is commonly known as the balance of power.

The Balance of Power

The term *balance of power,* however, is not perfectly descriptive of what its proponents mean. For one thing, they are not talking about balancing all forms of power, but only coercive power. They might better speak of *balance of fear*. Diplomacy and concessions will never civilize thugs without first intimidating them.

Nor does the word *balance* do justice to the complexity of countering threat with threat. Balancing power requires much more than a mere identity of force. Rather, an effective balance, one that will protect relationships from deteriorating into mindless ultimatums, requires *capability* and *commitment*—both a real opportunity to destroy the hostages of your adversary and the will to do so in the event your bluff is called.

Consider the importance of *capability*. Capability means that hostages must be virtually defenseless. If not in your actual possession, they must be highly vulnerable to assault. Otherwise, there is no balance of power. If an aggressive country has a large army and an unimpeded route to a nation in its neighborhood that has no army to fortify itself, then it is obviously capable of carrying out its ultimatum: "Surrender your territory [the ransom], or we will kill your citizens and plunder your possessions [the hostages]." If, however, the vulnerable nation has allies that do have sufficient force to defend it and its citizenry, the would-be invader's capability is thrown into question.

But capability has to be combined with a demonstrable commitment to exercise it. Or, as former secretary of state George Ball once put it, "The most important item in the calculus of [establishing a balance of power is] the relative strength of will of the parties."[2] Just as Stephen Field tamed anarchy in Marysville by publicly exhibiting the pleasure he would take in shooting the intimidating Judge Turner, one must combine the capability to harm with a convincing *willingness* to carry out one's threats, notwithstanding the dangers and costs of doing so.

Recall the concept of "face" in the previous chapter as a reputation for "ill will." To effect a real balance of power between nations, each of the adversaries must be able to convince the other that it will pursue vengeance unrelentingly for any injury done to it.

The notion of balance of power has application to a nation's domestic as well as its international affairs. Consider how Americans conduct labor relations. The laws of contract give an employer the capability—the *legal authority*—to fire employees (their paychecks are the boss's hostages) unless they work hard and otherwise behave themselves (the ransom). At the same time, different laws—in particular, the National Labor Relations Act—balance the company's coercive advantage by making it legal for employees to strike and bankrupt their employer's business (the hostage) unless the firm deals fairly with them (the ransom). By legitimizing mutual extortion, Congress established the foundation for an effective balance of power. Consequently, today neither labor nor management is likely to act contemptuously. They first resort to negotiating, bargaining in good faith and educating each other about their needs and interdependence. In other words, American factory workers and industrial bosses, once violent adversaries, have called a truce and (at least, relatively speaking) are peaceable with one another. Compared to yesteryear, today's labor-management relations are without violence, orderly, and productive. Underlying this civility is a balance of power, the result of carefully crafted legislation.

If we look elsewhere—at a crime-free neighborhood, an abuse-free marriage, or a store full of satisfied customers—we will detect other balances of power subtly and quietly underlying those happy conditions.

There are those who challenge the necessity for a balance of power, insisting that there exist less risky ways than mutual threats to stop aggressive bullies. "Think of the success," their argument runs, "of passive resistance in colonial India, or of the nonviolent civil rights movement right here in our own country."

The Shortcomings of Nonviolent Resistance

But are they right? Is it true, for example, that by merely turning the other cheek, Mahatma Gandhi (1869–1948) and his followers overwhelmed Britain with moral goodness and induced it to give up its colonial rule?

Not exactly. In fact, Gandhi was a skilled and perceptive practitioner of the balance of power. By peacefully refusing to resign himself and his followers to colonial rule (as the Indian people once had), he took hostage an asset Great Britain held very dear—its international reputation for civilized behavior, a reputation it thought vital to its commercial relationships throughout the nontyrannical world. Were the British to have jailed or injured the nonviolent Gandhi and his followers, the carefully cultivated image of a decent Great Britain—its "good will"—would have been in tatters.

A similar explanation accounts for the success of the civil rights movement in the American South. With the development of television and its dramatization of the news, civil rights leaders like Martin Luther King Jr. (1929–1968) found that they could hold the southern economy hostage. By countering the fearsome power of segregationists with threats of harsh publicity broadcast to the world, they convinced most of the white leaders to start negotiating.

Contrast the effectiveness of Gandhi and King with the impotence of nonviolent resistance in Nazi Germany, the Soviet Union, or Communist China. Instead of standing down to nonviolence, their armies slaughtered the unarmed resisters. Why? Because those three regimes maintained their international dominance by fear, not by moral example or commerce. Instead of caring about a reputation for decency, they valued being known for their ruthlessness. They were the perfect thugs, having nothing to lose but their appearance of implacability. A brutal response to nonviolence, far from damaging that reputation, would only enhance it.

In other words, nonviolence succeeds only when one's adversary holds its reputation for decency in high regard.

NOTES

1. Abraham Lincoln to Eliza P. Gurney, September 4, 1864, as quoted in Doris Kearns Goodwin, *Team of Rivals: The Political Genius of Abraham Lincoln* (New York: Simon and Schuster, 2005), 562.
2. George W. Ball, "The Trap of Rationality," *Newsweek*, July 26, 1971, 43.

4

THE POLICE POWER

*Most people . . . assume . . . policing is uniquely human. But they
would be wrong. . . . [M]onkey societies also have police. [A few
high-ranking individuals in the pig-tailed macaque monkey spe-
cies] do not just defend their own interests. . . . [T]hey also intervene to break up conflicts between lower-ranking individuals in an
apparently disinterested way. Moreover, removing these police
makes such societies less happy places . . . result[ing] in the
remaining monkeys grooming fewer others, playing with fewer
others and dividing up into cliques as the social network that held
the troop together broke down. The number of aggressive incidents
also increased. . . . [T]he role of policing in these monkeys is to
allow individuals to socialise widely at little risk and thus hold a
large troop together, since the police will intervene if things get out
of hand.*

The Economist (January 28, 2006)

A Division of Labor

The realistic question is not *whether* the balance of power is necessary to
deal with the power of terror, but *how* the balance of power is to be
employed skillfully. Establishing peaceful order in the face of threats of violence is so difficult that societies develop a division of labor. Communities

recruit and train "a particular class of citizens"[1] in the use of coercion. They equip this cadre of specialists with the police power—with lethal weapons, prisons, and laws legitimating their use. When America's founders met in Philadelphia in 1787 to design a new Constitution, they established a national government strong enough to "insure domestic tranquility" and "provide for the common defence." They gave it the powers to raise an army and a navy and to levy the taxes to pay for a military to counter anarchy within and without their new nation.

As the legal scholar Hans Kelsen points out, however, they and their political successors "attache[d] certain conditions to the use of force . . . authorizing the employment of force only by certain individuals and only under certain circumstances."[2] They limited the use of the police power with definite rules of engagement.

The question endures: did the conditions attached to the police power make it too weak to frighten the thugs into submission? Or, on the contrary, were the restrictions on the police power so ineffective that communities were left at the mercies of their police guardians? Did America get the balance right?

Experience has taught us that when the police are too weak, either because they lack capability or commitment, thugs will run amok, so endangering the society that it will look elsewhere for protective services and be willing to pay heavily for them. On the other hand, history also teaches that when insufficiently restrained, police will violate the liberty and property of ordinary persons and become tyrants.

At both these realities we now look.

Weak Police and the Rise of Warlords

In the early decades of the twentieth century the Italian neighborhoods in New York City received virtually no police protection. The Irish political machine that dominated New York City government controlled the police department, and it had little interest in protecting people living in areas they condemned as "Little Italy." Few cops were sent to patrol the streets. Without police protection, the residents fell prey to thugs and extortionists, and anarchy reigned in this "inner-city" neighborhood.

In his novel The Godfather,[3] Mario Puzo dramatizes what filled the vacuum of public police protection. The pivotal event occurs when Vito Corleone (his last name derived from the village where he was born in Sicily) is confronted by a small-time hoodlum, Fanucci, the neighborhood terrorist who extorts "protection money" from the grocers and other businessmen in the neighborhood. Fanucci is "a brutal-looking man and he had done nothing to disguise the circular scar that stretched in a white semicircle from ear to ear, hooking under his chin."

Accustomed to subservience, Fanucci bluntly demands that Vito give him five hundred dollars, and he opens his coat to reveal a gun stuck in his waistband. Vito, instead of submitting to Fanucci, murders him. To Vito's surprise, his neighbors treat him as a savior. Soon, several of Fanucci's former victims come to Vito and offer him payments to safeguard them from other vicious predators in the neighborhood. Vito accepts their offers and soon finds more and more willing customers in need of protective services. Most of his paying clients run harmless businesses that happen to be outside the law: gambling establishments, brothels, and speakeasies (it is the Prohibition era). Because they provide illegal commodities, they cannot call on official police, yet they need police-like services to protect against robberies and disturbances within their establishments. Vito responds to this increasing demand by hiring several young men and training them in supplying effective protective services.

In time, he finds he is running a large private police force, the duties of which mirror those of public law enforcement agencies. Its men are protecting a sizeable clientele from danger and disruption and are on call twenty-four hours a day, seven days a week. Like other growing businesses, Vito's firm—he calls it The Family—encounters financial squeezes from time to time. His costs mount while services expand. On his payroll are numerous "enforcers" (i.e., the equivalent of patrol officers) and elite security personnel ("hit men"), managers, accountants, bill collectors, auditors, and lawyers. All these costs Vito has to meet reliably even during periods of business downturn. Moreover, Vito has to make capital investments (for housing, offices, cars, weapons, and the acquisition of legitimate businesses), expend resources on recruiting and training of employees, and fund research and development. Furthermore, Vito has to enter into independent contracts for outside services—deals with police officers, inspectors, judges, government officials, and labor leaders to turn a blind eye to the outlaw actions of The Family.

Caught in a cost squeeze, Vito has to find new revenue sources. He considers expanding the firm's clientele beyond relatively harmless businesses. His need for new markets tempts him to extend The Family's protection services to drug dealers, but he eventually rejects this opportunity out of scruples for the harm drugs do to children. (His decision provokes a rebellion within The Family, which he has to suppress violently.)

Vito, however, has no scruples against pursuing an enhanced business plan—gaining a monopoly position in the protection market, so that he can raise his fees for services. He "wipes out" local competitors and enters into noncompete agreements with mobs established elsewhere, who promise to confine their activities to prescribed geographical areas.[4] He also augments his business strategy in another way: he heightens the demand for The Family's services. He targets the moneyed and deep-pocketed customers—construction companies, filmmakers, and shipping lines—and persuades them to avail themselves of protection against arson, sabotage, labor strikes, and pilfering, the very harms he threatens to cause in the first place.

Puzo's novel about Vito and the business he godfathers (subsequently turned into *two* Academy Award–winning films) has become a classic because it illuminates the destinies of real-life private policing groups worldwide—not only the Mafia, but gangs of virtually every ancestry (like Oakland's Hell's Angels, the Black Panthers, and the Aryan Brotherhood), labor unions before legislation made their activities legal, the fire department of Julius Caesar, and contemporary "warlords" abroad. Virtually all of them have begun as private guardians, but finding their expenditures exceeding their revenues they resort to unacceptable practices—shakedowns, monopoly, and murder. Over time, their presence results not in order and safety, but in community oppression and the corruption of civilized morality.

Youngstown, Ohio

Consider Youngstown, Ohio. Youngstown is a city of 75,000 persons and sits in the Mahoning Valley, near the Pennsylvania border. In the first half of the twentieth century, jobs at its numerous steel mills attracted migrants from Poland, Greece, Italy, and Slovakia. Exhausted from their work and with money in their pockets, the steelworkers would flow into after-hours joints to drink and gamble late into the night. Mafia families from nearby big cities moved in to "protect" the illegal bars and gambling parlors. The local police and politicians pliably looked the other way and let the mob maintain order in the immigrant community, whose inhabitants, accustomed to the arbitrary and violent police power of their old countries, impotently accepted their lot.

In 2000 David Grann, an investigative reporter, went to Youngstown and found a city and environs now completely dominated by the mob and deserted by a fearful middle class. Grann visited Mark Shutes, an anthropologist at the local university, who described the moral rot that had resulted from the Mafia's usurpation of the police power.[5] Grann reported:

> Shutes contends that, after so many years of eroded civic institutions, the community has come to rely increasingly on mobsters, who play the same role in civic life the police and the political establishment do in other cities. "We have socialized ourselves and our offspring that this is the way the world is," he says. "This is our little safe part, with our community and church, but in order for it to be safe, you need these people to be brokers." Indeed, in a world where corruption is normal, he says, values prized in other cities are, in [Youngstown], deemed counter-productive. "We don't see high ideals as being a benefit," he explains. "We see [them] as being a weakness. There is no sense in this community in which gangsters are people who have imposed their will on our community. Their values are our values."

The parallel with the frontier Marysville of Stephen Field's account and the "Little Italy" in Mario Puzo's novel is almost eerie. Youngstown's police power was too weak to guarantee public safety; hoodlum warlords imposed a kind of order based on brute threat. As a result, the community's moral order got inverted, and civilization degenerated into lawless barbarism: "Their values are our values."

Police Tyranny in the South

On the other hand, when the police power is too strong and unfettered by restrictions, police departments grow dangerous. As law enforcement specialists, police officers have to survive in an intimidating world where they exercise threat to suppress the threats of others. Without effective limits on their use of force, some start descending a slippery moral slope. Lacking effective external controls, they find that the character-shaping claims of the four paradoxes of coercion turn them harsh and cynical, and they begin to suspect and brutalize the citizenry whose personal safety they should be protecting. In no place was this more the case than in our southern states throughout the century-long aftermath of the Civil War.

Easy as it is to forget the details of that place and time, it is perilous to ignore them. *Brown v. Mississippi*, a case decided by the U.S. Supreme Court in 1936, is one of those terrifying instances of where police power was unrestricted because the officials and attentive groups expected to control it failed to do so.

At night in the spring of 1934 three black sharecroppers in eastern Mississippi were taken from their homes by a local deputy sheriff named Cliff Dial, who accused them of murdering a white farmer. Aided by an unofficial and terrifying posse of white men, Sheriff Dial hung one of the suspects by his neck from a limb of a tree, not once but twice, before letting him down so that he would not strangle to death. He then proceeded to whip his victim without mercy. Two days later Sheriff Dial returned and arrested the fellow and took him to the police station, where he whipped him again, threatening that "the whipping would continue until he confessed."[6] Upon agreeing to admit to anything that the sheriff demanded, the accused was locked up, awaiting trial.

The other two suspects were arrested, jailed, and whipped with a leather strap with buckles, and "their backs were cut to pieces." They then agreed to confess "in all particulars of detail so as to conform to the demands of their torturers." In the course of the next four days, they were arraigned, tried, convicted, and sentenced to death, the only evidence of their guilt being the "confessions that were extorted from them."

Although Sheriff Dial admitted to compelling the confessions by torture, neither the trial judge nor the prosecutor condemned him or imposed limits on the state's police power. Nor did a majority of the Mississippi Supreme Court.

If one wants to understand what tyranny is really like, one needs do no more than immerse oneself in the facts of this case—police searches and arrests in the dead of night, lynchings, whippings, false testimony, forced confessions, perversion of the judicial process, and no effective restraints on a government abusing its monopoly of the police power and turning it to horrible purpose.

Thankfully, the U.S. Supreme Court reversed the convictions and set the defendants free, condemning Mississippi's then-common police practices. "It would be difficult to conceive," wrote Chief Justice Charles Evans Hughes, "of methods more revolting to the sense of justice than those taken to procure the confessions of these petitioners, and the use of the confessions thus obtained as the basis for conviction and sentence was a clear denial of due process."

"How Do You Control Power?"

The events set out in *Brown v. Mississippi* occurred more than sixty years ago, and the *systematic* tyranny that then afflicted the people of Mississippi no longer occurs there or anywhere in the United States.[7] But attention must always be paid to the possibility of the police power being misused. Whenever a society, in order to protect the people, creates a class of specialists with a monopoly in the exercise of coercive power, how can it be confident that the protectors won't turn into tyrants?

The experience of the twentieth century has not been a reassuring one. It has given us horrifying examples of official abuse. While nations engaged in two murderous world wars and innumerable local conflicts, the frightening fact is that, between 1901 and 2000, more people were killed by their own governments than by the armies of enemy nations. At the least, 20 million Soviet citizens (some say 40 million) were liquidated in internal purges; seven million innocent citizens of Germany, Poland, Austria, and other middle European countries were annihilated by the ruling Nazi regime of Adolf Hitler; nearly two million Cambodians were slaughtered by the brutal Pol Pot government; and in the three decades between 1949 to 1980 the Chinese communist regime was responsible for the deaths of 30 (or more) million Chinese, a population nearly as numerous as all of California's. In addition, police in Iraq,[8] North Korea, Iran, Afghanistan, Cuba, Rwanda, the Congo, Sudan, Zimbabwe, Libya, Burma, and Malaysia killed and plundered countless numbers of their own nationals. The magnitude of the slaughter staggers the mind; it's all the more jolting because the twentieth century began with such high hopes for enlightenment and real peace.

Several years ago Communist China permitted a group of its political scholars to visit the United States without the supervision of its secret police. Their first academic destination happened to be the University of California, Berkeley. Several of us were invited to join them for lunch. As we walked to the Faculty Club to meet our visitors, we guessed what might be their first question about America: Would it be how the free market works? Or would they ask why there appeared to be so much poverty in the midst of our abundance? Or would they inquire about America's real

intentions internationally, and especially toward China? None of our spec-
ulations proved right.

I will never forget the question they asked. Almost apologetically, the
oldest member of their delegation inquired, "How do you control power?"

The American experience offers an answer to that challenging problem.

Notes

1. Adam Smith, the eighteenth-century moral philosopher and economist whose
   insight into the importance of the division of labor was profound, comments
   on the development of professional armies and police in modern societies:

   > The first duty of the sovereign, that of protecting the society from the violence
   > and invasion of other independent societies, can be performed only by means of
   > a military force. But the expense both of preparing this military force in time of
   > peace, and of employing it in time of war, is very different in the different states
   > of society, in the different periods of improvement.
   >
   > Among nations of hunters, the lowest and rudest state of society, such as we
   > find it among the native tribes of North America, every man is a warrior as well
   > as a hunter. . . . In a yet more advanced state of society, among those nations of
   > husbandmen who have little foreign commerce, and no other manufactures but
   > those coarse and household ones which almost every private family prepares for
   > its own use, every man, in the same manner, either is a warrior or easily becomes
   > such. . . .
   >
   > In a more advanced state of society, two different causes contribute to render
   > it altogether impossible that they who take the field should maintain themselves
   > at their own expense. Those two causes are, the progress of manufactures, and
   > the improvement in the art of war.
   >
   > Though a husbandman should be employed in an expedition, provided it
   > begins after seed-time and ends before harvest, the interruption of his business
   > will not always occasion any considerable diminution of his revenue. Without
   > the intervention of his labour, nature does herself the greater part of the work
   > which remains to be done. But the moment that an artificer, a smith, a carpen-
   > ter, or a weaver, for example, quits his workhouse, the sole source of his revenue
   > is completely dried up. Nature does nothing for him, he does all for himself.
   > When he takes the field, therefore, in defence of the public, as he has no revenue
   > to maintain himself, he must necessarily be maintained by the public; but in a
   > country of which a great part of the inhabitants are artificers and manufacturers,
   > a great part of the people who go to war must be drawn from those classes, and
   > must therefore be maintained by the public as long as they are employed in its

service. [Moreover, as] the art of war . . . becomes . . . complicated. . . , it is necessary that it should become the sole or principal occupation of a particular class of citizens, and the division of labour is as necessary for the improvement of this as of every other art. [*Wealth of Nations* (1776), book 5, chap. 1, 301–304]

2. Hans Kelsen, *General Theory of Law and State* (New York: Russell and Russell, Inc., 1961 [1945]), 18–21.

3. Mario Puzo's *The Godfather* (originally published in 1969 and, in my opinion, the best *political* novel of the last half-century) was essential in informing the public about the origins and the methods of the Italian Mafia in America.

4. One problem with The Family's monopoly strategy is that its principal competitor is the legitimate police department, which is subsidized by taxes and nearly invulnerable to assassination. To avoid competition from the legitimate police, Vito has to buy its leadership off, which adds to operating costs.

5. David Grann, "Crimetown, USA: The City That Fell in Love with the Mob," *New Republic*, July 10 and 17, 2000, 28–31. Grann's report details the extent of mob control:

> The mob, which had once competed with the valley's civil society, largely became its civil society. As late as 1997, in the [nearby suburb] of Campbell, [mob boss] Strollo controlled at least 90 percent of the appointments to the police department. He fixed the civil-service exam so he could pick the chief of police and nearly all the patrolmen. The city law director literally brought the list of candidates for promotion to Strollo's house so the don could select the ones he wanted. "Strollo," says an attorney familiar with the city, could "determine which murderers went to jail and which ones went free."
>
> In 1996, while three mob hit men, including Mo Man Harris, were on their way to kill their latest target, they were pulled over by the Campbell police for speeding, according to people in the car. In the vehicle the cops found an AK-47 rifle, a .357 Magnum revolver, and a 9 mm pistol. One of the killers used his cell phone to call Jeff Riddle, who rushed to the scene and told the police the men were running an errand for Bernie the Jew [the mob's accountant]. The cops let them go.

6. All the quoted language is taken from Chief Justice Charles Evans Hughes's majority opinion in *Brown v. Mississippi*, 297 U.S. 298 (1936), where Hughes incorporated in its virtual entirety the dissent of the two justices on the Mississippi Supreme Court, a nearly unprecedented acknowledgment of the power of their written opinion.

7. An important turning point in improving American police practices was the "Due Process Revolution." Courts began to exclude evidence gained by unconstitutional compulsion and encroachment on privacy. Lest they lose convictions, police departments began instructing their officers on how to

regulate their conduct so as to conform to constitutional restrictions. The landmark case in this Due Process Revolution was *Mapp v. Ohio*, 367 U.S. 643 (1961). See Chapter 19 for a further explanation.

8. For an invaluable, if horrifying, account of the atrocities of Saddam Hussein against his own Iraqi nationals, see Chris Kutschera, ed., *Le Livre Noir de Saddam Hussein* (Paris: Oh! Editions, 2005).

5

THE AMERICAN CONSTITUTION

In framing a government which is to be administered by men over men, the great difficulty lies in this: you must first enable the government to control the governed; and in the next place oblige it to control itself.

James Madison, *Federalist* No. 51 (1788)

Before the invention of modern democracy, back as recently as Machiavelli's time, the time-honored check against a government turning tyrant was regicide. Regicide literally meant the killing of kings. The threat of assassination was the primary restraint that kept kings from being vicious and oppressive. Rulers like Nero and Caligula made themselves so objectionable that they were murdered or forced to flee, and their fate served as a warning to other would-be tyrants.

But with each passing century, those wielding the police powers of governments became stronger, their capacity for violence and destruction enlarged, and the circles of safety within which they could withstand rebellion were made infinitely more secure. In the twentieth century, most tyrants survived assassination attempts and outlived their domestic enemies. As those in authority developed a greater capacity for self-protection, regicide became a weaker, less dependable check on tyranny.

The unique contribution of the United States to the science of politics was devising a more efficient restraint on tyranny, our special American variation of democracy.

The Articles of Confederation

Like most reforms, the American invention was born of trial and error. Two years before the armies of George Washington subdued the British in 1783, the thirteen American colonies negotiated what they called "a firm league of friendship." They drew up the Articles of Confederation to regulate their relationship with one another.

In seven striking ways, the articles resembled the present-day charter of the United Nations (UN). For one, their expressed purposes were similar: first, to serve as a gathering place of diplomats representing independent states; and second, to arrange for collective action against threats to the peace.[1] Both the American Confederation and the United Nations were intended to be alliances, not governments.

Second, neither the American Confederation nor the United Nations extended their authority to persons; both claimed only to restrain states.[2]

Third, their powers to act were sharply circumscribed. Both the American Confederation and the United Nations were denied the authority to interfere in the internal affairs of the states that comprised them.

Fourth, they each lacked a unitary executive, but instead embraced a rule of unanimity among their several members on any matter requiring forceful action, thereby rendering them indecisive. Just as each of the five major powers on the UN Security Council enjoys an absolute veto over every proposal of major significance, so any of the thirteen American states could prevent the Confederation from taking any action.[3]

Fifth, each was denied the power to tax the people directly. Like the UN today, the Confederation could assess the "sovereign, independent, and free" governments that composed it for its funding, but if any state refused to contribute, it could refuse with impunity.

Sixth, neither the UN nor the American Confederation had the power to raise armies.

And seventh, both provided for international courts of such limited and contingent jurisdiction as to be rendered insignificant.

The point to keep in mind is that when Americans first gained their independence and designed a regime, their Articles of Confederation tried to solve the problem of tyranny by establishing a contradiction—a national government that had no police power. Their thinking was no police power, therefore no tyranny. But without a police power, there was no civil order, no national security, and no civil liberties. Instead, there were mutually extortionate practices by the states, armed internal rebellions, barbarism on the frontiers, piracy on the high seas, and predatory practices by the major European powers.[4]

In the summer of 1787, sixty-five highly respected political leaders, disturbed by the growing domestic anarchy and the Confederation's military weakness internationally, gathered in Philadelphia. To keep reporters from prying into their deliberations, they met in private, bolting the doors and shutting the windows of their hall, despite the summer heat. By September, they had negotiated agreement on a document they called the Constitution of the United States of America.

A Domestic Balance of Power

Both its letter and its spirit were a total departure from the libertarian principles underlying the anemic regime of the Confederation. It created a national government that had, at least on paper, a strong police power, supported by the authority to tax individual persons and raise armies. Its purposes, to correct the shortcomings of the Articles of Confederation, were set out with the greatest clarity in its preamble:

> We, the People of the United States, in Order to form a more perfect Union, establish Justice, insure domestic Tranquility, provide for the common defence, promote the general Welfare, and secure the Blessings of Liberty for ourselves and our Posterity, do ordain and establish this Constitution of the United States.

To achieve these six purposes, the Constitution gave the central government the right to regulate much of the commercial activity of the individual states, and it made provision for a national judiciary with a robust jurisdiction over them and their citizens. Moreover, it created a strong, unitary executive[5] and removed every vestige of the rule of unanimity from the document, enabling the new central government to take decisive action in spite of dissent.[6]

The thirty-nine delegates who signed the Constitution then had to submit it to the states for ratification. They expected vigorous resistance to their innovation and assigned themselves the task of returning to their home states to direct the campaigns for ratification. It happened that there was only one signatory to the Constitution from rich and populous New York, the state that was expected to mount the most vigorous opposition. He was Alexander Hamilton, a former top aide to General George Washington during the Revolutionary War and a highly respected lawyer. In New York, however, he was distrusted as a partisan "centralist"—someone who wanted to enlarge the power of the national government at the expense of New York and its dominant position in the Confederation. As the local manager for ratification, the solitary Hamilton knew he needed help; so he asked James Madison, a Virginia delegate, to join him in the New York campaign.

Together, they devised a strategy of writing a series of essays for publication in four of the five newspapers circulating in New York City. Every third day, for a period of nine months, Hamilton or Madison would write a "paper," justifying a particular section of the proposed Constitution. Their collaboration (augmented briefly by the participation of John Jay, who early became ill) produced eighty-five different essays.[7] So popular were they that upstate newspapers began reprinting them, and even before the ratification process was over, they were assembled in two hardcover volumes and sold throughout the thirteen states under the title of *The Federalist*. As a result, they developed a wide readership and structured the public debate.

The essays were memorably eloquent, carefully detailed, and coherent. Most importantly, they set out the political theory underlying the Constitution. Its framers, they wrote, had sought to steer the American nation between the perils of anarchy and tyranny: "[Y]ou must first enable the government to control the governed; and in the next place oblige it to control itself."[8]

Alexander Hamilton and James Madison

Even now, more than two centuries later, judges, government officials, and laypersons alike treat *The Federalist* as the definitive explanation of the Constitution. Who were these two men who authored the essays that provided such profound understanding of governing a free people? What were Alexander Hamilton (1755–1804) and James Madison (1751–1836) like?

They were as unlikely a pair of collaborators as one could imagine. Temperamentally, Hamilton was aggressive, conspicuous, and boundlessly energetic. Madison was "paralyzingly shy," diffident, and sickly throughout much of his life. Despite serving heroically on the battlefield during the revolution (General Washington selected him to be his aide-de-camp and promoted him to lieutenant colonel), Hamilton admired the British, their commercial ingenuity, and their form of government. Madison, on the other hand, did not fight on the battlefields of the Revolutionary War, but never abandoned his mistrust of all things English (Madison did serve as a delegate to the Continental Congress from 1775 to 1779). Hamilton condemned civil disorder; Madison feared the possibility of governmental tyranny. Yet each had exceptional political gifts. President Theodore Roosevelt, no intellectual slouch himself, thought Hamilton was "the most brilliant American statesman who ever lived, possessing the loftiest and keenest intellect of his time."[9] And of the five-foot, four-inch, hundred-pound Madison, a contemporary observer wrote, "Never have I seen so much mind in so little matter."[10]

Historian Joseph Ellis, in his perceptive account of the nation's *Founding Brothers: The Revolutionary Generation*, contrasts the two men with colorful detail. Of Hamilton, he writes:[11]

[He] had a light peaches and cream complexion with violet-blue eyes and auburn-red hair, all of which came together to suggest an animated beam of light. . . . [He] conveyed kinetic energy incessantly expressing itself in bursts of conspicuous brilliance. . . . [His] dashing and consistently audacious style developed as a willful personal wager against the odds of his impoverished origins. John Adams, who despised Hamilton, once referred to him as "the bastard brat of a Scotch pedlar." While intended as a libelous description, Adams' choice of words was literally correct. Hamilton had been born on the West Indian island of Nevis, the illegitimate son of a down-on-her-luck beauty of French extraction and a hard-drinking Scottish merchant with a flair for bankruptcy. In part because of his undistinguished origins, Hamilton always seemed compelled to be proving himself; he needed to impress his superiors with his own superiority. Whether he was leading an infantry assault against an entrenched British strong point at Yorktown—first over the parapet in a desperate bayonet charge—or imposing his own visionary fiscal program for the new nation on a reluctant federal government, Hamilton tended to regard worldly problems as personal challenges, and therefore as fixed objects against which he could perform his own isometric exercises, which usually took the form of ostentatious acts of gallantry.

And Professor Ellis's description of Madison is equally compelling:[12]

"Little Jemmy Madison" had the frail and discernibly fragile appearance of a career librarian or schoolmaster, forever lingering on the edge of some fatal ailment, overmatched by the daily demands of ordinary life. When he left his father's modest-sized plantation at Montpelier in Virginia to attend

Princeton in 1769 . . . the youthful Madison had confessed to intimations of imminent mortality, somewhat morbidly predicting his early death. . . . Not only did he look like the epitome of insignificance—diminutive, colorless, sickly—he was also paralyzingly shy, the kind of guest at a party who instinctively searched out the corners of the room.

Appearances, in Madison's case, were not just massively deceptive; they actually helped to produce his prowess. Amid the flamboyant orators of the Virginia dynasty, he was practically invisible and wholly unthreatening, but therefore the acknowledged master of the inoffensive argument that just happened, time after time, to prove decisive. He seemed to lack a personal agenda because he seemed to lack a personality, yet when the votes were counted, his side almost always won. His diffidence in debate was disarming in several ways: He was so obviously gentle and so eager to give credit to others, especially his opponents, that it was impossible to unleash one's full fury against him without seeming a belligerent fool; he was so reserved that he conveyed the off-putting impression of someone with an infinite reservoir of additional information, all hidden away, the speaker not wishing to burden you with excessively conspicuous erudition; but, if you gave permission, fully prepared to go on for several more hours; or until your side voluntarily surrendered. His physical deficiencies meant that a Madisonian argument lacked all the usual emotional affectations and struck with the force of pure, unencumbered thought.

These two men—Hamilton, the man of affairs, and Madison, the man of ideas—pooled their experience and scholarship to convince generations of Americans. This fortuitous collaboration of diverse minds, written with the very practical purpose of winning ratification, made for a work of genius.

The Principle of Popular Sovereignty

Hamilton and Madison recognized that one foundation of the Constitution was the principle of popular sovereignty, by which the electorate could check the lawmaking power invested in government officials. By providing the people with the vote and the opportunity to cast it in a free election, the Constitution permitted the governed to hold hostage the careers of their governors. Through their votes, the people could dash the hopes of professional politicians to retain their offices beyond the next election. Democracy as regicide—a bloodless assassin, to be sure, and a deliberative one, but nonetheless one that could eliminate any official who attempted to turn tyrant—that was the way Hamilton and Madison viewed democracy.

We will return to the topic of the external check of electoral democracy in later chapters. Suffice it to say at this point that neither Hamilton nor Madison nor any member of the Constitutional Convention in 1787 really felt confident that this innovation of popular sovereignty would work satisfactorily, but they were certain of one thing: that the future of their nation should not depend solely on it to check governmental abuse.

And I believe they were right. Anyone who counts on elections alone to check tyranny is like a nation that disbands its army and depends for its defense on its cache of nuclear bombs. Electoral defeat is both too big and too undependable a threat to check the minor infractions of officials—too big because the voter usually wants only to tame an official's career, not end it, and too undependable because it takes widespread awareness of the official's shortcomings to execute it. The threat of electoral defeat is not an efficient way to check the small and invisible abuses of power that may gradually accumulate into tyranny.

The Necessity of Internal Checks

Instead, as *The Federalist* makes clear, those who framed the Constitution gave virtually all their attention to the structure of the new regime. The key to their thinking was to establish numerous internal restraints within a strong central government. Wherever the Constitution conferred on the national government the authority to exercise coercion, at least two independent departments within it had to concur in its particular exercise. The Constitution, in effect, applied the theory of the international balance of power to the construction of a domestic government. In Madison's words, "Ambition must be made to counteract ambition,"[13] much like one suspicious nation counteracts another in foreign politics. For every power conferred on one branch of government, a counterpower was given to another.[14]

The essays of Hamilton and Madison explain how this constitutional balance of power depended on two vital principles. One was the separation of powers. Governmental power was to be distributed among distinct departments—the executive branch, the judiciary, two legislative houses, and the several state governments (each of which, in turn, would employ its own system of separated powers).

The phrase *separated powers* referred to the virtual invulnerability of individual members of each department to *personal* threats from any of the other departments. The Constitution created safe havens within which constitutional officers could protect themselves and their personal possessions from being taken hostage. For example, the Constitution put every official's salary in sanctuary—outside the hostile reach of any other department but his own.[15] As *Federalist* No. 51 expresses it, "Were the executive magistrate, or the judges, not independent of the legislature in this particular [that is, in the matter of cutting or enhancing their salaries], their independence in every other would be merely nominal." (The same applied for the independence of state officials; their compensation could not be affected by Congress.)

For another example, both the president (by virtue of executive privilege) and members of Congress (by virtue of congressional immunity) were provided constitutional sanctuary, shielding each branch from the hostile interference of the other in their deliberations.

The other principle was that of checks and balances, which referred to the fact that in every significant matter, authority would be shared. For the government to act, two or more of these "separate," personally invulnerable departments had to acquiesce. The president and the Senate had to agree on all major executive and judicial appointments. The House of Representatives, the Senate, and the president needed to concur in the passage of all tax measures. As for funding government programs, the Constitution required that the House, Senate, and president arrive at a consensus regarding any decision to cut or enhance spending. The congressional power to investigate was made dependent upon the judiciary's willingness to issue subpoenas to compel testimony and production of documents. The executive's regulatory power was not enforceable without the sanction of courts. And so on.[16]

The principle of checks and balances meant that American government was conducted in the open and not closeted in any one department. The constitutional requirement of the joint approval of two (or more) independent departments effectively compelled public, transparent negotiations in which officials had to persuade one another of the rightness of their actions.

The Consequences of Internal Checks

In such a system, serious disagreements are bound to come to the surface, but they are regulated and resolved in a variety of forums—sometimes in courts (when the national government sues the states, and vice versa); at other times through legislative procedures (including conference committees where rival legislative houses hammer out compromises); and at still other times within political parties, loyalty to which motivates officials to transcend the boundaries separating the several branches.

Foreign observers unused to this elaborate system of balanced powers frequently express distress at what seems to them an endless deadlock. They point out that Americans have gone too far in avoiding the possibility of active tyranny. They claim that the Constitution, in fact, permits a tyranny of governmental *inaction*. They pointedly ask, "When government fails to act in a timely fashion to cure an unjust status quo, isn't that an equal or worse danger?"

But is their critique reasonable? There are three arguments why it is not.

First, the American system is surprisingly supple. The activity level of governments in the United States appears as high as in the free societies of Canada, Great Britain, and France, each of which concentrates lawmaking power in a single elective parliament. The United States confronts and resolves its public problems with surprising quickness because activists can take their initiatives to any of fifty-four independent government departments.[17] If the U.S. House of Representatives refuses to act on a measure, for example, the U.S. Senate may prove more receptive—or an executive agency, or the courts, or (most likely of all) one of the fifty state legislatures. Consider, for instance, the American response to the needs of the disabled for public access: compare the timely action in the United States with that of any parliamentary democracy, and one is left suspicious of the criticism of American deadlock and inaction.

Second, in America government actions tend to gain wholehearted acceptance by the people as a result of the openness of the debate between the separate elements of government. The negotiations between them educate the general public and prepare it to accept the need for new laws. Public negotiation of agreements is not wasted time.[18]

Third, the resulting policies are virtually always smart. Big glitches are rare, and little ones are quickly repaired. Of course, reasonable people might question whether better policy results from America's compound government than from the unitary ones of other democracies, but there is a plausible argument supporting the proposition. If two or more departments must be swayed before the government can enact a law, then broader public support must be enlisted for its passage. Imagine a hypothetical situation (admittedly an overly simple one, but accurate enough for our purposes): one sector of the public (say, lawyers) has a dominating influence in the legislative department, while a different sector of the public (say, religious clerics) is weightier in the executive. To get a measure affecting both professions passed by Congress *and* signed by the president, a mutually agreeable policy must be developed, one more likely to harmonize the interests of the two than help one at the expense of the other.

Of course, proponents of such contentious reforms as gun control, tax simplification, automobile fuel economy, universal access to health care, and more amply funded welfare-to-work programs become distressed by their inability to effect immediate change. In their frustration, they point their fingers at the complexity of our governmental institutions and decry the "special interests" that outwit them.[19]

But a more convincing explanation of the deadlock they lament is the ambivalence of the electorate. Until a significant majority of the public is ready to acquiesce to a specific solution of these devilishly difficult issues, Americans are inclined to resist compulsion of any kind. The cause of inaction is the lack of the consent of the governed, not the complexity of the government.

Even if the critics of complexity are partly right, however, they miss the point. The value of protecting against tyranny (and impulsive resort to government's coercive powers) outweighs the cost of laggard response. There are trade-offs in life. Nothing—not even shielding a citizenry from an oppressive and unjust government—comes free. Alexander Hamilton put the matter well in the concluding *Federalist* paper, No. 85: "I never expect to see a perfect work from imperfect man."

But we fail to see the whole picture if we focus exclusively on the checks and balances within government. For those who participated in the Constitutional Convention believed that the private marketplace, if robustly competitive and free of private and public monopolies, could perform tasks that only governments theretofore had attempted. Hamilton and Madison explained in *The Federalist Papers* that the framers of the Constitution set out to create a republic where "the commercial character of America"[20] would flourish and private enterprise would fulfill duties once thought to require state action. Competition among suppliers and customers, they foresaw, would create countless little balances of power. In this respect, the contemporary United States has exceeded Hamilton and Madison's wildest hopes. Not only do private entities produce the nation's goods, spread information, manage the flow of money, dole out capital, grow food, transport goods and travelers, put citizens to work, manage religious life, and train workers, but they also compete with government to deliver the mail, educate youngsters, and recycle the garbage.

In addition, private enterprises compete among themselves to do the government's business of equipping the nation's military, building its highways, and managing official data. For our founding fathers, socialism—government domination in meeting public needs—was anathema, not because of its aspirations, but because of its imprudent concentration of power. The theory of socialism, they would have argued, neglected the central principle of a free society's government: for every conferral of power, create a counterpower to check it.

Summary

The American Constitution framed a novel system of government, an intricate balance of numerous powers. The Americans who wrote it had experienced and rebelled against the harshness of English colonial rule. They had also witnessed the Confederation's weakness, which had provoked public fear and anger. As a consequence, the founders designed a new kind of government, one that was both strong enough to subdue anarchy and circumscribed enough to check tyranny.

The premise of the Constitution is a deep distrust of coercive power, a suspicion of man's temptation-prone nature, and a horror of combining the one with the other without the most careful regulation. Its framers were determined to design a government that could accommodate such human flaws as avarice, fear, jealousy, and vengeance.

History has supported their prudence. It is no accident that for more than two centuries the American Constitution has survived in spite of human nature's dark side. The framers paid attention to the reality of selfishness and evil in human existence and took precautions to baffle it. As the mindful Madison said so sensibly,[21]

It may be a reflection on human nature that such devices [as the separation of powers and checks and balances] should be necessary to control the abuses of government. But what is government itself but the greatest of all reflections on human nature? If men were angels, no government would be necessary. If angels were to govern men, neither external nor internal controls of government would be necessary.

NOTES

1. Articles of Confederation (1781): "The said states hereby severally enter into a firm league of friendship with each other, for their common defense. . . " (Article III). United Nations Charter (1945): "The Purposes of the United Nations are: (1) To maintain international peace and security, and to that end: To take effective collective measures for the prevention and removal of threats to the peace, and for the suppression of acts of aggression or other breaches of the peace, and . . . (4) To be a center for harmonizing the actions of nations in the attainment of these common ends" (Chapter I, Article 1).

2. *Federalist* No. 15:

   Government implies the power of making laws. It is essential, to the idea of a law, that it be attended with a sanction; or, in other words, a penalty of punishment for disobedience. If there be no penalty annexed to disobedience, the resolutions or commands which pretend to be laws will in fact amount to nothing more than advice or recommendation. This penalty, whatever it may be, can only be inflicted in two ways; by the agency of the Courts and Ministers of Justice, or by military force; by the coertion of the magistracy, or by the COERTION of arms. The first kind can evidently apply only to men—the last kind must of necessity be employed against bodies politic, or communities or States. It is evident, that there is no process of a court by which their observance of the laws can in the last resort be enforced. Sentences may be denounced against them for violations of their duty; but these sentences can only be carried into execution by the sword. In an association where the general authority is confined to the collective bodies of the communities that compose it, every breach of the laws must involve a state of war, and military execution must become the only instrument of civil obedience. Such a state of things can certainly not deserve the name of government, nor would any prudent man choose to commit his happiness to it.

3. Even amending the articles required the consent of every member state.

4. For a definitive account of the conditions during the years of the Confederation, see Gordon S. Wood's Bancroft Prize–winning history, *The Creation of the*

American Republic 1776–1787 (Chapel Hill: University of North Carolina Press, 1998 [1969]).

5 The most compelling justification of a strong American executive is Alexander Hamilton, *Federalist* No. 70: "Decision, activity, secrecy, and dispatch," especially, are vital to the successful conduct of war; "the executive is the bulwark of the national security."

6. For a full understanding of the Constitution and its making, I highly recommend Akhil Reed Amar's uniquely informative, highly readable *America's Constitution: A Biography* (New York: Random House, 2005).

7. John Jay was then the most distinguished delegate in Philadelphia (excepting Benjamin Franklin and George Washington). He wrote six of the essays, the bulk of which described the geostrategic peril of the American Confederation in a world of covetous great powers, particularly France, Spain, and Great Britain.

8. *Federalist* No. 51.

9. As quoted in Ron Chernow, *Alexander Hamilton* (New York: Penguin Press, 2004), 7.

10. As quoted in Joseph J. Ellis, *Founding Brothers: The Revolutionary Generation* (New York: Alfred A. Knopf, 2001), 54.

11. Ibid., 21–22.

12. Ibid., 54.

13. *Federalist* No. 51.

14. Ibid. In a celebrated passage, Madison makes explicit the prudential assumptions that guided the Constitutional Convention:

> [T]he great security against a gradual concentration of the several powers in the same department, consists in giving to those who administer each department, the necessary constitutional means, and personal motives, to resist encroachments of the others. The provision for defence must in this, as in all other cases, be made commensurate to the danger of attack. Ambition must be connected with the constitutional rights of the place. . . .
>
> This policy of supplying, by opposite and rival interests, the defect of better motives, might be traced through the whole system of human affairs, private as well as public. . . . These inventions of prudence cannot be less requisite in the distribution of the supreme powers of the state.

15. The president's compensation "shall neither be increased nor diminished during the period for which he shall have been elected"; the compensation of federal judges "shall not be diminished during their continuance in office"; the compensation of lawmaking senators and representatives is "to be ascertained by law" (that is, by themselves); and, of course, the payment of state officials is determined by each state.

16. For a discussion of federalism, see Chapter 24.

17. That is, fifty states, plus the four departments of the national government (presidency, House of Representatives, Senate, and federal courts).

18. Hamilton, while less an enthusiast of legislatures than his collaborator Madison, pointed up their value: "In the legislature, promptitude of decision is oftener an evil than a benefit. The differences of opinion, and the jarrings of parties in that department of the government, though they may sometimes obstruct salutary plans, yet often promote deliberation and circumspection; and serve to check excesses in the majority." *Federalist* No. 70.

19. The recession of 2008—arguably the product of too little regulation of the marketing of unaffordable home mortgages and the bundling of good and bad mortgages in an innovative form of marketable security—might be evidence of the danger of American governmental "deadlock." Parliamentary democracies, however, while free of a separation of powers and elaborate checks and balances, were no more timely in enacting safeguards against the potential dangers leading to the recession.

20. *Federalist* No. 11.

21. *Federalist* No. 51.

6

THE DECLARATION OF INDEPENDENCE

It was not man who implanted in himself the taste for what is infinite and the love of what is immortal; these lofty instincts are not the offspring of his capricious will; their steadfast foundation is fixed in human nature, and they exist in spite of his efforts. He may cross and distort them; destroy them he cannot. The soul has wants which must be satisfied. . . .

Alexis de Tocqueville, *Democracy in America* (1840)

No one will ever accuse the authors of *The Federalist* of holding an idealized picture of human nature: they never forgot that "men are ambitious, vindictive, and rapacious."[1] But human nature is more complicated than simply a troubling tendency toward evil, and American political philosophy reflects that complexity. In fact, the premise of America's other founding document, the Declaration of Independence, is that people are "good" and "patient" and endowed by "nature's God" with the necessary self-discipline to be free.

When speaking of the Declaration of Independence, we come on a name not mentioned in our discussion of the Constitution. Thomas Jefferson was the principal draftsman of the Declaration of Independence. In the Constitutional Convention, however, he played no part; in 1787 he was in Paris as the American Confederation's emissary to France.

Thomas Jefferson

Born in 1743 into a prominent, up-country, land-owning Virginia family, Jefferson early displayed a marked aptitude for mathematics and the natural sciences, but he was intent on a career as a lawyer and politician. By 1767, when he concluded his legal studies, Virginia was growing impatient with its English governor and his repeated failures to heed the warnings of the colonial legislature that taxes were too high and commercial regulation too severe.

The young Jefferson collaborated with other activists to organize a political resistance, developing a broad network of correspondence. By 1774, Jefferson and others had hatched the idea of convening a Continental Congress from all thirteen of the North American colonies, and in 1775 the first Congress met in Philadelphia, bringing the thirty-two-year-old Jefferson into face-to-face contact with representatives from the other colonies.

Grievances against English rule accumulated, and when the Continental Congress met for a second time in 1776, its members made the fateful decision that the colonies should cut their ties to the mother country. Out of twin concerns to rally the colonists' spirit of resistance and to enlist foreign support, the Congress established a writing committee to compose a public justification for rebellion. Jefferson's colleagues knew him to be a forceful and eloquent writer; so, despite his youth and habitual reticence, they appointed him to the writing committee, along with two New Englanders, John Adams and Roger Sherman; a New Yorker named Robert Livingston; and the greatly respected Benjamin Franklin from Pennsylvania.

Jefferson sought out and won the job of composing the first draft. He explained that his object was to put in plain words what he thought was the common sense of Americans of that period. As he told a friend, the Declaration of Independence "was intended to be an expression of the American mind. . . . All its authority rests then on the harmonizing sentiments of the day, whether expressed in conversation, in letters, printed essays, or in the elementary books of public right."[2] His views of the "sentiments of the day" were deeply colored by his education at the College of William and Mary, where he had encountered the philosophy of the Scottish Enlightenment and particularly that of Francis Hutcheson, the influential moral philosopher who lectured at the University of Glasgow from 1729 to 1746.[3]

Jefferson's fellow committee members carefully went over each word of his draft, with an eye to winning the approval of the Congress as a whole. They then passed their handiwork on to the Congress for further consideration and amendment. Eventually, after considerable debate and several more changes, the document gained the unanimous approval of the Congress and was officially made public on July 4, 1776.[4]

The Declaration consisted of two parts, the second reading like a criminal indictment. It charged the English king with several dozen misdeeds, ranging from "imposing taxes without our consent" to inciting the Indians to attack "the inhabitants on our frontiers."

The first part of the Declaration—a kind of preamble to the indictment—is what Americans remember. It was philosophical in temper and began, "When in the course of human events, it becomes necessary for one people to dissolve the political bands which have connected them with another, and to assume, among the powers of the earth, the separate and equal station to which the laws of nature and of nature's God entitle them, a decent respect to the opinions of mankind requires that they should declare the causes which impel them to the separation." It then set out the four principles—the "self-evident truths"—that justified the rebellion:

> . . . that all men are created equal; that they are endowed by their Creator with certain unalienable rights; that among these are life, liberty, and the pursuit of happiness[; and t]hat, to secure these rights governments are instituted among men, deriving their just powers from the consent of the governed.

These four "truths" warrant careful consideration, for they are embedded deeply in the way Americans have thought and still think. They are the American creed.[5]

At the outset, note the ambiguity in the Declaration's initial assertion about human nature: "all men[6] are created equal." Equally what? Equally prone to the vices of overweening ambition, vindictiveness, and violence, as *The Federalist* would declare a decade later? Or equally virtuous? Or equally free to choose between vice and virtue?

The second and third truths in the Declaration clarified these ambiguities. Individuals were equally "endowed by their Creator with certain unalienable rights." Jefferson and his colleagues, trained as they were in moral philosophy, had a special understanding of the meaning of the word *rights.* "Rights" referred to conditions of existence, which, if threatened, any person could defend with legal impunity. For example, if someone were to threaten another with a gun, the latter's right to live would privilege him to defend himself by assaulting his assailant, even kill him, notwithstanding any human laws to the contrary. That right of self-defense proceeded from God, the Creator of Nature. It, along with the other "natural" rights, was designed by God to perfect human society here below and, hence, were superior to the fallible (and sometimes malicious) handiwork of mortal legislators.

These natural rights were "unalienable" in the sense that they could not be taken away by coercion, nor limited by legislation, nor traded away voluntarily. Just as the right to vote cannot legally be handed over to someone else (even for money), so natural rights were nontransferable.

The right to "life" was the right to resist anarchy—the right of personal security against the kinds of threats and dangers encountered in Marysville, California, and Youngstown, Ohio. The right to "liberty" was the right to resist tyranny—the kind of official oppression carried out by Sheriff Dial in *Brown v. Mississippi.*

"The Pursuit of Happiness"

But what about the third right, the right to "the pursuit of happiness"? It is certain that neither Jefferson nor any of the colonists assembled in the Continental Congress in 1776 meant the pursuit of pleasure.[7] They did not think that God gave His creations an unalienable right to act out their lustful impulses, or satiate their gluttony or greed, or laze about as couch potatoes day in and day out.

What is certain is that Jefferson intended a very Scottish understanding of happiness. Happiness was the product of the personal commitment of one's faculties to purposes of enduring and justifiable value. As Jefferson put the matter in a letter to his friend Thomas Law, "[G]ood acts give us pleasure, but how happens it that they give us pleasure? Because nature hath implanted in our breasts a love of others, a sense of duty to them, a moral instinct, in short, which prompts us irresistibly to feel and to succour their distresses."[8]

The right to pursue happiness meant the personal freedom to do good acts as our "moral instinct" (one's sense of empathy and one's craving to matter to others[9]) enabled us to know the good.

Erik Erikson and His Theory of Identity

For anyone familiar with the horrors perpetrated in the last century by the likes of Hitler, Stalin, and Mao Tse Tung, or even for anyone with ears attuned to the warnings of *The Federalist*, Jefferson's outlook that individuals were universally "endowed" with an instinctive desire to "feel and to succour [the] distresses" of others might sound naive. Yet his observation strangely resonates with modern insights.

Among American psychologists, Erik Erikson probably ranks as the most influential. Born in Germany in 1902 and introduced to psychoanalysis by Sigmund Freud and his very talented daughter Anna Freud in 1927, Erikson came to the United States in 1933. In the course of teaching and writing over the next half-century, he grew increasingly skeptical of Freud's emphasis on the overwhelming influence of infancy and early childhood. To the contrary, he observed that healthy individuals took control of their personal destinies around mid-adolescence. He inferred from these clinical observations that people are *genetically constituted* to progress through an increasingly complex series of stages of personal development, which he called "crises." During each crisis the individual would concentrate his emotional energies on shaping a particular trait that would then be incorporated into his character.[10]

For example, the individual's central concern during infancy is whether to trust others. Later, during adolescence, his attention, genetically guided, turns to whether and how to work industriously.

The fifth of these eight stages, the "identity crisis," is central to Erikson's theory. During the late teens, the individual begins to take stock of his talents and asks the question, *To what useful goal can I commit my grown-up years?* A healthy person emerges from the identity crisis with some degree of assurance that there is a fit between his aptitudes and an honorable purpose for his life. His object may be to become an excellent parent, or to explore the causes of mental disorder, or to be the best plumber possible. Whatever the purpose to which he commits, it thereafter functions as the measure of his personal worth. By that act of commitment to a future, adults free themselves from their past, their energies surge, and they assert control over the narratives of their lives.[11]

Jefferson never abandoned his belief in the universality of the moral instinct and the individual's capacity for self-government. In 1826, just months before he died, he wrote, "[T]he mass of mankind has not been born with saddles on their backs, nor a favored few, booted and spurred, ready to ride them legitimately by the grace of God."[12]

Revolutionary Implications

Jefferson's argument that people were driven by a moral instinct rang true to multitudes. Moreover, it had revolutionary implications. Prior to Jefferson's time, political systems in Europe and virtually everywhere else functioned on the aristocratic principle, namely, that because commoners lacked the capacity to pursue enlightened purposes of their own devising, a superior few—kings, landowners, the clergy, the "state"—should be trusted to decide for them. (Note that I use *aristocratic* in a less conventional, more expansive sense to denote any class-based social order of superiors and inferiors, whether the regime is tyrannical or benign. Thus the term embraces regimes as brutal as Nazi fascism and Soviet communism and as gentle as Anthony Trollope's Britain because they are *not* socially egalitarian.)

If Jefferson were right, however, if individuals were naturally capable of pursuing an enlightened self-interest for themselves, then there would be no need for a superior elite to monopolize rule. *And*—and this was a big addition to the vision of Jefferson's nonaristocratic society—the state was duty-bound to assist individuals in *their* pursuit of *their* own purposes.

That was why the fourth self-evident truth contained in the Declaration of Independence was so radical. When Jefferson wrote "governments are instituted among men," not to rule them but "to secure" their right to pursue their self-defined purposes, he sowed the seeds of a revolution against aristocracy that continues to unfold to this day.

While in an aristocratic regime it was the duty of the individual to pursue the purposes of the "state" (or the party or the nobility), in the society that Jefferson envisioned it was the duty of the state to help individuals accomplish what they freely wanted to achieve. We call Jefferson's conception of society "individualism."

The great contribution of the Declaration of Independence was that it incorporated this optimistic vision of self-controlled individualism into the American way of thinking. The belief that ordinary persons might legitimately pursue their self-interest and be ennobled by their dedication to it was an elevating estimate of human nature. Of course, whether any particular person used his freedom to extend himself to live usefully or, on the other hand, submitted to the darker, distrustful impulses the *Federalist* authors identified, was his personal responsibility. All free individuals were equally burdened with this choice.

For Jefferson, the urgent task of a self-governing, individualistic civilization was to expose persons to the range of purposes to which they might aspire. It was a proper function of government to provide education in the sciences and the humanities so as to elevate the technical and spiritual vision of each generation.

NOTES

1. *Federalist* No. 6. *The Federalist Papers* have a far more balanced view of human nature than sometimes is attributed to them, however. Consider *Federalist* No. 55:

   > As there is a degree of depravity in mankind which requires a certain degree of circumspection and distrust: So there are other qualities in human nature, which justify a certain portion of esteem and confidence. Republican government presupposes the existence of these qualities in a higher degree than any other form. Were the pictures which have been drawn by the political jealousy of some among us, faithful likenesses of the human character the inference would be that there is not sufficient virtue among men for self-government; and that nothing less than the chains of despotism can restrain them from destroying and devouring one another.

2. Letter to Henry Lee, "The Object of the Declaration of Independence," May 8, 1825, in *Thomas Jefferson: Writings* (New York: Library of America, 1984), 1501.

3. "Francis Hutcheson . . . was concerned with showing . . . that moral judgment cannot be based on reason and therefore must be a matter of whether an action is 'amiable or disagreeable' to one's moral sense. . . . Hutcheson's moral sense does not find pleasing only, or even predominantly, those actions that are in one's own interest. On the contrary, Hutcheson conceived moral sense as based on a *disinterested benevolence* [emphasis added]. This led him to state, as the ultimate criterion of the goodness of an action, a principle that was to serve as the basis for the Utilitarian reformers: 'that action is best which procures the greatest happiness for the greatest numbers.'" *Encyclopaedia Britannica*, "Ethics: The Climax of Moral Sense Theory: Hutcheson and Hume." For more on Hutcheson and his profound influence in America, see Arthur Herman, *How the Scots Invented the Modern World* (New York: Crown Publishers, 2001), especially 66–69.

4. When Thomas Jefferson submitted his draft of the Declaration of Independence to the Continental Congress for approval, it underwent considerable debate and criticism. Years afterward, Jefferson recalled his discomfort:

> [T]here were two or three unlucky expressions in it, which gave offense to some members. The words, "Scotch and other foreign auxiliaries," excited the ire of a gentleman or two of that country. Severe strictures on the conduct of the British King, in negating our repeated repeals of the law which permitted the importation of slaves, were disapproved by some Southern gentlemen, whose reflections were not yet matured to the full abhorrence of that traffic. Although the offensive expressions were immediately yielded, these gentlemen continued their depredations on other parts of the instrument.
>
> I was sitting by Dr. Franklin, who perceived that I was not insensible to these mutilations. [Franklin quietly remarked to me,] "I have made it a rule, whenever in my power, to avoid being the draughtsman of papers to be reviewed by a public body. I took my lesson from an incident which I will relate to you. When I was a journeyman printer, one of my companions, an apprentice hatter, having served out his time was about to open shop for himself. His first concern was to have a handsome signboard, with a proper inscription. He composed it in the words, 'John Thompson, Hatter, makes and sells hats for ready money', with a figure of a hat subjoined; but he thought he would submit it to his friends for their amendments. The first he showed it to thought the word 'Hatter' tautologous, because followed by the words, 'makes hats,' which showed he was a hatter. It was struck out. The next observed that the word, 'makes,' might as well be omitted, because his customers would not care who made the hats. If good and to their mind, they would buy by whomever made. He struck it out. A third said he thought the words, 'for ready money,' were useless, as it was not the custom of the place to sell on credit. Everyone who purchased expected to pay. They were parted with, and the inscription now stood, 'John Thompson sells hats.' 'Sells hats,' says his next friend. 'Why nobody will expect you to give them away, what then is the use of that word?' It was stricken out, and 'hats' followed it, the rather as there was one painted on the board. So the inscription was reduced ultimately to 'John Thompson' with the figure of a hat subjoined." [Letter from Thomas Jefferson to Robert Walsh, April 13, 1818, 5, in *Thomas Jefferson: Writings*]

5. Cf., Samuel P. Huntington, *Who Are We? The Challenges to America's National Identity* (New York: Simon and Schuster, 2004), 338: "The principles of the [American] Creed—liberty, equality, democracy, civil rights, nondiscrimination, rule of law—are markers of how to organize a society."

6. By "all men" Jefferson meant all humans, male and female, as do I throughout this book whenever I use the masculine pronoun generically.

7. "[S]cholars, theologians and politicians have wrangled over the definition of happiness and, more specifically, what makes people happy. Is it sensory pleasure? Satisfied desires? Freedom from sorrow or pain? Purposeful labor or a life

of leisure? Is it luck? Money? Goodness? Or is it just an accident of biology, some people seemingly born cheerful, others innately crabby?" Cynthia Crossen, "Déjà Vu," *Wall Street Journal*, March 6, 2006, B1. See a more expansive discussion in Darrin M. McMahon, *Happiness: A History* (New York: Atlantic Monthly Press, 2006).

8. Letter from Thomas Jefferson to Thomas Law, June 13, 1814, in *Thomas Jefferson: Writings*, 1337. Cf., public policy scholar Arthur C. Brooks's definition of happiness as a feeling of "earned success"—of creating "value in our lives or in the lives of others." *The Battle: How the Fight between Free Enterprise and Big Government Will Shape America's Future* (New York: Basic Books, 2010), 75.

9. In her poem "To Be of Use," the American Marge Piercy concludes with this lovely couplet (in *Circles on the Water*, New York: Alfred A. Knopf, 1982):

   The pitcher cries for water to carry/and a person for work that is real.

10. Perhaps the most succinct description of his theory is in Erik Erikson, *Identity: Youth and Crisis* (New York: W. W. Norton, 1968), chap. III, "The Life Cycle: Epigenesis of Identity."

11. Recent medical research relating to schizophrenia and depression has begun to support Erikson's (and Jefferson's) insights. For example, a summary of that research, offered by Dr. Daniel Weinberger of the National Institutes of Mental Health, refers to "the brain's dopamine system [as] a neurotransmitter that seems to be involved in feelings of achievement and motivation. Learning and planning rely critically on this system because if you don't know what you like and what you want and don't enjoy becoming more competent, you won't be able to function well in the world." "The Search for Causative Factors: A Profile of Daniel R. Weinberger, M.D.," *NARSAD Research Newsletter* 13, no. 1 (spring 2001): 2. In other words, according to Dr. Weinberger, the latest biomedical discoveries indicate that a particular system is at work in the human brain that regulates the formation of purpose in life ("what you like and what you want to do . . . competent[ly]"). The dopamine system is the seat of "the pursuit of happiness," the site of the "moral instinct."

12. Letter to Roger C. Weightman, June 24, 1826, in *Thomas Jefferson: Writings*, 1517. These words were virtually the last Jefferson wrote; he died within two weeks of composing them.

7

TOCQUEVILLE AND MARX

The Anglo-American relies upon personal interest to accomplish
his ends and gives free scope to the unguided strength and common
sense of the people; the Russian centers all the authority of society
in a single arm. The principal instrument of the former is freedom;
of the latter, servitude. Their starting-point is different and their
courses are not the same; yet each of them seems marked out by the
will of heaven to sway the destinies of half the globe.

Alexis de Tocqueville, *Democracy in America* (1835)

Individualism and Aristocracy

The history of the nineteenth and twentieth centuries has been one where a select few nations transformed themselves from lethargic, impoverished, and resentful societies into bustling, prosperous, and public-spirited ones. The secret to expanding the wealth of these nations was the unlocking of human energies by giving ordinary individuals the opportunity to "pursu[e] happiness." Growth came to those countries that entrusted their citizens with setting their own goals and then gave them the freedom to overcome the inevitable obstacles they encountered in pursuing them. (Thomas Jefferson once summed up the connection between individual freedom and prosperity, "Nothing is troublesome that we do willingly."[1])

Tensions were bound to occur between individualistic regimes and the aristocratic ones they surpassed. The very success of the former undermined the acceptability of the latter. As a consequence, the twentieth century was afflicted by two deadly world wars and a forty-five-year Cold War, in which nations adhering to the older, aristocratic ways sought to regain dominance over their prospering, egalitarian rivals.

In an uncannily accurate way, two remarkable thinkers, each highly influential over the last 150 years, anticipated this conflict. They were born within eighteen years of each other; they started with opposite views of human nature; they employed highly different methods of observation and reasoning; but they reached much the same conclusion—that there would be an inevitable struggle between aristocracy and individualism for world domination. I speak of Alexis de Tocqueville and Karl Marx.

Alexis de Tocqueville

Tocqueville, a Frenchman, was the older of the two. Born in 1804, he came of an aristocratic family, several of whose members had been executed in the Terror that followed the first stages of the French Revolution. If a prodigy is a young person with extraordinary gifts, Tocqueville was a political prodigy. Before reaching adulthood, he foresaw that the French aristocratic tradition was doomed; no longer would the French people submit to a system in which large landholding families were deemed superior.[2]

He further saw that such would not just be the fate of France, but of all of Europe. If the nations of Europe could devise a new basis for social order, however, they could avoid chaos and barbarism. But what might that new society look like, and what could Europe's political leaders do *now* to lead their nations to freedom, knowledge, and prosperity?[3]

In 1831, at the age of twenty-six, Tocqueville went to the United States to observe Americans and their novel system of individualism—"social democracy" was what he called it. His nine-month journey left him deeply impressed by the "common sense" of people who would have been dismissed as mere commoners in France.[4]

Key to America's well-being, Tocqueville perceived, was Jefferson's insight that all people were possessed of a moral instinct. Almost in awe, he witnessed ordinary Americans, without benefit of *rulers*, creating an energetic, robust, unimaginably prosperous society. He concluded that aristocracy, by wasting the energies latent in individuals, would stay poor, doomed to grow weak and inferior. He marveled:

On passing from a free country [i.e., a socially democratic one], into one which is not free [i.e., an aristocratic society], the traveler is struck by the change; in the former all is bustle and activity; in the latter everything seems calm and motionless. In the one, amelioration and progress are the topics of inquiry; in the other, it seems as if the community wished only to repose in the enjoyment of advantages already acquired. Nevertheless, the country which exerts itself so strenuously to become happy is generally more wealthy and prosperous than that which appears so contented with its lot; and when we compare them, we can scarcely conceive how so many new wants are daily felt in the former, while so few seem to exist in the latter.[5]

He returned home, confident in the principle of individualism. In two remarkable volumes entitled *Democracy in America* and published, respectively, in 1835 and 1840, he advised Europe's leaders to educate their people and then set them free to pursue their self-interest.[6]

Karl Marx

Karl Marx was younger than Tocqueville by fourteen years. Born in 1818 in a western province of what is now Germany, Marx grew up in a professional family. He attended the University of Berlin, where his studies challenged the traditional Christian training of his youth. He converted to atheism, embraced an academic philosophy called "dialectical materialism," and received a doctoral degree in 1841. Thereafter, he spent his life writing (as journalist, editor, and scholar) and fleeing (first from Prussia and then from France) to escape punishment for what he published. Ultimately he settled in England, where he lived in such wretched poverty that two of his children died and his wife broke down mentally.

His writings were voluminous, his learning encyclopedic, and his willingness to explore the implications of ideas boundless. Like Tocqueville,[7] he was appalled by the cycles of misery that beset factory workers at the outset of the Industrial Revolution. But unlike Tocqueville, who called for ameliorative legislation, universal education, and managerial vision, Marx urged "the violent overthrow of the bourgeoisie,"[8] by which he meant the murder of those who owned substantial properties and the expropriation of their assets by the state.

But as radical as his vision sounds, in an ironic way, Marx's thinking was reactionary. His proposal for a "dictatorship of the proletariat" was nothing more than a throwback to the aristocratic principle that

Tocqueville foresaw as doomed. Marx renounced the possibilities of individualism and embraced an image of a world in which a few superior persons[9]—he called them a "vanguard"—would define the public interest and the commoners would be instructed to carry it out. Marx's utopia was aristocracy, with a new crowd in charge. He sympathized with the misery of factory workers but did not trust them to solve their problems. Rather, the members of the proletariat were to relinquish control of their destiny to their superiors in virtue. The "masses," as Marx derided them, had only blind instincts, were uneducable, and were incapable of developing a worthy self-interest.[10]

The views of these two men were incompatible. Tocqueville urged education and self-improvement, and Marx, murder and indoctrination.

Who Was Right?

Of the two, Tocqueville proved the more prophetic. He was certain that the individualistic principle at work in the United States would gather strength and some day supplant aristocracy throughout Western Europe. At the same time, he predicted that the aristocratic principle would survive in Russia. And so, in 1835, a year when the United States was a nation of barely 12 million people and Russia was a clumsy, largely illiterate country on the edge of Europe, he predicted an eventual clash for world dominion between these two countries and their contending views of human society:[11]

> There are at the present time two great nations in the world, which started from different points, but seem to tend towards the same end. I allude to the Russians and the Americans. Both of them have grown up unnoticed; and while the attention of mankind was directed elsewhere, they have suddenly placed themselves in the front rank among the nations, and the world learned their existence and their greatness at almost the same time.
>
> All other nations seem to have nearly reached their natural limits, and they have only to maintain their power; but these are still in the act of growth. All the others have stopped, or continue to advance with extreme difficulty; these alone are proceeding with ease and celerity along a path to which no limit can be perceived. The American struggles against the obstacles that nature opposes to him; the adversaries of the Russian are men. The former combats the wilderness and savage life; the latter,

civilization with all its arms. The conquests of the American are therefore gained by the plowshare; those of the Russian by the sword. The Anglo-American relies upon personal interest to accomplish his ends and gives free scope to the unguided strength and common sense of the people; the Russian centers all the authority of society in a single arm. The principal instrument of the former is freedom; of the latter, servitude. Their starting-point is different and their courses are not the same; yet each of them seems marked out by the will of heaven to sway the destinies of half the globe.

Tocqueville wrote those lines more than a century before the beginning of the Cold War, the confrontation between America and Russia that lasted nearly half a century and ended with the collapse of the Russian empire in 1991 and its aspiration "to sway the destinies of half the globe."

It was a profound piece of prophecy.

NOTES

1. Letter from Thomas Jefferson to Thomas Jefferson Smith, February 21, 1825, *Thomas Jefferson: Writings* (New York: Library of America, 1984), 1500. President Ronald Reagan relished collecting stories to define the difference between an individualistic society, like the United States, and those, like the former communist nations, that adhered to the aristocratic principle. One anecdote he especially enjoyed concerned the American ambassador to the then–Soviet Union. In returning to Moscow, he had taken a taxi in New York City to Kennedy Airport and on the way to the airport began a conversation with his taxi driver, a young man about twenty-five years of age.

   "What are you going to do with your life?" he inquired.

   "I don't know," said the cabby, "I haven't made up my mind yet."

   The ambassador caught his plane, flew to Moscow, and took a cab to the American embassy. As they drove along, he put the same question to the young Russian driver: "What are you going to do with your life?"

   "I don't know," he responded. "*They* haven't made up their minds yet."

   For the Russian taxi driver, deciding on what private purpose to pursue—the question central to Erikson's "identity crisis"—was relegated to the periphery of his concerns, for the Soviet state would make his decision for him. He would serve whatever purposes the commissariat set. For the American taxi driver, however, the question was at the core of his being. Were he not to develop his own personal set of objectives, there would be only drift. It depended on him to develop meaningful goals.

2. The most concise and, in my opinion, insightful biography of Tocqueville is Joseph Epstein's *Alexis de Tocqueville: Democracy's Guide* (New York: Harper-Collins, 2006). Longer recent works are Andre Jardin, *Tocqueville: A Biography*, trans. Lydia Davis with Robert Hemenway (New York: Farrar, Straus and Giroux, 1988), and Hugh Brogan, *Alexis de Tocqueville: A Life* (New Haven: Yale University Press, 2006). The indispensable account of Tocqueville's journey to America in 1831–1832 is George Wilson Pierson, *Tocqueville in America* (Baltimore: Johns Hopkins University Press, 1996), and originally published by Oxford University in 1938, under the title *Tocqueville and Beaumont in America*.

3. Tocqueville's final words in his majestic two-volume work on American society were those in the epigraph heading the introduction of this book. See Alexis de Tocqueville, *Democracy in America,* trans. Henry Reeve (New York: Bantam, 2000 [1840]), vol. II, book 4, chap. 8.

4. Nothing surpasses the masterful account of Tocqueville's travels by George Wilson Pierson, *Tocqueville in America* (Baltimore: Johns Hopkins University Press, 1996 [1938]). In 1979 columnist Richard Reeves followed Tocqueville's footsteps and wrote a discerning and enjoyable chronicle, *American Journey: Traveling with Tocqueville in Search of "Democracy in America"* (New York: Simon and Schuster, 1982).

5. Alexis de Tocqueville, *Democracy in America,* trans. Henry Reeve (New York: Bantam, 2000 [1835]), vol. I, chap. 14.

6. "The first of the duties that are at this time imposed upon those who direct our affairs is to educate democracy, to reawaken, if possible, its religious beliefs; to purify its morals; to mold its actions; to substitute a knowledge of statecraft for its inexperience, and an awareness of its true interest for its blind instincts." Tocqueville, *Democracy in America,* vol. I, "Author's Introduction."

7. Tocqueville, *Democracy in America,* vol. II, book 3, chap. 7:

> When competition or some other fortuitous circumstance lessens his profits, [the manufacturer] can reduce the wages of his workmen almost at pleasure and make from them what he loses by the chances of business. Should the workmen strike, the [manufacturer], who is a rich man, can very well wait, without being ruined, until necessity brings them back to him; but they must work day by day or they die, for their only property is in their hands. They have long been impoverished by oppression, and the poorer they become, the more easily they may be oppressed; they can never escape from this fatal circle of cause and consequence. [F]or this very reason no circumstance is more important or more deserving of the special consideration of the legislator. . . .

8. Karl Marx and Friedrich Engels, *Manifesto of the Communist Party* (1848; trans. Samuel Moore, 1888), Part I.

9. Ibid. "[S]o now a portion of the bourgeoisie goes over to the proletariat, and in particular, a portion of the bourgeois ideologists who have raised themselves to the level of comprehending theoretically the historical movement of the whole."

10. Ibid. The "masses" included the proletariat ("wage laborers") and what Marx called the *Lumpenproletariat:* ("[T]he social scum, that passively rotting mass thrown off by the lowest layers of old society").

11. Tocqueville, *Democracy in America*, vol. I, chap. 18.

8

RECIPROCAL POWER

[T]he passions of human nature . . . are inalterable [and] 'twou'd be in vain, either for moralists or politicians, to tamper with us, or attempt to change the usual course of our actions, with a view to public interest. And indeed, did the success of their designs depend upon their success in correcting the selfishness and ingratitude of men, they wou'd never make any progress, unless aided by omnipotence, which is alone able to new-mould the human mind, and change its character in such fundamental articles. All they can pretend to, is, to give a new direction to those natural passions, and teach us that we can better satisfy our appetites in an oblique and artificial manner, than by their headlong and impetuous motion. Hence I learn to do a service to another, without bearing him any real kindness, because I foresee, that he will return my service, in expectation of another of the same kind, and in order to maintain the same correspondence of good offices with me or with others. And accordingly, after I have serv'd him, and he is in possession of the advantage arising from my action, he is induc'd to perform his part as foreseeing the consequences of his refusal.

David Hume, *A Treatise of Human Nature* (1739)

How does a society based on individualism work? How does an individual pursuing his personal interest get anything done? Most importantly, if he has what Thomas Jefferson called a "moral instinct" and Alexis de

Tocqueville called a "soul," a motive that aspires to "lofty"[1] achievements, how does the "body" find the assistance to accomplish them?

The stubborn fact is that attaining virtually any object of consequence depends on collaboration. Without teamwork, no children can be conceived, no buildings built, no products produced. Escaping ignorance, healing illness, serving God: all these require people to combine their efforts. A single individual needs the services of others to augment his. Even the lonely contemplation of a trout stream or a solitary walk through a quiet meadow requires the assistance of others, if only to provide security from violent assault.

The Problem of Collaboration

Slavery is a form of human collaboration, a vile form of persons working together to achieve something. It is enabled by coercive power. The pyramids of Egypt testify to what slavery can accomplish, even when the cooperation involved is involuntary, inefficient, and contingent on the continuous application of threats.

In gentler, land-based, aristocratic societies, extended family ties were the basis for enlisting collaboration. In those so-called traditional societies, nobles and commoners alike depended upon parents, uncles, aunts, cousins, landlords, and tenants for protection, friendship, capital, labor in the fields, and help in emergencies. There were no banks, no insurers, and no trustworthy police, and in their absence individuals could not stray beyond the boundaries of family and village.

In modern individualistic societies, however, the miracle is that virtually any person can find teams of people outside their family circle willing to assist them. Consider the number of persons who cooperate on our behalf when we write and mail a letter. Even the lowly pencil is the product of a collaboration of woodcutters, sawyers, graphite miners, rubber manufacturers, tinsmiths, and makers of fabricating equipment.[2] In addition, countless persons enlist to provide the paper we write on, deliver the letter we compose, and teach the language that enables our correspondents to understand one another.

The fact is that there takes place an astonishing amount of cooperation in an individualistic society. Here are two of our finest political scientists, Wallace Sayre and Herbert Kaufman, describing their hometown, New York City. They marvel at the availability of help to be found there. New York, they write, has a huge white collar work force; but it also has a million industrial workers, a huge number of small and independent factory owners, and a large population of small shopkeepers. There is a large reservoir of unskilled laborers and domestics, but there is probably nowhere in the world such a collection of practitioners of the skilled trades as may be found here, nor such a concentration of professional manpower—legal, medical, engineering, scientific, teaching, and the like. Indeed, with relatively few exceptions—farming, ranching, mining, for instance—one is likely to find in New York *somebody routinely producing precisely the goods or performing exactly the services one needs, no matter how specialized or unusual.*[3] [Emphasis added.]

Their point is that New Yorkers, no matter how idiosyncratic their pursuits might be, can team up with "precisely" the kinds of associates they want at virtually any moment they need collaborators.

The two political scientists go on to make a second point—that all this precise assistance available to them exists amid a staggering diversity of national origins, customs, religious faiths, and individual purposes. "The City is fascinating," they write,

in that it does afford each individual a realistic hope of fulfilling himself in his own way. It is important as a social experiment in that it manages to provide these opportunities despite the enormous number of different values and patterns of living that must somehow be accommodated with each other. If New York were administered like a military camp—with standardized clothing, diet, architecture, living routines, types of work, recreation, and so on, and with tight control over the movement and disposition of interrelations of personnel—the technological operation of feeding, sheltering, clothing, amusing, and keeping order among eight million people crammed into a little over 300 square miles of land area would constitute a remarkable achievement. New York City accomplishes all this without sacrificing the variety, the multifarious customs, the divergent interests, or the competing objectives of its people.[4]

New York City, the embodiment of extreme individualism, bustles with teamwork.

The Marketplace

It is markets that provide the means by which New Yorkers build personal teams of collaboration. In free market–capitalist societies like New York City and America, in general, individuals do induce others to do what needs

to be done. Their power is the power of reciprocity. The marketplace facilitates reciprocity; it serves as a mechanism by which Americans everywhere
connect in relationships of voluntary exchange.

When we earlier analyzed coercion, we saw that its major defect in
inducing cooperation was that it evoked resistance. When coerced, people
cooperate unwillingly and unimaginatively—and as soon as the threat is
relaxed, teamwork stops.

In contrast, reciprocal power does not repel, but attracts persons capable
of help. It motivates you and me to cooperate, often creating lasting bonds
of mutually beneficial collaboration. It produces what is happily labeled a
"win-win" situation.[5]

The peculiar feature of reciprocity is that we get our way with others by
permitting them to get their way with us.

Reciprocity is so important to our understanding of freedom in
American society that we must take some time to examine it and its
paradoxical nature with the same scrutiny we paid to the subtleties of
coercion.

The Paradox of Scarcity

In 1776 a moral philosopher named Adam Smith looked down from his
ivory tower and made sense of the seeming babble and bickering in the
marketplace below him. His explanations struck many of his readers as
paradoxical, defying common sense. Today, his paradoxes have grown in
acceptance, but not so much that we don't need reminders of them. Let
me mention four of those paradoxes. I call them the paradox of scarcity,
the paradox of abundance, the paradox of equality, and the paradox of
freedom.

First, the **paradox of scarcity**: *the scarcer the supply, the higher the price;
the higher the price, the more is supplied.* In Smith's time, it was conventional
wisdom that the price of goods and services was based upon the cost of
producing them. Even today, many people still think that there is a "just
price" for things (like gasoline). But that seeming truth is just plain wrong.
A commodity's price rises or falls depending on its scarcity—on its supply
relative to demand for it.[6]

High prices attract new efforts to meet the needs of others. For the entrepreneur, "a problem is nothing more than an opportunity in work clothes,"
as Henry Kaiser once said.[7] *Someone else's* problem is a road to prosperity for
any of us who can help solve it. And so we get good at stepping into the

shoes of people who need help; we empathize with them, seeing their troubles from their point of view. Then we improve our skills so that we can assist them by inventing a solution to fill their need: a gas-saving car, a better air-conditioning system in their building, a cure for cancer. What, in fact, we do in a commercial society is work constantly to improve our abilities to make the lives of others better. The paradox of scarcity, in short, develops two vitally important virtues—empathy for others and the habit of continual self-improvement.[8]

It should be noted that some critics allege a moral objection to reciprocity. They claim that it makes people greedy.[9] This objection, however, is hollow. Granted, reciprocity legitimates acquisitiveness. In routine matters a regime of reciprocity heavily depends on its members' appetites, not on their selflessness. Idealists find it disturbing that in a free-market capitalist society the most reliable way to obtain collaboration is by appealing to self-interest rather than to the common weal.[10]

Compared to coercion, however, reciprocity is unquestionably superior; people who extort rather than exchange are the very embodiment of greed, and I, for one, prefer a civilized materialism to brutal rapacity. Moreover, as reciprocal relationships mature over time, they are more marked by generosity than avarice. Finally, significant forces in the United States countervail against greed—particularly religion, with its doctrine of love and its spur to charity.

While the paradox of scarcity shapes the character of persons engaging in reciprocity, it also creates a distinctive kind of society. It leads invariably to a division of labor. In a commercial society we come to depend on the competencies of others to fulfill our needs, which in turn frees up time for us to develop our special talents, improve our skills, and enter demanding vocations. For example, it's hard to believe that anyone would freely choose to specialize in capping out-of-control oil wells. That is outdoor work and heavy lifting in the extreme, and the supply of persons who would make the effort to perfect such a unique skill, much less repeatedly employ it, might seem minuscule—maybe even nonexistent. By its willingness to pay a high price, however, the oil industry attracts sufficient individuals and motivates them to develop these extraordinary skills and put them to work under dangerous and emergency circumstances.

In turn, the oil capper now needs others to perform the tasks that he no longer has the time or talent to complete. He must depend on others with their different, complementary skills to produce much of what he needs.[11]

To Adam Smith, nothing was more important than this increase in interdependency in the modern world. Nations prospered when "every man . . . lives by exchanging, or becomes in some measure a merchant."[12]

The Paradox of Abundance

The second of our paradoxes is the **paradox of abundance:** *the more resourceful our competitor, the worse, but the more resourceful our customer, the better.* Think about it. As a general rule, I don't envy the success of others, but (to the contrary) am made happy by their prosperity because their success in their chosen field enriches me. If I'm a winemaker in California, I cheer when car sales rise in Detroit because a set of my customers, wine-drinking auto engineers, are working and making money. Because of *their* increased buying power of my wines, I profit and experience an increase in my profits—*my* buying power. Conversely, when auto sales slump, alas, so do my wine sales; auto engineers start scrimping and drinking tap water. My fortunes decline when my customers suffer misfortune, and it is my sincerest wish that they will get back on their feet.

The moral consequence of the paradox of abundance is a huge increase in social good will. Since most people are potential customers, not competitors, participants in a commercial society are cheered by the successes of virtually everyone. Envy, the green-eyed monster that inhabits the darkest regions of the human heart, diminishes and human fellowship flourishes.

The Paradox of Equality

The third of our paradoxes is the **paradox of equality:** *people hang out with others with whom they can be mutually useful.* Let me explain it in slightly more detail.

One might think that in free markets persons with few skills or resources to exchange for assistance would be ignored and left destitute. Doubtless, in the past the needy sometimes were regarded as useless and became invisible. But in today's commercial and social life, partly *because* of the empathy generated by the habits of exchange, the more fortunate frequently hold out a hand to those in great need. Consider how creditors extend repayment periods and negotiate their bills downward or how employers devise jobs for the least fortunate to do and lend encouragement and training in how they might improve themselves—not always, but surprisingly often. We tend to be patient even when a person has not lived up to his end of the bargain. Out of self-interest, we want others to succeed.[13]

More interestingly, in a free-market system the indebted person usually will want to terminate his needy relationship as soon as he can to regain his self-respect. The anthropologist Elliot Liebow saw as much when he spent years observing homeless men. He became particularly interested in the ups and downs of the affectionate relationships between a dozen unemployed vagrants and their "nice," attractive girlfriends. In contrast to the men, the women held paying jobs and lived in clean, well-lit apartments. Liebow was surprised when the homeless men "broke off" these affairs against the wishes of their attractive girlfriends. Then it dawned on him that the men acted the way they did out of need to maintain their self-respect. So pervasive in American society is the notion of "giving fair weight," so intertwined in the definition of being worthwhile is the duty to reciprocate, that they were ashamed of being over their heads in social indebtedness. And so these homeless men walked out on the sweet deals their girlfriends offered them and returned to their community of vagrants, where they regained what Liebow called a "sanctuary for those who can no longer endure the experience or prospect of failure."[14] They retreated to less demanding relationships, where their jokes, their scavenging, their patient listening and consolations were appreciated by their peers. By voluntarily retreating to a less demanding status, they transformed themselves from good-for-nothings to good-for-somethings, able to reciprocate the lesser obligations they incurred. At that level, by caring for others whom they could assist, they experienced success.

As a consequence of this tendency to seek out a comfort level, people in commercial societies tend to drift into separate but self-respecting communities. Individuals of one set of abilities tend to withdraw willingly from individuals with different sets or levels of talents; we cluster with individuals more like us. Birds of a feather flock together and begin feeling good about one another. Within our distinctive communities (in the words of Garrison Keillor) we all end up thinking we're "above average." Self-esteem rises within the segment of society to which we assign ourselves.[15]

The Paradox of Freedom

And finally, the fourth paradox, the **paradox of freedom:** *liberty requires limits*. While most Americans observe the norm of reciprocity most of the time, it is not fail-safe. In all of us the obligation to give fair weight breaks down once in a while, and in a few of us it breaks down much too often. We take without paying back. Theft by robbery is the classic instance of the refusal to reciprocate, but theft occurs in many other forms as well. When individuals do not deliver on their promises, or create nuisances, or refuse to pay their fair share of taxes for national defense, public safety, highways, clean air, and universal education, they are taking without paying back.

When theft (in whatever form) increases, free exchange is threatened, for theft erodes trust and frightens people into hiding their skills and products instead of letting customers know about them. Exchange depends on trust. With those who lack internal restraints on the temptation to take something for nothing, government has to use its police power: the patrol officer to threaten the robber, the judge to threaten the promise breaker, the regulator to threaten the nuisance maker, the taxman to threaten the tax evader.

So liberty requires limits. The moral consequence of suitable limits is personal honesty. We can prosper and avoid the coercive restraints of the policeman, the judge, the regulator, and the taxman by restraining ourselves. In a commercial society we are rewarded for being honest by being left alone by the restraints of government.

A Paradise, Not Perfect but as Good as It Gets

These are the moral consequences of the four paradoxes of the dynamic of reciprocity in a commercial society—the paradox of scarcity makes us empathetic, inventive, and self-improving; the paradox of abundance makes us supportive of our fellows and neutralizes envy; the paradox of equality confers self-respect on all who try; and the paradox of freedom rewards honesty and self-restraint. To put the same points negatively, free markets neutralize four of mankind's deadliest sins—sloth, detachment, dishonesty, and (most importantly) envy.

If one were to conceive of a utopia in the real world—a paradise not perfect, but as good as it gets—it probably would look like a society that motivated the bulk of its members to want to make themselves better so that they could help others. A commercial society in which voluntary exchange enables collaboration is precisely that utopia.

America's founders envisioned creating what they called a "commercial republic" because they had this one central insight: *a free-market society motivates its members to improve themselves.* In a society where the good fortune of others multiplies our own, there would be a material foundation to live by the golden rule—to do unto others as we would have them do unto us.

Government has a critical role in making free markets work. Besides curtailing the liberty to swindle and steal, a skilled government maintains a stable currency, the lubricant of exchange. It collaborates as both supplier and customer in providing universal education, national defense, and highways for hauling commerce. It also remedies extreme differences in bargaining power with antitrust and labor laws. It motivates private charity and augments private generosity with public funds as "the charity of last resort."

But when government carries out these essential tasks, the free market-place is a superb device for enabling collaboration. It gives individuals the personal freedom to pursue their own purposes without requiring the collective assent of others. It enables individuals to get the precise assistance they need to accomplish their purposes. It diminishes government's temptation to coerce by reducing our dependence on government. And most importantly, it rewards service to others and, in doing so, reinforces a morality that motivates self-improvement and becoming useful to others, while discouraging laziness and envy. The most important product of free markets is not that they make more goods, but that they make more good people.

Not a bad bottom line.

A Material Foundation for the Golden Rule

Walter Lippmann (1889–1974) was for four decades considered America's wisest observer, honored universally as no single political pundit is today.[16] Lippmann preached the importance of reciprocity to a free society. His message is worth pondering:[17]

> We have become insensitive and forgetful about the revolutionary change in human life [based on the reciprocal and mutually profitable exchange of specialized labor and] only by recapturing the original insight of the pioneer liberals can we fully appreciate the evangelical fervor with which they preached that the freedom of trade was a new dispensation for all mankind. For the first time in human history men had come upon a way of producing wealth in which the good fortune of others multiplied their own. It was a great moment, for example, in the long history of conquest, rapine, and oppression, when David Hume could say [in 1742] at the conclusion of his

essay, "Of the Jealousy of Trade": "I pray for the flourishing commerce of Germany, Spain, Italy, and even France itself. I am at least certain that Great Britain, and all those nations, would flourish more, did their sovereigns and ministers adopt such enlarged and benevolent sympathies toward each other." It had not occurred to many men before that the Golden Rule was economically sound. Thus the enlarged and benevolent sympathies of the eighteenth and nineteenth centuries had a material foundation in the self-interest of men who were growing richer by exchanging the products of specialized labor in wide markets.

They actually felt it to be true that an enlightened self-interest promoted the common good. For the first time men could conceive a social order in which the ancient moral aspiration for liberty, equality, and fraternity was consistent with the abolition of poverty and the increase of wealth.[18]

Summary

Until Adam Smith and his fellow moral philosophers made the dynamics of free markets understandable (and until laws and universal education combined to increase equality of bargaining power in the marketplace), the difference between coercion and reciprocity as inducements to collaboration was vastly underestimated. Today it grows ever clearer that coercion rewards vicious qualities like destructiveness, detachment, cruelty, and ignorance, thereby corrupting constructive morals. *Reciprocity does just the opposite.* It reinforces, even elevates, the human urge to be energetic, creative, empathetic, generous, knowledgeable, and cooperative, with the result that a commercial society is vital and develops robust and self-reliant personalities, truly capable of self-government.[19]

NOTES

1. Alexis de Tocqueville, *Democracy in America,* trans. Henry Reeve (New York: Bantam 2000 [1840]), vol. II, book 2, chap.12.
2. Henry Petroski, *The Pencil: A History of Design and Circumstance* (New York: Knopf Borzoi, 1989).
3. Wallace S. Sayre and Herbert Kaufman, *Governing New York City: Politics in the Metropolis* (New York: Russell Sage Foundation, 1960), 28.

4. Ibid., 25–26.

5. That commerce is a "win-win" relationship was the great insight of Adam Smith's *An Enquiry into the Nature and Causes of the Wealth of Nations* (1776), book 3, chap. 2:

> The town, in which there neither is nor can be any reproduction of substances, may very properly be said to gain its whole wealth and subsistence from the country. We must not, however, upon this account, imagine that the gain of the town is the loss of the country. The gains of both are mutual and reciprocal, and the division of labour is in this, as in all other cases, advantageous to all the different persons employed in the various occupations into which it is subdivided. The inhabitants of the country purchase of the town a greater quantity of manufactured goods, with the produce of a much smaller quantity of their own labour, than they must have employed had they attempted to prepare them themselves. The town affords a market for the surplus produce of the country, or what is over and above the maintenance of the cultivators, and it is there that the inhabitants of the country exchange it for something else, which is in demand among them. The greater the number and revenue of the inhabitants of the town, the more extensive is the market which it affords to those of the country. . . .

6. Scarcity elevates the value of an asset above its "natural price" (i.e., the whole value of rent, labor, and profit) for one reason worth special mention: technological balance. Most of the things we want are compounded of many elements. For example, in the assembly and propelling of autos to take Americans to work, there must be as many nuts as there are bolts, as many brake systems as there are power systems, as much refined gasoline as there are engines that run on it, and sufficient highways to drive on. If there is an imbalance so that one of these elements is in short supply, then all the other elements become excessive and will lie idle. It then is in the interest of the suppliers with excess on their hands to induce the person holding the scarce resource to direct it their way, and they do so by offering to pay a higher price.

7. Adam Smith expressed the same thought: "It is not from the benevolence of the butcher, the brewer, or the baker that we expect our dinner, but from their regard to their own interest. We address ourselves, not to their humanity but to their self-love, and never talk to them of our own necessities but of their advantages. Nobody but a beggar chooses to depend chiefly upon the benevolence of his fellow-citizens." Smith, *Wealth of Nations*, book 1, chap. 2.

8. Likewise in the politics of elective democracy, candidates running for office try to discover what each voter wants—a job, a zoning permit, a safe street, a new park, shelter for a family whose house has burned down, a chance for a young man with a fine tenor voice to sing at the neighborhood Fourth of July celebration. By supplying what a voter hankers after, a candidate gains what he values—votes and loyalty—in exchange. As a traditional New York "machine

boss" once put it, "You gotta know human nature and act accordin'." William L. Riordan, *Plunkitt of Tammany Hall* (New York: E. P. Dutton, 1963 [1905]), 25.

9. Adam Smith had a different concern. He worried lest the division of labor inhibit moral and intellectual development:

> The man whose whole life is spent in performing a few simpler operations, of which the effects are perhaps always the same, or very nearly the same, has no occasion to exert his understanding or to exercise his invention in finding out expedients for removing difficulties which never occur. He naturally loses, therefore, the habit of such exertion and generally becomes as stupid and ignorant as it is possible for a human creature to become. The torpor of his mind renders him not only incapable of relishing or bearing a part in any rational conversation, but of conceiving any generous, noble, or tender sentiments, and consequently of forming any just judgment concerning many even of the ordinary duties of private life. Of the great and extensive interests of his country he is altogether incapable of judging, and unless very particular pains have been taken to render him otherwise, he is equally incapable of defending his country in war. The uniformity of his stationary life naturally corrupts the courage of his mind and makes him regard with abhorrence the irregular, uncertain, and adventurous life of a soldier. It corrupts even the activity of his body, and renders him incapable of exerting his strength with vigour and perseverance in any other employment than that to which he has been bred. His dexterity at his own particular trade seems, in this manner, to be acquired at the expense of his intellectual, social, and martial virtues. But in every improved and civilized society this is the state into which the labouring poor, that is, the great body of the people, must necessarily fall, unless government takes some pains to prevent it. [*Wealth of Nations*, book 5, chap.1, part 3.]

10. Other critics of reciprocity will say that the downtrodden have such urgent wants that they are disproportionately obliged to fill someone else's needs. Because their bargaining power is weak, they are forced to join teams of which they are never captain. It is true that some persons have markedly worse bargaining positions than others. But most healthy individuals can devise ways to make or do something that others can use, once they come to understand "the rules of the game" are to take the initiative. But in rectifying extreme bargaining disadvantages, skillful legislators have an important role to play. Recall the earlier discussion in Chapter 3 of the National Labor Relations Act and how it adjusts the bargaining positions of management and labor.

11. The paradox of scarcity draws inventive individuals to things no one else wants because unwanted things come with lower price tags. Reciprocity, in effect, gives discounts to persons for being different and for developing oddball, idiosyncratic tastes and ways to use people and commodities that others have believed of no value. Those who can find a use for things in long supply and

short demand—that is, things that are not scarce, like junk or snakes or bad houses in bad neighborhoods—find that they can get others to provide them at very little cost. They can "play it cool" in negotiating terms of exchange because virtually no one else competes for what they want. Reciprocity advantages the creative eccentric, and his presence makes for a society with a richly textured and imaginative culture.

12. Smith, *Wealth of Nations,* book 1, chap. 2. The division of labor in America affects every aspect of everyday life. As the columnist and one-time manager of *Foreign Affairs* magazine, Fareed Zakaria, recognized, "American culture celebrates and reinforces problem-solving, questioning authority, and thinking heretically. . . . It rewards self-starters and oddballs." Fareed Zakaria, *The Post-American World* (New York: W. W. Norton, 2008), 195.

13. These habits, nurtured by commerce, explain the astounding amount of philanthropy in the United States; over $300 billion annually and countless hours of voluntarism are extended by Americans to charitable and cultural causes. For further on American charitable giving, see Chapter 23.

14. Elliot Liebow, *Tally's Corner: A Study of Negro Streetcorner Men* (Boston: Little, Brown, 1960), 167. See also Robert E. Lane, *Political Ideology* (New York: Free Press, 1962), chap. 5, "The Fear of Equality."

15. Author and *New York Times* columnist David Brooks calls himself a "comic sociologist" but is perhaps America's most discerning and loving observer. With a touch of the truth, he once chuckled, "90% of Americans have way too much self-esteem." David Brooks, *On Paradise Drive: How We Live Now (And Always Have) in the Future Tense* (New York: Simon and Schuster, 2004), 73.

16. Walter Lippmann was a one-time socialist, an American delegate to the Versailles Peace Talks after World War I, and an intimate adviser to President Franklin Roosevelt, besides being the writer of a twice-weekly column and the author of at least four books *still* considered major classics—*A Preface to Politics* (1913), *Public Opinion* (1922), *The Good Society* (1937), and *Essays on the Public Philosophy* (1955).

17. Walter Lippmann, *The Good Society* (New York: Grosset and Dunlap, 1956 [1937]), 193–194.

18. Perhaps the most celebrated formulation of the social benefits of the pursuit of self-interest is that of Adam Smith and his metaphor of the "invisible hand":

> As every individual, therefore, endeavours as much as he can both to employ his capital in the support of domestic industry, and so to direct that industry that its produce may be of the greatest value; every individual necessarily labours to render the annual revenue of the society as great as he can. He generally, indeed, neither intends to promote the public interest, nor knows how much he is promoting it. By preferring the support of domestic to that of foreign industry he intends only his own security and by directing that industry in such a manner as its produce may be of the greatest value, he intends only his own gain, and he

is in this as in many other cases led by an invisible hand to promote an end which was no part of his intention. Nor is it always the worse for the society that it was not part of it. By pursuing his own interest he frequently promotes that of the society more effectually than when he really intends to promote it. I have never known much good done by those who affected to trade for the public good. It is an affectation, indeed, not very common among merchants, and very few words need be employed in dissuading them from it. [*Wealth of Nations*, book 4, chap. 2.]

19. The habits of reciprocity that Americans develop in the economic marketplace carry over into our governmental institutions. Skills cultivated to negotiate fair exchange of goods and services, for example, are perfectly suited to arranging political compromise over laws and programs. If Americans are used to getting their way by giving way, by returning "fair weight," we should not be surprised that they practice reciprocity in their official institutions—and especially so might that be the case in the quintessential democratic institution, their legislatures. We should anticipate reciprocity with all its implications—that legislators will have wants they desire to satisfy by exchange, that they will develop a scarce and desirable specialty, that a division of labor will develop, that a willing stratification separating the superior from the inferior legislators will emerge, and mechanisms will emerge to prevent political forms of theft. For more on this topic, see Chapter 16. See also William K. Muir Jr., *Legislature: California's School for Politics* (Chicago: University of Chicago Press, 1983).

9

MORAL POWER

In order that society should exist and, a fortiori, that a society should prosper, it is necessary that the minds of all the citizens should be rallied and held together by certain predominant ideas; and this cannot be the case unless each of them sometimes draws his opinions from the common source and consents to accept certain matters of belief already formed.

Alexis de Tocqueville, *Democracy in America* (1840)

Were we to think that human collaboration in American society depended only upon coercion and reciprocity, we would miss an even more dominant feature of American society and its politics—the importance of persuasion with ideas. We now turn to this third, and last, inducement to cooperation—the power of ideas.

If coercion is the power of the sword and reciprocity the power of the purse, we might call this third power the power of the pen. I prefer, instead, the term *moral power,* for it emphasizes that we get others to act as we want them to by influencing their most deeply held ideas—their moral beliefs. Moral power—commonly called leadership[1]—relies heavily on the written and spoken word (sometimes combined with images) to shape the ideas of others.

Unless one appreciates the complexity and effects of exercising moral power, one cannot understand the dynamics of America's healthy, self-governing society and the dangers it risks—and avoids. So this chapter is given over in its entirety to clarifying the nature and function of those strongly felt beliefs by which we steer our lives—our individual "morality"— the do's and don'ts of ethics and etiquette, the systems of belief and expectation, and the codes of honor and shame by which each of us measures whether our lives count for something—in other words, our ideas.

What Is an Idea?

An idea is a statement of fact about the way two concepts act upon one another. By a concept I mean a class of similar things. Freedom, for example, is a concept; it embraces numerous events, like traveling wherever we wish, reading an uncensored newspaper, speaking critically of government without fear of reprisal, quitting a bad boss, and choosing among thirty-one flavors of ice cream—activities that, while different in many particulars, are identical in at least one essential way: individuals doing them are acting of their own accord, without undue external compulsion or unreasonable limits upon their pursuit of their goals.

Any two concepts can be combined into an idea by connecting them *causally*.[2] When we come to think that one concept is "good for" or "bad for" another, we have generated an idea. For example, "freedom defeats ('is bad for') tyranny" and "freedom promotes ('is good for') vitality" are ideas.

Certain general ideas, the ones we hold deeply, share three special features: they are tinged with emotion, they are balanced psychologically, and they are tangled in a web of interconnections.[3] Let's examine each of those characteristics, one at a time.

Emotional, Balanced, and Interconnected

Ideas are charged with feeling. For instance, you and I have a deep fondness for, and feel protective toward, the notion of "freedom" and the countless acts embraced within it (like feeling unafraid or having a choice among those thirty-one different flavors of ice cream). Freedom is a *positively* felt concept; we feel positive—happy—about ourselves when we take some action that increases the amount of it in the world (like freeing a trapped bird, or hearing about an American immigrant's success story). Conversely, we abhor freedom's opposite, "tyranny," and the repellent acts that notion denotes (like bullying or torture). Tyranny is charged *negatively*, and we feel badly—unhappy with ourselves—if we let it exist or listen while someone says something in support of an instance of it.

Second, we are made uneasy when a general idea of ours feels out of balance. Ideas charged with emotion adhere to a special logic, a psycho-logic of *equilibrium*. For example, they feel true ("self-evident") whenever positive concepts are good for other positive concepts. "Good things happen to good people" is the classic idea-in-equilibrium, and we are comfortable believing it and its offspring (like "prosperity flows to free people," "success results to those who persevere," and "Americans support underdogs").

Likewise, we're comfortable with ideas where something positive is supposed to harm despicable things (as in "freedom defeats tyranny") or something negative does bad things (as in "ruthless bosses eventually get their comeuppance"). Generally, the logic of equilibrium is satisfied when positive concepts increase good things and diminish the bad, and negative concepts produce bad things and diminish the good.

Compare our emotional comfort regarding beliefs-in-equilibrium with our disquiet when we confront an idea where harm is believed to happen to things we like. Such ideas, like "the good die young" and "no good deed goes unpunished," may please cynics, but they upset the bulk of humanity. It is no accident that the story of Job—the kindly Old Testament figure who is beset by loss of wife, children, business, and health—is the most troubling tale in the Bible, for it implies a general idea that violates the psycho-logic of equilibrium.

And third, intellectually, general ideas interconnect with one another in systems of belief. General concepts (like "freedom") causally connect to a variety of objects. For example, freedom stimulates personal vitality, increases a nation's prosperity, defeats tyrants, and requires self-restraint. These four ideas *interconnect* because they share the common concept of "freedom."

A troubling problem arises when an individual changes his mind about one of these emotionally charged, interconnected ideas. For example, living in America, a young man is brought up with a love for freedom. As he reaches young adulthood, he goes to a college in an urban setting, where he encounters troubling numbers of poor people living "in the streets." The idea that some of his fellow Americans are being left behind disturbs him because it contradicts his emotion-laden idea that freedom enables individuals to prosper; the reality he views implies that freedom (which he loves) causes poverty (which he hates). When compelled to confront the incompatibility of these two beliefs—say, by a professor putting him on the spot in a classroom—he may resolve it by altering his feelings about one of the concepts; for example, he might try convincing himself that poverty is a good thing (because it prods those who suffer it to try harder).

More likely, however, he will question the value of freedom, coming to believe that freedom is just another word for exploitation by the evil rich. In other words, he will reverse his feelings about an element of his belief system.

Whenever such a reversal involves a concept so central to an individual's belief system as "freedom," serious consequences begin to flow. Changing one idea about freedom creates imbalances in all the other ideas associated with it. If, for example, his sense of personal responsibility has been founded on his love of freedom—"living in a free country requires everyone to hold himself responsible for choosing between virtuous and wrong actions"—his sudden demeaning of freedom may "demoralize" him. He may come to think that "only the gullible believe in self-restraint." Or, to take another example, if his personal honesty promotes what he now sees as an exploitative, greedy country, then why should he act honestly? In confusion, he loses all self-confidence, sinks into self-accusation, and finds himself painfully alienated from family and friends. When those feelings come over college students, we used to call it "sophomore slump." Today, we perhaps call it by other names—depression, anomie, alienation—but it's all the same thing.

Now why does changing our minds have such consequential, often quite devastating effects? The answer has to do with the three important functions general ideas fulfill. They enable us to have "hunches." They make life meaningful. And they enable voluntary cooperation.

The Paradox of Perception

For one thing, ideas enable the healthy person to ascertain the unknowable—to predict the future, to see the invisible, to fill in the gaps in what he knows. His attitudes supply him with hunches about cause-and-effect and clue him in on what is going to happen and what to do about it. Think of the idea embedded in the age-old rhyme, "Red sky at night, sailors' delight; red sky in the morning, sailors take warning." That piece of lore—that idea—enables people to prophesy the weather from a telltale horizon and to act confidently on the basis of that prediction. This simple folk belief enables them to choose between going on a picnic or going to a movie and puts an end to indecision. Likewise, if one "knows" that "freedom promotes vitality," it is not hard to foresee that a nation that frees itself from the shackles of totalitarianism (as the Polish people did in 1989) will experience a great surge of vitality and national economic growth, even though one has never been to Poland or met a Pole.

In short, foreseeing storms and prophesying prosperity are just two instances of the **paradox of perception:** *beliefs enable seeing.* Anyone who has experienced the world (including our most creative scientists) knows that belief has to come first so that he or she knows what to look for. Ideas predict the presence of what is invisible to the eye. For example, no one "saw" molecules until molecular theory suggested their existence and where they would likely be visible. For another example, a judge cannot see the effect of leniency when he sentences a wrongdoer; he only has hunches, ideas about a reality that has not yet materialized.

So when people change a deeply held belief, they undermine their powers of foresight. The person who starts demeaning freedom as nothing more than plutocratic trickery, for example, is left without a clue as to what might happen to a liberated Poland or any other nation that regains its freedom. At best, he will have no clue as to what will happen. At worst, he will be dead wrong in his prediction. Averse to feeling uncertain, he will vigorously defend, rather than change, his convictions.

The Paradox of Responsibility

Second, in addition to being intellectually disorienting, changing one's general ideas alters the moral meaning of one's past, for these big beliefs are the basis of determining whether your deeds honor or shame you. Take, as an example, your volunteering several nights a month assisting at a homeless shelter in your community. If you have a positive concept of personal freedom, you may "see" your activity as helping to liberate homeless persons from the terrors of the street; by connecting what might otherwise seem to be little deeds to a bigger and cherished value, your sacrifice of time and effort enhances your self-respect, which in turn inspires even greater dedication to your duties.[4]

But change your evaluation of freedom for the worse, and you run the risk of changing the moral value of your past actions. Your altered feelings about freedom nullify the honor of your work with the homeless, premised as it was on an idea you have come to dismiss.

That example may be a bit trivial, but the point is not. Heroic soldiers who killed an enemy in a "good" war of liberation are transformed into dishonored murderers by revisionist historians who redefine the war as a "bad" one of exploitation. Dedicated Soviet generals, disillusioned by the end of the Cold War and the revelations of communism's evils, committed suicide.

You can't undo your past, but you can degrade it. And since nobody wants earlier deeds dishonored or previous sacrifices made vain, people naturally resist changes in beliefs that would demean their past. This intellectual firmness is summed up in the **paradox of responsibility:** *the more irrevocable the deed, the more irreversible the idea that sired it.*

The Paradox of Social Order

Third, and finally, general ideas are the basis of human cooperation, and most importantly, they enable collaboration on a large scale. People with the same outlook and values—who "share the same culture"—know they can count on each other to behave predictably.[5]

Consider Shakespeare's image, life as theater:[5]

All the world's a stage,

And all the men and women merely players:

They have their exits and their entrances;

And one man in his time plays many parts. . . .

What Shakespeare observed was that social life resembles a stage play. In a variety of circumstances, individuals act as if they were following a fixed script. They constitute a cast in a drama. People play their "many parts"— their roles as wives (or husbands), parents (or children), teachers (or students), coaches (or players), bosses (or employees), even jailors (or prisoners).[6] Each role incorporates a set of general, moralized ideas that guides the individual in his or her performance. We learn our parts, thanks to families, kindergartens, churches, high schools, professions, and businesses. Despite our individualism, we cooperate supportively and accomplish things of value as long as we follow our scripts. Our families interact smoothly, our schools succeed, our sports teams adhere to victorious "game plans," our firms profit, our orchestras sound harmonious, our prisons become orderly, and our military accomplishes miracles in peace and war. And all this cooperation is gained without "forcing" anyone, without coercion. And no price needs to be paid to achieve cooperation. A "common sense" makes human collaboration possible.

In these relationships participants hold a mutual authority over one another. Each "actor" expects his fellow players to perform according to the scripted beliefs they share. If one of them makes a wayward move, the others feel entitled to compel him to mend his ways—to conform to the part as scripted.

In a play, should a participant adopt a new attitude, like Juliet deciding to speak Lady Macbeth's lines to Romeo, the scene falls apart. In the interest of preserving order, the other participants will act to get Juliet back into her role. In like manner, human relationships, from the family unit to the nation, are stabilized by social pressures to conform. As with a theater company, so with societies. Societies invariably resist a rebel tinkering with the general ideas that bind their members together in voluntary, trusting cooperation. Such is true of all societies, even in times when they know that their group has to adapt to new conditions, or they will become extinct. They fear, and therefore resist, surrendering their traditional ways even though their customs have become obsolete.

The British statesman Edmund Burke (1729-1797) warned that to conserve itself, a society may have to modernize the scripts of its culture.[7] Consider the application of Burke's advice in the American context: in the aftermath of World War II many white southerners knew that the racially segregationist traditions and beliefs of their region were not sustainable—and should not be sustained. But the dilemma they faced was that in making changes in the numerous roles defined by their southern culture, people would disconnect from one another, would get out of synch. Change would damage vital collateral values and undermine gentle cooperation. New beliefs about racial equality, while much needed, would leave people unsure about their relationships with others; social pressures to conform and collaborate would weaken and chaos would come, lasting decades.

In fact, sociologist Charles Murray, among other insightful observers, has persuasively argued that that is just what happened: new ideas—noble ideas—created incompatible (and ambiguously defined) roles, leading to a decade of chaos, riots, and criminality that occurred in the late 1960s and early 1970s.[8]

Thus, while it may be necessary in some instances to tinker with cultural scripts to preserve a society, the process of change is likely to be accompanied by serious disorientation and disorder. A community's tendency to shy away from changing established roles is called the **paradox of social order:** *social order abhors change, even when change is necessary to preserve it.*

The Dangers of Moral Disorder

The poet Robert Frost (1874–1963) gives us a memorable image of the importance of these general ideas to an individual and the larger society in which he is embedded. He calls these widely shared "truths"—these cultural scripts—the forces that maintain the "sureness of the soul" in a poem where he likens the human personality to a "silken tent" held upright by its guy ropes:

> She is as in a field a silken tent
> At midday, when a sunny summer breeze
> Has dried the dew and all the ropes relent,
> So that in guys it gently sways at ease,
> And its supporting central cedar pole,
> That is its pinnacle to heavenward
> And signifies the sureness of the soul,
> Seems to owe naught to any single cord,
> But strictly held by none, is loosely bound
> By countless silken ties of love and thought
> To everything on earth the compass round. . . .

Undoing any of those "countless silken ties of love and thought"—those deeply felt, emotion-laden moral beliefs—is risky business. Ineptly done, adjusting them can topple "the supporting central cedar pole" and the "soul" it signifies. Excising and replacing those stays of personality can accidentally cause severe, paralyzing depression.

When large numbers of a society experience such confusion, despair, and alienation, we say that a condition of *social anomie* exists. Anomie imperils a society's capacity for collaboration. At such times, a moral vacuum occurs, and leaders may arise who will have the opportunity to reshape people's thinking for good—or, more direfully, for ill—where demagogues such as Hitler, Stalin, Saddam Hussein, and Osama bin Laden can convince a demoralized people they have an answer to their confusion, despair, and alienation.

NOTES

1. See William Ker Muir Jr., *The Bully Pulpit: The Presidential Leadership of Ronald Reagan* (San Francisco: ICS Press, 1992).
2. This discussion of the nature of ideas derives largely from Robert Abelson and Milton Rosenberg, "A Model of Attitudinal Cognition," in Milton J. Rosenberg, C. I. Hovland, et al., *Attitude Organization and Change* (New Haven: Yale University Press, 1960).
3. General ideas are also invariably flawed. Tocqueville cautions, "General ideas are no proof of the strength, but rather of the insufficiency of the human intellect; for there are in nature no beings exactly alike, no things precisely identical, no rules indiscriminately and alike applicable to several objects at once. The chief merit of general ideas is that they enable the human mind to pass a rapid judgment on a great many objects at once; but, on the other hand, the notions they convey are never other than incomplete, and they always cause the mind to lose as much in accuracy as it gains in comprehensiveness." Alexis de Tocqueville, *Democracy in America,* trans. Henry Reeve (New York: Bantam, 2000 [1840]), vol. II, book 1, chap. 3.
4. For a superb study of the moral basis of volunteer work, see Robert S. Ogilvie, *Voluntarism, Community Life, and the American Ethic* (Bloomington: University of Indiana Press, 2004).
5. William Shakespeare, *As You Like It*, Act II, Scene 7.
6. See Richard McCleery's insightful study of a maximum security prison, "Correctional Administration and Political Change," in Lawrence E. Hazelrigg, ed., *Prison within Society* (Garden City, N.Y.: Doubleday/Anchor, 1969), 115–149.
7. Edmund Burke, *Reflections on the Revolution in France* (Garden City, N.Y.: Doubleday/Dolphin, 1961 [1790]).
8. Charles Murray, *Losing Ground: American Social Policy* (New York: Basic Books, 1986). For more on the disruptive effects of desegregation in the black community, see Chapter 29.

10

DEMAGOGUERY

Systems of belief resemble a thick matting of roots under the floor of the forest which if cut may result in the withering of some distant bush or a whole tree. The man who intrudes into another culture, or way of life, . . . is like one who cuts bothersome roots without being aware of their functions and interconnections. The people of the other culture, however, like the trees of the forest, even if themselves ignorant of the functional nature of their system of belief, nevertheless feel it when their roots are cut.

Alexander Leighton, *The Governing of Men* (1945)

No political novel better illustrates the dynamic of widespread disorientation—social anomie—than Robert Penn Warren's *All the King's Men*.[1] Its setting is the United States, but among Warren's motives in writing it was to understand the rise of the Nazi dictator Adolf Hitler and his transformation of Germany's cultured and civilized society into a people who embraced a bizarre ideology of hatred and murder.

The central character of *All the King's Men* is Willie Stark, "The Boss." In creating Stark, Warren drew heavily on incidents in the life of Huey Long, one-time governor and U.S. senator of Louisiana in the 1930s and unquestionably the most powerful demagogue in American history. (But for his assassination in 1935, Long might have been elected president in 1936.) In Warren's judgment, Huey Long (and his fictional counterpart, Willie

Stark) was the American Hitler, the closest thing the nation had to the German Führer.

Stark owed his political ascent to the support—the devout support—of the downtrodden small farmers in a state where an aristocracy of financial and landed wealth dominated all its institutions. Before Stark came on the political scene, these small farmers acquiesced in their oppression. They believed they were inferior by virtue of their illiteracy and poverty. In their minds, they were shameful, common "hicks," and their superiors, the sophisticated aristocracy downstate, had every right to make them subservient.

Stark set out to reverse their submissive acceptance of poverty. His purpose was to arouse a collective anger against the rich and powerful elite, whom he despised. His means were words. With soaring oratory, he exposed them to the "truth" of the democratic idea—the very beliefs about human equality and just government that Thomas Jefferson expressed in the Declaration of Independence.

The pivotal scene in the novel takes place at a country fair. Stark is campaigning for governor, but minutes before the action takes place he's learned that the gubernatorial candidate of the aristocratic party, Joe Harrison, has tricked him into playing the "spoiler." When he realizes that if he continues running for governor he will split the vote of Harrison's opponents, enabling Harrison to win, Stark decides to pull out of the race and to urge his supporters to give their votes to the rural candidate, MacMurfee.

The Speech

From an elevated platform Stark confronts a gathering of farmers. He begins to talk by articulating the aristocratic point of view that he knows country folk have submissively accepted—a belief that shames them: hicks are inferior in brains and virtue. "Look at your pants," he tells them. "Have they got holes in the knee? Listen to your belly. Did it ever rumble for emptiness? Look at your crop. Did it ever rot in the field because the road was so bad you couldn't get it to market? Look at your kids. Are they growing up ignorant as you and dirt because there isn't any school for them?"

Having brought to the surface the self-hating ideas of his audience, Stark goes on to tell his personal story, admitting that he, too, once shared their outlook about a superior few being entitled to lord it over ordinary folk, who lacked the "stuff and character" to run their own lives.

It's a funny story. . . . Get ready to laugh. Get ready to bust your sides for it is sure a funny story. It's about a hick. It's about a red-neck, like you all, if you please. Yeah, like you. He grew up like any other mother's son on the dirt roads and gully washes of a north-state farm. He knew all about being a hick. He knew what it was to get up before day and get cow dung between his toes and feed and slop and milk before breakfast so he could set off by sunup to walk six miles to a one-room, slab-sided schoolhouse. He knew what it was to pay high taxes for that windy shack of a schoolhouse and those gully-washed red-clay roads to walk over—or to break his wagon axle or string-halt his mules on.

Stark continues, recollecting his attempt to improve himself and depicting the personal pride he took in his effort to elevate himself out of the "hick" class into membership among the superior few.

Oh, he knew what it was to be a hick, summer and winter. He figured if he wanted to do anything he had to do it himself. So he sat up nights and studied books and studied law so maybe he could do something about changing things. He didn't study that law in any man's school or college. He studied it nights after a hard day's work in the field. So he could change things some. For himself and for folks like him. I am not lying to you. He didn't start out thinking about all the other hicks and how he was going to do wonderful things for them. He started out thinking of number one, but something came to him on the way. . . .

He then details the political dirty trick that had humiliated him and caused his personal transformation. Years before, he tells the crowd, he had gained local respect for trying to reveal the public corruption involved in building a new brick schoolhouse, whose defective construction caused the death of several students.

People were his friends because he had fought that rotten brick. And some of the public leaders down in the city knew that and they rode up to his pappy's place in a big fine car and said how they wanted him to run for Governor, . . . and that hick swallowed it. He looked in his heart and thought he might try to change things. In all humility he thought how he might try. He was just a human, country boy, who believed like we have always believed back here in the hills that even the plainest, poorest fellow can be Governor if his fellow citizens find he has got the stuff and the character for the job.

Those fellows in the striped pants saw the hick and they took him in. They said how MacMurfee was a limber-back and a dead-head and how Joe Harrison was the tool of the city machine, and how they wanted that hick to step in and try to give some honest government. They told him that. But . . . do you know who they were? They were Joe Harrison's hired hands and lickspittles and they wanted to get a hick to run to split MacMurfee's hick vote.

Having confessed his gullibility, Stark announces his withdrawal from the race for governor, "not because my little feelings are hurt. They aren't hurt, I never felt better in my life, because now I know the truth." And he declares that "truth," the democratic idea that hicks aren't "dirt" but God's creatures with just as much "stuff and character" as anyone else. "What I ought to known long back. Whatever a hick wants he's got to do for himself. Nobody in a fine automobile and sweet-talking is going to do it for him. . . . The truth is going to be told and I'm going to tell it. I'm going to tell it over this state from one end to the other if I have to ride the rods or steal me a mule to do it, and no man, Joe Harrison or any other man, can stop me. For I got me a gospel."

His is a radical gospel—not individual self-improvement but social revolution, not love but hate, not forgiveness but revenge, not passivity but war, not brotherhood but enmity.

He stood on schoolhouse steps, and on the top of boxes borrowed from the dry-goods store and on the seats of farm wagons and on the porches of crossroads stores, and talked. "Friends, red-necks, suckers, and fellow hicks," he would say, leaning forward, leaning at them, looking at them. And he would pause, letting the words sink in. And in the quiet the crowd would be restless and resentful under these words, the words they knew people called them, but the words nobody ever got up and called them to their face. "Yeah," he would say, "yeah," and twist his mouth on the word, "that's what you are, and you needn't get mad at me for telling you. Well, get mad, but I'm telling you. That's what you are. And me—I'm one, too. Oh, I'm a red-neck, for the sun has beat down on me. Oh, I'm a sucker, for I fell for that sweet-talking fellow in the fine automobile. Oh, I took the sugar tit and hushed my crying. Oh, I'm a hick and I am the hick they were going to try to use and split the hick vote. But I'm standing here on my own hind legs, for even a dog can learn to do that, give him time. I learned. It took me a time but I learned, and here I am on my own hind legs." And he would lean at them. And demand, "Are you, are you on your hind legs? Have you learned that much yet? You think you can learn that much?"

The Resolution of Anomie

Then, as only a great writer can, Warren describes the intense reaction of his "hicks" on hearing his "gospel": first resistance, then confusion, then paralyzing anomie, and at last, electrifying transformation.

[Stark] gave them that, and they stood there in front of him, with a thumb hooked in the overall strap, and the eyes under the pulled down hat brim squinting at him as though he were something spied across a valley or cove, something they weren't quite easy in the mind about, too far away to make out good, or a sudden movement in the brush seen way off yonder across the valley or across the field and something might pop out of the brush, and under the eyes the jaw revolved working the quid with a slow, punctilious, immitigable motion, like historical process. And Time is nothing to a hog, or to History, either. They watched him, and if you watched close you might be able to see something beginning to happen. They stand so quiet, they don't even shift from one foot to the other—they've got a talent for being quiet, you can see them stand on the street corner when they come to town, not moving or talking or see one of them squatting on his heels by the road, just looking off where the road drops over the hill—and their squinched eyes don't flicker off the man up there in front of them. They've got a talent for being quiet. But sometimes the quietness stops. It snaps all of a sudden, like a piece of string pulled tight. One of them sits quiet on the bench, at the brush-arbor revival, listening, and all of a sudden he jumps up and lifts up his arms and yells, "Oh, Jesus! I have seen His name!" Or one of them presses his finger on the trigger, and the sound of the gun surprises even him.

In the remaining chapters of *All the King's Men*, Warren narrates how the moral unity that Stark's words generate results in a devotion to him personally, for he has convinced his listeners that they are no one's inferior. Then, in a strange irony, they commit their prodigious energies to follow him blindly into his own oppressive totalitarianism.

The key to Stark's moral power—as it was to Hitler's—is the intellectual and moral confusion created by his "gospel." With their abandonment of their belief in class distinction, the "hicks" lose confidence in the values interconnected with it—virtuous ideas like love, honesty, kindness, forgiveness, hard work, and reasonableness. Stark's certainties fill up the philosophical vacuum they experience, dispelling their disorientation. His values become their values, his hatemongering definition of society their definition, and his way their way.

Warren's fictionalized account of the rise of a demagogue teaches an important lesson about social anomie. In particular, it contains a timely warning: whenever a formerly aristocratic society stops believing that a small elite rightfully is its master, it becomes vulnerable to anomie. Widespread moral confusion invariably results from intruding new ideas into a timeworn culture. This is especially so with people totally unexposed to the democratic idea. As they feel the undoing of "their countless silken ties of love and thought," as they sense the former "sureness" of their souls tumbling into self-doubt, they can offer little resistance to demagogues who promise a return to the stability of an aristocratic order. This time, however, the demagogue's aristocracy is of a different, more virulent kind than that which had been thrown over; the new aristocracy is a regime of fascist Führers, nationalist zealots, communist apparatchiks, or militant mullahs.

By no means is such a result inevitable. When nations recognize the possibly demoralizing effects of the transition to the democratic idea and address the intellectual, social, and (especially) moral tumult that can result, then they may make a humane transition to freedom and social democracy.

Japan transformed itself into a free society following its defeat in World War II. The United States, anticipating that it would need to occupy postwar Japan and realizing how little it understood Japanese culture, established a task force of academics years before the war came to an end. Headed by anthropologist Ruth Benedict, its mission was to explain the customs and belief systems American occupation authorities would encounter. The scholars supplemented the available literature by commissioning studies of the experience of the Japanese who had been forcibly interned in camps in several western states in 1942. The task force's conclusions helped guide the American occupation after the war.[2]

The most notable of the internment studies it commissioned was anthropologist Alexander Leighton's analysis of the failed Japanese relocation center in Poston, Arizona. There, Leighton had witnessed the demoralization of several thousand Japanese and Japanese Americans in a camp governed by a "kindly" American administrator, whose policies (e.g., arranging dances for teenaged boys and girls, which affronted Japanese traditions of deference to one's elders, even in matters of courtship and matrimony) were premised on his own American, individualistic ideas. Leighton identified the causes of an organized strike, with the internees refusing to work and cooperate. To Leighton, it became clear that it arose from the cultural clash between the administrator's naive assumptions and the internees' traditions (with the unintended demeaning of the authority of the elders and the consequent moral uncertainties). Likening the effect of the administrator's alien notions of individual freedom on the traditional belief systems inside the camp to "cut[ting] bothersome roots without being aware of their functions and interconnections"[3] to some distant tree, Leighton exhorted the members of Benedict's task force, "Never forget the strength there may be in a system of belief and the fact that no matter how foreign, useless or destructive it seems it may still be interconnected with those things upon which the security and capacity of the people depend."[4]

Partly as a consequence of the task force's report and the cautions it uttered against impatience and abrupt action, the American occupation authorities left the Japanese emperor in his position as chief of state in recognition of his central place within the Japanese moral culture. His retention calmed anxieties, giving the people time to fit new ideas of individual freedom into their own "common sense."

But the difficulties of accomplishing successful change must not be underestimated. If they are not confronted and delicately overcome, the "blood-dimmed tide" of anarchy is likely, and the tragedy of a "center [that] cannot hold" is very great.

From recent experience, it is important for Americans to recollect how disabling the moral disorder was that beset the nation during the Vietnam War (1962–1975). The riots, legal disobedience, and flaunting of authority should be an instructive, if harsh, lesson of the power of ideas. All things fell apart in those times, not because there was policy disagreement as to whether and how to fight the war (though there was plenty of that), but because there was broadcast a contradictory definition of the American democracy, causing people to doubt their moral foundations. Was America an essentially good society waging a just war for freedom, or was it a gullible society that had done worldwide harm, thanks to the manipulations of elitist knaves ("the best and the brightest," as the administrations of Presidents Kennedy, Johnson, and Nixon were derisively labeled)? The harsh attack upon America's definition of itself threw into doubt what it meant to be a good American and thereby undermined the basis of social collaboration.

Ideas have real consequences.

NOTES

1. Robert Penn Warren, *All the King's Men* (New York: Harcourt Brace, 1946).
2. Professor Benedict later made the gist of the task force available to the public in her *The Chrysanthemum and the Sword: Patterns of Japanese Culture* (Boston: Houghton Mifflin, 1946).
3. Alexander H. Leighton, *The Governing of Men* (Princeton: Princeton University Press, 1945), 292.
4. Ibid., 294.

11

SOCIAL PLURALISM

There were thirty-eight different stations broadcasting on the AM band of the car radio. Revolution was being preached. . . . I heard offered a consensus of opinion that the public policy of the United States was deliberately designed . . . to subjugate twenty-six Black Americans. . . . From Lexington, Massachusetts, on WROL, a Protestant evangelist named Kathryn Kuhlman, who had been dead for three years, was on tape that could play until eternity, vigorously attacking all recipients of government welfare. . . . Four stations were broadcasting nothing but news. . . . Five stations were broadcasting only religious programming. . . . That was one hour on the AM band of one radio—and I have recorded only a tiny fraction of the information and opinion on concerns from stock to sex that I heard in that hour.

Richard Reeves, *American Journey* (1982)

By its constitutional protections of free speech and press, America's open society permits the advocacy of beliefs of every kind. Labor unions and business associations, evangelical churches and atheists, environmentalists and developers, government spokespeople and government critics, and mavens of every conceivable cause broadcast countless ideas into the public space, daily battling for dominance.

As a result, Americans live amidst a lot of noise. William James, perhaps America's premier student of psychology, resorted to adjectives like *cacophonous* and *booming* to capture the ceaseless intellectual and moral chatter besetting them.[1]

The American "Tumult"

To an outsider suddenly come to our shores, the din is daunting. Of his first impression of America in 1831, Alexis de Tocqueville wrote,

> No sooner do you set foot upon American ground than you are stunned by a kind of tumult; a confused clamor is heard on every side, and a thousand simultaneous voices demand the satisfaction of their social wants. Everything is in motion around you: here the people of one quarter of a town are met to decide upon the building of a church; there the election of a representative is going on; a little farther, the delegates of a district are hastening to the town in order to consult upon some local improvements; in another place the laborers of a village quit their plows to deliberate upon the project of a road or a public school. Meetings are called for the sole purpose of declaring their disapprobation of the conduct of the government, while in other assemblies citizens salute the authorities of the day as the fathers of their country. Societies are formed which regard drunkenness as the principal cause of the evils of the state, and seriously bind themselves to give an example of temperance.[2]

Tocqueville grew to admire the energy and skill with which Americans rallied their neighbors to collaborate in "the satisfaction of their social wants." The ability of ordinary people voluntarily to team up sharply contrasted with the passivity of Tocqueville's French countrymen, who would wait for government officials to take the initiative. The difference, he observed, stemmed from the feeble character of American government at national and local levels. As a consequence, the American people were obliged to master what he called "the principle of association"—the skills of arousing and focusing volunteer efforts to build improvements like churches, schools, libraries, theaters, and hospitals. "Americans of all ages, all conditions, and all dispositions" developed a knack for motivating volunteers to participate in the conception, organization, and completion of public undertakings—rebuilding a family barn, aiding a widow, or planning a public celebration.

Tocqueville discerned something else. The motivational skills of the citizenry, so impressive in attaining practical ends, were no less useful in promoting moral—that is, belief-changing—objectives. "Americans," said Tocqueville, "constantly form associations. They have not only commercial and manufacturing companies, in which all take part, but associations of a thousand other kinds. . . . *If it is proposed to inculcate some truth or to foster some feeling by the encouragement of a great example, they form a society.*"[3] (Emphasis added.) What struck Tocqueville so forcefully about this new democratic society was how much Americans cared about what their fellow citizens thought. The cause, he believed, was that to achieve anything of any magnitude one needed to shape a supportive public opinion. As he ruefully quipped, "The people reign in the American political world as the Deity does in the universe."[4] Where the people reign, it is the better part of wisdom to attend to what they think and educate their thinking.[5]

Since Tocqueville's time, governments have grown more capable, doing more and with greater skill. Instead of reducing the need for public persuasion, however, as the public administration has improved, its assistance has become more highly prized—and securing it for individual projects has required winning over the electorate's support for them.[6]

As we saw in the last chapter, intruding a new "truth" into the belief system of even one individual is a task of considerable difficulty. Changing the minds of large numbers of people compounds the difficulty and requires sophisticated organization. As soon as one looks about for such organizations, one is stunned by their multitude and omnipresence in America. These groups play a central part in its politics and give it its special quality—a character that is called pluralism[7]—social pluralism.

Essential Characteristics of Moral Organizations

They have many critics, who decry them as the "special-interest industry." But these special interests are exactly the "societies" that Tocqueville found so vital to the life of a democracy (although, you will recall, that James Madison denounced them as "factions").[8] Today, as yesterday, they attempt "to inculcate some truth" they care about. There are groups to spread truths about the environment,[9] women's role in society,[10] and America's international obligations.[11] There are thousands of local labor unions convincing the public of the value of hard work and of those who do it, and there exist countless more associations to inculcate truths about firearms, tobacco, drug abuse, illiteracy, parenting, and mental illness.

Although these advocacy organizations virtually always require financial resources to get their word out effectively, they are not commercial in nature; they are not organized to promote the sale of goods and services. On the contrary, they are *moral organizations*; their object is to cultivate moral beliefs in others and challenge prevalent attitudes contrary to their own.

Tocqueville also mentioned societies organized "to foster some feeling." Assemblages of citizens of every background, determined to change or reinforce popular attitudes, line our sidewalks and our campuses with their card tables, pamphlets, and posters. Just naming a tiny fraction of them reminds us of their importance in fostering feelings of tolerance, among them the National Association for the Advancement of Colored People, the (Jewish) Anti-Defamation League, the Italo-American Anti-Defamation League, the Japanese American League, the American Civil Liberties Union, and the Roman Catholic Church. There is also the mass of local service organizations like Rotary, Kiwanis, Lions, and Masons—all serving to promote positive feelings about their communities.

These moral organizations, be they local or national in their reach, share six essential characteristics.[12] One, they virtually always have a *text*, an authoritative document that is amendable only with difficulty. The text may be a formal legal charter. In other instances, it may simply be the mission statement contained in the written materials that the organization distributes door to door and on the streets. The important point is that a text invariably exists, is publicly accessible, and contains essential principles that can be invoked by any adherent in the organization.

Two, moral organizations have an *authoritative interpreter* of the text. Since texts speak in general principles (like "Take control of our borders," "Love thy neighbor," and "Think globally; act locally"), ambiguities pop up in their application to specific problems. Interpreters bridge the gaps between the abstractions of the text and the particulars of circumstance.

In most organizations, these final authorities are executive boards, but the more sophisticated moral organizations delegate this crucial task of interpretation to a judicial-like body, one specialized in justifying the group's activities by the words of the text.

Three, moral organizations perpetuate themselves by developing *procedures to recruit, train, and inspire* new adherents in how to teach the texts and their applications to the larger world. These missionaries perform the job of converting the public, sometimes on a one-on-one basis, sometimes in small groups, where they personally facilitate, counsel, and hold the hands of individuals during the sometimes painful and difficult process of embracing new truths and altered feelings.

Four, moral organizations have *means of oversight*, whereby they discipline their adherents to stay current with the latest interpretation of their text and to incorporate its implications into their teaching.

Five, moral organizations institutionalize procedures to provide their activist adherents effective (*not* sham) participation and influence in the interpretive process. They permit the members who are teaching the public to *feed back* to the leadership the public's reactions.

Finally, moral organizations cultivate a *sense of fraternity* among their adherents. The means they use to promote feelings of a shared destiny may be as simple as awarding a lapel pin or a card to be carried in the wallet, or as conspicuous as entitling them to wear a T-shirt or a common uniform. Sometimes, a moral organization may require a public act of commitment, like putting one's name on a letterhead or requiring a year of missionary work. Whatever the symbol or sacrifice, it is intended to develop among the adherents a sense of interdependence—an *esprit de corps.*

While these six features of text, interpretation, recruitment, discipline, participatory mechanisms, and bonding can be discerned in even the most local and temporary collaborations, they can best be examined in America's two most established moral organizations.

The Law Profession as a Moral Institution

Arguably, the most influential of America's idea-disseminating associations is the law profession—its million or so lawyers, together with its elaborate judicial system, hundreds of law schools, and numerous publishing houses. Virtually every lawyer reveres the U.S. Constitution, with its sweeping abstractions enjoining every government official—from the jailer in the smallest hamlet to the chief executive in the White House—from depriving "any person of life, liberty or property without due process of law."

The law profession, for all its seeming diversity, acknowledges the U.S. Supreme Court as the singular interpreter of that text. The widely published opinions of the Supreme Court authoritatively connect the generalities of the Constitution to concrete situations.

As for recruitment and training of its adherents, hundreds of accredited schools exist throughout the United States to attract and train candidates in the spirit and language of the law; in their classes law students are evaluated by how well they master the text and the justices' rendering of it.

As for organizational oversight of the profession after law school, there are disciplining devices to root out heretical ways. Lawyers can lose their licenses and, even more importantly, their cases, if their thinking strays too far from the law, either by intention or by ignorance. Moreover, clients oblige attorneys to know the law and lay it out understandably so they can conform their actions to it. Likewise, lawyers are expected to teach the law's ideas where and when they sit on corporate and charitable boards, city councils, school boards, and legislative committees.

Between judges and lawyers, there is a tradition of respectful mutuality. Judges are obliged by the norms of their profession to read the briefs containing the attorneys' ideas and to incorporate them into their opinions. When they do, lawyers are filled with a strong sense of identification with the legal system.

Finally, while only the judges wear a distinctive uniform in America, lawyers display their licenses to practice, speak, and think in distinctive ways, all leading to personal pride and a fraternal feeling.

No other moral organization is so perfectly suited as the law to voice ideas in a disciplined way and disseminate them.[13] Consequently, virtually every American belief has arisen in or been deeply influenced by the law—ideas about freedom, fairness, personal responsibility, human nature, the good life, the nobility of labor, reciprocity, and the importance of truth. No one understood the moral power of the legal community better than Tocqueville. "Scarcely any political question arises in the United States that is not resolved, sooner or later, into a judicial question," he observed. "Hence all parties are obliged to borrow, in their daily controversies, the ideas, and even the language, peculiar to judicial proceedings. As most public men are or have been legal practitioners, they introduce the customs and technicalities of their profession into the management of public affairs. . . . The language of the law thus becomes, in some measure, a vulgar tongue; the spirit of the law, which is produced in the schools, gradually penetrates into the bosom of society. . . ."[14]

The Religious Community as a Moral Organization

Compared to the legal community, rival moral organizations have shortcomings, either because they lack its size, resources, comprehensive text, unity of interpretation, training and disciplinary mechanisms, or feedback mechanisms. Even large and seemingly resourceful competitors, like the media, entertainment business, and education community pale in comparison because they all lack a comprehensive text and a singular interpretive authority.

One institution, however, does rival the law in moral influence and in the scale and intricacy of its organization. The religious community—and here I refer to the approximately 350,000 members of the formal clergy, plus lay missionaries and evangelicals, devoted congregations, the religious press, and religious broadcasters—manages to suffuse Americans' belief systems with values that soften the malign effects of coercive and recipro-cal power—vindictiveness, on the one hand, and acquisitiveness, on the other—in the daily life of the nation. So important is the religious commu-nity that it would be foolhardy to overlook its vital role in America's pluralist society.

From a purely spiritual aspect, the religious community meets in seem-ingly divisive sects. But seen from a political perspective, these numerous religious assemblages all inculcate much the same truths about how to live a good life; their adherents spread the word that the right behavior now will entitle them later to a happy afterlife (however defined); and the American religious community, despite its apparent divisions, has arrived at an unex-pected consensus on what constitutes the worthy life.[15]

It is true that religions elsewhere differ in their definitions of the earthly actions that earn entry into the Kingdom of Heaven, requiring of their adherents deeds as different as implacable revenge at one extreme, to utter indifference to worldly matters at the other. In the United States, however, virtually every theology promotes the idea that heavenly acceptance depends on making the lives of others better. By being charitable to the needy, personally responsible to one's neighborhood and nation, and (most importantly) respectful of the value of all human life, religious Americans think they assure themselves of some form of immortality beyond death. These three duties—charity, responsibility, and respect—are the requirements of the good life and constitute what is known as the imperative of love.[16]

This consensus among a seeming variety of religious sects has many causes, the most important of which is the religious competition existing in the United States.[17] With no single church assured of a religious monop-oly, and with religious freedom legally guaranteed, each sect competes with the others for members. Like rivals everywhere—like Toyota and Gen-eral Motors or the Yankees and the Red Sox—they begin to resemble each other in their essentials. In building their congregations, churches "cher-rypick" the most agreeable features of their competitors. They adjust their theologies in socially acceptable ways and find themselves converging on the kind of behavior that the public respects as appropriate keys to God's kingdom—deeds that accord with the imperative of love.

Widespread agreement on the word of the religious community partially mitigates the lack of an acknowledged authority to give a definitive interpretation of doctrine. In other respects, religion's organizational features closely parallel the law's. It has a text, a widely accessible Bible that is full of general principles that apply to virtually every human action.[18] It has a system to attract fresh clerical recruits, enticing youngsters with special youth ministries and offering scholarships to religious colleges and graduate schools of theology, which more often than not take pride in their ecumenism and admire the same theological heroes, like C. S. Lewis, Mother Teresa, Reinhold Niebuhr, Martin Buber, Sören Kierkegaard, Dietrich Bonhoeffer, Elie Wiesel, and the pope. It employs mechanisms for supervising and disciplining the clerics, once they have been "licensed" to minister to the public: the "defrocking" of heretical priests, the dismissal of wayward clerics by traditionalist congregations, and the stripping of ministers' pension, health, and sabbatical benefits.

The religious community also provides a system of commentary that enables the clergy in their parishes to interact with, and feed back timely information to, the central religious authorities. The proliferation of religious radio, television, bookstores, and book clubs creates opportunities for ordinary clerics and laypersons to express their ideas forcefully to their churchly hierarchies. Of even greater importance, the central authorities cannot isolate themselves from ministers and religious laypersons because they financially depend upon the funds sent them by the local churches. "Who pays the piper calls the tune" is no less true in religious circles than in other human endeavors. Thus religious groups have learned not to change their doctrines impulsively, but only after deliberate and widespread consultation. The freedom to interact so frequently and easily with bishops (or their equivalents) gives those who actually are spreading the gospel an identification with their community no less strong than that of lawyers with theirs.

Moreover, the clergy has an *esprit de corps,* a feeling of fraternity. Priests, ministers, rabbis, and the like wear a clerical collar, or some clearly detectable equivalent. Like lawyers, they carry in their heads a special learning that enables them to read and apply biblical precedents and precepts with which to counsel their parishioners. They are set apart from the public by these factors and enjoy a special social prestige as a result.

Religion thus turns out to be a moral organization that performs with pervasive effect. It is no accident that virtually all the great social movements in the United States have had religious roots.[19] Religion has been *the* key in spreading the ideas that undermined established ways of thinking regarding slavery, child labor, drunkenness, war, labor-management relations, racial segregation, family irresponsibility, abortion, and capital punishment.[20]

By virtue of unity and numbers, the legal and religious communities are the most influential participants in America's moral life, but they exist among a vast multitude of moral organizations, each one ready to contest for public opinion. Inevitably, for every organization ready and able to convince Americans to change their minds in one direction, there is another trying to inculcate a contradictory belief. When a Ku Klux Klan—a KKK—arises to spread the idea of white supremacy, a National Association for the Advancement of Colored People—an NAACP—is organized to combat it. If there is an American Civil Liberties Union to persuade the nation of the importance of legal safeguards for alleged criminals, a Citizens for Justice group arises to convince the public that victims have rights too.

The Consequences of Social Pluralism

This heady and robust collision of ideas and values—what we've called social pluralism—sometimes produces confusion and harsh feelings. Conflict seems perpetual, discontent is constantly expressed,[21] serious culture wars break out, personal animosities result, and sometimes it seems as if some eternal truths are attacked so harshly that they almost shrivel up and die. But, in my mind, the good far outweighs the bad. Let me specify seven benefits of this robust social pluralism.

To begin, because these moral organizations are in constant need of active adherents to spread the word, they actively recruit volunteers. They train the volunteers in teaching, political skills, and empathy, the last because the spreading of beliefs requires them to talk with people outside their intimate circle of family and business colleagues.

Next, a moral organization gives social and philosophical support to its members, who, finding others who share their ideas, are relieved of their feelings of aloneness and impotence.

Third, when individuals participate in a moral organization, they fortify the moral principles by which they live their lives. They find themselves able to withstand the capricious public opinion of the moment.

A fourth consequence: consensus often emerges as groups with competing beliefs look for common ground. In the time it takes for consensus to develop, competition has tested (and strengthened) the ideas they are propagating and vetted them of their most serious flaws.

A fifth effect: the rules of social pluralism decry violence (although limited instances of it do occur). The weapons of moral organizations are words, their means persuasion. And while words can be upsetting, a culture war is preferable to a violent war.

Sixth, the ease with which a moral organization can enter into the public space means that there will virtually always arise healthy counterbalances to check runaway ideas. Great personal energy and considerable savvy may have to be devoted in starting up an effective local association to get its beliefs noticed, but there is little required in the way of monetary resources. Even when substantial capital is necessary to reach a national audience, the barriers to entry still are not insuperable. Incentives in the tax code, inexpensive bulk mail services, charitable habits, and the availability of private wealth in so many hands all assist in overcoming those barriers. It is no accident that when an AIPAC (American Israel Public Affairs Committee) starts to tout the virtues of a democratic Israel, a CAIR (Council on American-Islamic Relations) appears to dispute the claim and remind the media to tell the "other side" (e.g., that the Palestinians in Gaza are suffering). Likewise, the presence of a liberal weekly like the *New Republic* provokes a William F. Buckley to start up a conservative weekly like *National Review*. As a result of these countervailing organizations, Americans as a people get smart.

Last (and most important of all), social pluralism means that these competitively toughened organizations are capable of resisting a resource-rich government, which has its own formidable, attitude-shaping techniques. Social pluralism is an antidote to tyranny.

NOTES

1. William James, *The Varieties of Religious Experience* (New York: Modern Library, 1999). Cf. Richard Reeves, *American Journey: Traveling with Tocqueville in Search of "Democracy in America"* (New York: Simon and Schuster, 1982), 20–22.

2. Alexis de Tocqueville, *Democracy in America*, trans. Henry Reeve (New York: Bantam, 2000 [1835]), vol. I, chap. 14.

3. Alexis de Tocqueville, *Democracy in America*, trans. Henry Reeve (New York: Bantam, 2000 [1840]), vol. II, book 2, chap. 5.

4. Tocqueville, *Democracy in America*, vol. I, chap. 4.

5. Cf. President George Washington in his farewell address (1796): "In proportion as the structure of a government gives force to public opinion, it is essential that public opinion should be enlightened."

6. Putting the matter more invidiously, Pulitzer Prize–winning columnist George Will recently opined, "High-stakes government that directly dispenses trillions of dollars and influences, with tax benefits and regulations, the flow of trillions more, elicits an influence industry. Thoughtful people who recoil from many repugnant aspects of contemporary politics should squarely face the fact that big government begets bad politics." *Washington Post* Writers Group, May 14, 2006.

7. "Pluralism" has a variety of meanings; here it refers to *social* pluralism. For an enlightening discussion of *political* pluralism, see David Alan Sklansky, *Democracy and the Police* (Stanford: Stanford University Press, 2008), chap.1.

8. *Federalist* No. 10.

9. E.g., the Sierra Club, the League of Conservation Voters, the Southwest Legal Defense Fund, and the Boy Scouts of America.

10. E.g., the National Organization of Women, "Dr. Laura," the Planned Parenthood League, the National Association of University Women, the Junior League, the Queens Bench, and the Gay, Lesbian, and Bisexual League.

11. E.g., the United Nations Association, the World Affairs Council, and America First.

12. These six characteristics obtain as well in professional bureaucracies that need to give their members wide discretion to act. Cf. Herbert Kaufman's classic account, *The Forest Ranger* (Baltimore: Johns Hopkins University Press, 1960), from which this chapter largely derives.

13. In their study of tolerance in America, Herbert McClosky and Alida Brill found that lawyers were not only significantly more tolerant than any other group, but also that their attitudes on toleration were far more uniform than any other class of citizens. *Dimensions of Tolerance: What Americans Believe about Civil Liberties* (New York: Russell Sage Foundation, 1983).

14. Tocqueville, *Democracy in America*, vol. I, chap. 16.

15. In this regard, see Samuel P. Huntington, *Who Are We? The Challenges to America's National Identity* (New York: Simon and Schuster, 2004), especially chap. 4, "Anglo-Protestant Culture," and chap. 5, "Religion and Christianity."

16. E.g., Father Anthony Greeley and Professor Michael Hout show how similar the beliefs are (with the exception of attitudes about sexuality) of "conservative Christians" and other Christian Americans in their book, *The Truth about*

Conservative Christians: What They Think and What They Believe (Chicago: University of Chicago Press, 2006).

17. Max Lerner, in *America as a Civilization* (Simon and Schuster, 1964), makes this point with great force.

18. Admittedly, scholars argue over what constitute the real Muslim and Buddhist "texts."

19. Huntington, *Who Are We?* 15: "The twenty-first century, however, is dawning as a century of religion. Virtually everywhere, apart from Western Europe, people are turning to religion for comfort, guidance, solace, and identity. . . . Violence between religious groups is proliferating around the world. People are increasingly concerned with the fate of geographically remote co-religionists. In many countries powerful movements have appeared attempting to redefine the identity of their country in religious terms. In a very different way, movements in the United States are recalling America's religious origins and the extraordinary commitment to religion of the American people."

20. Ibid., 365: "Religiosity distinguishes America from most other Western societies. Americans are also overwhelmingly Christian, which distinguishes them from most non-Western peoples. Their religiosity leads Americans to see the world in terms of good and evil to a much greater extent than others do. The leaders of other societies often find this religiosity not only extraordinary but also exasperating for the deep moralism it engenders in the consideration of political, economic, and social issues."

21. Discontent is *not* a recent feature of American society. In his journey through the United States in 1831–1832, Tocqueville observed, "In America I saw the freest and most enlightened men placed in the happiest circumstances that the world affords; it seemed to me as if a cloud habitually hung upon their brow, and I thought them serious and almost sad, even in their pleasures." *Democracy in America,* vol. II, book 2, chap. 13. In time, he saw that this discontent was the cause of the nation's energy and prosperity.

12

POLITICAL DEMOCRACY

Then let's rejoice with loud Fal la
That Nature always does contrive
That every boy and every gal
That's born into the world alive
Is either a little Liberal
Or else a little Conservative!

William S. Gilbert, *Iolanthe* (1882)

We have left unmentioned the moral institution of greatest significance to the functioning of American government: our system of competing political parties. Two major parties have dominated the political landscape since the nation's founding. By and large, every national election since John Adams defeated Thomas Jefferson for the presidency in 1796 has consisted of the rivalry between the Democratic Party and the organization we now know as the Republican Party (through its several incarnations, it has been called the Federalist Party and the Whig Party). As rival moral organizations, they have promoted the two competing belief systems that frame political debate in the United States.

American political parties are the product of a democratic procedure so familiar to us that we often take it for granted: the requirement that legislatures make their decisions by majority rule. Before any proposal becomes law, it must receive the support of 50 percent plus one of the lawmakers.

Legislative majority rule burdens those who want to lead the government with two demanding tasks. They must first recruit candidates for political office and convince them to subscribe to a particular set of ideas; and they must then secure the election of those candidates by recruiting activists (and the candidates themselves) to go forth to persuade the bulk of the public that their set of ideas is sound. Hence, like lawyers and clerics, democratic political leaders have to organize a moral institution—a political party—to get the word out.[1]

Political Parties

Political parties in America are numerous and varied. They come in two sizes.

Large: the Republican and Democratic Parties are national in their extent and numerous in their membership. Their adherents are government officials, campaign managers, media specialists, pollsters, political activists, and fund-givers. The members of these two large parties are intent on winning national and state elections so that they can staff governments with officials who share their philosophies.

And small: there are hundreds of little parties throughout the United States. Some only operate locally, like the two in my hometown of Berkeley, California, which have vied for electoral victories in what officially is a "nonpartisan" system but actually isn't; in recent times they called themselves the "ABC's" (which stood for All Berkeley Coalition) and the "BCA's" (which stood for Berkeley Citizens Action). In other localities, you will find parties that divide along such lines as Growth and No Growth, or High-Taxes-and-Abundant-Services and Low-Taxes-and-Minimal-Services. Of a different character are ideological parties, like the Peace and Freedom, the Libertarian, the Socialist, the Communist, the American Independence, and the Green Parties. They are not organized to win elections, not even local ones (although once in a rare moment they will). Rather, they use the election season to propagate their ideas in a forum where, and at a time when, they can catch public attention.

But, whether large or small, all political parties specialize in convincing the electorate to embrace their beliefs. And, like other effective moral institutions, political parties are organized to spread their truths. They will invariably have a written text—their platforms, a final interpretive authority—their platform committees, recruitment and training devices—including leadership schools, conventions, formal debates, and meetings (where members will learn, and practice, using rules of parliamentary procedure); disciplining devices like the awarding and denying of campaign funds and other assistance; a feedback process, which requires party officials to compete for election and solicit funds from the membership; and distinctive, publicly displayed logos and colors.

"50 Percent Plus One"

Recall the conception of democracy discussed briefly in Chapter 5 as institutionalized assassination—or, rather, the *threat* of institutionalized assassination. Through periodic elections, democracy extends to the electorate the power to take the careers of elected officials hostage and threaten them, "Govern well, or else. . . ."

Think of it: *every day* every elected official, at least any with hopes of pursuing his or her political career, looks down a figurative muzzle of a gun. The trigger on that gun can be pulled by an electoral majority—50 percent plus one of the voters. Politicians in a democracy never know how many voters are enough to fire the gun. If few people vote, 50 percent plus one can be a very small number of constituents—which magnifies the threatening effect of even one dissatisfied citizen.[2]

Democracy creates an armed standoff between the people and their elected officials. While officials can summon the police power to do great damage to the people (or a segment of them), the people can use their voting power to terrify officials into desisting. Like two gunmen facing each other with guns drawn, they may decide to start talking and listening instead of committing mutual suicide. That's how political democracy works.[3]

Electoral majority rule has significant consequences, the most important of which is that it requires contending political parties to appeal to diverse constituencies. Otherwise, they will fall far short of winning 50 percent plus one of the votes, the magic threshold of certain victory. Hence, they have no choice but to develop ideas that attract individuals of widely varied casts of thought. A political party that appealed only to Rotarians or subscribers of the *New York Review of Books* would certainly be homogeneous intellectually and morally, but it would not achieve its object of winning office. To reach majority support in a nation as extensive as the United States, a large party has to embrace all sorts of strange bedfellows and coalesce—unite—them with an overriding, general political idea that transcends the issue differences among them.[4]

The Liberal Idea of Equality

The intellectual glue uniting the Democratic Party over the centuries has been the moral idea of equality. Most people who consider themselves Democrats have embraced the notion that in ancient Greece was called "distributive justice." Democrats have invested their energies in teaching that "liberal" idea to the public.

Democrats may disagree among themselves on what should be equalized, and to what extent—dignity, income, opportunity, education, social status, or legal defense—but they unite behind the belief that equality is good for America because it diffuses comfort and wealth to the have-nots. The Democratic Party, as a moral organization, spreads that singular "truth" wherever and whenever it can: "leveling the playing field" will make America great, while individual disadvantage is bad for the nation. Virtually always, that belief links up with two complementary ideas: that government is the engine of equality, and that human nature is basically good, but is corrupted by material and social disparities. The idea of equality, so powerfully expressed by Jefferson in the Declaration of Independence, had its partisan formulation as early as 1792 when James Madison, one of the two principal authors of *The Federalist Papers,* engineered the formation of the Democratic-Republican Party (as the Democrats then called themselves) and urged an egalitarian program. Laws, he wrote, should "reduce extreme wealth towards a state of mediocrity, and raise extreme indigence towards a state of comfort."[5] Within reasonable limits not specified, Madison's formulation of the Democratic liberal credo boiled down to ". . . to each according to his need."

Today, the diverse elements that constitute the Democratic Party still justify their political objectives on the basis of Madison's idea of distributive justice—of equality of condition. Its internal debates are conducted in the shadow of this single imperative notion, and its members assess every domestic policy in terms of how it affects the distribution of earnings or wealth.

The Conservative Idea of Personal Freedom

The Republican Party, on the other hand, unites around a rival idea, a competing truth no less compelling than material equality. It is the "conservative" idea of personal freedom. Liberty is good for America because it motivates individuals to improve themselves so as to behave usefully and with vigor. Persons who consider themselves Republicans agree that the one dependable engine of human betterment is an enlightened self-interest acting in free markets that makes (to repeat Walter Lippmann's felicitous phrase) "the Golden Rule . . . economically sound."

Republicans may disagree among themselves on how best to enlighten the self-interest of its participants. In this respect, some emphasize the necessity of religion, some the family, others the law, and still others education as the vehicle of connecting individual self-interest to the general welfare. But almost every Republican ties the idea of personal freedom to two related beliefs: that human nature is free to choose between good and evil and ought to be held responsible for its choices, and that government power is always suspect because the coercion inherent in the police power will corrupt the moral instinct of the officials who exercise it.

And just as the idea of equality united "liberal" Democrats at the nation's founding, so the idea of personal freedom coalesced the "conservatives" of the time in a rival political party called the Federalists. The principal spokesman for the party was Alexander Hamilton, James Madison's one-time collaborator. Hamilton was President Washington's closest confidant and served as the young nation's secretary of the Treasury from 1789 to 1796. When Washington completed his two terms as America's first president, Hamilton drafted his farewell address to the nation, where we find expressed the credo of personal freedom, that key to a nation's success are enlightened self-interest, personal responsibility, and reinforcement of individual consciences in choosing good over evil:

> Of all the dispositions and habits which lead to political prosperity [Washington declared], religion and morality are indispensable supports. . . . A volume could not trace all their connections with private and public felicity. Let it simply be asked—Where is the security for property, for reputation, for life, if the sense of religious [and moral] obligation desert [us]?[6]

As a result of this consensus about personal freedom, Republicans take heed of the impact of public policy on the people's sense of moral obligation. They believe devoutly that attention must be paid to the "moral hazards" that lie hidden away in laws—those unintended but very real incentives to resign ourselves to uselessness and even to do harm to our fellow human beings. Republicans energetically use their every resource to spread the word. Beware, they warn, when government institutes policies that reward neediness and not usefulness, for their effect will be to subvert the morality that produces "private and public felicity."

Now keep in mind that these two fundamental and rival ideas—the liberal belief in distributive justice ("to each according to his need") and the rival conservative belief in personal freedom ("to each according to his usefulness to others")—are both embraced in our national creed. Recall the words of the Pledge of Allegiance:

> I pledge allegiance to the flag of the United States of America, and to the Republic for which it stands, one nation, under God, indivisible, with *liberty* [the Republican idea] and *justice* [the Democratic idea] for all.

For more than two hundred years, the two political parties that Madison and Hamilton founded have endured, their members uniting around and teaching one or the other of these rival worldviews. In a word, the two-party system has organized all the countless little divisions that have afflicted this nation into a pair of politically equal moral institutions that compete to shape the nation's public philosophy.

Political Democracy and *The Federalist Papers*

Recall that *The Federalist Papers* barely mentioned the details of political democracy and how the universal franchise might actually work in practice. While both Hamilton and Madison knew from their readings in history about the effect of *internal* checks on government (separation of powers, checks and balances, an independent judiciary), they were in the dark about the consequences of the *external* check of sovereignty of a numerous popular electorate because the world had had hardly any experience with it (and none in an extensive nation).

They could not have anticipated the American two-party system, but it is precisely the opposition of Republicans and Democrats that has supplied a balance of power *within* the electorate. In the several centuries since the writing of *The Federalist*, these two large political parties have checked one another by pointing to their rival's acts of tyranny, corruption, inattention, or stupidity. Moreover, they have taught the people their competing and fundamental perspectives of freedom and equality, all the while bringing them to bear on our social and economic problems and the policies to solve them.

Maintaining our two-party democratic system and the freedom to choose between them requires five conditions.

First. *An effective marketplace.* Free economic markets have enabled Americans to exercise reciprocal power and to team up voluntarily, without having to seek the permission or the assistance of officials. By facilitating most of their social and economic activities, markets have diminished the importance of politics and government in their daily lives. Who cares who the secretary of commerce or labor is if an individual can pursue his or her happiness without the approval of government? When elective office is really of limited importance, the citizenry can tolerate political opposition and the changing of governments from election to election.[7]

Second. *A competent legislative institution.* It is up to American legislatures to create the legal foundation for an efficient and fair marketplace. In the enactment of intelligent laws, nothing has proved more important than open legislative procedures and adequate staff in informing legislators of the likely effects of its proposals and the real consequences of laws.[8]

Third. *Protections of the freedoms of speech and assembly.* These two freedoms have protected the existence of rival moral organizations and have permitted them to thrust their ideas into what Justice Oliver Wendell Holmes called the American "marketplace of ideas," where they challenge each other for dominance. An active judiciary, with independent judges disciplined by their training to give due process and equal treatment, has proved crucial to ensuring these freedoms.[9]

Fourth. *Education.* Each succeeding generation of Americans has needed to be educated in literacy, skills, wisdom, and capacity for independent thought. Education has a moral function, elevating our notions of self-interest, and a practical function, expanding the pool of potential collaborators to assist us in our endeavors. Education also has direct political consequences. As President Washington wrote in his farewell address in 1796, "Promote, then, as an object of primary importance, institutions for the general diffusion of knowledge. In proportion as the structure of a government gives force to public opinion, it is essential that public opinion should be enlightened."[10] In fact, Americans have promoted post-secondary education opportunities (extension courses, colleges, universities, churches, and enlightened workplaces) in such diverse forms and varieties that individuals can "go to school" throughout their lifetimes. No early learning "failures" prevent Americans from gaining further education whenever they become ready for it. The result is an educated electorate, capable of comprehending rival arguments and their implications.

And fifth. *Order and personal safety.* The history of the United States has not been devoid of episodes of domestic disorder. Nor has it escaped the dangers of foreign aggression. However, with the major exception of the American Civil War (1861–1865), ordinary Americans have lived secure from violence. Unlike the peoples of most other nations, they have not suffered the destitution of defeat, with homes razed, businesses looted, universities sacked, and lives crushed. Political debate is a luxury unaffordable in the presence of terror.

***

We have now finished familiarizing ourselves with the three techniques of power and the complexities of exercising them. We have examined eleven of the paradoxes they present. The founders of the American democracy fully understood them, as we must today: the vicious cycle set in motion by coercion, the gentling effects of reciprocity, and the problematic effect of moral power on belief systems.

We are now prepared to examine eight of America's most consequential institutions. The majority of them are governmental, but three of them—the market economy, media, and political parties—are "private." How does each of them enable those working within them to exercise the power they have to have in order to do what they want? How do Americans, be they a president or mere citizen, cope with the eleven paradoxes of power and even turn them to advantage? Who benefits and who is disadvantaged by the present distribution of power? And finally, do the nation's institutions and its present distribution of power enhance or diminish the personal freedom of Americans?

NOTES

1. I have always relied for an understanding of political parties on Moise Ostrogorski's classic and wonderfully readable *Democracy and the Organization of Political Parties*, trans. Frederick Clarke (New York: Macmillan, 1902), vol. 2. Another stimulating book on parties is Anthony Downs, *An Economic Theory of Democracy* (New York: Harper and Row, 1997), whose fanciful

(and utterly unrealistic) assumptions of party competition prove to be brilliantly suggestive. For more on Ostrogorski, Downs, and American political parties, see Chapter 20.

2. Witness the legendary story of Sen. Oliver Johnston of South Carolina. Johnston, who was coming up for reelection, was troubled by his lack of anything substantial to write about in his congressional newsletter to his constituents. Finally, he said to his assistant, "Why don't we write something about communism?" His aide agreed and came back with a crackerjack column exposing the evils of "godless, atheistic communism," putting the good senator four-square for Americanism and against communism.

   Johnston read the prepared draft and nodded his approval. As the aide went out the door, Johnston called him back. "Wait a second. How many communists do you think we have in South Carolina?" "About five or six," said the aide. "Well," said the senator, "you make sure that the piece doesn't get sent to any of them! Ya hear?"

3. Of course, democracy is not easy to establish. In nondemocratic, aristocratic systems, officials get used to holding all the cards and don't tolerate attempts to institute a system to assassinate them, even if it's only a metaphorical assassination. Once established, however, democracy works and appears almost self-perpetuating. If one looks at present-day Poland, one finds ex-communists tamed by democracy.

4. See Chapter 20, which details the nature of the rivalries between and *within* the Democratic and Republican Parties.

5. Richard Hofstadter, *The Idea of a Party System: The Rise of Legitimate Opposition in the United States, 1780-1840* (Berkeley and Los Angeles: University of California Press, 1969), 81, quoting James Madison, *Writings*, vol. VI, 86, 87, 104–105, 106–113. (Madison's sentiments were published in the Democratic-Republican newspaper, *The National Gazette*.)

6. George Washington, farewell address, 1796. President Washington did not deliver the address. Rather, it was printed and first appeared in the *American Daily Advertiser*, September 19, 1796.

7. See Chapter 22 on American free-market capitalism.

8. See Chapter 17 on the increased competency of Congress.

9. See Chapter 19 on the conditions under which courts, and especially the U.S. Supreme Court, can be effective protectors of personal freedoms.

10. Washington, Farewell Address.

PART II

INSTITUTIONS OF FREEDOM

13

THE PRESIDENCY

In the legislature, promptitude of decision is oftener an evil than a benefit. The differences of opinion, and the jarrings of parties in that department of the government, though they may sometimes obstruct salutary plans, yet often promote deliberation and circumspection, and serve to check excesses in the majority. [But differences of opinion] constantly counteract those necessary ingredients in the Executive which are the most necessary ingredients in its composition—vigour and expedition, and this without any counterbalancing good. In the conduct of war, in which the energy of the executive is the bulwark of the national security, every thing would be to be apprehended from its plurality.

Alexander Hamilton, *Federalist* No. 70 (1788)

The founders of the American nation envisioned that the mission of government was to "secure" ordinary persons in their freedom so that they could pursue their happiness as they chose. In this respect their first stab at establishing such a government was a failure. The defective Articles of Confederation made no provision for an executive to provide the people with the order and safety necessary to their freedom. Nor did the articles grant the national government any authority to protect the nation, nor did they provide for taxing powers to pay for national defense. Consequently, early America existed in geostrategic peril.

Life has a way of demonstrating that defective ideas are defective by producing failed results. And fail the articles did. Only six years after establishing the articles, as *Federalist* No. 4 lamented, the United States was too weak militarily to defend itself against foreign encroachments: "Spain thinks it convenient to shut the Mississippi against us on the one side, and Britain excludes us from the Saint Lawrence, on the other; nor will either of them permit the other waters which are between them and us to become the means of mutual intercourse and traffic." America's lack of a reliable army and navy under a single commander left the nation powerless to control its own destiny. Hamilton put the matter bluntly: "The rights of neutrality will only be respected, when they are defended by an adequate power. A nation, despicable by its weakness, forfeits even the privilege of being neutral."[1]

Creating a Unitary Presidency

So, in 1787, the founders gathered in Philadelphia to reform the articles. They wanted a strong central government, with an executive department sufficiently empowered to defend the nation and carry out the laws. They debated the powers and tenure of a strong executive. Hamilton, for one, suggested a lifetime appointment of one man—a monarch, though one with defined powers. Others wanted an elected executive council—a kind of UN Security Council—to administer the government and collectively serve as plural commanders in chief. Ultimately, the question resolved itself—and for reasons that Hamilton powerfully summarized in *Federalist* No. 70. One person with relative security of tenure in office can act *decisively*, *quickly*, and *energetically*, whereas a plural executive cannot. "Vigour and expedition . . . is the bulwark of the national security."

Those same qualities also could serve domestic politics. By providing concrete initiatives, a chief executive could focus an otherwise divided and dilatory body of representatives and enable it to react and decide. The executive's "promptitude of decision" would serve to "counteract" a legislature's tendency toward endless debate.

The President's Nine Powers

The Constitution sketched out the job description of the president. Article II was explicit about six of his powers. Two of them he exercised in concert with the U.S. Senate: the treaty-making power and the power to appoint officials. Four of his powers were his exclusively to exercise. One was the authority to act as commander in chief of the military. A second power was to "take care that the laws be faithfully executed." A third power was to hold responsible "the principal officer of each [executive] department." The fourth was the power to grant pardons.

The seventh of his powers was lodged not in Article II, but in Article I, the part of the Constitution that dealt with the lawmaking authority. There the president was provided the so-called veto power, enabling him to heighten the legislative requirement for turning a bill into law. Ordinarily, each legislative house would need the approval of a majority of its members (50 percent plus one) to pass legislation. The president, however, was given the constitutional power to increase the requirement of a mere majority to an extraordinary majority (two-thirds of the membership of each congressional chamber).

The eighth presidential power was couched in the guise of a duty. Article II required him to "recommend to [Congress's] consideration such measures as he shall judge necessary and expedient." Therein lay the president's agenda-setting power, a power that Franklin Roosevelt and all modern presidents since him would exploit to seize the public's attention, and hence to dominate Congress.

The ninth and last of the president's powers was his "bully pulpit." The Constitution required him to provide (and Congress and the public to hear) "information of the state of the union." This rhetorical power, which was his alone to exercise, would enable him to teach, inspire, and unify the public—to be a moral leader. In *Federalist* No. 71, Hamilton emphasized the crucial importance of the rhetorical power of the presidency in checking the people's misjudgments:

> It is a just observation the people commonly *intend* the PUBLIC GOOD. But [only an] adulator [would] pretend that they always *reason right* about the *means* of promoting it. They know from experience that they sometimes err; and the wonder is that they so seldom err as they do, beset as they continually are, by the wiles of parasites and sycophants, by the snares of the ambitious, the avaricious, the desperate, by the artifices of men who possess their confidence more than they deserve it, and of those who seek to possess rather than to deserve it. When occasions present themselves, in which the interests of the people are at variance with their inclinations, it is the duty of the persons whom they have appointed to be the guardians of those interests, to withstand the temporary delusion, in order to give them time and opportunity for more cool and sedate reflection.

With his presidential voice, the chief executive was to enlighten public opinion with his vision of the general welfare.

A Uniter and a Divider

Inherent in the founders' conception of the American president was a central contradiction. His rhetorical power enabled him to lead the nation. His agenda-setting power required him to lead his party against the opposition party. He was at once uniter and divider. "The roles seem almost designed to collide," warns presidential scholar Fred Greenstein.[2]

Every president since George Washington has had to confront this painful dilemma. Each has adapted to it in his own way. Most historians now agree that the chief executive most successful at harmonizing the two roles was America's thirty-fourth president, Dwight Eisenhower (1953–1960), who, while *appearing* to the electorate to be a kind of neutral presiding officer, would detail the strategy by which his party would vanquish its political adversaries. In this latter capacity, he acted with such secrecy that he was only found out two decades after he had left office and his presidential files became public.[3]

A comparison with Great Britain puts this collision of roles in perspective. There the prime minister is the acknowledged partisan leader of the dominant faction of Parliament. He is an out-and-out divider, taking on all persons at odds with his party. The monarchy, on the other hand, is above partisanship. The queen (or king, as the case may be) is the leader of the nation—she holds an office that symbolizes and expresses unity.[4] In the United States the president is both monarch and prime minister.

The Pre-1933 Presidency

Prior to 1933, the president had a minute White House staff (other than household servants). In 1861, for example, the year Abraham Lincoln came to Washington in disguise lest he be assassinated before he was inaugurated, the presidential staff consisted of two personal secretaries; that was all.

President Lincoln oversaw four agencies—State, Treasury, War, and Justice. He could seek the advice of the employees of those departments—experts in diplomacy, finance, force, and law—but he had to keep in mind that his cabinet secretaries owed their dominant loyalty to Congress, which managed their budgets.

He also had no revenues to speak of. There was no income tax; the federal government was dependent on customs fees, postal stamps, and profits from the sale of western lands. He had few official jobs to dole out to his supporters as patronage, at least that amounted to much: postmasterships, customs inspectors, and the like—peanuts.

Nor did he have the means of communicating his ideas to the wider public except through newspapers, over which he lacked control. Traveling out of Washington to talk to audiences took time and was often impractical.

Admittedly, unlike today, when presidents are limited to serving two four-year terms, Lincoln and those pre-1933 presidents never needed to be "lame ducks." Theoretically, they could run for reelection for their lifetimes, but they would have to be nominated by their political party, which would be totally dominated by local political bosses.

These pre-1933 presidents had no supportive institutions and virtually no personnel wholeheartedly allegiant to them. There was no National Security Council to give the president advice on international affairs; the NSC would not come to be until 1947. There was no Office of Management and Budget (OMB) to oversee the budget requests of his government agencies and monitor their performance; there was not even a rudimentary presidential budget bureau until 1937. There was no Council of Economic Advisers to inform him about the nation's economy; the CEA would not come into existence until 1946. And the president, assisted by his two overworked secretaries, wrote his own speeches: he did not give many, anyway, because until modern times there was no radio, television, Internet, or airplane to connect him to the American public.

Although the pre-1933 presidency was a thankless and relatively insignificant office, the prescient Alexis de Tocqueville a century earlier had noted that it would not remain so when America emerged as a world power. He wrote:

> It is chiefly in its foreign relations that the executive power of a nation finds occasion to exert its skill and its strength. If the existence of the Union were perpetually threatened. . . , the executive government would assume an increased importance in proportion to the measures expected of it and to those which it would execute. [Presently], the President . . . is the commander-in-chief of the army, but the army is composed of only six thousand men; he commands the fleet, but the fleet reckons but few sail; he conducts the foreign relations of the Union, but the United States is a nation

without neighbors [or] enemies, and its interests rarely come into contact with those of any other nation of the globe. This proves that the practical operation of the government must not be judged by the theory of its constitution. The President of the United States possesses almost royal prerogatives, which he has no opportunity of exercising; and the privileges that he can at present use are very circumscribed. The laws allow him to be strong, but circumstances keep him weak.[5]

The Modern Presidency and the Welfare State

The year 1933 is regarded as the turning point in the development of the presidency, the time when the presidential office began to exploit its "almost royal prerogatives."

The four administrations of Franklin Delano Roosevelt (1933–1945) constituted the first modern presidency. The severity of the Great Economic Depression (1929–1940) and the complexity of the military mobilization for World War II (1939–1945), together with the activist inclinations of Roosevelt himself and his dramatic use of radio and film, centered public emotions on "That Man in the White House." Since then, each successive president has taken on additional responsibilities.

Tocqueville had identified one reason: America's enhanced role in international affairs. No longer protected by the British navy (as was the case throughout the nineteenth century), the United States was compelled to take its place in the community of nations and assume responsibility for policing a dangerous world. It armed itself to balance the arms of potential adversaries, and that, in turn, made the government become a major customer in the domestic economy as well.

There was a further reason, however. President Roosevelt's Democratic presidency brought us the welfare state, with its ever-greater concern about material inequality within the American community. Consider his remarks in 1944, where he urged the public to oblige the federal government to take on responsibility for stabilizing the nation's economy:[6]

We have accepted, so to speak, a second Bill of Rights under which a new basis of security and prosperity can be established for all—regardless of station, race, or creed. Among these are:

The right to a useful and remunerative job in the industries or shops or farms or mines of the Nation;

The right to earn enough to provide adequate food and clothing and recreation;

The right of every farmer to raise and sell his products at a return which will give him and his family a decent living;

The right of every businessman, large or small, to trade in an atmosphere of freedom from unfair competition dominated by monopolies at home or abroad;

The right of every family to a decent home;

The right to adequate medical care and the opportunity to achieve and enjoy good health;

The right to adequate protection from the economic fears of old age, sickness, accident, and unemployment;

The right to a good education.

Roosevelt's point was a simple one: in advanced societies where the division of labor had become extremely sophisticated, the people expected their governments to assure against catastrophic disruption of the complex economic relations that coordinated them. But Roosevelt's vision of government as a kindly, adept, and responsible social engineer wrought a transformation of the presidential institution.

Presidential historian Forrest McDonald has convincingly demonstrated how the welfare state has provided the president with significantly greater resources, but has given him a fiendishly lengthened agenda on which to spend them; has enlarged governmental capacity, but has left him with a burgeoning, often uncontrollable, and always stubborn bureaucracy to manage; and has elevated him to a higher level of visibility, but created a greater potential that he will be made the public's scapegoat for anything going wrong. And, significantly, his new domestic duties require him to be a partisan leader, and hence there is greater possibility that he will become a virulently divisive force in the nation.[7]

Moreover, the modern president is limited to two terms in office, which means he is a "lame duck" immediately upon his reelection. And with the expansion of public presidential primaries, he now has to run a gauntlet of state party primaries against opponents within his own party, who usually have very little else to do.

It's a wonder that anyone wants to be president. The personal toll on the modern president, both physical and psychological, is intense and unimaginably draining. The added tasks he has to perform exact a horrific cost on the person elected to the office. Prime minister of the state, leader of the nation, commander in chief, head diplomat, and constant political campaigner, with an ever-decreasing margin of error, the modern president, as Woodrow Wilson remarked with rue, has to be "a wise and prudent athlete."[8]

Mediated Information

Now add one more detail to this picture of the presidency and his environment. As each president becomes more significant to the lives of Americans and also to the international community, he is exposed to greater personal danger. Power doesn't corrupt so much as it inspires fanatics to become assassins. That means he has to fortify himself, and hence he becomes more isolated from the lives of ordinary people. Ever more imposing gates, barricades, and fences around the White House symbolize that isolation.

Increasing isolation requires the president to obtain his information about what is occurring within and outside the United States through mediating channels. In foreign affairs, streams of facts and judgments converge on him from a multiplicity of independent sources: the CIA; the Defense Intelligence Agency; the Justice, Treasury, and Commerce Departments; the International Trade Representative; and, of course, the Department of State, with its countless regional bureaus and national desks. In the system's redundancy, in the overlap of foreign intelligence responsibilities, there was some assurance that a breakdown of one source would be offset by the operation of other sources. While not perfect in its reach and its results, it would be hard to imagine a better system for unearthing and analyzing hard-to-get information.[9]

But domestically, the irony is that there is so much information as to be confusing and, at times, unmanageable. Take one example—the unemployment rate. How many Americans have jobs, and how many don't? Are new jobs being created? Are old ones lost? The Labor Department alone conducts two different official surveys, with one canvassing large businesses, the other individual households. Significant discrepancies often result. For example, in 2005 the two estimates of new jobs differed by more than a million. When good information becomes so abundant and so at odds, it is hard to devise effective policy and convince others of its wisdom. Inflation rates, the extent of poverty, job estimates, trade deficit figures, the gross domestic product, and measures of contentment rates all depend on information dug up and interpreted by others. The president is left alone in his office to ponder their accuracy and their implications for policy.

NOTES

1. *Federalist* No. 11.
2. Fred I. Greenstein, *The Hidden-Hand Presidency: Eisenhower as Leader* (New York: Basic Books, 1982), 5.
3. Professor Greenstein was the first scholar to disclose this aspect of the Eisenhower presidency. It's also worth mentioning a second successful president, Franklin Roosevelt, who, thanks to world circumstances, managed to transform himself from a controversial divider in peacetime into a beloved uniter in wartime.
4. A recent movie, *The Queen,* beautifully orchestrates their division of labor. *The Queen* tells of the relationship between Queen Elizabeth II and Prime Minister Tony Blair. The film's climax comes when Prime Minister Blair realizes he cannot bring together the British people deeply saddened by the death of Princess Diana and passionately divided over how to honor her. Only the queen—the embodiment of national unity—can speak the words that can restore community and affirm the nation's common sense of itself. Blair, realizing his partisan office disables him from being effective in this moral crisis, persuades the queen to speak out and voice the people's common distress.
5. Alexis de Tocqueville, *Democracy in America,* trans. Henry Reeve (New York: Bantam, 2000 [1835]), vol. I, chap. 8.
6. Franklin Delano Roosevelt, remarks, "State of the Union," January 11, 1944, in *The Public Papers and Addresses of Franklin D. Roosevelt,* ed. Samuel Rosenman (New York: Harper, 1950), vol. XIII, 40–42.
7. Forrest McDonald, *The American Presidency: An Intellectual History* (Lawrence: University Press of Kansas, 1994), especially Part III.
8. Ibid., 475. Professor McDonald has noted that presidents who served before the Civil War lived to an average age of seventy-three, those after the war to an average of sixty-three, despite the enormous improvements in medical care.
9. As for this favorable assessment, thoughtful scholars may object. McDonald, ibid., 469, writes: "In one area, foreign affairs, the quantity and scope of information available is stupefying."

14

THE COERCIVE POWER
OF THE PRESIDENCY

*Therefore, a prudent prince will . . . [choose] the wise men of his
state and grant . . . only to them the freedom to tell him the truth,
but only concerning those matters about which he asks, and no
others. Yet he should question them about all matters, listen to
their opinions, and then decide for himself as he wishes. He should
treat these councils and the individual advisers in such a way as to
make it clear that their words will be the more welcome the more
freely they are spoken.*

Niccolò Machiavelli, *The Prince* (1513)

How do presidents get reliable information? How do they organize their
White House so that they can validate, and alter, their hunches about what
is presently happening in the real world? How do presidents *test* reality?[1]

All presidents come into the White House with some knowledge of
America and its people, if only because they have campaigned throughout
the land to win the presidency. Only a rare few, Dwight Eisenhower being
the most exceptional, have had previous careers that gave them a nuanced
understanding of foreign lands and their affairs.

But those understandings, whether limited to America or extended
beyond, quickly are made problematic by developing events. Once a president takes office, where does he get the information necessary to act
effectively?

Four sources exist within the White House to help him if—and it's a big *if*—he wishes to use them. Each has the potential to serve as an advisory council to the president—the kind of "wise men" Machiavelli recommended be "grant[ed] . . . the freedom to tell him the truth."[2] One is the National Security Council, which aids him in his exercise of coercive power. Next, the Office of Management and Budget is able to assist him in controlling his administration through reciprocity. The third is the Council of Economic Advisers to enhance his knowledge of the private economy so that he can influence the commercial marketplace. Finally, there is his communications department (and, specifically, his speechwriting department), which can help him make use of his moral powers by illuminating people's heartfelt attitudes.

The Personal Nature of the Presidency

No procedure in the White House is institutionalized in the sense that the president *must* listen to the information it offers him. The four sources of knowledge can be heeded or ignored at the president's whim. Contrast their erratic use in the presidency with the regular procedures of Congress. There, the members have a stake in seeing that their rules and their committees stay fixed, even as their leaders come and go. Likewise, in the Supreme Court, it would be hard to imagine the justices altering the institutionalized procedures by which adversary lawyers provide it with facts, contexts, arguments, and recommendations.

The presidency is, first and foremost, then, a personal institution, and how it is organized depends almost completely on the character and habits of the boss. In the White House nothing of consequence happens unless the president desires it.[3] A loner, like President Jimmy Carter (1977–1981), who prided himself on being his own chief of staff and administering to details of White House life, was free to discard the formal procedures and staff operations developed by his predecessors. In Carter's case, he ended up overwhelming himself with the demands of office and poorly apprehending what was going on in the Cold War, in the economy, in public opinion, and even in his own agencies. He seemed constantly surprised by events and consequently rarely responded to them in a timely or effective way. On the other hand, a team-builder like President Eisenhower, who had organized the greatest military operation in world history—the Allied invasion of Western Europe in 1944—could utilize staff to great effect. Eisenhower improved the presidency by appointing the first White House chief of staff, organizing the first Congressional Liaison Office, and mandating with particularity the procedures of his assistant for national security affairs (now called the national security adviser, a position that has been filled by such luminaries as McGeorge Bundy, Henry Kissinger, Zbigniew Brzezinski, and Condoleezza Rice).

Coercive Power and the National Security Council

The first responsibility of a president—the one he alone bears—is to keep the American people safe from foreign aggression. He is *the* commander in chief of the military. His constitutional duty requires him to employ coercive power to daunt aggressors and to overcome the opposition of world leaders to his plans.

The international realm is a lawless place and filled with a host of potential enemies. In a world policed by mutual threats, the president recurrently confronts the paradoxes of coercive power. He must get a grasp on what to do about the paradox of dispossession and "asymmetrical relationships," where America offers countless hostages and adversaries feel they have nothing to lose. He will be surprised by the paradox of irrationality, where jihadist suicide bombers appear to embrace death with the same avidity as rational persons embrace life. And, most importantly, he must come to understand the importance of "face," maintaining a mean reputation while spreading humane ideals. Foreign policy is an impending disaster for a naive president.[4]

Most Americans are relative neophytes when it comes to using threats; resorting to coercion and countering it play a small part in our normal routines, thank goodness. We live under a rule of law, a rule that has civilized and regulated the extent of threat's reach and accustomed us in habits of reciprocity. This is especially so in the political realm. A legislator, for example, is a master of give and take. He doesn't make violent threats to get his way with his colleagues: he has to attract, not repel his fellow legislators, whose assistance and votes he is going to need over a prolonged term.

How, then, might the typical elected president—often a former state governor or U.S. senator with little international experience—learn on the job how to cope with the lawlessness of foreign relations? I recall listening to the Washington correspondent for the *London Times* speak of how President Richard Nixon puzzled him. He had no liking for Nixon personally, but he admired, as did most Europeans, Nixon's skills in international matters. In the opinion of this Englishman, no American president ranked higher in his grasp of foreign affairs and in his adept use of diplomacy and threat in the pursuit of real peace. Where, he wondered, did Nixon, a conscientious Quaker with a small-town legal practice and limited experience as a junior congressman, learn the craft of coercion so skillfully?

The answer, this seasoned journalist concluded, was that Nixon observed President Eisenhower's conduct of foreign affairs. As vice president, Nixon was a member of the National Security Council (NSC). Seated next to President Eisenhower at the NSC's regular weekly meetings from 1953 through 1961, Nixon had intimate exposure to how Eisenhower, one-time commander of Allied forces in World War II and later NATO's chief, employed, and refrained from employing, the military power of the United States in a number of crises.

The NSC was established by Congress in 1947, partly as a response to Vice President Harry Truman's having been excluded from vital war information prior to President Roosevelt's death in April 1945. (Up to that time, vice presidents were isolated in a tiny office in the U.S. Senate and were rarely even invited to the White House for briefing or consultation.) When he was suddenly elevated to the presidency in the crucial last stages of World War II, he had no knowledge of confidential military developments, especially the building of the atomic bomb and its imminent use.

Congress designed the membership of the NSC so as to include future vice presidents in the making of the nation's foreign affairs. By statute, four officials were to have a place on the NSC—the president, his secretaries of state and defense, *and* the vice president, with the chairman of the Joint Chiefs of Staff as its military adviser. If the president wished to add more members, such as the director of Central Intelligence or the secretary of the Treasury, he could do so. The NSC was also provided a staff, with a special assistant to national security affairs to direct it.

The statute was silent as to the council's procedures, its use, or its influence. What it had done, however, was to give the vice president, *for the first time,*[5] an official duty in the presidency. That provision enabled Vice President Nixon to observe directly Eisenhower's skill in using threat in the conduct of foreign relations. Chalk one up for formal organization.

Ironically, President Truman virtually ignored using the NSC. Truman was not an adept organizer. His lapse left Eisenhower, his successor, with a free hand to design the NSC's proceedings from scratch.

Eisenhower established two separate units to serve the council. One he called the Planning Board, a committee of second-level officials in the foreign affairs departments, who crafted papers for the council members' discussion. The other he called the Operations Coordinating Board, a body to plan implementation of his foreign policy decisions.

Eisenhower scheduled regular weekly meetings of the NSC and required the Planning Board to prepare and present extensively informed, adversarial position papers on policy disagreements that he identified. These procedures—an adaptation of the adversarial procedures of law courts— constituted what has come to be called "multiple advocacy." His purpose was to generate a sharply joined, well-informed debate in his presence. Multiple advocacy, among other things, permitted him to play the role of judge.

Typical of the questions brought to the NSC was whether the United States should intervene unilaterally in Vietnam in the event that the French army were defeated there. By way of background, in 1954 the French, who regarded Vietnam as their colony, found their forces of occupation being attacked by rebel communist forces led by Ho Chi Minh. (The French were ultimately defeated at Dien Bien Phu and forced to abandon Vietnam.)

In anticipation of the French calling for assistance, the NSC met to decide what to do. One decision group of the NSC's Planning Board presented a paper arguing for intervention, concluding that "nothing short of military victory" was acceptable; the opposing position paper emphasized the great costs such an intervention would entail.[6] The advocates of each position, together with the NSC members themselves, then engaged in vigorous debate in front of Eisenhower. In the words of one observer, "[T]he president's ears seemed never to leave the discourse around him."[7] Eisenhower sometimes interjected his own remarks forcefully, but he always made it clear that he wanted his own views challenged, and challenged no less tenaciously than those of the other members. Moreover, Eisenhower assigned his national security adviser the task of "custodian manager" to ensure that the discussion was thorough and balanced.[8] The adviser's job was to stand back from the fray, to see that all disagreements got aired openly, and to raise questions that were being overlooked in the rough-and-tumble of debate.

At the end of the session Eisenhower, like a judge, took no vote. His general practice was to reserve final decision, supplementing the information and arguments developed in the NSC meeting with further, more informal discussions with outside advisers whom he trusted, like his brother Milton. Then he would arrive at his decision. This formal, adversarial, multiple advocacy system was crucial in strengthening his confidence that he knew the reality in Vietnam. It led him to withhold American assistance there.

To appreciate Eisenhower's innovative use of multiple advocacy, contrast the informal methods of President Lyndon Johnson (1963–1969) in assessing much the same issue when it arose a decade later, in 1965. Johnson's practices had been cultivated in the U.S. Senate, where he had been an extremely effective majority leader. Scholars have called him "master of the Senate"[9] and judged him to be perhaps the most successful Senate leader in the entire twentieth century.

However, as president, he bypassed the National Security Council and Eisenhower's formal procedures. Johnson's NSC met erratically and, for all practical purposes, never deliberated. Impatient with the whole idea of "multiple advocacy," he would pick out a single adviser and take him aside to discuss a particular matter. Given Johnson's character and his impatience with the details of policy, however, the result was that he invariably picked an adviser whom he knew would agree with him.

His procedure would have worried Machiavelli because it was a system prone to the danger of "flatterers." Those who had different points of view from Johnson—those advisers who were privy to different information or had recommendations that might have been at odds with Johnson's hunches—were relegated to an outer circle and never given an opportunity to air their disagreements. Just as importantly, the persons President Johnson did consult, lacking a process where they had to confront policy adversaries, were not compelled to articulate their own assumptions. Johnson's lack of organizational skill wasted the advisory resources available to him.

Machiavelli would have predicted the results: a piecemeal escalation of force in Vietnam, vaguely understood objectives, minimal anticipation of the enemy's resistance to the American presence, and inconsistency. Worst of all, Johnson's informal system failed to educate him in both the facts and the coercive perspective that gave them meaning.

If Eisenhower's use of the National Security Council was so successful, why didn't Johnson (and Presidents Kennedy and Carter, for that matter) maintain what they had inherited and make minor improvements on it as needed? Presidential scholars John Burke and Fred Greenstein suggest that it was in part "hubris"—a vanity that they were smarter than those who had preceded them, a vanity reinforced by those whose flattery they thrived upon. Perhaps it was their "scorn of red tape and brass hats that was generally shared by the World War II junior officers and enlisted men who took over political leadership in the 1960's."[10]

Whatever the reasons, the discontinuation of the "multiple advocacy" procedures demonstrates the fragility of institutions within the American presidency, shaped as it is by the unique personalities of those who temporarily occupy it.

NOTES

1. In this chapter I rely heavily on a splendid book by John Burke and Fred I. Greenstein, *How Presidents Test Reality: Decisions on Vietnam, 1954 and 1965* (New York: Russell Sage Foundation, 1989).
2. Niccolò Machiavelli, *The Prince*, trans. Daniel Donno (New York: Dell, 1996 [1513]), chap. 23.
3. In his landmark work, *Presidential Power: The Politics of Leadership from Roosevelt to Reagan*, rev. ed. (New York: Free Press, 1990), 10, Richard E. Neustadt reports President Truman's remark on what lay in store for the man about to succeed him in office, General Dwight "Ike" Eisenhower: "He'll sit here, and he'll say, 'Do this. Do that.' And nothing will happen. Poor Ike—it won't be like the Army. He'll find it very frustrating." Readers have often judged (mistakenly) from this anecdote that presidents lack control of their staffs' behavior. If Neustadt intended to say that, he may have been right about the weakness of Truman, an accidental president and (at that time) less distinguished than most of his cabinet secretaries. But as a picture of normally elected presidents controlling their White House staffs, it greatly distorts reality; presidents are dominant in the White House.
4. Labor-management negotiation is suited to teach the handling of threats. George Shultz, who had been a labor-management negotiator in private life and who turned out to be unquestionably in the first rank of American secretaries of state, once remarked:

   > You show me a union that will never strike, and I'll show you a union that isn't going to get anywhere. You show me a management that will never take a strike, and I'll show you a management that's going to get pushed around.

   His point: a few careers are potentially a good preparation for the foreign side of the presidency. While Secretary Shultz was never president, his success as presidential adviser demonstrated that his experience in industrial relations had taught him a thing or two about using threat effectively. Secretary Shultz went on to say: "One of the things I enjoyed with President Reagan was that he had been involved in union management and negotiations, as I had, and we used to talk over negotiation stories. It's right there. You learn those lessons." Daniel Henninger, "The Weekend Interview with George Shultz," *Wall Street Journal,* April 29, 2006, A8.

5. The vice president never before had any official duties other than his constitutional tasks of presiding over the Senate and casting a deciding vote in the event that the Senate was "equally divided."

6. Burke and Greenstein, *How Presidents Test Reality,* 14, 53–54, 70, 258.

7. Ibid., 63.

8. Ibid., 55.

9. E.g., Robert A. Caro, *Lyndon B. Johnson: Master of the Senate* (New York: Knopf, 2002).

10. Burke and Greenstein, *How Presidents Test Reality,* 281. Tocqueville, at the end of his second volume, speaks of the importance of procedures—what he calls "forms"—in a democratic age:

> Men living in democratic ages do not readily comprehend the utility of forms: they feel an instinctive contempt for them. . . . Forms excite their contempt and often their hatred; as they commonly aspire to none but easy and present gratification, they rush onwards to the object of their desires, and the slightest delay exasperates them. This same temper, carried with them into political life, renders them hostile to forms, which perpetually retard or arrest them in some of their projects. Yet this objection which the men of democracies make to forms is the very thing which renders forms so useful to freedom; for their chief merit is to serve as a barrier between the strong and the weak, the ruler and the people, to retard the one and give the other time to look about him. Forms become more necessary in proportion as the government becomes more active and more powerful, while private persons are becoming more indolent and more feeble. Thus democratic nations naturally stand more in need of forms than other nations, and they naturally respect them less. This deserves most serious attention. [Alexis de Tocqueville, *Democracy in America,* trans. Henry Reeve [New York: Bantam, 2000 (1840)], vol. 2, book 4, chap. 7.]

15

THE PRESIDENCY'S RECIPROCAL AND MORAL POWERS

Whose bread I eat, his song I sing.

German proverb

Domestic affairs present a president different problems and require a different form of power to manage them. Unlike foreign relations, where threat and intimidation are required in dealing with adversaries, in domestic matters coercion is ill-advised and ineffective. A president must depend on reciprocal power, exchanging the resources at his disposal (budgets, patronage, and celebrity) for compliance with his wishes.[1]

It is surprisingly difficult for a president to control his branch of government—the colossal agencies that administer policy. A source of his difficulty is the obvious bureaucratic pathology that officials protected by civil service do what *they* want to do, including making themselves comfortable. Bureaucratic disobedience is likely to be widespread and difficult to police. The officials whom the president finds acting contrary to his wishes are not a docile lot: they are tough, determined, and supported by fervent clientele.

Moreover, the president shares control of those agencies with Congress. It is Congress, not the president, that provides the appropriations for *their* programs. In the old days, an ambitious bureau chief, interested (for example) in a new tank or another national park, would plead his case in Congress. The price he'd pay for the funds he needed would be his willingness to do what Congress wanted him to do.

Instituting Clearance Procedures

In 1937 President Franklin Roosevelt developed a rudimentary procedure to stem this loss of control and turn executive agencies back to a greater dependency on him. He established a budget bureau to oversee the requests for appropriations being made by his agencies before they went to Congress.

The mission of the original budget bureau was to shake out waste. Over the years it expanded its function, a change reflected in its current name, the Office of *Management* and Budget (or OMB). It began to require each unit of government to undergo extended executive budget hearings as to whether its programs were consonant with the president's purposes. Only after the hearings before OMB were complete—and the adjustments that OMB required were made—would the agency's request be included in the *president's* budget submitted to Congress for approval.[2]

It was President Harry Truman who initiated this improvement whereby all agency requests were disciplined by the present executive clearance procedures. He honed his budgetary skills in the U.S. Senate, where he chaired a vital wartime committee charged with investigating the performance of government contractors in supplying military equipment. There he became acutely aware of the value of procedures for auditing and assessing government behavior and, doubtless, his Senate experience awakened him to the possibilities of presidential clearance. He recognized how OMB procedures would increase his bargaining power. He could compel the agencies to disclose what they were doing. With that knowledge, the president could use his check on their budgets to make sure they were in compliance with his wishes.[3]

Fortunately, when the Republican Dwight Eisenhower succeeded the Democratic Truman, he saw OMB's value and kept its high-quality staff in place, using it to shape the agencies of government to the discipline of *his* program.

OMB has proved itself so valuable to presidents in providing them knowledge of what their bureaucracies are doing that its future use is assured. Unlike presidents' sometime use of the NSC, no future president is likely to bypass OMB and its clearance procedures.[4]

The Council of Economic Advisers

The Council of Economic Advisers (CEA) is the other White House unit ready to provide presidents with information, meaning, and recommendations in the use of reciprocal power. The CEA was established by the Employment Act of 1946, with the legislative intent of giving presidents an "independent assessment" of the economy. The statute provided for a chair, two associate advisers, and a staff of economists. Their job was to gather and make sense of the flood of data churned out by the economy—to grasp the realities of America's economic life and draw out their implications for tax and monetary policy, regulatory changes, and commercial legislation.

The independence of the CEA did not last long. Presidents, it turned out, did not want economists around who saw economic realities in radically different ways from their own hunches. But within a certain range of philosophical tolerance, their economic advisers could help clarify the economic picture in their bosses' thinking, assess the quality of the available economic data, and position the information within a body of economic theory—if the president wanted such assistance.

Some presidents embraced their lessons in economics with enthusiasm. President John F. Kennedy's greatest economic success resulted from cuts in the tax rate in 1962 to ward off recession. Nothing in Kennedy's past as a liberal Democrat inclined him to reduce the tax burdens of "the rich," but he gradually came to understand the information and the arguments that his Council of Economic Advisers kept bringing to him. Finally convinced, he initiated the largest tax-rate cut in history with a speech that his friend, the liberal economist John Kenneth Galbraith, condemned with the quip, "That was the most Republican speech since McKinley."[5] (William McKinley, who was president from 1897 to 1901, has always symbolized the embodiment of the unregulated free market, laissez-faire.) Kennedy's tax-cut initiative was an instance where the institutionalization in the presidency of economic experts changed the picture of reality a president would have gotten by merely informal means.

Both Presidents Eisenhower and Gerald Ford (1974–1977) had great confidence in their economic advisers. Said Ford of Alan Greenspan, "I would pick his brains, and he would make suggestions. His advice on economic policy was invaluable."[6] Eisenhower asked his economic adviser, Arthur Burns, to meet each week to discuss economic developments and theorize about them.[7] For other presidents, economics took a back seat to politics, and the council and its chair simply became a device to rationalize economic decisions made on other grounds.

But for the most part the CEA has functioned to nurture the president's mastery of economics and his use of monetary and fiscal policies to prevent the cheapening of the nation's currency. Most importantly, his economic advisers have been ever-present to remind him of the connection between economics and liberty—that the key to personal freedom is reciprocal power, and the key to spreading reciprocal power is the public's access to credit; that the expansion of credit depends on a stable medium of exchange, and that when credit is spread, the citizenry's freedom to use their talents to create beautiful and useful things is enlarged.

The Bully Pulpit

Moreover, the president has his "bully pulpit" from which to exercise his moral power. In order to use it effectively, he must know what his people are thinking. Cooped up in his White House, how might he find out what is on the citizenry's minds?

Most presidents have very good hunches in this regard. They have been in politics much of their lives, and they have been successful because they have developed skills at reading people from clues that ordinary persons would find insufficient or baffling.

They have also learned to be skeptical of public opinion polls. They know from experience that the questions of poll-takers often bias the answers; the answers most people give to a pollster are rarely heartfelt because they are responses to inquiries on topics they don't much care about; and often, they would—and will—change their responses with the slightest additional information. Presidents know that public opinion, at least as described by most polling devices, is what the insightful Walter Lippmann called the opinion of a "phantom public."[8]

The device that many presidents rely on to verify their hunches is the reaction of audiences to their public remarks. A president will give countless talks from his "bully pulpit" in a year, amounting to over a half-million words prepared by his speechwriters.[9]

His audiences are diverse: on any one day, he might address remarks to an association of realtors and then to a group of clergy. The next day he might be off to talk at a West Point graduation, return to Washington to speak to an assemblage of liberal city mayors, and conclude by making a few remarks to members of a political action committee that has been scheduled as a "drop-by." He pays acute attention to the responses of each of these audiences, not merely their reactions to his explanation of things, but also the general attitudes underlying those reactions.

Audiences communicate to a speaker what's really on their minds. I recall New York governor Nelson Rockefeller's 1966 reelection campaign. It was struggling and lacked a compelling purpose until one day the governor spoke to a group of mothers residing in a typical "inner-city" neighborhood on New York City's Lower East Side. The women's response to his campaign pitch was tepid; they were restless and largely inattentive, but just as Rockefeller was wrapping up, almost as an aside he mentioned illegal drugs. In an instant, his audience was rapt, their attention riveted on the governor. For those women, *the* issue was drugs. They cared passionately about the growing availability and promotion of heroin in their neighborhoods, and they were frightened by the damage drugs were doing to their children. "Drugs" overshadowed all other matters, and Rockefeller soon thereafter made his proposals to control them the most prominent part of his platform. He was reelected.

No poll asking the generic question of a randomized sample of the public, "What issue is of greatest concern to you?" could have provided a more convincing picture of public opinion than that instant reaction.[10]

Some presidents are extremely skilled at assessing their audiences' reception of what they say. Consequently, they select their speechwriters with great care (and they pay their writers high salaries in order to keep them around). For such presidents, speechwriters are important because their words pry a hole into the real public opinion and enable the president to see the heartfelt beliefs of their citizenry. Other presidents don't use this device; Lyndon Johnson dismissed any talk that wasn't about his policies as "Rose Garden garbage." But if he actually felt that way, he was wasting his best opportunity to know what the public honestly and deeply thought.

A trustworthy grasp on public opinion was especially important to presidents who sought to alter the common sense of the public—to elevate it, for example, out of despair or confusion or feelings of helplessness. No president in the last half-century sought to do that with greater effort than President Ronald Reagan, and no recent president has ever been more successful than he in his purposes. He did so by assembling half a dozen writers who were more literary than policy wonks—who loved Chaucer and Shakespeare and Dickens, those gifted seers into the human heart. And he made sure that his schedulers found occasions where soulful remarks were appropriate. There, he would "poll" for the general ideas people lived by and in turn would provide them words to express those ideas. By his countless speeches, he would attempt to shape the public's minds to resemble his and then test to see if his effort had succeeded.

Eisenhower's Achievements

Two final thoughts. First, the reader may have noticed how frequently I have held up President Eisenhower as a model president. That may strike some as a surprise, but it should not. This extraordinary man had a passion for organization, and he brought his special skills to the White House at a time when the president's responsibilities were expanding. He sought to find ways accurately to inform the institution of the presidency so that the nation's chief executive could exercise the powers of his office to good effect.

At the time presidential watchers did not perceive the consequences of those organizational reforms. Although he was popular among the people when he left office, the bulk of Washington insiders and academics dismissed him as a lightweight. For example, American historians in their rankings of past presidents as Great, Near Great, Average, Below Average, and Failures, put Eisenhower in the Below Average class; not a James Buchanan (1857-1861) or an Andrew Johnson (1865-1869), but maybe another Ulysses S. Grant (1869-1877).

No longer: scholars have come to recognize Eisenhower's achievements and gifts to the presidential office. The last appraisal of a similar group of historians was that Eisenhower was a Near Great, up with Teddy Roosevelt (1901-1909), Thomas Jefferson (1801-1809), Woodrow Wilson (1913-1921), Harry Truman (1945-1953), and Ronald Reagan (1981-1989).[11] That's probably where he belongs, just below George Washington (1789-1797), the man who created the American presidency; Franklin Roosevelt (1933-1945), that "Man in the White House" whose undaunted spirit brought America through both the Great Depression and World War II; and Abraham Lincoln (1861-1865), the noblest of them all.

The Lingering Effects of Abraham Lincoln

Finally, I can't conclude these chapters on the presidency without mentioning the abiding influence of the man most Americans consider their greatest president.

For the most part, American presidents—and especially our modern ones—have been impressive individuals. Getting to the White House requires a lifetime record of successes, often in the face of tough odds, plus a strong character, a perceptive insight into the human condition, a very tough skin, a staying power, purposefulness, and courage to stand in the spotlight and take responsibility. As a result, Americans get a very self-assured individual as their chief executive.

But if you were to ask any president, I think he would tell you that when he walked into the White House for the first time, he was humbled by the spirit that haunts the place. He would say he felt like a midget when he measured himself beside Abraham Lincoln. I would bet that, as a result, he started rededicating himself to the purposes that Lincoln expressed so indelibly in the Gettysburg Address: "that this nation, under God, shall have a new birth of freedom—and that government of the people, by the people, for the people, shall not perish from the earth."

Furthermore, I would wager that he prayed that he wouldn't screw up. As he grew in the job and became more comfortable doing it, he read and reread America's greatest testament, Lincoln's second inaugural address, given one month before General Robert E. Lee's surrender at Appomattox and the conclusion of a Civil War that had taken more than 600,000 lives.

This is what Lincoln said the day he took the oath of office to begin his second term as president (1865):

Fellow Countrymen: At this second appearing to take the oath of the Presidential office there is less occasion for an extended address than there was at the first. Then a statement somewhat in detail of a course to be pursued seemed fitting and proper. Now, at the expiration of four years, during which public declarations have been constantly called forth on every point and phase of the great contest which still absorbs the attention and engrosses the energies of the nation, little that is new could be presented.

The progress of our arms, upon which all else chiefly depends, is as well known to the public as to myself, and it is, I trust, reasonably satisfactory and encouraging to all. With high hope for the future, no prediction in regard to it is ventured.

On the occasion corresponding to this four years ago all thoughts were anxiously directed to an impending civil war. All dreaded it, all sought to avert it. While the inaugural address was being delivered from this place, devoted altogether to *saving* the Union without war, urgent agents were in the city seeking to *destroy* it without war—seeking to dissolve the Union and divide effects by negotiation. Both parties deprecated war, but one of them would *make* war rather than let the nation survive, and the other would *accept* war rather than let it perish, and the war came.

One-eighth of the whole population were colored slaves, not distributed generally over the Union, but localized in the southern part of it. These slaves constituted a peculiar and powerful interest. All knew that this interest was somehow the cause of the war. To strengthen, perpetuate, and extend this interest was the object for which the insurgents would rend the Union even by war, while the Government claimed no right to do more than to restrict the territorial enlargement of it.

Neither party expected for the war the magnitude or the duration which it has already attained. Neither anticipated that the *cause* of the conflict might cease with or even before the conflict itself should cease. Each looked for an easier triumph, and a result less fundamental and astounding.

Both read the same Bible and pray to the same God, and each invokes His aid against the other. It may seem strange that any men should dare to ask a just God's assistance in wringing their bread from the sweat of other men's faces, but let us judge not, that we be not judged. The prayers of both could not be answered. That of neither has been answered fully. The Almighty has His own purposes.

"Woe unto the world because of offenses; for it must needs be that offenses come, but woe to that man by whom the offense cometh." If we shall suppose that American slavery is one of those offenses which, in the providence of God, must needs come, but which, having continued through His appointed time, He now wills to remove, and that He gives to both North and South this terrible war as the woe due to those by whom the offense came, shall we discern therein any departure from those divine attributes which the believers in a living God always ascribe to Him?

Fondly do we hope, fervently do we pray, that this mighty scourge of war may speedily pass away. Yet, if God wills that it continue until all the wealth piled by the bondsman's two hundred and fifty years of unrequited toil shall be sunk, and until every drop of blood drawn with the lash shall be paid by another drawn with the sword, as was said three thousand years ago, so still it must be said "the judgments of the Lord are true and righteous altogether."

With malice toward none, with charity for all, with firmness in the right as God gives us to see the right, let us strive on to finish the work we are in, to bind up the nation's wounds, to care for him who shall have borne the battle and for his widow and his orphan, to do all which may achieve and cherish a just and lasting peace among ourselves and with all nations.

Six weeks after his second inaugural address, Lincoln was assassinated. He left as his legacy his vision of reconciliation and national dedication to fulfill the Almighty's "purposes" of enabling all persons to live free and unafraid. His belief in freedom influences Americans to this day, as the noted scholar Walter Berns tells us: "Ordinary Americans are moved by these words, sometimes to tears; I have seen it happen. Lincoln speaks to them as only a great poet can speak, reminding them of the cause that binds the generations, that freedom is more than being left alone, that there is a price to be paid for it, and that they are indebted to those who have already paid it."[12]

NOTES

1. Richard E. Neustadt, *Presidential Power: The Politics of Leadership from Roosevelt to Reagan*, rev. ed. (New York: Free Press, 1990), 40.
2. And when Congress, on its members' own initiative, enacted a program, OMB would analyze it in light of the president's priorities and then recommend approval or a veto.
3. Aaron Wildavsky's *The Politics of the Budgetary Process* (Boston: Little, Brown, 1964), even if the facts are now dated, is incomparable.
4. Furthermore, if an OMB director were to develop standards of assessment too much at odds with his president's, he would doubtless be asked to resign. For example, President Ronald Reagan could not get his first OMB director, the obdurate David Stockman, to stop objecting to his program of lowered tax rates and heightened military spending—and fired him.
5. As quoted in Carl M. Brauer, "The Endurance of Inspirational Leadership," in Fred I. Greenstein, ed., *Leadership in the Modern Presidency* (Cambridge, Mass.: Harvard University Press, 1988), 122.
6. Roger B. Porter, "A Healing Presidency," in ibid., 224.
7. John Burke and Fred I. Greenstein, *How Presidents Test Reality: Decisions on Vietnam, 1954 and 1965* (New York: Russell Sage Foundation, 1989), 13.
8. Walter Lippmann, *The Phantom Public* (New Brunswick, N.J.: Transaction Publishers, 1993 [1922]).

9. William Ker Muir Jr., *The Bully Pulpit* (San Francisco: ICS Press, 1992), 107.

10. Political scientist Herbert Kaufman tells a similar story from his days as a college student at the City College of New York. He and his classmates took a psychology course, where the professor described "conditioned learning," by which he meant the effects of rewards and punishment on one's behavior. Kaufman and his friends conspired with the rest of the class to experiment. Every time the professor stood at the dais or walked to the left side of the stage, the students would squirm, drop their pencils, and put their heads down on the desk. Every time he walked to the right side, they would sit bolt upright, be absolutely quiet, and write down everything the professor said. Moreover, the further he went to the right, the more erect they would sit, the faster they would write, and so on. The bet was how long it would take before the professor stood immobile and pinned to the extreme right side of the stage. Five minutes: that was all it took before the students' behavior worked its influence.

11. See William A. Degregorio, *The Complete Book of U.S. Presidents* (New York: Gramercy Books, 2001).

12. Walter Berns, *Making Patriots* (Chicago: University of Chicago Press, 2001), 98.

16

LEGISLATURES AS SCHOOLS

It is not possible that an assembly of men called for the most part from pursuits of a private nature, continued in appointment for a short time, and led by no permanent motive to devote the intervals of public occupation to a study of the laws, the affairs and the comprehensive interests of their country, should, if left wholly to themselves, escape a variety of important errors in the exercise of their legislative trust.

James Madison, *Federalist* No. 62 (1788)

When Alexis de Tocqueville, a man who appreciated persons "intellectually and morally superior,"[1] visited the Capitol in 1832, his impression of the people's legislature was distinctly unfavorable. "On entering the House of Representatives at Washington, one is struck by the vulgar demeanor of that great assembly," he wrote. "Often there is not a distinguished man in the whole number. Its members are almost all obscure individuals, whose names bring no associations to mind. They are mostly village lawyers, men in trade, or even persons belonging to the lower classes of society. In a country in which education is very general, it is said that representatives of the people do not always know how to write correctly."[2]

His uncomplimentary impression of the House would differ little from the recitals of today's snootier commentators. "Vulgar," "illiterate," "village lawyers" (Rep. Abraham Lincoln was a village lawyer), "persons belonging to the lower classes" (Lincoln was that, too) are phrases that, I'm sure, would flow from the computers of some of today's "chattering class" of reporters and public intellectuals if their editors didn't override them with better judgment.

Journalists' scorn is based on external appearances. There is a homely adage much closer to the truth: "Connoisseurs of good sausage and lovers of good laws have one thing in common: they should never watch either being made." To those who watch from the sidelines and have never participated in democratic government, the work of a legislature—and particularly of Congress—proceeds at an agonizingly slow pace. But those very features they complain of—unhurried consideration and complex procedures that afford so many representatives the chance to talk and stymie—are among its best attributes.

Congress (along with America's numerous state legislatures) is the quintessential democratic institution, and we who live in a democracy would be wise to understand how legislatures work from an insider's perspective.[3]

We must start with several basic facts about the U.S. Congress. As is well known, it consists of two houses. One, the Senate, has two representatives from each of the fifty states: two from California with its 37 million people, two from Wyoming with its 550,000 people. The House of Representatives has 435 members, distributed to the various states in proportion to their populations, with each member on average representing a district of 700,000 people.

The different sizes of the Senate and the House compel different procedures within them: less debate time per member in the larger House, and more committee assignments in the smaller Senate, for example. The Constitution also assigns the two bodies different responsibilities. The Senate alone shares with the president the treaty-making and appointive powers, and consequently it is more active and influential than the House in foreign affairs and the appointment of federal judges. On the other hand, the House is more influential in the area of taxes and government budgets because the Constitution specifies that all tax bills—and by custom all budget bills—must originate in the House. On taxes and spending decisions, the Senate plays a subordinate role, serving more as a court of appeals for those groups aggrieved by the prior actions of the House. Thus a member who has ambitions to matter in the Senate will seek a seat on the Foreign Relations or the Judiciary Committee. In contrast, if the member were a representative in the House, he or she would seek out membership on the "money" committees: Ways and Means for taxes or Appropriations for spending.

But legislative bodies are legislative bodies, and their similarities are far more important than their differences. What goes on in an American legislature?

What Is a Legislature Like?

Ask what the Congress of the United States is like and you will hear it likened to an arena, assembly, back alley, balance, bawdy house, body organ, branch of a tree, brokerage firm, bunch of horse traders, butcher shop, card game, cash register, circus, citadel, club, cockpit, collection agency, conciliator, dance hall, debating society, decision maker, engine, errand boy, family, forum, house, inquisition, judge, jury, linchpin, locus of pressures, machine, magnet, marketplace, medium, mirror, moral midwife, nightclub, pork barrel, pride of lions, rat race, referee, sausage maker, seminar, small town, social fabric-mender, stage, struggle, theater, and zoo. Metaphors all, they recur in our conversations and reflect our different notions of what legislators do—and should do—in a legislature.

We've already seen it likened to a sausage factory, blending sordid elements into palatable compromises. The factory metaphor inheres in our common parlance; we say that Congress is a "lawmaking" body, implying that unless it produces law in high volume its workers are behaving inefficiently.

Madison's Vision of a Legislature as a School

In no way was that the view of James Madison. In *Federalist* No. 53 he likened Congress to a school. Madison insisted on the importance, not of turning out more laws, but of turning out more good lawmakers. Madison identified certain procedures necessary to the education of elected representatives in learning how to govern well. He emphasized "the importance of the knowledge requisite for federal legislation." Even the smartest representative who thoroughly knows the district he represents needs to acquire a grasp of "the affairs, and even of the law of all the states" so that federal laws can be "accommodated to the different laws and local circumstances . . . in the different states." On top of that, he needs a "knowledge . . . of foreign affairs." Madison concluded with a warning that the legislative institution itself must be equipped to teach every one of its members the knowledge and skills required of democratic leaders: "Some portions of this knowledge may, no doubt, be acquired in a man's closet [i.e., his office]; but some of it also can only be derived from the public sources of information; and all of it will be acquired to best effect by a practical attention to the subject during the period of actual practice in the legislature."

Madison had no illusions about the initial caliber of the individual representatives, selected as they would be from parochial circumstance, deficient in the theory and practice of public affairs, and lacking "due acquaintance with the objects and principles of legislation." He uttered this caution, which serves as the epigraph to this chapter:

> It is not possible that an assembly of men called for the most part from pursuits of a private nature, continued in appointment for a short term, and led by no permanent motive to devote the intervals of public occupation to a study of the laws, the affairs, and the comprehensive interests of their country, should, if left wholly to themselves, escape a variety of important errors in the exercise of their legislative trust.[4]

Legislative misrule, according to Madison's way of thinking, would stem from incompetence more than from a lack of "upright intention"[5]—from blunders of "the heads rather than the hearts."[6]

To avoid such blunders, democratic legislators had to be made to master three fundamental competencies. First, they had to be taught sympathy for the circumstances of all their constituents. They had to learn about the concerns not only of partisans and neighbors but also of opponents and strangers. *Patriotism* was Madison's term for this enlargement of identification. A legislator was patriotic if he regarded every constituent as one of his people. If a legislator lacked patriotism, if he were too lazy or too parochial to study the affairs of all the diverse individuals in his district—farmers and laborers, rebels and contented, young and old, like-minded partisans and political opponents—then he would serve the legislature poorly. Representatives had to understand the hopes and dilemmas of all the citizenry if they were to avoid passing oppressive laws. If representatives were ignorant of particular circumstances in their own districts, *a fortiori* they could not anticipate the subtle consequences of applying general policies to a highly diverse people.

Second, individual legislators had to learn to manage legislation and discipline themselves to do it fairly, openly, and in the face of opposition. This skill of public negotiation Madison called the *love of justice*. It was the ability to act as a good judge would, hearing all the parties out and "protect[ing] all parties, the weaker as well as the more powerful."[7] Love of justice signified a representative's insistence on the integrity of the legislative process, so that "all parties" touched by a governmental policy would have a real say in influencing its design.

Third, legislators had to learn to take personal responsibility for a discrete segment of the legislative load. By specializing and giving "constant attention" to a particular area of public policy, each representative would develop an expert's competence. The specialist would choose a division of the legislature's work and develop a vision of the public interest in that area more subtle than that of his fellow legislators, who would then be permitted to become masters of other problems. The specialist legislator would bear the primary responsibility for preparing "a succession of well-chosen and well-connected measures" in the area of his concern. In order to move his "train of measures" through the legislature, the specialist would have to bring together a number of informed and committed citizens who would persevere in enacting the whole program.[8] *Wisdom* was Madison's term for the specialist's capacity to conceive and realize an idea in a democratic society. Wisdom was the social skill of building enduring coalitions. A wise legislator understood the republican genius of representative government and grasped the fact that ideas and vision and hard work could prevail in a republic only by building agreement over time among a community of the truly concerned. Wisdom was knowing how to establish, and become the center of, a broad network of trustworthy individuals.

In short, Madison's solution to the problem of democratic caprice—the problem he called "majority tyranny"—consisted of designing legislative institutions that educated their members to become political professionals "whose wisdom may best discern the true interest of their country, and whose patriotism and love of justice will be least likely to sacrifice it to temporary and partial considerations."[9]

He saw one danger lurking in such a solution. A legislature would be a poor school if it played favorites among its students. Unless it was egalitarian in the best sense, unless all legislators had an equal opportunity to learn how to be professionals, he warned, "the countenance of the government [might] become more democratic, but the soul that animates it [would] be more oligarchic."[10] An oligarchic legislature, consisting of only a few well-informed members with the rest remaining ignorant, not only muffed its chance to teach the educable; it also ran the danger of becoming corrupt. Concentrate influence in a few legislators, and they may become "perhaps not unwilling to avail themselves of those advantages."[11] Rather, a good legislature will devise procedures to deepen the intellects of *all* its members and place within their reach the mastery of public affairs necessary to check their colleagues' temptation to personal corruption.

Madison saw a second advantage in increasing the competence of all the representatives. As legislators improved their skills in conducting the public business, their commitment to a career in politics would harden. As a result, they would stand for reelection. Their competence, if they had taken the trouble to nurture it, would stand out boldly against the inexperience of any challengers. The electorate would discern the difference and tend to return incumbents to office, thus giving the legislature an institutional continuity. Madison was convinced that democratic government could be stable (and a good society possible) only if most legislators were veterans, were "members of long standing."[12] The ideal legislature was one in which "the bulk of the members" were experienced political incumbents, and in which the few new representatives entering the legislature each term would be schooled, equally and systematically, in the subtle arts of leading democracy. Madison would have despised term limits.[13]

The Modern Congress

If Congress is conceived as a school, lobbyists turn out to be their teachers. Clem Miller was an articulate and highly respected three-term member of Congress from Northern California. He customarily wrote letters to his constituents back in his district, depicting the everyday life of Congress. In one of those letters, he explained the usefulness of lobbyists to him:

> Generally at 9:00 comes the first office appointment: A trade association to discuss an industrial problem, or a lobbyist to explain his position on a bill. I invite them to come in. Right now, I am wrestling mightily with the problem of what to do about fair trade laws. I invite interested parties to meet with me and discuss their point of view. I have just recently concluded a similar study on the Administration's proposals for taxing cooperatives. . . . I invite them to my office to speak frankly about their problems. I learn faster, and feel better. . . .

He continued:

> A good lobby, with its technical resources, can speak to a congressman on his own terms. It is not diverted by irrelevancies, and if it is, then it is not a good lobby. A good lobbyist is one who knows his legislative objectives, who

has the facts firmly in hand, who can separate the facts from his prejudices, and proceed to the matter at hand with directness. . . . Many citizens may best help themselves legislatively if they will select those organizations which represent their aspirations and then back them with some of their treasure to carry forward the work.[14]

Lobbyists frame the intellectual issues, point out subtleties, and proffer solutions. Teaching in an intellectually adversarial context, they advocate the pros and cons of competing views, both theirs and others. There are lobbyists for nearly everybody—old and young, wealthy and poverty-stricken, boss and worker, farmer and rancher, citizen and immigrant, isolationist and foreign trade representative.

There are lobbyists to represent governmental interests as well: cities, states, nations, the judiciary, public employees, executive agencies (like the Federal Communications Commission), and, of course, the president. Lobbyists come with all kinds of formal and informal titles: "special interests," "public-interest advocates," "presidential liaison and cabinet secretaries" (the titles of the president's lobbyists).

But, in common, they are all professional educators of the legislature, and they roam the corridors of Congress day in, day out, on perpetual call to respond to their students' requests for "basic information" about the "real world" within and beyond Washington, D.C.

Lobbyists can be effective teachers for the same reasons that any professor can be an effective teacher of a subject. They specialize, they repeat the lessons over and over again, and they cram beforehand so they can stay a few pages ahead of their students. They capitalize on their different strengths. Some get their students' attention because they speak for well-organized and well-heeled constituencies; some by the warmth of their personalities; some by their enthusiasm for their subject matter; some by the power of their ideas, the reliability of their facts, or the touching quality of their cause. But every effective lobbyist educates.

The rule of the congressional legislative school is "the open door." No House members or senators would think of refusing to let a lobbyist take up a matter with their staffs or (if time is available) with themselves. That is, a lobbyist is welcome to enter any legislative office—unless the lobbyist has previously lied, and virtually no experienced lobbyist does that.

The lobbyists' formal classrooms are "in committee." Scattered throughout the Capitol and the House and Senate office buildings are several dozen committee rooms, looking like lecture halls. Here the seats of the legislators are positioned so the lobbyist or expert speaking to them can scrutinize their faces to see if they are paying attention.

In these classroom-like settings the formal courses of the legislative school take place. The subjects are taught in the committees and subcommittees to which the legislators are assigned. In the House, for example, the normal load of each member is two committees (and as many as four subcommittees); typically, senators take more committee and subcommittee assignments than their House colleagues (which means they cannot delve so deeply into any one subject as the representatives). The courses deal with virtually every aspect of life: agriculture, business and finance, labor, law, science, transportation; education, health, housing, welfare; youth, old age, Indian affairs; energy, land, water; foreign affairs, national defense, veterans' affairs; the high seas, the post office, the District of Columbia; government funding, government spending; public administration, government personnel; and the management of the legislature itself.

In committees, the legislators learn the concepts, substance, and vocabulary of the subject matters. They also make the acquaintance of the executive agency heads, the labor union representatives, the leaders of commerce, the welfare rights lawyers, the foreign affairs experts, and the other key people in the field, who, as witnesses, give guest lectures and then follow up with conversation with individual legislators.

There are first-rate, second-rate, and third-rate committees. The best are committees in which the chairpersons are fair and think educationally; the worst are those in which the opposite is the case. Great chairpersons establish standards of admiration by which other chairpersons are praised and condemned. Of Wayne Aspinall (1898–1983), for twenty years the head of the House Interior Committee, it was said, "[He] is fairness personified"; "he's kind of like a schoolteacher who likes to explain a lot of background stuff for the members"; "[he] is fair, thorough, a helluva guy [and] spends as much time [training] the freshmen Republicans as . . . the freshmen Democrats." One admirer summed up the reasons for Aspinall's greatness: "Wayne Aspinall is an old schoolmarm. He gives us civics lectures up there in the Committee about the three coordinate branches. He tells us we don't have to accept the administration bill or the Senate bill—that we are going to take our time and do it in our own way. We are schooled in that philosophy of independence."[15]

According to congressional scholar Richard Fenno, Aspinall would introduce his House colleagues to the subject matter of the Interior Committee—defined as the stewardship of the land owned by the U.S.

government—by holding "what he variously calls an 'orientation,' 'indoctrination,' or 'get-acquainted' session with the Secretary of the Interior and his top-level aides, primarily for the education of new members. During the session, all members have the opportunity to 'ask questions which may be pertinent to general matters or which may be pertinent to matters within their own districts.' Aspinall primes the executive officials to tell the newcomers how accessible they are and how they can be reached. And he prods them to emphasize their special willingness 'to give the facts whenever any problems arise within a member's district.'"[16]

Some of the courses are more complicated than others; there are "varsity" and nonvarsity curricula. The business courses, for example, are intellectually challenging because commercial occupations are so various: banking and international commerce are topics that stretch the mind. Some are wide-ranging in their intellectual sweep: to be effective on the energy committee, a member has to bone up on books on nuclear energy and geology, for example. On the other hand, the subject matter of some committees tends to the technical or parochial.

Furthermore, the courses vary in the pedagogical quality of the lobbyists. The business courses are taught by some of the most gifted teachers in town, and notables in the world of finance and industry travel to Washington to share their knowledge and experience. On the other hand, when the teachers are mundane and the members of the committee themselves are neither interested nor diverse, the discussion is dull, and potentially interesting material is left unexplored.

One last difference among the committees is their policy or fiscal function (i.e., appropriating the funds to pay for the policies). Most problems undergo two distinct committee examinations in each house (which means a successfully resolved problem usually passes four congressional committees in all). The first examination takes place in any one of a number of policy committees, where technical questions arise such as: Is there a real problem to be solved? Do the assumptions about cause and effect make sense? Will the proposed solution work? Are the details of the legislation logical and practical? In policy committees, legislators function to design the best "orange" or "apple" possible.

Once a policy committee has perfected the solution's technical efficiency and has "authorized" it, its handiwork is handed over to a second committee, where it is subjected to a "fiscal"—or "money"—examination. Fiscal committees (House Appropriations and Senate Finance) weigh the merits of the various policy proposals and appraise them comparatively. In fiscal committees questions arise such as: Will the good results of Committee P's solution to problem X outweigh the good results of Committee Q's solution to problem Y? Choices have to be made because there are always limits to the funds, manpower, and energy of government. Is a technically good farm program more valuable than a nicely designed freeway or an innovative military weapons program? Fiscal committees choose whether the good "orange" designed by one policy committee is more desirable than the good "apple" developed elsewhere in Congress.

Fiscal committees "appropriate" money to fuel the programs they deem most deserving and leave the other programs to wane away quietly without funds. Their authority to kill the handiwork of the policy committees requires their members to have earned reputations for being intellectually versatile, skilled, and hard working. Consequently, their members predominantly are senior in service. Most have had exposure to a half-dozen or so issue areas by having sat on policy committees and important subcommittees earlier in their legislative careers. If there are senior honors seminars in the legislative school, they are the fiscal committees.

The fiscal committees are where the action is. They establish priorities. In judging what proposals are to be fueled with dollars, they are deciding which substantive programs the government deems the most important; they are deciding the pecking order of programs, departments, and governmental careers.

The point to remember is, there are two legislative tasks in solving virtually every problem. The first task is to design a solution—the "authorization" process. The second is to provide it with human energy (which requires money)—the "appropriations" process. These tasks are performed in Congress's committee system.

The Effect of the Vote

While legislators speak repeatedly of how much they learn in the committees they serve—and of their likeness to college courses, they insist on one contrast with the conventional school: in the legislative school, the professional faculty is subordinate to the students—*because the legislators have the vote*. Their teachers want their students' votes; the livelihood of each faculty member depends on how his or her efforts please the students. (In college, of course, the professors have the grading power, and the students need good grades.)

It is a crucial point in understanding the dynamics of Congress. The legislator's privilege to vote in committee and on the floor means that interesting people with interesting problems and interesting things to say want to teach them. It means that the legislative students feel entitled to ask questions—endless questions about the reasons and consequences of things. It means that each lobbyist will do his or her utmost to provide the members the knowledge they desire. It means that the students can say, "Put it in writing," so that they can take the lobbyists' knowledge home and study it. Their vote is bestowed on those who give them the best, most accurate, most comprehensive knowledge.

The drawing power of the legislative vote is so obvious in understanding a legislature that an observer might overlook its magnetic effect. Absent it, no lobbyist would take the time to educate legislators. But once the members possess this extraordinary resource—the privilege to say yes or no in a meaningful way—they are then visited, importuned, and enlightened by skilled teachers.

Insofar as each member has legislative votes, Congress is an egalitarian institution. Every member starts with a set of resources: each legislator receives pieces of the franchise—like vouchers—to come to school with, to grant, withhold, and signal for attention. The dominant feature of the committee system in Congress—and the bulk of congressional decisions will be made by committees because of the division of labor—is its egalitarian character. There is no poverty; no legislator is a have-not.

"Study Hard"

Despite the drawbacks of the legislative life—the loneliness, the constant travel, the loss of privacy, the insecurity of tenure, and the constant demand for study—members of Congress enjoy their work. A former representative named Jim Rogan gave what I consider the most convincing explanation. But first, a little background.

The aristocratic Tocqueville would have considered Rogan a person "belonging to the lower classes"; he was raised by a single mother—a cocktail waitress who was later convicted of welfare fraud. (His bartender-father abandoned her before Rogan was born.) Brought up in San Francisco's Mission District, as a kid Rogan traveled with a tough circle of friends; after years of borderline delinquency, he was expelled from high school, thereafter becoming a porn theater bouncer and then a bartender at a strip joint and Hell's Angels bar. Next he joined the Merchant Marine, got a GED (a high school graduate equivalent degree), enrolled in a community college, and eventually went on to university and law school.

Then, in succession, he became a prosecuting attorney, a judge (the youngest ever appointed in California), a state legislator and minority leader (in a poll of journalists he was named both the most effective legislator and also the one having the greatest integrity), and then a Republican member of Congress.

In his memoir, *Rough Edges: My Unlikely Road from Welfare to Washington*,[17] he describes his introduction to legislative life. He had just been elected as a member of the state assembly (California's legislature) and had been taken to greet the speaker of the assembly, Willie Brown. Here, in Rogan's own words, is what happened:

> To California Republicans, Willie Brown was the Great Satan. Love him or despise him, nobody dared underestimate him. Born into poverty in the racially segregated town of Mineola, Texas, this young African-American got his education while working as a shoeshine boy, janitor, and crop picker. Moving west to California with his belongings in a cardboard suitcase, he worked his way through college and law school, and then began a successful San Francisco practice. Elected to the Assembly when I was seven years old, Willie served there for over three decades and held the longevity record (fifteen years) as speaker. He was the "most" of everything: the most charming, the most savvy, the most successful, the most cunning, the most skilled orator, and (when he wanted to be) the most ruthless. He had a reputation for enjoying the exercise of raw political power, once calling himself the "Ayatollah of the Assembly." His legislative might matched his penchant for flashy cars and expensive suits. Forever amused by rumors of corruption surrounding his lavish lifestyle on a legislator's modest salary, Willie wasn't crooked and didn't need to be: He maintained a lucrative law practice on the side. Republican candidates for years ran against Willie Brown as much as they ran against taxes and big government. I was no different, but privately I couldn't wait to serve with him. To me he was the most fascinating man on the American political scene.

> When [the Republican minority leader] escorted me to Willie's office, he rose from his desk and greeted me warmly. The broad smile on his face looked a tad suspicious. Wrapping his arm around my shoulder, he walked me to the rear of his conference room: "Come, Judge, I'd like to show you something." He opened a door leading directly to the Assembly floor.

Pointing to the members now collecting at their desks for the start of session, he asked, "Do you know what most of those people are?"

"Assemblymen?"

"Very good," Willie responded. "Do you know what most of them did before coming here? They were lawyers. Do you know why lawyers come here? To get to know a governor who will appoint them to the bench. In this room, we have many assemblymen wanting to be judges; until now, I never met a judge wanting to be an assemblyman. So, Judge Rogan, I'm curious: what made you give up the bench to come here?"

Assuming this was an esoteric question, I gave an esoteric answer: "Well, the legislature is where our laws are written. Although I loved the bench, I thought this opportunity would give me a chance to serve in a different venue. I wanted to have a hand in drafting laws to make our state a better place for my children."

Like a cat playing with his mouse before eating it, Willie toyed with me before pouncing for the kill: "Judge, let me share with you some arithmetic: There are 80 members in this body. I lead 47 Democrats; [the minority leader] leads 33 Republicans. I have what we call *a majority*; you have what we call *a minority*. 'Passing laws'—we do those things. On rare occasions, when a bill requires a two-thirds vote, I may consult with a few members of your caucus.

"Of course," Willie added, "don't feel you gave up the bench for nothing. You have an important role to play. Please show up on time, which helps my majority to make a quorum, so *we* can pass those laws that make better the lives of *your* children. And don't forget to collect your salary and per diem check.

"Judge Rogan," the Speaker concluded with a wide grin, "welcome to the California State Assembly!" As we shook hands, I couldn't help but smile. The schoolmaster had just tutored his new assembly-boy with a verbal hickory switch. This was my introduction to a man I came to respect, like, and fear in equal measure. Say what you will about Willie Brown: For my money, each day I wished he was on our side.

For Jim Rogan, what was likeable about legislatures? Working with "the most fascinating man on the American political scene"; the good-natured fun and the sporting challenge that made him "smile" as he said his adieux to Speaker Brown; the competition with "savvy," "successful," "skilled," even "cunning" men and women; and the satisfaction of mastering the political process to fight for what he believed in. Those are the things that good legislators like.

Representative Rogan's book ends on a poignant and instructive note. When he, a Republican from California, was first elected to Congress, he received a congratulatory note from his longtime political hero, Democratic senator Hubert Humphrey of Minnesota, who, after a lifetime of legislative accomplishment, was ravaged by cancer that would take his life four months later. Here was the concluding paragraph of that note:[18]

> We need good, progressive, honorable young people in government and politics. So, go to it! Work hard; study hard; fight the good fight; and, my friend, be of good cheer!

None of those words were clichés. They were, rather, the conclusions of an experienced legislator and great man who had guided significant legislation into law—laws like the Civil Rights Act of 1964—and had narrowly missed being elected president of the United States. And two words in his letter stand out: "Study hard."

NOTES

1. Alexis de Tocqueville, *Democracy in America,* trans. Harry Reeve (New York: Bantam, 2000 [1835]), vol. I, chap. 13.
2. Ibid. To be fair, it must be added that he was more impressed by the U.S. Senate than by the House of Representatives (to his way of seeing, the Senate was comprised of "statesmen whose arguments would do honor to the most remarkable parliamentary debates in Europe").
3. Besides, Congress is an evolving institution. A healthy synergy exists between Congress and its state counterparts. Most members of Congress have had prior state legislative experience, and when they arrive in Congress, they bring certain habits and expectations from their prior legislative experiences. They focus on reforming congressional practices that they think work less well than those they know function well in their particular state. For example, the precursor of the Congressional Budget Office, which makes crucial data and analyses available to *every member* of Congress, was the Legislative Analyst's Office in the California state legislature. Alumni of that legislature knew its value and worked successfully to "Californianize" Congress and make

information readily available. In fits and starts, Congress keeps reforming its procedures and itself.

4. *Federalist* No. 62.
5. *Federalist* No. 53.
6. *Federalist* No. 62.
7. *Federalist* No. 51.
8. *Federalist* No. 63. Madison elaborates: "The objects of government may be divided into two general classes; the one depending on measures which have singly an immediate and sensible operation; the other depending on a succession of . . . measures, which have a gradual and perhaps unobserved operation." In the latter category would fall subjects like air quality and military readiness.
9. *Federalist* No. 10.
10. *Federalist* No. 58.
11. *Federalist* No. 53.
12. *Federalist* No. 62.
13. In 1992, two years before the public voted to replace the incumbent Democratic majority in Congress with many new Republicans, the often insightful George Will published *Restoration: Congress, Term Limits, and the Recovery of Deliberative Democracy* (New York: Free Press, 1992). In it Will advocated term limits on the grounds, among others, that making longtime members of Congress move on would lead to budgetary responsibility (less spending), reduction of taxes, enhanced legislative power vis-à-vis the president and federal judges, increased voter turnout, the end of "careerism," and introduction into politics of people with worldly experience and principles to resist the "addled" thinking of the voting public. While Congress did not succumb to Will's proposal, several states, among them California, did. I think it fair to say that *none* of the hoped-for consequences occurred. In California, government spending skyrocketed, the state went (figuratively, if not legally) bankrupt, the influence of the governor became greater, legislative staff ("careerists") succeeded to the seats of their termed-out bosses, and the membership lacked the foresight to see obvious and disastrous problems in bills advanced by the governor to solve complex problems like energy.
14. Clem Miller, *Member of the House: Letters of a Congressman*, ed. John W. Baker (New York: Charles Scribner's Sons, 1962), 66–67, 72–73.
15. This discussion of Rep. Wayne Aspinall is drawn from political scientist Richard Fenno's splendid *Congressmen in Committees* (Boston: Little, Brown, 1973).
16. Ibid., 119.
17. James E. Rogan, *Rough Edges: My Unlikely Road from Welfare to Washington* (New York: Regan Books, 2004), 300–301.
18. Ibid., 308.

17

CONGRESS AS DEFENDER OF FREEDOM

Asia was rich in the intellectual and institutional traditions that would provide fertile grounds for democracy. What Asia did not have was the organizations of representative democracy. The genius of the West was to create the organizations, a remarkable accomplishment that has greatly advanced the history of humankind.

> Kim Dae Jung, president of South Korea,
> on receipt of the Nobel Peace Prize (2000)

A theme common to both James Madison and Alexis de Tocqueville was their fear of majority tyranny—namely, that a democratic people would abridge the freedoms of a discrete and unpopular minority living amongst them. Out of fear, greed, or impatience, the prevailing majority would use the instruments of government to silence the dissenters, rob the productive, and crush the nonconformists.[1]

Warned Tocqueville: "Democratic republics extend the practice of currying favor with the many and introduce it into all classes at once; this is the most serious reproach that can be addressed to them. This is especially true in democratic states organized like the American republics, where the power of the majority is so absolute and irresistible that one must give up one's rights as a citizen and almost abjure one's qualities as a man if one intends to stray from the track which it prescribes."[2]

Tocqueville had little confidence that any elective official would resist the impulses of the many. The politicians he encountered in his nine months in America proved to be spineless and abject when facing a determined mob representing the majority. He found "few [officeholders] who displayed that manly candor and masculine independence of opinion which frequently distinguished the Americans in former times."[3] In fact, he likened members of Congress to the sycophantic courtiers to King Louis XIV at Versailles.[4]

Tocqueville was no pessimist, no believer in the inevitability of majority tyranny. He looked to the American law profession to cool the people's rash impatience. The training of lawyers, their procedures, and their conservative habits, he thought, might succeed in opposing the majority's first ardent impulse to do injustice.[5]

Where Madison and Tocqueville Diverge

Madison did not share Tocqueville's dismal assessment of democratically elected officials. Rather, he placed his hopes on an enlightened national legislature to inhibit the majority's tendency toward oppressive extremism. Congress would be the principal obstacle to the public's acting impetuously. As you may recall from Chapter 16, it could, under the right circumstances, "refine and enlarge the public views, by passing them through the medium of a chosen body of citizens, whose wisdom may best discern the true interest of their country, and whose patriotism and love of justice, will be least likely to sacrifice it to temporary or partial considerations."[6]

Madison's Metaphor of a Filter

Madison's metaphor of "a medium" likened Congress to a filtration process removing impurities—the impurities of passion and ignorance—from "the public views." That's a useful analogy because it focuses attention on a productive question: Is it possible to keep the filter from becoming soiled? What is to be done to prevent Congress from stimulating majority tyranny, providing them fuel for public malevolence and fear? Madison answers those questions in *Federalist* Nos. 52 through 66. But before we explore his solution, let's take a moment to make sure we fully appreciate what was expected of that ideal congressman Madison envisioned, with his mastery of the three competencies of patriotism, love of justice, and wisdom as those competencies would actually have to be practiced in the real world.

The Demands of the Madisonian Vision

Recall that Madison, when he spoke of *patriotism*, was referring to a legislator's sympathy for the circumstances of *all* his constituents and not just for those who supported him. Patriotism entailed the duty of discovering the real problems people faced and lending a compassionate "ear" to their dilemmas and goals.

That's a demanding obligation and requires unusual self-discipline. In the real world, it takes immense amounts of time to get to know people who are outside the legislator's immediate circle of family and professional acquaintance. That means little time left for family duties, not to mention for sleep. It is emotionally exhausting to travel recurrently between Washington and his constituents back home, listen mindfully to a steady parade of problem-filled situations, and develop realistic solutions to them.

The second competency Madison expected of his ideal legislator was a *love of justice.* Love of justice boiled down to a respect for the values of due process, which entail *listening* to opposing sides of a conflict, *arranging* for those opponents to air their disagreements openly in front of one another, and *judging* their controversy fairly. Consider President Dwight Eisenhower's counsel to future chief executives:

[There is] only one way in which you can be sure you've done your best to make a wise decision. That is to get all of the people . . . with their different viewpoints in front of you, and listen to them debate. I do not believe in bringing them in one at a time, and therefore being more impressed by the most recent one you hear than the earlier ones. . . . You listen, and you see if there's anything been brought up, an idea that changes your own view and enriches your view or adds to it.

Eisenhower's advice to executives has equal application to legislators trying to do "justice": take the time to give people the chance to air their disagreements openly and in front of one another. Be humble about your grasp of what is really going on. Be open to new facts and reasons. Don't prejudge any matter. That's what Madison was getting at with his phrase, "love of justice."

Finally, Madison expected *wisdom* from members of Congress. What he meant by wisdom was an ability to combine technical skill with political skill. The technical skill was an ability to craft legislation that did not overreach the problem it was intended to solve. By keeping coercion to the absolute minimum and framing laws that depended for their effectiveness on positive incentives, a wise legislator crafted laws that were easy to enforce and difficult to disobey.

But good solutions never enacted into legislation count for little. That's where political skill comes into play. The ideal legislator must combine his good proposals with a skill in overcoming opposition to them. He must learn to build coalitions, bringing diverse groups of potential supporters along every step of the way, serving as a hub of communication, searching out common ground they may share, and unifying the coalition around an agreed course of action.[7]

These two skills—legislative competence and coalition building—are complex in the extreme, and their exercise is an art gained not in a class-room, but in an apprentice system. One who aspires to the Madisonian ideal has to observe those who have mastered the skill and participate beside them, letting them mentor and correct his efforts.

Much is demanded by the Madisonian ideal in the way of patience, effort, and skill. Little wonder that actual legislators often fall short of the Madisonian ideal. We must add one more wrinkle, however, to our picture. The ideal legislator is a *representative* of the people. He is the embodiment of the principle we have called the sovereignty of the people. But what people does the representative represent? The voters in his district—that is, his constituents? Or "we the people"—that is, the nation as a whole? (Or perhaps all of humankind?) To the service of *which* people does his duty extend?[8]

Is It Possible?

Given the realities of democratic political life, Madison expected nearly superhuman dedication. Madison would have his ideal legislator be patriotic, just, and wise while operating in a real world where he would be perpetually tired, invariably pressed to act before all the facts were in, often on call at the center of coalitions that would be always about to fall apart, sometimes bedeviled by moral conflict, and always needing to survive and rise in a competitive political world of rivals.

Is it possible to motivate legislators to put out such sustained and extraordinary effort? Or, as Tocqueville thought, is such a hope an illusion, doomed to disappoint? What power might motivate members of Congress to function as Madison would want them to?

In my experience, the external control of competitive elections—the threat of defeat at the polls—can only serve as a secondary incentive. There are two reasons for the ineffectiveness of electoral coercion. One is that the relatively few voters who closely observe the slipshod ways of a bad legislator tend to care only about his responsiveness to their particular issues. The second is that coercion from outside the legislature is exercised too bluntly and too unreliably to compel the extraordinary dedication Madison hoped for. In every American legislature one can find members who are lazy, incompetent, and unresponsive to real problems. They spend their days more attentive to their golf game than to their homework. A lazy legislator quickly learns that a few regular visits to senior citizens' centers in his district will reap enough votes to offset the ballots cast against him by those disserved by his shortcomings.

As evidence, witness the fact that at one time or another there have been American legislatures somewhere that declined into dysfunction, where the bulk of their members were passive, narrow, and politically clumsy dolts, yet the voters kept voting them back into office.

For example, here was the 1960 Texas state legislature, as observed by the late Willie Morris. Morris, a former Rhodes scholar and founder of the *Texas Observer*, the most admired political journal in the state, described the representatives in these disheartening terms:

> I was simply not prepared for it. It is difficult to convey exactly the way I reacted those first days [reporting the activities of the Texas legislature], but I remember it as a kind of physical sickness, the result of a continuing outrage, for which even writing was no outlet. . . . Texas was a state which ranked first in the nation in oil. . . ; first in gas. . . ; first in cattle, first in cotton, first in everything from livestock and mohair to goats and pecans. Yet in basic social services the State of Texas ranked first in caseload per state social worker. . . ; 40th in literacy, 50th in vocational rehabilitation for injured workers; and close to the bottom in educational services. Despite its impressive beauty, its state parks were a travesty, and it could be judged nothing less than criminal in its neglect of the mentally ill. Such arguments . . . were greeted, depending on the moment, with smugness, high hilarity, inattention, or a simple lack of intelligence.

That was not the sort of legislature that was going to resist a majority committed to run roughshod over the lives and freedoms of the politically weak.

Reciprocity

Readers will be relieved to know that the Texas state legislature is no longer disgracefully indifferent and incompetent. Reform has come to Texas, but not because the voters scared their legislators into doing their work.

However, that it has improved—that legislatures can get better—brings us to the question, Can a legislature like Congress be shaped so as to elevate its members to a sturdy independence of unjust public demands on them? What can be done to motivate them to behave patriotically, fairly, and wisely?

The solution to legislative improvement is the skilled use of reciprocity. The kind of Madisonian dedication we have discussed cannot be compelled, nor can it be the result of urging legislators to be selfless. Reform, if and when it comes, results from changing the circumstances within the legislature so that the legislators discover that it is in their self-interest to become competent.

Why is reciprocity the only kind of power that is effective in a legislature? Because a legislature is a small, inescapable community of individuals dependent on one another over an extended period of time. Were a leader (or any member) to practice coercion to get his way with his colleagues, he would repel them, beget their resistance, and defeat any hope of enlisting their collaboration in the future. In a community as small and self-contained as 100 members, or even of 435 representatives, the life of a would-be extortionist with a reputation for "ill will" would become a never-ending series of unfriendly and unproductive encounters. Thus the only long-term means by which a member can get his way within such a close-knit community is to accommodate others and gain his colleagues' respect for his "good will." Thus anyone who wants to reform his colleagues' conduct has to resort to the practice of give-and-take and understand the possibilities that the paradoxes of reciprocal power offer him.

The Paradox of Scarcity, Redux

The first of those paradoxes is the paradox of scarcity (*the scarcer the supply, the higher the price*). Reciprocators mutually submit, and the degree of each submission depends on how much one desires the other's help. A legislative leader seeking increased dedication from colleagues must know their unmet needs and fill them.

Think back to the story of freshman legislator Jim Rogan in his first days in the legislature. What did he want? Money? Not likely, for if it were so, any lawyer with his talents would surely pursue a more lucrative career than politics. Was it higher social status, or domination, or the satisfaction of being a benefactor? To achieve any of those goals, his immediate need would be information. He would be anxious to get, as Madison put it, "the knowledge requisite to the business of . . . legislation."[9] From experience in the Continental Congress, Madison had learned that the "novelty and difficulty" of making law for the entire nation required more than "the store of knowledge brought by a Congressman from his experience in the district." Without information and an understanding of the likely consequences of a policy they proposed, legislators like the young Rogan would foul up. Their uninformed proposal would be defective and, if enacted, would produce a failed result, earning the scorn of their colleagues and their constituents.

On the other hand, if they had adequate information and knew what they was doing, they would begin to be effective as a legislator.

Sufficient knowledge, it turns out, is power. It gives a legislator a sense of self-control. He has a vote, and when coupled with information and understanding, he can use it so as to bring about results he desires. Moreover, his knowledge attracts others who want to hear what he has to say; he can efficiently teach other legislators in exchange for their giving him the information they have mastered. With knowledge and with the trust his colleagues give him, he can guide the votes of his fellow members to support legislation he thinks beneficial.

Furthermore, a knowledgeable legislator can explain things to journalists and members of the public, from CEOs to irate constituents, who will keep coming back to take his informed advice.

When Information Becomes Easily Accessible

Finally, knowledge is the one resource he can derive from his experience in Congress that he can take elsewhere—whether to the Senate or an executive agency, to the judiciary or the world of commerce, or to a career as a legislative lobbyist. A portfolio of expertise is portable and useful to others; hence, because the depth of his understanding is rare, it will command a high price from businesses or other political institutions who desire it.

Suppose, however, that assembling a portfolio of expertise in Congress demanded too much effort, especially in light of all the other demands besetting a member of Congress for constituency service and fighting off rivals. For example, suppose that Congress resembled the kind of oligarchic institution that Madison warned of in *Federalist* No. 53, where "a few of the members . . . will possess superior talents; will, by frequent re-elections, become members of long standing; will be thoroughly masters of the public business and perhaps not unwilling to avail themselves of those advantages." In this travesty of a legislature, this "superior few" would keep what they know to themselves; they would monopolize the supply of knowledge—and the more they obstructed the education of their colleagues, the more they could dictate what the legislature enacted—and turn their domination to "avail themselves of advantages."

Or suppose that Congress were the informational desert that Walter Lippmann described in 1922:[10]

The main reason for the discredit [of popularly elected legislatures], which is world wide, is to be found in the fact that a congress of representatives is essentially a group of blind men in a vast, unknown world. With some exceptions, the only method recognized in the constitution or in the theory of representative government, by which Congress can inform itself, is to exchange opinions from the districts. There is no systematic, adequate and authorized way for Congress to know what is going on in the world. The theory is that the best man of each district brings the best wisdom of his constituents to a central place, and that all these wisdoms combined are all the wisdom the congress needs. Now there is no need to question the value of expressing local opinions and exchanging them. Congress has great value as the market place of a continental nation. . . . But even if the theory were applied and the districts always sent their wisest men, the sum or a combination of local impressions is not a wide enough base for national policy, and no base at all for the control of foreign policy. Since the real effects of most laws are subtle and hidden, they cannot be understood by filtering local experiences through local states of mind. They can be known only by controlled reporting and objective analysis. . . . So bad is the contact of legislators with necessary facts that they are forced to rely either on private tips or on that legalized atrocity, the Congressional investigation, where congressmen starved of their legitimate food for thought, go on a wild and feverish manhunt, and do not stop at cannibalism.

The cleverest and most industrious representative cannot hope to understand a fraction of the bills on which he votes. The best he can do is to specialize on a few bills and take somebody's word about the rest. I have known congressmen when they were boning up on a subject, to study as they had not studied since they passed their final examinations, many large cups of black coffee, wet towels, and all. They had to dig for information, sweat over arranging and verifying facts, which, in any consciously organized government, should have been easily available in a form suitable for decision.

In that kind of frustrating environment, it might not take long for a new member like Jim Rogan to despair of his ideal and shift goals to personal profit—a quick buck in his personal bank account by using his vote as his leaders told him to, or a cushy patronage job in some inconsequential government agency by submitting to the president. Might not he give up on his ambition to be a legislator who could stand up against an impulsive public opinion and who would persevere to make a beneficial difference in other people's lives?

An Abundance of Information

Now, think what would happen if into this desert of information came a bounty of significant knowledge and analysis that would make it possible for him and *all* his colleagues to get a handle on matters of importance. Then, imagine the reaction of those few legislators "of long standing" who had once monopolized information of the budget and governmental programs, once they lost their monopoly.

No longer the only informed persons in a vale of ignorance, those powerful few—oligarchs, as Madison called them—would have to compete to maintain their influence. And in those circumstances, in order to compete for influence they would find it in their self-interest to advertise their expertise and their availability to teach it to anyone who wanted it. Their self-interest would be in educating each of their colleagues in the hopes that he or she would come to see things as they did. In other words, abundant knowledge that is available to all the legislators changes the entire dynamic of a legislature. It transforms the "superior few" from oppressors of their colleagues into their teachers. It equalizes all by elevating all.

In sum, the secret of realizing Madison's ideal legislature is to make the retrieval of essential information possible and the obtaining of useful analysis easy.

Steps to Reform

In this light, a legislative leader with a reform bent would take these first steps. He would enlarge important committees and provide smart and energetic committee staffs. He would give each legislator a personal staff. He would hire professionals to update his colleagues on new developments in science and technology. He would establish a nonpartisan office to provide expertise on matters of the government's budget and the private economy. He would distribute written papers on public policy topics. He would develop relationships with nearby libraries to have reference librarians on call to help out legislators. He would give all members access to legal counsel. And, of course, all these resources would be available on a nonpartisan basis.

That is precisely what has happened since Walter Lippmann wrote about Congress back in 1922. No longer is Congress "essentially a group of blind men." Members of Congress now have personal and committee staff; they now are served by a nonpartisan Congressional Budget Office that churns out analyses of the economy and the president's budget; they now have professionals at the Library of Congress who respond quickly and amply to any member's request; there was (until recent budget cuts) an Office of Technology Assessment to teach any member of Congress about the most abstruse scientific matter; and each member can now avail himself of the services of an Office of Legal Counsel to bring him up to speed on legal matters.

Moreover, members have budgets that allow them to fly off to foreign lands, to observe directly otherwise strange and befuddling geographies and cultures. The result is that Congress has developed what Lippmann hoped for: a "systematic, adequate and authorized way for Congress to [understand] what is going on in the world." Taxpayers bemoan all this expense, but good government is not cheap government.[11]

Now, imagine what might further result from this bounty of information. As the legislators became better informed, the lobbyists trying to influence them would be obliged to bring them more and better information and package it more accessibly. Moreover, abundant knowledge would energize *all* the members to share and to advertise *their* expertise.

Colleagues, assisted by their staffs, would start writing informative memos, distributing them widely throughout Congress. They would spend nights preparing for floor debates, digging out reliable evidence that others might never have considered. They would pass on gossip or tips to colleagues, providing each other telling insights into the personalities and circumstances of both allies and adversaries. They would take the time to mentor rookies in the procedures and mores of the institution.

And, most importantly, an effective and highly skilled division of labor within the legislature would develop. As the amount of information to which each legislator had access grew, the more time he would need to devote to maintaining his portfolio of expertise on which he traded. He no longer would have the luxury of being an amateur jack-of-all-trades. In order to become a master of aerospace science, for example, he would have to delegate to others the task of becoming experts in the countless other concerns of the nation—highways, taxes, banking, agricultural subsidies, African trade problems, and so on. He would encourage (and expect) them to do their homework in their area of expertise as carefully as he would do his.[12] He would look to colleagues to supply him expert advice in these areas and would have every reason to trust it. As a consequence, Congress would be able to elevate both the quantity of work and the quality with which it would be performed. Each legislator would bear his or her fair share of the load.

With all the good things that would stem from reciprocity—the promotion of initiative; the development of better, more sophisticated public policy; the increased camaraderie of the legislators resulting from a useful division of labor; the greater sense of purpose and the heightened morale among members—what would happen to those legislators who had lesser talents? One would anticipate that the talented and knowledgeable legislators would start hanging out with one another, while those who were less able to assimilate complexities would feel dishonored as good-for-nothings. Being treated indifferently, those who were less fast in comprehension or less able to assimilate complexities would cluster with other less talented representatives.[13] Potential "failures" all, made to feel worthless, they might begin to misbehave, as neglected students will do. They would still have a vote to cast on legislation, after all, which they could sell or use counterproductively, in spite.

Good legislative leaders, however, could learn to develop ways of honoring the lesser tier among the membership by parceling out responsibilities consistent with their limited talents—a limited area of public policy, perhaps, or a less abstruse one, at which they wouldn't fail. By being sensitive to their need for self-esteem, by making them feel like contributors, leaders could avoid the peril of demoralization.

And all this improvement would occur, not from the legislators' noble intentions, but out of their self-interest.[14]

In real life things never go as smoothly or benignly as I've depicted here. Human imperfection, bitter partisanship, and flawed legislative leadership occur even in the most benign of circumstances. But here is the important point about the modern Congress: its present and future shortcomings should not blind us to the fact that it is a reasonable realization of the Madisonian ideal.[15] An intellectually confident and politically skilled assembly of legislators is capable of being the "medium" that cleanses public opinion of the angry, passionate, and misinformed fears that impel majorities to scapegoat vulnerable minorities.

One final observation: while the partisan arguments within Congress often sound harsh, its successful members achieve their goals as legislators not by threatening colleagues, but by gaining their trust. To put that fact into perspective, recall Machiavelli's lament that in his anarchic time it was necessary, if one were to succeed in politics, to be feared—much more than to be loved. But if that were so because the defective institutions of sixteenth-century Italy "compelled" a leader to use coercion to get his way, notice that a congressperson today can thrive from developing a reputation for "good will," for being a trustworthy partner in reciprocity. That development is a change of real consequence, made possible by making information universally available in our legislatures. We have made hearts and minds trump, not clubs.

This progress from threat to reciprocity is sometimes hard for Americans to appreciate, but for persons elsewhere who have always lived under regimes whose rulers survived by threat, the advancement is obvious. That is why Americans should keep in mind the remarks of President Kim Dae Jung of South Korea. On accepting the Nobel Peace Prize in 2000, President Kim, once a political prisoner during the authoritarian regime that preceded South Korean democracy, told the world, "Asia was rich in the intellectual and institutional traditions that would provide fertile grounds for democracy. What Asia did not have was the organizations of representative democracy. The genius of the West was to create the organizations, a remarkable accomplishment that has greatly advanced the history of humankind."

The "organizations of representative democracy"—legislatures function-ing as schools for an enlightened, nonviolent politics—have "greatly advanced the history of humankind." That's an idea to take your hat off to.

NOTES

1. Madison's and Tocqueville's fears are timely and important. Legal scholar Amy Chua's *World on Fire: How Exporting Free Market Democracy Breeds Ethnic Hatred and Global Instability* (New York: Doubleday, 2003) chronicles instances of majority tyranny in countries that have recently democratized— the Philippines, Thailand, Malaysia, and Indonesia. Fear of majority tyranny, no doubt, lay at the bottom of the misgivings that reasonable Sunni moderates originally had about democratizing Iraq.
2. Alexis de Tocqueville, *Democracy in America*, trans. Henry Reeve (New York: Bantam, 2000 [1835]), vol. I, chap. 15.
3. Ibid.
4. Ibid. Tocqueville mocked the spinelessness of American legislators:

    > I have heard of patriotism in the United States, and I have found true patriotism among the people but never among the leaders of the people. This may be explained by analogy: despotism debases the oppressed much more than the oppressor: in absolute monarchies the king often has great virtues, but the court-iers are invariably servile. It is true that American courtiers do not say "Sire," or "Your Majesty," a distinction without a difference. They are forever talking of the natural intelligence of the people whom they serve; they do not debate the question which of the virtues of their master is pre-eminently worthy of admira-tion, for they assure him that he possesses all the virtues without having acquired them, or without caring to acquire them; they do not give him their daughters and their wives to be raised at his pleasure to the rank of concubines; but by sac-rificing their opinions they prostitute themselves. . . . The sycophants of Louis XIV could not flatter more dexterously.

5. Ibid., chap.16:

    > The more we reflect upon all that occurs in the United States, the more we shall be persuaded that the lawyers, as a body, form the most powerful, if not the only, counterpoise to the democratic element. In that country we easily perceive how the legal profession is qualified by its attributes, and even by its faults, to neutral-ize the vices inherent in popular government. When the American people are intoxicated by passion or carried away by the impetuosity of their ideas, they are checked and stopped by the almost invisible influence of their legal counselors.

These secretly oppose their aristocratic propensities to the nation's democratic instincts, their superstitious attachment to what is old to its love of novelty, their narrow views to its immense designs, and their habitual procrastination to its ardent impatience.

6. Madison was making the distinction between direct democracy and representative democracy. Here is the entirety of his remarks:

> One of the] great points of difference between a Democracy and a Republic [is] the delegation of the Government, in the latter, to a small number of citizens, elected by the rest. . . . The effect . . . is . . . to refine and enlarge the public views, by passing them through the medium of a chosen body of citizens, whose wisdom may best discern the true interest of their country, and whose patriotism and love of justice, will be least likely to sacrifice it to temporary or partial considerations. Under such a regulation, it may well happen that the public voice pronounced by the representatives of the people, will be more consonant to the public good, than if pronounced by the people themselves convened for the purpose. [*Federalist* No. 10.]

7. For a case study of the effort expended in coalition building, see former Federal Trade Commissioner chair Michael Pertschuk's *Smoke in Their Eyes: Lessons in Movement Leadership from the Tobacco Wars* (Nashville: Vanderbilt University Press, 2001), detailing the legislative failure of the antismoking coalition.

8. It must be said that frequently a representative's notions of the welfare of his constituents and the welfare of the nation coincide, or at least they don't directly collide with each other. But collisions do happen. Issues like abortion, conservation, waging war, and extending free trade are the kind of passion-filled topics that occasionally confront a representative with a dilemma of choosing between his constituents and a conscience that enjoins him to think of the well-being of those outside his district.

Take an example from half a century ago: civil rights. That's an issue so dramatic as to make the conflict between constituency and conscience very clear. Imagine the ethical quandary of a moderate, reform-minded representative from a southern state who represents a strongly racially segregationist district. How should he vote on the Civil Rights Act of 1964, a proposal that would make it a federal crime for a private hotel keeper or a restaurant owner to deny service to a customer on the basis of race?

Our hypothetical representative's moral dilemma would be stark: whether to respond to his constituency (and hence vote against the bill) or his conscience (and hence cast his vote for the bill). Here were two widely varying answers given by two respected legislators of the time. The first was that of a crusty New England legislator, whose moral integrity was admired during his fifty years of political life, Sen. Ralph Flanders of Vermont. "There is a saying to the effect that 'a Senator's first duty is to get re-elected.' This sounds a bit cynical, but there is a real vein of truth in it. If I were a Southern Senator and were facing [that question], I would be strongly moved to avoid the extreme segregationist position, but would also avoid crusading for anti-segregation. I would join the moderates [in mildly opposing the bill and would vote against it] and hope for re-election, knowing that if I were defeated in the primaries my place would be taken by a rabid segregationist."

In other words, he recommended voting in the way that the bulk of a legislator's constituents would want him to vote, both out of prudence and also out of principle: the voters entrusted him to represent them, not to represent people embraced within his personal sensitivities.

The second opinion was that of an equally admired midwestern legislator, who, through years of study, had become the acknowledged foreign-policy authority within the House of Representatives. His answer was very different: "I think that Congressmen and Senators are expendable rather than indispensable, and no Congressman or Senator should cast a vote he knows is wrong in order to be reelected. It makes no difference whether the wrongness is on a moral, legal, economic or other issue. . . . I think that if a Southern Senator is opposed morally to segregation he should vote his convictions and take his medicine. For one thing, he might be surprised to find how many people admire that kind of courage." William Benton, "The Big Dilemma: Conscience or Votes," *New York Times Magazine*, April 26, 1959, 12-ff.

9. *Federalist* No. 63.
10. Walter Lippmann, *The Phantom Public* (New York: Harcourt, Brace, 1922), 288–291.
11. Many of these reforms originated first in the California state legislature under the leadership of a political genius named Jesse Unruh. When its alumni went to Washington and found that Congress was defective, they fought to introduce California practices into Congress. Thus the contagion of reform is spread from state to nation through the genius of federalism, an institution that we will examine in Chapter 24.
12. Recall a second paradox of reciprocity, that of abundance: *the more resourceful our customer, the better; the more resourceful our competitor, the worse.*
13. Keep in mind the third paradox of reciprocity, that of equality: *people hang out with others with whom they can be mutually useful.*
14. In any reciprocal system, there is always the danger of theft. In Congress theft can take the form of corruption—of accepting illicit goods and services in exchange for votes and insider information. Corruption can also take the form of misbehavior of other sorts, including the practice of blackmail and extortion within the membership. Who in Congress is the policeman who keeps an eye out for unscrupulous members?

Policing is the job of the leaders: the Speaker of the House and Majority Leader in the Senate. Both are given considerable authority to investigate and punish members' improprieties—and bring down on them the condemnation of their colleagues. In 2006, when former House Speaker Dennis Hastert failed adequately to heed rumors that a representative was making aggressive homosexual overtures to former House "pages" (youths serving as messengers), he—and only he—was held responsible; he had been negligent in fulfilling his indispensable role as the House's policeman.

15. The thoughtful Fareed Zakaria, among others, does not share my optimism about Congress. In his *The Post-American World* (New York: W. W. Norton, 2008), 211, he writes: "The problem today is that the American political system seems to have lost its ability to create broad coalitions that solve complex issues. . . . A set of sensible reforms could be enacted tomorrow to trim wasteful spending and subsidies, increase savings, expand training in science and technology, secure pensions, create a workable immigration process, and achieve significant efficiencies in the use of energy. . . . It has developed a highly dysfunctional politics. An antiquated and overly rigid political system to begin with—about 225 years old—has been captured by money, special interests, sensationalist media, and ideological attack groups." In rebuttal, one must ask, "Dysfunctional" compared to what? To the Congresses of yesteryear? To the British, Indian, or French parliaments? To the Kremlin in the former Soviet Union?

18

THE SUPREME COURT AS FREEDOM'S PROTECTOR

*No legislative act . . . contrary to the constitution can be valid.
[The] courts were designed to be an intermediate body between the
people and the legislature in order, among other things, to keep the
latter within the limits assigned to their authority. The interpretation of the laws is the proper and peculiar province of the courts.
A constitution is in fact, and must be, regarded by the judges as
a fundamental law.*

Alexander Hamilton, *Federalist* No. 78 (1788)

If James Madison depended on an enlightened Congress to protect personal freedom from majority tyranny, his *Federalist* collaborator Alexander
Hamilton thought otherwise. He opted to rely on the federal courts[1] to prevent political officials, and especially those of the new national government, from treating people unjustly. As he wrote in *Federalist* No. 78,
federal judges at every level would be duty-bound to review the constitutionality of laws touching on all cases brought to them and "pronounce
[any] void [if] contrary to the constitution."[2] By doing so, the federal
courts would act as an effective check on democratic majorities and compel them to reconsider "the effects of [their] ill humours."[3] Without the
courts' power of "judicial review," none of the constitutional limits on the
new government (such as the prohibition of bills of attainder and *ex post
facto* laws) could "be preserved in practice."

In drafting the Constitution, Hamilton and his fellow delegates at the Constitutional Convention in Philadelphia knew full well that the courts, and especially the Supreme Court of the United States, would encounter powerful political adversaries who would resent judicial interference and resist compliance. To enable the judiciary to defend itself against retaliation, the Constitution provided that "The judges, both of the supreme and inferior courts, shall hold their offices during good behavior." This conferral of lifetime tenure, Hamilton felt, was key to the Court's remaining independent and capable of resisting (in *The Federalist*'s delicate phrasing) "a disposition to consult popularity."

Getting to the U.S. Supreme Court

The Supreme Court today is understood to have the final say on constitutional matters. Whenever anybody feels that an official has denied him the personal freedom that he believes the Constitution guarantees, he can raise his objections in a court of "original jurisdiction" (popularly called a trial court). Should he lose, he is entitled to at least one appeal in a court of "appellate jurisdiction." This latter court will nearly always consist of three or more judges, whose job it is to assess (among other matters) whether the trial judge correctly determined any questions of constitutionality.

Should the complainant lose his appeal, he may, under some circumstances, be provided still further avenues of lawful redress, but eventually when they too are exhausted and he's left unsatisfied, he has the right to petition the U.S. Supreme Court to hear his case.

In the course of a year, several thousand such petitions come to the Supreme Court, all claiming to raise issues "arising under the constitution" and federal law. With nearly absolute discretion, the justices of the Court will pick among them and choose to review a few dozen. [4] (The process by which the Supreme Court selects a particular case for review is called *certiorari*, the Latin word for "to be made certain.") The Court can thus fashion its own agenda; it can even signal its future willingness to hear cases that raise issues of current concern to it.

In the beginning the Supreme Court appeared a "feeble" reed to oppose popular and legislative majorities determined to get their way. Indeed, whether the Court would survive its responsibilities was early in doubt. The first years were hardly auspicious. Its agenda was so trivial that several of the original justices, including Chief Justice John Jay, resigned from boredom. Symbolizing its lack of consequence was its first quarters. Tucked away in the bowels of the Capitol building in Washington, its courtroom was a thoroughly disagreeable space below the Senate chamber.[5] Here is a newspaper account of it:

> The apartment is not in a style which comports with the dignity of that body, or which wears a comparison with the other Halls of the Capitol. In the first place, it is like going down cellar to reach it. The room is in the basement story in an obscure part of the north wing [i.e., the Senate chamber]. In arriving at it, you pass a labyrinth and almost need the clue of Ariadne to guide you to the sanctuary of the blind goddess. A stranger might traverse the dark avenues of the Capitol for a week, without finding the remote corner in which justice is administered to the American republic, . . . a room which is hardly capacious enough for a ward Justice. . . . It is a triangular, semi-circular, odd-shaped apartment with three windows, and a profusion of arches in the ceiling. . . . Owing to the smallness of the room, the judges are compelled to put on their robes in the presence of the spectators, which is an awkward ceremony, and destroys the effect intended to be produced by assuming the gown.[6]

John Marshall, Chief Justice

However inconsequential were the Court's beginnings, over the centuries it has gained popular respect, coming to be accepted as the authoritative interpreter of the Constitution. The secret of its survival in its various confrontations with the elective branches of government has been a political prudence, a lesson the Court learned from its third chief justice, John Marshall, who presided over its affairs for thirty-four years, from 1801 to 1835.

Marshall was a Virginian and Thomas Jefferson's first cousin, but he and Jefferson despised each other. A mutual mistrust early developed between them, arising largely out of bitterly opposed political views. Marshall, a Federalist, was convinced that a vigorous central government was essential if the country were going to thrive commercially. Jefferson, an opponent of Federalist policies, was no less certain that a strong central government would be a danger to the country if it were to prosper agriculturally.

Marshall served America's second president, John Adams, as secretary of state. When Jefferson defeated Adams in the presidential election of 1800, Marshall and the outgoing president used the three-month hiatus between their defeat and Jefferson's inauguration to "pack" the judiciary.

The lame-duck Federalist Congress passed legislation that created new judgeships, which Adams and Marshall proceeded to fill with sympathetic partisans. Moreover, the president named Marshall to take the vacant position of chief justice of the Supreme Court.

The newly elected Congress was predominantly pro-Jefferson, and on taking office, it repealed the new judiciary act the previous Congress had just passed. It also refused to pay any of the new judges, in effect, abrogating their constitutionally guaranteed life tenure. It did not deny Marshall his seat on the Supreme Court, however, because doing so would have raised an even more troublesome constitutional question. The Supreme Court, unlike the inferior federal courts, which were created by statute, was established by the Constitution. Hence it seemed more dubious that appointments to it could be "repealed" by a congressional act.

Whatever the reasoning, the Jeffersonian legislature let Marshall's appointment stand. However, it forbade the Court to meet for the next two years, thereby preventing the justices from convening until 1803 and keeping Marshall and his colleagues from objecting to its high-handedness.

That Congress could so readily usurp the Court's authority did not bode well. It would take all of Marshall's cunning to save the Court.

From his position of grave political weakness, Marshall refrained from confronting the Jeffersonians directly, a battle he knew the Court could not win. He accepted the two-year moratorium demanded by Congress.

Marbury v. Madison

When the justices finally did convene in 1803, among the first cases on the Court's agenda was a matter entitled *Marbury v. Madison.*[7] *Marbury* presented the following facts. The final days of the Adams presidency in March 1801 were filled with frantic activity. In the offices of the secretary of state, Marshall and his staff were trying to complete the details of dozens of last-minute judicial appointments. They had had to find willing Federalists to appoint as judges, get their nominations to Congress for confirmation, and give each successful appointee his commission, consisting of a written document officially validating him as a federal judge.

Scribes prepared these commissions for the appointees in descending order of importance. At the lowest level were the minor judgeships, the justices of the peace who would be serving in the still inchoate District of Columbia. They had only a narrow authority to marry couples, punish misdemeanors, and resolve minor property disputes; in fact, they were so minor that they received no salary, but instead gained their livelihood from the fees and fines they levied for each transaction. Their dockets were penny-ante stuff.

When midnight rang on the last day of Adams's presidency, Jefferson's supporters rushed to the White House, evicted Marshall from his office, and locked the doors, behind which lay Marbury's commission, still undelivered.

Marbury was without a job unless he could get that document, but what was he to do? In theory, his recourse was to sue the secretary of state's office (now headed by James Madison) to compel the delivery of his commission. But in what court was he to originate his suit in 1801? No local courts existed in the District of Columbia, because the Jeffersonian Congress had repealed the legislation that had created them.

Marbury decided to bring his case to the only court in town, the Supreme Court of the United States, presided over by John Marshall, the very person who, as secretary of state, had failed to deliver the commissioning document in the first place.

Creating a Conflict of Laws

Consider the dilemma the case presented to Marshall. If he and his Court ordered Secretary of State Madison to turn the commission over to Marbury, Madison predictably would refuse to comply. That would demonstrate the Court's real impotence and set a dangerous political precedent of disobedience. If the Court denied Marbury his commission, its inaction would signify its subservience to the politically powerful and not to the rule of law.

Marshall turned his dilemma into a triumph. He did so by creating a conflict of laws. He construed—"distorted" might be a better word—the Judiciary Act of 1789, the one creating the federal judicial structure at the outset of the United States, so as to provide Marbury the right to originate his suit in the Supreme Court, and then found that that provision (as Marshall had interpreted it) violated the Constitution (as Marshall interpreted it), limiting the Supreme Court to hearing cases only on *appeal*. Having manufactured this constitutional conflict, Marshall's opinion *upheld* Madison and denied poor Marbury his day in court. At the same time, it claimed the Court's power of judicial review and the authority to void all legislation that it found was in violation of the Constitution.

He began the concluding part of his opinion with the (then) incontestable premise: "That the people have an original right to establish, for their future government, such principles as, in their opinion, shall most conduce to their own happiness, is the basis on which the whole American fabric has been erected. . . ." Continuing, he reminded "the people" that, in their new nation, "the powers of the legislature are defined and limited; and that those limits may not be mistaken or forgotten, the constitution [was] written." Then he posed this question: "To what purpose are powers limited . . . if these limits may, at any time, be passed by those intended to be restrained?" He provided this answer:

> The distinction between a government with limited and unlimited powers is abolished if those limits do not confine the persons on whom they are imposed and if acts prohibited and acts allowed are of equal obligation.

And to make sure that no one missed the point, he added:

> If an act of the legislature, repugnant to the constitution, is void, does it, notwithstanding its invalidity, bind the courts and oblige them to give it effect? Or, in other words, though it be not law, does it constitute a rule as operative as if it was a law? This would be to overthrow in fact what was established in theory, and [is] an absurdity too gross to be insisted on. . . .

And finally, with a flourish, he added the key assertion—the Supreme Court alone has the ultimate authority to interpret and apply the Constitution: "It is emphatically the province and duty of the judicial department to say what the law is. . . ."

In short, Marshall "rigged" the case so as to oblige future generations to accept the Court's distinctive role as protector of personal freedom from majority rule. Yes, the Jeffersonians won the inconsequential battle over Marbury's commission, but lost their war against the Hamiltonian principle that the Court was the ultimate guardian of the Constitution. As such, it had the authority to nullify legislation it thought to be oppressive.

For the remaining thirty-two years of his tenure Marshall combined a prudent regard for political realities with a tactical dexterity *and* a long-range vision of a central government strong enough to promote commercial freedom across the continent in the face of efforts by the states to confine it.[8] He used his brilliant legal mind to persuade his fellow justices to adopt his Federalist vision. In the Washington boarding house where the justices slept, ate, and spent countless hours together, discussing the law and the future of their new country, his influence over his colleagues was magnified.

The Power of Judicial Review

In the coming centuries the Court would use its power of judicial review to safeguard all kinds of personal liberty—the freedoms of slaveholders, employers, unpopular spokespeople, crusading publishers, ethnic minorities, women, and religious sects.[9]

The justices have not always gotten their way. President Andrew Jackson refused to renew the charter of the Bank of the United States after the Court upheld its constitutionality. Moreover, the American Civil War "reversed" the notorious decision in *Dred Scott v. Sandford*, which had upheld the freedom of slaveholders to retain their slaves in "free" states. Seventy years later President Franklin Roosevelt, a Democrat, appointed his kind of justices to overrule earlier decisions protecting employers' freedom to contract with their workers.[10] Twenty years after that, the Court had to depend on the willingness of President Dwight Eisenhower, a Republican, to send the National Guard into Little Rock, Arkansas, to enforce the integration of black students in a previously all-white high school.[11] And as recently as 1992, stiff legislative resistance compelled the Court to retreat from a line of decision that had given women unconditional discretion to terminate their pregnancies.[12]

But generally, when the Supreme Court has handed down a decision, effective opposition has never materialized: critics have often looked formidable in anticipation, but then quietly submitted in the event. Think about *Bush v. Gore*,[13] the case that put an end to the litigation concerning the presidential election in 2000. For more than a month, the ballot counts in several Florida counties were disputed in both the state and federal courts, with Al Gore, the Democrat, sometimes prevailing on the legal issues and George W. Bush, the Republican, sometimes emerging victorious. Then the Supreme Court stepped in and essentially said, "Stop all further recounts, and stop *now*. Bush wins." Law school critics and disappointed Democratic activists said the opinion was defective; the *New York Times* reacted with passion and verbal abuse, declaring the Court guilty of judicial tyranny. And the people's reaction? They appeared calm, acquiescent, and appreciative that the Court had used its authority to put an end to a disruptive conflict.

Why? What explains such ready submission to the Court's judgments? What enables the Court to get its way?[14] To that question, we now turn.

NOTES

1. Article III of the Constitution reads, in part: "The judicial power of the United States, shall be vested in one supreme court, and in such inferior courts as the Congress may, from time to time, ordain and establish. The judges, both of the supreme and inferior courts, shall hold their offices during good behavior. . . . The judicial power shall extend to all cases . . . arising under this Constitution, the laws of the United States, and treaties . . . made under their authority [and] between citizens of different states. . . ."

2. All quotations in this section, unless otherwise attributed, come from *Federalist* No. 78.

3. "This independence of the judges is . . . requisite to guard the constitution and the rights of individuals from the effects of these ill humours which the arts of designing men [i.e., demagogues] or the influence of particular conjunctures, sometimes disseminate among the people themselves and which, though they speedily give place to better information and more deliberate reflection, have a tendency in the mean time to occasion dangerous innovations in the government, and serious oppressions of the minor party in the community." *Federalist* No. 78.

4. The remainder of the Court's annual agenda of seventy-five (or more) consists of matters relating to the interpretation of *federal* statutes and regulations.

5. Short of funds, Congress had never appropriated moneys to build the courthouse originally planned. The Court continued to conduct its business in this abysmal basement hole until 1935, when a separate Supreme Court building finally was constructed across the street from the Capitol.

6. *New York Statesman,* February 7, 1824, as quoted in Charles Warren, *The Supreme Court in United States History,* rev. ed. (Boston: Little, Brown, 1926), vol. 1, 460–461.

7. *Marbury v. Madison,* 5 U.S. 137 (1803).

8. E.g., *McCulloch v. Maryland,* 17 U.S. 316 (1819), protecting the Bank of the United States from a state's effort to put it out of business.

9. E.g., *Dred Scott v. Sandford,* 60 U.S. 393 (1856), holding that a slaveholder has a right to retain ownership of his slave, no matter the state of his residence; *Lochner v. New York,* 198 U.S. 45 (1905), holding that an employer and his workers are free to negotiate the terms of employment regarding hours of work; *Feiner v. New York,* 340 U.S. 315 (1951), asserting that local governments must protect speakers from a "hostile audience"; *Near v. Minnesota,* 283 U.S. 697 (1931), nullifying a restraint on political criticism prior to its publication; *Brown v. Board of Education,* 347 U.S. 483 (1954), upholding black students'

right to go to public schools with white ones; and *Akron v. Akron Center for Reproductive Health, Inc.,* 462 U.S. 416 (1983), upholding a woman's freedom to have an immediate abortion without having to wait twenty-four hours.

10. The New Deal's "Court-packing" efforts are superbly chronicled in Joseph Alsop and Turner Catledge, *The 168 Days* (Garden City, N.Y.: Doubleday, 1938).

11. Henry Hampton's magnificent television documentary *Eyes on the Prize* preserves the memory of this tumultuous event (and of similar confrontations during the Kennedy and Johnson presidencies).

12. *Planned Parenthood of Southeastern Pennsylvania v. Casey,* 505 U.S. 833 (1992), sustaining five important legislative regulations governing the provision of abortion services.

13. *Bush v. Gore,* 531 U.S. 98 (2000).

14. Gerald N. Rosenberg's *The Hollow Hope: Can Courts Bring about Social Change?* (Chicago: University of Chicago Press, 1991) thoughtfully addresses this same question.

19

THE MORAL POWER OF THE COURTS

[T]he judiciary, from the nature of its functions, will always be the least dangerous to the political rights of the Constitution. . . .

Alexander Hamilton, *Federalist* No. 78 (1788)

In *Federalist* No. 78 Hamilton declared that courts would be "the weakest of the three departments of power," suffering "the natural feebleness of the judiciary" and "constantly in danger of being overpowered":

> The Executive . . . holds the sword of the community. The legislature . . . commands the purse. . . . The judiciary, on the contrary, has no influence over either the sword or the purse; no direction either of the strength or of the wealth of the society; and can take no active resolution whatever. It may truly be said to have neither FORCE nor WILL, but merely judgment; and must ultimately depend upon the aid of the executive arm even for the efficacy of its judgments.

That is, if the federal judiciary encountered political resistance to its orders, it had neither coercive power ("influence over the sword") nor reciprocal power ("influence over . . . the purse") to compel compliance. It "merely" had moral power ("judgment") to get its way. Unless it could convince others to embrace its ideas and act on them, it would be stymied.

But reality is not quite so simple as Hamilton made it sound. The judiciary's moral power may not be so weak as he suggested if the justices of the Supreme Court would employ political skills of a high order to augment their "judgments." By way of illustration, I want to contrast two instances: one where the Court succeeded in shaping attitudes, and the other where it badly botched its attempt at social change.

The Due Process Revolution

Characteristically, policing in the United States has been a local affair. There has never been a national police department with general jurisdiction. The control of "crime," as we normally think of it (murder, robbery, burglary, and the like), is left to local police departments.

Admittedly, over the centuries Congress has established units to enforce laws relating to particularized subject matters: immigration, prohibition of alcohol in the 1920s, and interstate racketeering, for example. The Constitution's Fourth, Fifth, and Sixth Amendments directly apply to federal agencies and regulate their practices—their arrests, searches, interrogations, and trial procedures.

These same limits, however, did *not* apply to state and local law enforcement. Regulating the behaviors of municipal, county, and state police was understood to be the sole responsibility of local jurisdictions. So long as local police didn't deprive anyone of their "liberty *without due process of law*," the relatively permissive standard set out by the Fourteenth Amendment, their actions passed judicial scrutiny. As a result, police practices varied widely throughout the nation. Some departments were scrupulous in training and overseeing their officers' actions. Elsewhere, particularly in the southern states, where police functioned to maintain an extralegal system of racial oppression, officers were notorious for abusing persons with impunity. And the bulk of American law enforcement agencies simply left their patrolmen and detectives alone to devise their own practices in accord with the desires of the local political culture.

That was largely the case until 1961, when the Supreme Court transformed these widely variant operations. Case by case, it prescribed a uniform set of procedures limiting police discretion and condemning a range of enforcement methods previously accepted as legitimate. The Court "incorporated" the limits applicable to federal officers into the Fourteenth Amendment's requirement of "due process." It specified that the public had rights to be free from unreasonable searches, strenuous interrogations, and biased judicial treatment—even from certain practices that had been praised by experts the decade before. Observers of the Court dubbed its effort to reform America's policing the "Due Process Revolution."

Earl Warren, Chief Justice

The heart and soul of this "revolution" was the Court's chief justice, Earl Warren. Born in 1891, Warren grew up in Bakersfield, California, a town then known for being tough and vice-ridden. Following graduation from law school and service in the First World War, he went to work as a prosecutor in the Alameda County district attorney's office in Northern California. His boss was well regarded for his insistence on competence, honesty, and regard for suspects' rights; the office, for example, established the nation's first public defender program in 1919 to provide free legal counsel to indigent criminal defendants.

As a prosecutor, Warren met and befriended a local police chief named August Vollmer. Vollmer was a visionary, and in numerous discussions with Warren he pointed out the reforms he was making in his relatively small Berkeley police department; he was requiring a college education of his officers, giving them extensive training throughout their careers, and establishing internal procedures to investigate and discipline cases of police abuse or corruption.

In time Warren was elected the county's district attorney and gained a national reputation for being tough and fair. In 1938 he won statewide election and became California's attorney general. As such, he was the state official who concurred in the federal government's decision to evacuate all persons of Japanese ancestry living near the Pacific coast in the aftermath of Japan's attack on Pearl Harbor, Hawaii, in December 1941[1]—a decision he later deeply regretted.

In 1942 Warren, a Republican, went on to become governor of California, and he was reelected twice more—in 1946 and 1950. He was instrumental in the Republican National Convention that nominated Dwight Eisenhower for president in 1952, swinging the state's delegation behind the former general.

Then, in September 1953, less than a year after Eisenhower's inauguration as president, the unexpected occurred, one of those fortunate events that lead foreign observers to declare America the luckiest nation on Earth. It happened that the landmark civil rights case *Brown v. Board of Education*,[2] which questioned the constitutionality of racial segregation in public schools, had been argued before the Supreme Court in 1952. Several of the justices, unable to have the case decided to their satisfaction, requested additional argument, and the matter was set over for rehearing in the next term. The chief justice at the time was Fred Vinson, a former representative from Kentucky. Of the justices, he was the most opposed to overturning the "separate but equal" doctrine that permitted governments to segregate black Americans from white Americans throughout the South. All during his long political career he had favored segregation of the races. Regrettably for Vinson, but propitiously for the nation, he died on September 8, 1953, just three weeks before the Court was scheduled to begin its 1953 term. President Eisenhower acted quickly to give Warren an interim appointment as chief justice to replace Vinson (there was insufficient time for Senate confirmation). On December 7, 1953, Warren was in place to preside over the reargument of *Brown v. Board*. In the next five months Warren convinced his colleagues that, whatever the Court decided, the opinion must be a unanimous one.[3] On May 17, 1954, Warren as author announced the opinion of the Court that governmentally enforced separation of the races was unconstitutional. Virtually every observer of the Court has concluded that were it not for Warren's influential presence, the opinion would not have been unanimous; nor would it have been as compelling and forceful.[4]

That is, Warren's presence as "the Chief" (as he came to be called) mattered in 1953, and thanks to his leadership over the next sixteen years the Court went on from its decision in *Brown* to further the civil rights of minorities in other ways. Every manifestation of legalized racial discrimination was obliterated from the law books; the voting process was cleared of the obstacles that had long prevented minorities from fully participating in elections—the poll tax, literacy tests, citizenship tests, differently sized legislative districts that diluted the black vote, and the like.

And they were years when the Court—through literally dozens of decisions—civilized police treatment of black Americans and other vulnerable minorities.[5]

Transforming Police Attitudes

One could hardly imagine a more difficult job than transforming police behavior and the attitudes underlying it. Policing is the archetypical profession; the very definition of policing is individual discretion. Police work involves personal danger to the officer and is performed under circumstances that vary every day. One day officers confront the homeless and denizens of skid row; the next they're dealing with family beefs, in which spouse is pitted against spouse, or kids against parents, or brother against brother, and doing it in the family's home where only family members know where the knives and guns are; the day after that they're dealing with gang warfare or a neighborhood beef; and the next day they are confronting a crowd of juveniles shoplifting.[6] There is no effective way to control police with rules; it's their outlooks, personal courage, ingenuity, and self-restraint that effectively govern how ably they're going to handle these constantly changing conditions. To change police behavior, it's necessary to transform the deeply held ideas of the individual police officer—and transformation is a problem of moral power.

Earl Warren's prior career in law enforcement and his enduring friendship with Chief Vollmer were ideal preparation for understanding the typical police officer's mindset, with its particular standards of honor and its possible shortcomings in doling out justice in minority communities. That he came from California also helped, for in many ways that state was ahead of its times in "professionalizing" its police departments. By 1960 many of its principal cities had begun to follow Vollmer's example and instituted training programs for their recruits, had eliminated most police corruption, and had set higher recruiting standards in terms of formal education and psychological balance. The state had also reformed its rules of criminal procedure, established an effective public defender's office in every county, imposed limits on the means of obtaining confessions and the conduct of searches, and enforced those limits by excluding at trial all illegally obtained evidence.

When opponents later objected to the reforms that the Warren Court incorporated into the Constitution, Warren had a ready answer: personal experience. He had prosecuted cases under those rules and won convictions. That was a convincing rebuttal.

In six years, from 1961 to 1966, the Warren Court selected numerous cases raising questions about local police practices—for example, warrantless searches of suspects in their homes, tricking or frightening suspects into confessing, detaining them in solitary custody without lawyers, arresting suspicious persons on unarticulated hunches, and using a defendant's choice not to take the witness stand as evidence of guilt. (Some of these practices were taught in academies and police textbooks as "best practices.") Of these cases, the two crucial ones were *Mapp v. Ohio*[7] and *Gideon v. Wainwright*.[8] They were the foundations of the Due Process Revolution.

The Capability to Take Hostages

Warren and his Court anticipated resistance by police, prosecutors, judges, and the general public. They knew that unless threatened, those in opposition would simply disregard the Court's orders. But to threaten the police into paying attention, the Court had to "take hostages"—had to demonstrate it had both the capability and the will to injure something that the police themselves valued. The hostage it identified was the individual cop's moral passion to remove "bad guys" from the streets and prevent them from doing further harm to people.

The key was to condition conviction and incarceration on police officers' compliance with the new limitations on their behavior. In that way the Court could "extort" adherence to its standards. In *Mapp v. Ohio* (1961), the Warren Court ruled that evidence seized by local police in a wrongful search and seizure was constitutionally inadmissible in state courts. That meant that unless the police officer was willing to risk the exclusion at trial of important incriminating evidence (like the murder weapon, illegal drugs, gambling paraphernalia, and child pornography), he would have to go to a judge and obtain a warrant specifying what he was looking for and where he intended to search for it.

In many cities up to that time, police had never needed a search warrant. The typical police officer probably did not even know what he had to do to get one. He undoubtedly also suspected—rightly—that if he went to get one, spies in the courthouse would tip off the intended subjects of the search to clear out before the police arrived. After *Mapp*, however, his passion to win a conviction usually overpowered any temptation to cut procedural corners.

The Commitment to Harm Hostages

But there was a big "if" in the Court's threat. The Supreme Court, sitting in Washington, D.C., needed the state courts to investigate allegations of police misconduct, exclude evidence, and let an obviously harmful person go free. How would the "will" of local judges to carry out the threat of freeing wrongdoers be demonstrated to the police?

The answer was to provide criminal suspects with skilled legal counsel who were capable of identifying offensive police practices and were committed to eliminating them, no matter the cost. Most criminal suspects, however, were too poor to pay for competent lawyers.

Here was where the Court's unanimous decision in *Gideon v. Wainwright* (1963) was key. The facts involved a down-on-his-luck vagrant named Clarence Earl Gideon, who had been charged with stealing coins from a cigarette vending machine and convicted of burglary. To all appearances, the case seemed open and shut: Gideon had a long criminal record of petty thievery. He didn't have a job. And his pockets at the time of his apprehension were full of nickels, dimes, and quarters—the stuff of vending machines. Moreover, there was an eyewitness who saw Gideon break into the saloon and pry open the vending machine in question.

Fortunately for Gideon, however, he had asked the trial judge to provide him a lawyer at the state's expense, a request the judge had refused. After Gideon was convicted, he appealed. Eventually his case reached the U.S. Supreme Court, which reversed his conviction, holding that states must provide free legal assistance to any indigent defendant charged with a felony.[9] The Court, lacking the power of the purse, had to leave it to the states to figure out how to fund these legal services.

Needless to say, requiring the states to spend taxpayers' money to pay for skilled criminal defense lawyers did not sit well with the general public or the legislators who represented them. It offended groups who thought more money should be spent on improving things that mattered, like better schools, highways, and health and welfare programs. Compared to those needs, most taxpayers thought it a waste of their taxes to *defend* society's predators.

But Warren and his colleagues on the Court knew a practical thing about the law profession. They anticipated that lawyers would see in the *Gideon* decision a potential bounty of steady income. Criminal defense lawyers would have more paying clients, and prosecutors would have to enlarge their legal staffs to handle bigger caseloads. Lawyers would use their political clout and knowledge of legislatures and their appropriations committees to lobby for funding with great effectiveness. The Court guessed right: once the lawyers descended on state capitals and made their case, resistance to funding public defenders' offices wilted.

With lawyers, poor defendants began regularly insisting on their rights. (And in case any state court failed to recognize those rights, the Supreme Court developed a procedure whereby defendants could appeal to a local federal judge to overrule their convictions and set them free.[10]) In response, trial courts throughout the nation established a procedure that has become standard today. It works by transforming every prosecution into a double trial. The first trial is of the police officers involved in the case—who are, in effect, charged (by the defendant) with misconduct.

Only if the police defeat the charges would there be a second trial, that of the alleged murderer, rapist, robber, or assailant. To a Martian, this "double trial" might seem ludicrous. Contemporary Americans—even police themselves—have become accustomed to it.

I have oversimplified the story—but not much. Despite my omission of some interesting details, the reader can accurately assess the Court's political ingenuity in maneuvering the coercive and reciprocal power of state judges and legislatures. Once police departments were faced with the prospect of losing convictions, they expanded their training programs carefully to teach their officers the restrictions the Court was imposing on searches, arrests, and interrogations.

Moreover, the instructors of constitutional law in police academies tended not only to teach the rules but also embraced the reasons—the ideas—underlying them. And to augment the formal training, judges and prosecutors would take time to explain to police officers the value and workability of the constitutional limitations.

Confronting the Paradoxes of Moral Power

This careful teaching by trustworthy instructors was vital to overcoming the paradoxes of moral power. Keep in mind that experienced police—the veterans who entered their profession before the Warren Court's Due Process Revolution began—had taken pride in keeping people safe by anticipating the crimes that cunning, "street-smart" bad guys were intending to do, nipping their wrongdoing in the bud. The best officers were proud of the investigative practices they had developed and found effective, and they sensed the Warren Court's due process decisions as attacks on their self-esteem; the justices' opinions seemed to suggest that police were bullies and that the criminals they outwitted were really ignorant unfortunates. The paradox of responsibility, that people resist dishonoring their past actions, came into play.

So too did the paradox of perception—*believing is seeing*. When the Warren Court began requiring police to specify with greater exactitude the clues behind their hunches, they became confused and uncertain. Heretofore, suspicious individuals could be identified by certain telltale indications—their race, joblessness, or loitering; their being "out of place"; and their having a "bad attitude." The Warren Court's rules about searches and arrests, often administered by local judges who lacked "street" experience, required police to articulate the reasons for their hunches. Experienced officers were left to wonder if the Warren Court's rules oblige police to blind themselves to the clues they previously looked for—signs that, if detected, might save their lives and those of others?

Finally, the paradox of social order—*social order abhors change, even when change is necessary to preserve it*—functioned to strengthen police solidarity. Any cop tempted to justify the Court's way of thinking to his fellow officers was likely to be condemned as a renegade, an outcast in a profession that depended on selfless teamwork to survive in a dangerous world. The pressures to conform to the beliefs prevalent in a police department were hard to resist.

Many observers of the Warren Court lamented that its efforts to transform police thinking would fail. They called the reforms it was attempting a "self-inflicted wound."[11] Their predictions proved wrong, however, for the Warren Court understood the political nature and limits of judicial power.

The Successful Exercise of Moral Power

The Court was assisted by lucky accidents. One piece of good fortune was a best-selling book about *Gideon v. Wainwright*, elegantly and accessibly written by journalist Anthony Lewis. His *Gideon's Trumpet*[12] became required reading in America's high schools and colleges and helped tip public opinion to embrace the Court's ideas. The public's support in turn influenced the police to change. Lewis's character sketch of Gideon turned a harmless ne'er-do-well into a national saint. The book told how a harmless American, wrongly convicted of a crime when he lacked legal representation, was able to establish his innocence when he had court-appointed counsel. (Making the story even more dramatic, the principal witness against Gideon, on cross-examination, all but admitted that it was he who had broken into the vending machine—fitting testimony to the value of a competent lawyer.[13])

A second stroke of luck was that *Mapp* and *Gideon* won the praises of professors in the nation's numerous law schools. The opinions were coherent and, more importantly, they set out rules and defined procedures that academics had anticipated. Law professors' sympathetic embrace of the pair of opinions in turn engendered a favorable reaction in their students— the future law profession.

It is undeniable, nevertheless, that the Court created some of its own luck. One example is a case it selected in 1968, *Terry v. Ohio*,[14] for review. The facts involved a policeman with thirty-five years of experience, a detective named Martin J. McFadden, who had stopped and searched two young men on the basis of a hunch that their suspicious behavior "didn't look right to me." McFadden surmised that they were "casing" a jewelry store before they robbed it at gunpoint; he then confronted them, patted them down, and found two revolvers concealed in the pockets of their coats, whereupon he arrested them. Warren personally wrote the opinion, commending Detective McFadden's work. The officer, according to Warren, had "confined his search strictly to what was minimally necessary to learn whether the men were armed and to disarm them once he discovered the weapons"; his was "the tempered act of a policeman who in the course of an investigation had to make a quick decision as to how to protect himself and others from possible danger." Warren also emphasized the risks police officers run and their courage to serve despite them ("American criminals have a long tradition of armed violence, and every year in this country many law enforcement officers are killed in the line of duty, and thousands more are wounded"). Finally, Warren set out a detailed mode by which policemen could do their job safely and effectively. He concluded his opinion this way:[15]

> We think on the facts and circumstances Officer McFadden detailed before the trial judge, a reasonably prudent man, would have been warranted in believing petitioner was armed and thus presented a threat to the officer's safety while he was investigating his suspicious behavior. The actions of Terry and Chilton [the suspects] were consistent with McFadden's hypothesis that these men were contemplating a daylight robbery—which, it is reasonable to assume, would be likely to involve the use of weapons—and nothing in their conduct from the time he first noticed them until the time he confronted them and identified himself as a police officer gave him sufficient reason to negate that hypothesis.

Warren's opinion in *Terry v. Ohio* accomplished three important goals. First, it resolved the paradox of perception by clarifying much of the confusion regarding the legitimacy of the policeman's "hunch" (his unrefuted "hypothesis"). Second, it honored the public service and courage of police work, thereby taking the sting out of the paradox of responsibility. And three, it capitalized on the paradox of social order by providing a workable standard around which police might unite (commending Officer McFadden as a role model).

In short, *Terry v. Ohio* undercut police resistance to the Due Process Revolution. As an exercise of effective moral power, Warren's opinion was a practically perfect example.

Moral Power with Little Forethought

For contrast, let's briefly look at the Court's later bumbling in transforming the public's moral attitudes about abortion. Four years after Earl Warren retired as chief justice, the Court decided *Roe v. Wade* (1973),[16] in which the Court voided all state laws pertaining to medical procedures terminating "unwanted" pregnancies prior to birth. Even today, almost four decades later, *Roe* remains the cause of passionate social contention, even violence; it has polarized our political parties as no other issue has since slavery; and it still undermines respect for the Court in many quarters.

What went wrong? First, *Roe*, by voiding government restrictions on abortions in the name of the "privacy" of the doctor-patient relationship, made no connection to what Hamilton called "the manifest tenor"—the words—of the Constitution. Whereas in *Mapp* and *Gideon* the Court invoked the language of the Bill of Rights condemning unreasonable searches and denial of legal counsel, the opinion in *Roe v. Wade* invoked a right—"privacy"—not mentioned anywhere in the Constitution. As a result, the decision seemed arbitrary and beyond the Court's legal competence.

Second, the opinion surprised lawyers. It left the legal community without a set of arguments adequate to the task of disarming public revulsion toward abortion. Its failure to assess the competing moral values involved left lawyers with nothing convincing to say to their troubled clients (e.g. hospitals and nurses) about the acceptability of killing "babies." Consider, for example, the paralyzing dilemma facing an obstetrical nurse who, one day, might spend eight emergency-filled hours saving a prematurely born child, yet the next day be required to participate in the abortion of an equally developed infant.[17] Nowhere in the Court's opinion in *Roe* did the justices confront the moral argument that unborn children are living beings whose existences were being snuffed out with premeditation.

Third, law faculties, while generally approving the outcome of *Roe*, heaped scorn in their classrooms and legal periodicals on the clumsiness of its legal reasoning. Under these circumstances, where the Court exercised its moral power with so little forethought, is it any wonder that the Court's attempt at peaceful social change was doomed to fail?[18]

"What Enables the Court to Get Its Way?"

We return to the question we asked at the end of the previous chapter: What enables the Supreme Court to get its way? If all it possesses is the power of "judgment," as Hamilton insisted, success would seem impossible, for moral power requires the alteration of deeply felt beliefs. In the case of police, the Warren Court sought to change an entire culture, a tangled and deeply embedded web of attitudes bearing on the officers' demanding and dangerous work, and to do it without disabling their skills of anticipation, dishonoring their earlier achievements, or undermining their teamwork. That the Warren Court was successful in avoiding widespread demoralization—*anomie*—is the measure of its real political skill. By finding ways to mobilize allies to use *their* power on its behalf and then providing police and prosecutors the language with which to change their attitudes, it transformed law enforcement in the United States.

One cannot overstate the significance of the Warren Court's accomplishment, for it is necessary to keep in mind three truths: personal freedom depends on social order; social order depends on "a well-regulated"[19] police power; and, lastly, a badly regulated police is a terrible danger to personal freedom. If a society's professional protectors—the police officer, the sheriff, the soldier—lack the right beliefs to curb the discretion that comes with their authority, they become oppressors. Then the people, lacking safety and the specialists required to provide it, have no choice but to build their own safe havens and devote the bulk of their time and energies to maintaining them.

NOTES

1. The constitutionality of the Japanese American internment was upheld in *Korematsu v. United States*, 323 U.S. 214 (1944). In 1988 Congress formally apologized for the injustice done and voted to give $20,000 to each surviving Japanese American internee.
2. *Brown v. Board of Education*, 347 U.S. 483 (1954).
3. The story is vividly told in Richard Kluger, *Simple Justice: The History of* Brown v. Board of Education *and Black America's Struggle for Equality* (New York: Knopf, 1976).
4. No one can be certain that Warren's decisive leadership resulted from his regret over his role in relocating innocent Japanese Americans at the outset of World War II. In 1969 Warren, now retired, taught several courses at his alma mater. During one seminar, he remarked that the biggest mistake of his political career was agreeing to the internment of the Japanese Americans. For me, it

is certainly conceivable that that "mistake" fixed his determination to get the African American case "right."

5. Not everybody was enthusiastic about Warren's leadership, including a few of his colleagues. In an interview in 1983, retired justice Potter Stewart said, "I think that Chief Justice Warren, for whom I have great admiration and great affection, sometimes was guided by what he thought was right or wrong rather than by the law. His best friend or greatest admirer would not say he was a great lawyer or great legal scholar. He wasn't and he didn't pretend to be. That was part of his greatness. But I think he went wrong sometimes." "The Law and Potter Stewart," *American Heritage Magazine* 35, no. 1 (December 1983).

6. See William K. Muir Jr., *Police: Streetcorner Politicians* (Chicago: University of Chicago Press, 1977).

7. *Mapp v. Ohio,* 367 U.S. 643 (1961).

8. *Gideon v. Wainwright,* 372 U.S. 335 (1963).

9. It ruled that the Fourteenth Amendment had incorporated the Sixth Amendment's right of the accused "to have the Assistance of Counsel for his defense."

10. The procedure, known as *habeas corpus,* permitted defendants, convicted on the basis of "inadmissible evidence," to appeal to federal district court and be set free, even when the states' highest courts had decided otherwise. See, for example, *Fay v. Noia,* 372 U.S. 391 (1963).

11. For example, Fred Graham, CBS's commentator on the Supreme Court, wrote a book he called *The Self-Inflicted Wound* (New York: Macmillan, 1970). Eight years later, in its revised second edition, the book had been retitled *The Due Process Revolution: The Warren Court's Impact on Criminal Law* (New York: Haydon Books, 1978).

12. Anthony Lewis, *Gideon's Trumpet* (New York: Random House, 1964).

13. To appreciate the Court's good fortune, suppose Lewis's book had been about a vicious defendant (unlike Gideon) who, on release as a result of some "legal technicality" dreamed up by an unscrupulous defense lawyer, had returned to society and immediately massacred a family. The general public's reaction to the Court's Due Process Revolution might have been considerably different.

14. *Terry v. Ohio,* 392 U.S. 1 (1968).

15. Ibid., 392 U.S. 1, at 28.

16. *Roe v. Wade,* 410 U.S. 113 (1973).

17. This and other illustrative instances of moral conflict resulting from *Roe v. Wade* appear in Kristin Luker's revealing book, *Abortion and the Politics of Motherhood* (Berkeley: University of California Press, 1984).

18. Furthermore, the Court encountered bad luck. There was no *Gideon's Trumpet* to sing its praises. Quite the contrary: when Kristin Luker, a sincere feminist and proponent of legalized abortion, wrote her influential book, *Abortion and the Politics of Motherhood,* she was compelled by her research to characterize the

women who opposed *Roe v. Wade* as heroic and selfless defenders of the sanc-
tity of human life. A second piece of bad luck: Jane Roe, the plaintiff in *Roe v.
Wade,* far from being a saint like Gideon, turned out to have lied about how she
became pregnant. Worst of all, she later converted to fundamentalist Christianity and confessed her remorse over killing her unborn child.

19. I have borrowed the phrase from the Second Amendment to the Constitution:
"A well-regulated militia [i.e., national guard] being necessary to the security
of a free state, the right of the people to keep and bear arms shall not be
infringed."

20

POLITICAL PARTIES: MACHINES, COALITIONS, CHURCHES

> *[A] pure Democracy, by which I mean, a society, consisting of a small number of citizens, who assemble and administer the Government in person, can admit of no cure for the mischiefs of faction. A common passion or interest will, in almost every case, be felt by a majority of the whole; a communication and conceit results from the form of Government itself; and there is nothing to check the inducements to sacrifice the weaker party, or an obnoxious individual.*

James Madison, Federalist No. 10 (1787)

In *Federalist* No. 51 Madison stated the central issue addressed by the Constitutional Convention:

> In framing a government which is to be administered by men over men, the great difficulty lies in this: you must first enable the government to control the governed; and in the next place oblige it to control itself. . . . A dependence on the people is no doubt the primary control on the government. . . .

But Madison had reservations about democratic elections. For one thing, no great nation had ever tried truly democratic elections in which every man had the right to vote. The second reason was more theoretical.

The people would have no obvious political restraint, nothing to check and balance their power. What would check the "people" if they were ever to be startled by "a common passion or interest"? Suppose that the public, once invested with the vote, turned tyrannical?

Certainly, the one nonelective department, the courts—the weakest branch of government—would be no match for a misled, panicked, or enraged citizenry denying freedom to a few. Therefore, Madison throughout his *Federalist* essays promoted what he called "auxiliary" controls—a balance of power within the government itself:

> [E]xperience has taught mankind the necessity of auxiliary precautions. This policy of supplying by opposite and rival interests, the defect of better motives, might be traced through the whole system of human affairs, private as well as public. . . . These inventions of prudence [are] requisite in the distribution of the supreme powers of the state.

Madison gave fullest expression to his anxieties relating to democratic tyranny in *Federalist* No. 10. One must assume, he wrote, that the people will organize into a multiplicity of groups based on like-mindedness and common interests. Shoemakers, old people, lawyers, environmentalists, persons of faith, and the like—these he called "factions." Today we call them "interest groups" or, more invidiously, "the *special* interests." Although Madison decried factions for "the mischiefs" they might do, he had no doubts that they were an inevitable part of a free society, remarking that "[t]he latent causes of faction are . . . sown in the nature of man."

In fact, however, he worried very little about interest groups, foreseeing that their clashes would in all likelihood generate fruitful and just compromise between them. Rather, the nightmare that haunted him was majority tyranny: What would happen if there were no competing factions to balance one another? What if all the people, save a few, were of one mind and demanded the satisfaction of their interests at the expense of those few outsiders? What would check an overwhelming public opinion that subscribed to Nazism, racial apartheid, or radical Islamic fundamentalism? Madison expressed the possibility this way:

> A common passion or interest will . . . be felt by a majority of the whole; a communication and conceit results from the form of Government itself; and there is nothing to check the inducements to sacrifice the weaker party, or an obnoxious individual. Hence, it is, that such democracies have ever

been spectacles of turbulence and contention; have ever been found incompatible with personal security, or the rights of property; and have in general been as short in their lives, as they have been violent in their deaths.

What did Madison prescribe to "cure" this danger inherent in a free society? He urged his fellow Americans to "extend the sphere": that is, they should open up the frontier, expand into new territories, and flood the continent with a civilization founded on personal freedom. By so doing "you take in a greater variety of parties and interests." That is, you increase the diversity of opinion and multiply the number of factions, heightening the competition among them.

Consider how radical Madison's thinking was. From the times of ancient Greece to the European Enlightenment of the eighteenth century, the conventional wisdom had been that small was beautiful—that the ideal size of a free republic was modest, about the size of present-day Montenegro or Switzerland. Any state much more extensive made popular participation in government impossible. That position Madison rejected (just as he would condemn its present-day incarnation in the principle of national self-determination, which has justified the breakups of such nations as the Soviet Union, Yugoslavia, India, and Czechoslovakia).

America took Madison's advice and expanded its sphere westward, and the resulting regional differences, arguably, have reduced the possibility of majority tyranny at the federal level. But in this chapter a case is made that an even greater safeguard against the "mischiefs of faction" has been the development of America's *national two-party* political system.

A Competitive Two-Party System

Political parties are private organizations. The Constitution makes no mention of them, and they have no official authority. George Washington, in his farewell address in 1796, inveighed against them, declaring them "truly the worst enemy" of democracies. Madison initially felt likewise, decrying parties in *Federalist* No. 10 because they caused "instability, injustice, and confusion" in "the public councils." Parties, in his experience, inhibited the exercise of independent judgment on the part of the representatives. They tended to thrust into leadership not "enlightened statesmen" but, rather, "ambitious" politicians, "contending for pre-eminence and power," who dictated that party members had to vote together as a unified group without regard for "the public good."

(The irony, of course, is that within a half-decade of writing *Federalist No. 10*, Madison, having denounced political parties and their "bosses," organized the Democratic-Republican Party, which endures to this day as the Democratic Party.)

Have American political parties contributed to political instability, injustice, and confusion (as Madison *feared*)? Or have they actually benefited the nation (as Madison arguably *came to believe*) by providing the missing balance necessary to check and moderate the force of public opinion?

To answer those questions, it is important to understand what parties actually do in a politically *competitive* two-party system. Keep in mind the word *competitive*.

As the legendary elephant was perceived by the blind men, so political parties have been seen to operate in three very different ways: as machines, coalitions, and churches.

Parties as Machines

Typically, journalists adopt the first view: a party operates like a "political machine." To their way of thinking, each party is in the business of exchanging patronage for support—for votes or the resources necessary to attract votes. It doles out promises in order to woo the electorate away from its competitor party. In exchange for such goodies as a drug prescription plan, an air force base in a congressional district,[1] a judgeship, a decision to withdraw the military from "harm's way," or "earmarks" to fund a local museum or a bridge to nowhere, a party wins support for its candidates from a region, interest group, or influential individual (who presumably has contributed campaign funding necessary to winning the elections).

In this give-and-take, economic[2] view of things, the two rival parties (Republicans on the one hand and Democrats on the other) act like a pair of giant corporations competing for market share in the marketplace they dominate. They do market research by sending out "representatives" to discover the current needs of their customers, the electorate. Then they produce the products (or the promises of products) the electorate wants and are repaid in support. In this perspective of reciprocity, the rival parties pursue no other goal but to stay in office—the equivalent of turning a profit.

Accordingly, one would expect Republicans and Democrats to behave like General Motors and Toyota or Safeway and Lucky's Markets. They would converge.

To illustrate how a commercial duopoly operates, consider a typical suburb. Let's call it Jeffersonville. Two suburbs bracket it—Madison on its west and Hamilton Creek on its east. Jeffersonville's major thoroughfare runs six miles, west to east, and its population is distributed evenly along the way, with half its citizens on one side of the thoroughfare's three-mile post and half on the other side.

Imagine being the planner of a new Safeway supermarket, authorized to build a store in Jeffersonville. Your initial decision is to establish it close to the town's west border, the one it shares with Madison (say, the one-mile post) because your distributors are all located in the metropolis further to the west. Positioning your store on the west side of Jeffersonville will mean the Safeway trucks delivering the merchandise will need to travel fewer miles than if the store located further east. That is, you pick a site for *your* convenience.

Then competition arrives in Jeffersonville. Lucky's Markets plans to establish a store of its own. On price and quality of its commodities, it will match Safeway's in every particular. Lucky's believes it can gain a competitive edge over Safeway by being the closer market for most shoppers. That would rule out placing Lucky's on the east side of town. Even the town's center (the three-mile post) as a site could be improved upon. Best would be to pick a moderately western location, say, at the one-and-a-half-mile post, because, there, nearly *five-sixths* of residents would find Lucky's the nearer of the two. So Lucky's commits to construction.

As Safeway's manager, you react. When Lucky's begins to build, you will sell your store to a car dealer and start building a new one just east of Lucky's. That is, you will "leapfrog" to seize back market share and leave that upstart Lucky's in the lurch. Of course, Lucky's will then do likewise, "leapfrogging" east of the new Safeway, with the process repeating itself until the two stores are situated cheek-by-jowl exactly at the town's center, each with 50 percent market share.

This tendency toward the middle is the nearly inevitable result of economic competition, and it serves the public well. Unlike the earlier locations, the final site of the two stores means that no Jeffersonville resident has to drive more than three miles to get groceries. A quick look at American suburbs bears this tendency out. Competing supermarkets virtually always cluster together at a town's population center.

Substitute the Republican and Democratic Parties for Safeway and Lucky's, and the prediction will be that each party will scramble toward the political center of the electorate. Each party will match the other's promises to deliver what the majority demands—growth or environmentalism, universal health care or lower taxes, victory in Afghanistan or exit from it. The parties, thereby, will come to look like Tweedledum and Tweedledee, just as Safeway and Lucky's do; there would not be, as they say, "a dime's worth of difference between them."

For two reasons, however, small distinctions inevitably do pop up. Market research in politics isn't a perfect science, and the parties' sales representatives—say, Senator Doe of the Democrats and Governor Roe of the Republicans—may assess public opinion erroneously. But both are *trying* to find where majority opinion lies.

The second reason why the parties may diverge is their need for capital. Each party needs investors to provide advertising and other campaign resources. In order to please its investors, each party has to pay a bit greater heed to their preferences. But on the decisive issues a political party *must* respond to the tastes of a majority of the citizenry, or it will lose the election.

Two predictions result from seeing parties as competitive corporations in a political marketplace. First, elective officials will care little about principle; what the people want determines what politicians promise and deliver. They will habitually hold their fingers up to discern the political winds.

Second, the incumbent party will usually lose to its challenger. The underlying logic is that the party in power enjoys less flexibility to adapt its promises to changing demand. Like Safeway, an incumbent party has certain "sunk costs" in the programs it has implemented, like a military intervention in Afghanistan or a costly pursuit of full employment. If things start going badly in Afghanistan or its job stimulus program results in hyperinflation, it can't extricate itself from these earlier commitments quickly enough to satisfy the voters who want change. When the electorate reverses its preferences, the challenger simply promises to meet the new desires—get out of Afghanistan or stop the extravagant spending. The result is the incumbent loses the next election.

This conception of political parties as "machines," with bosses trading favors for votes, may sound familiar. But alas for the pundits who hew to this view, their predictions often prove false. Then those who adhere to the view of parties as patronage-dispensing machines write books like *What's the Matter with Kansas?*,[3] whose author was mystified that the Democratic Party keeps losing in Kansas even though it promises Kansans more patronage than the Republicans do—more subsidies, more government jobs, and more entitlements.

The view of American parties as "machines" reflexively adopting every position favored by a majority and the public shifting to the rival party every four years doesn't square with the historical facts, for when one looks at our American competitive two-party system over time, there is no pattern of continuous alternation. Rather, the picture is one of surprising continuities. From 1800, when Madison's Democratic Party prevailed over Alexander Hamilton's Federalist Party, until 1860, at the onset of the Civil War, the Democrats dominated elections, continuously attracting the support of a majority of the voters time and time again. The Federalist Party, which later morphed into the Whig Party, never gained support from more than a minority of voters.

From 1860 to 1932, the Republican Party, the party of Abraham Lincoln, was rarely defeated at the national level. The Great Depression of 1929 was blamed on the Republicans, and from then until 1980, the Democrats returned to the saddle of events, with a majority of voters identifying as loyal Democrats. Those protracted periods of political dominance can't be explained in terms of parties outpromising one another.

Parties as Coalitions

That anomaly suggests that parties behave in more complex ways than simple patronage machines. Fortunately for our understanding, other close observers of politics have drawn our attention to the role of factions. [4]

They emphasize the fact that political parties have embraced specific interest groups. Both the Democratic and Republican Parties consist of "a great variety of interests"—a diverse collection of "bedfellows" who do not see eye to eye. One faction thinks there are too few jobs, another too much development, a third too great neglect of the inner cities, another too great neglect of the military, a fifth too low crop prices, and still another too high food prices, and so on. While sharing one common purpose—to win the next election and gain control of government—these factions, each with their single interest, struggle amongst themselves to dominate their party's choice of direction.

For example, the coalition assembled by the Democratic Party under President Franklin Roosevelt in the 1930s consisted of twelve distinct interest groups: farmers and organized labor, white southerners and northern blacks, Roman Catholics and Jews, Irish Americans and Italian Americans, young voters and older voters, intellectuals and the most poorly educated. [5]

Note that these dozen groups were antagonists of one another. Farmers were unhappy with the low prices of their crops and the high cost of the farm machinery they had to buy and wanted policies like crop restrictions and tariff reductions that would serve these goals. Organized labor, on the contrary, believed food cost too much and wanted artificial price support (in the form of tariffs) for the machines they manufactured. White southerners passionately resisted racial integration of any sort, while northern blacks resisted racial segregation with equal intensity. Catholics and Jews were historical enemies. Irish Americans thought it their birthright to dominate local big-city politics; Italian Americans felt otherwise and thought it their turn to use political channels to rise from the basement of American society into the sunshine. The young urged inflationary policies because they decreased the real costs of their indebtedness; oldsters urged on deflationary policies because they increased the real purchasing power of their savings. Liberal intellectuals loved change (at least, when it didn't affect their lives) and envisioned countless ways to make America better—permissive child-raising, subsidies to enable single mothers to stay at home, food stamps, school busing, maximum feasible participation in the governance of cities, race-based affirmative action, gender parity, and industrial reorganization—all of which undermined established standards of status, customary ways of coping, and traditional ladders of success for the poor and least educated. In other words, the Roosevelt coalition was in constant civil war: debate raged, and differences were compromised within the Democratic Party structure.

Coalitions are definitely not well-oiled "machines." They more closely resemble a herd of cats in their unruliness, but with this difference: "political cats" not only despise being herded; they despise each other, to boot. The wry comic of the Roosevelt era, Will Rogers, quipped, "I ain't a member of any organized political party. I'm a Demmycrat."

Note that when we speak of an interest group like organized labor or "the Irish" or "the old," we mean the leaders of particular groups, persons whose stature, knowledge, or barrels of ink have equipped them to be worthy of the trust of large numbers of like-minded followers to guide their voting decisions. In a party coalition these group leaders know one another, assemble with one another, and negotiate with one another in promoting their priorities in the legislatures and executive offices their collective votes have won. The negotiating power that each leader carries to the table is a function of his ability to mobilize his followers to vote in a given direction.

Armed with his group's potential voting power, each leader demands that his preferences be served, or else. . . . Or else, he will direct the voting power of his faction to support the rival party. If his colleagues in *his* party won't heed his threat and call his bluff, he will have to walk out. He and his followers, to preserve their credibility over the long run, must "bolt," as the saying goes, with the intention of bringing his fellow partisans down to defeat in the upcoming election.

His "bolt" sets in motion a counter dynamic of cohesion. The groups he has left behind now have a compelling incentive to unite to defeat his threat, for if they don't and lose, they face the prospect that the wayward leader and his faction will only rejoin the party after the election at a price: they will have to accede to his demands.

For example, during the Vietnam War (1964–1974), "the young" wanted their party to promise a policy to "cut and run" from further military involvement. Their demands were ignored and they "bolted"; labor, oldsters, the Irish, and other factions united to attempt to win the 1968 election *in spite of* the young's walk-out. Had they succeeded, the young would have had no alternative but to return to the Democratic coalition, chastened and weakened by their failed threat. If, on the other hand, the young succeeded in defeating their own party, they would prove their vital importance to the party. Like a bully, they would be in a position to call the shots.

The danger was that if the young brought the Democratic Party down and then returned to it (as it happened), their leaders would overdo their superior bargaining position, thereby offending labor with their arrogance. They did, and labor despised their naively liberal ideas and "bolted" in the 1972 election, leaving the party in defeat once again.

Both American parties are characterized by this same dynamic: a member group makes its demands, which sometimes the coalition refuses, whereupon the group "bolts," inducing the remnants of the coalition to set aside their differences and unite in pursuit of victory. (The so-called Reagan Coalition in the Republican Party behaved in much the same way as did the Roosevelt Coalition in the Democratic Party.)

Parties as Churches

Viewing the two parties as coalitions would appear to explain their persistent character over sustained periods of time. But exclusive attention to the dynamic within the two parties, as illuminating as it is, does not explain the partisan rancor *between* competing parties. For this, we need to view their operations in a third way, to understand America's two political parties not as machines or coalitions, but as churches—secular churches, but churches with the full panoply of sacred texts, creeds, eloquent clerics, and evangelicals spreading the "good news."[6] Chapter 12 briefly introduced us to the notion that America's system of political parties shares a resemblance to the legal system and the religious community; it is a moral institution, spreading important political ideas. I want now to elaborate on that way of viewing political parties.

If one thinks of America's two-party political system as consisting of rival churches and listens for their opposing creeds, one will hear something like this. On the one hand, there is the creed of personal freedom, called conservatism:

> We believe in the drive of the individual as he seeks to be esteemed in the eyes of others. We believe in the free marketplace where individuals with diverse objectives can find assistance from others willing to be useful and where the desire to follow the Golden Rule of treating others as you would wish to be treated is reinforced by self-interest. We believe that coercion, on the other hand, excites the worst aspects of our nature and that it is good to confine the government (which has the exclusive right to use coercion legitimately) to only those few responsibilities strictly beyond the individual's capacity. We believe in the norm of reciprocity, in the education of all, in the stimulus of competition to improve our talents, and in a social order in which the good fortune of others multiplies our own good fortune.

The rival creed, liberalism, emphasizes not personal freedom but egalitarianism, which its partisans tend to call "justice":

> We believe in a government strong enough to use the words "love" and "compassion" and smart enough to convert our noblest aspirations into practical realities. We believe in encouraging the talented, but we believe that while survival of the fittest may be a good working description of the process of evolution, a government of humans should elevate itself to a higher order. We believe in a single fundamental idea, the idea of family. Mutuality. Sharing one another's blessings. Recognizing we are bound one

to another, that the problems of a retired school teacher in Duluth are our problems, that the future of the child in Buffalo is our future, that the struggle of a disabled man in Boston to survive and live decently is our struggle, that the hunger of a woman in Little Rock is our hunger, that the failure to provide what reasonably we might is our failure.

Perhaps those last words sound familiar. They were uttered in what many think was the most memorable keynote address ever given at a Democratic Party Convention, that of New York governor Mario Cuomo in 1984.[7]

In a view of political party operations that highlights ideas, we witness a religious-like clash between rival teams of evangelists, each team working every day throughout every year to "get out" the word. These evangelists are not sales representatives of political machines, doing market research, trying to find what the people want. Nor are they leaders of factions, threatening and bluffing rivals within their chosen party. Instead, they are intellectually sharp instructors of their respective faiths, spreading the "good news" to impel others to be "born again" and convert to their way of thinking.[8]

Both of these church-like parties constantly experiment in new techniques of spreading the word. Where ward heelers once roamed neighborhoods that they had lived in since childhood, nowadays spokespersons on radio, television, and the Internet serve as their equivalent. Republicans, with a Rush Limbaugh and a "Fox News" channel, and Democrats, with a Katie Couric and a National Public Radio network, spread their parties' faiths.

These two political churches, one conservative, the other liberal, are founded on unchanging principles that do not bend to the times, but rather adapt the times to them. Their followers highlight, rather than ignore, the permanent principles that distinguish their faith from the other.

Ideas endure,[9] and the organizations that spread them endure, sending their missionaries out to meet the citizenry in the public square and to prevail not by the sword or the purse, but by the word. And whether a party is inspired sufficiently to do hard missionary work depends on how inspiring its spokespersons are—its leaders and public intellectuals. What counts is their ability to articulate its credo and the application of that credo to contemporary problems from their bully pulpits.

Seeing parties as churches illuminates the importance of ideas. We come to understand the importance of the sermons of Abraham Lincoln, Teddy Roosevelt, and Ronald Reagan on the one hand, and of Franklin Roosevelt, John F. Kennedy, and Mario Cuomo on the other. Their oratory carries the two great competing faiths of personal freedom and material equality into the public square.

There is no one best way to think about political parties. Each perspective alone is defective. A political party *is* a machine, a coalition, *and* a church. Ignore any one of these three distinctive perspectives, and you will blind yourself to the whole picture.

People who see parties only as machines boil politics down to "It's the economy, stupid" (to borrow a currently pungent phrase). Promise the voters more than the other guy, and your party will win. Others, who see parties only as coalitions, discover the key to electoral victory in the pressure of the "interests"—the threats rival groups make against their fellow partisans. They boil everything down to "Mobilize your base." And those who see parties as churches understand that ideas have consequences; they insist to "Stand by your principles." In this light, the process of producing party platforms and finding ways to channel ideas into voters' minds are the things that really matter.

So are American political parties as bad as Madison feared? Or do they benefit the nation and keep majority tyranny in check? It is easy to think that Madison's baleful assessment of a political party is correct.[10] The one-party South that existed to 1965 enabled the Democratic Party to maintain racial oppression. But under circumstances where one party has to compete with another, the effects, it strikes me, are highly beneficial. There are numerous reasons to believe that parties are an antidote against majority tyranny and the "mischiefs of faction," but I only want to highlight one.

In the American two-party political system, each party competes to bundle together as many minority factions as it can by emphasizing one or the other of our two enduring, but often warring, values defining American civilization—liberty and equality. Then each coalition fights to balance the electoral might of the other. Each serves to check the excesses of the other; or, as Madison declared in *Federalist* No. 51, "[T]he private interest of [each party serves as] a centinel over the public rights." Thus just as the formal Constitution checks the power of each department of government with the power of the others, so the two political parties, each founded on enduring but warring beliefs, constitute a system of checks and balances within the electorate.

NOTES

1. See, e.g., Frank Lynn, "Legal, Normal Politics Is Continual Backscratching," *New York Times*, May 30, 1976, Section B (Sunday edition). (The political scientist Harold Lasswell once defined politics as "who gets what, when, and how.")

2. The discussion of "machines" derives in its entirety from a wonderfully provocative book by the economist Anthony Downs, *An Economic Theory of Democracy* (New York: HarperCollins, 1957).

3. Thomas Frank, *What's the Matter with Kansas?* (New York: Henry Holt, 2004).

4. See Samuel Lubell, *The Future of American Politics*, 3rd rev. ed. (New York: Harper/Colophon, 1965 [1951]), 190–210.

5. Amity Shlaes's *The Forgotten Man: A New History of the Great Depression* (New York: HarperCollins, 2007) is an account of Roosevelt's political tactics in assembling his coalition.

6. Moise Ostrogorski, *Democracy and the Organization of Political Parties*, trans. Frederick Clarke (New York: Macmillan, 1902), vol. 2.

7. "Text of Governor Cuomo's Keynote Address," *Congressional Quarterly Weekly Report*, July 21, 1984, 1781–1784.

8. Earlier, in Chapter 12, we called these church-like political parties "moral institutions."

9. Consider a reputable poll of activists engaged in the work of these two "churches." Jeane Kirkpatrick, *The New Presidential Elite* (New York: Russell Sage Foundation, 1976), Tables 10-1, 10-2, 10-3, and 10-7, as cited in James Q. Wilson, *American Government: Institutions and Policies*, 2nd ed. (Lexington, Mass./Toronto: D.C. Heath, 1983), 156:

   - Among Democratic—liberal—activists, 57 percent agreed that "no one should live in poverty whether or not they work." Among Republican—conservative—activists, only 10 percent thought so.
   - Among Democratic activists, 28 percent agreed that persons able to work should be required to work. Among Republican activists, 75 percent agreed. That is a difference of nearly 50 percent.
   - As to the criminal justice system, 78 percent of Democratic activists felt it was more important to protect the rights of the accused. Only 21 percent of Republican activists felt that way. Conversely, 56 percent of Republican activists felt the most important thing was to stop crime; only 13 percent of Democratic activists shared that view.
   - 43 percent of Democratic activists had an unfavorable attitude toward the military; only 4 percent of the Republican activists did.

   I would wager that partisan activists in 2011—37 years later—would respond in virtually the same way.

10. Perhaps the finest piece of twentieth-century academic political science (and certainly among the most consequential) is V. O. Key (with Alexander Heard), *Southern Politics in State and Nation* (New York: Random House/Vintage, 1949), which details the malign effects of the one-party system that came into existence in eleven southern states in the aftermath of the Civil War. Louisiana, the setting of Robert Penn Warren's *All the King's Men*, was one of those states, and the story of Willie Stark (and his real-life counterpart, Huey Long) demonstrates many of the worst consequences that stem from the absence of competing parties.

21

AMERICAN NEWSPAPERS AND IDEAS

In democratic countries . . . it frequently happens that a great number of men who wish or want to combine cannot accomplish it because as they are very insignificant and lost amid the crowd, they cannot see and do not know where to find one another. A newspaper then takes up the notion or the feeling that had occurred simultaneously, but singly, to each of them. All are then immediately guided towards this beacon; and these wandering minds, which had long sought each other in darkness, at length meet and unite. The newspaper brought them together, and the newspaper is still necessary to keep them united.

Alexis de Tocqueville, *Democracy in America* (1840)

By September 1787, the Constitutional Convention in Philadelphia had finished its business of writing a proposed Constitution. Alexander Hamilton and James Madison returned to New York, intending to manage the local campaign for ratification. They confronted a strongly entrenched opposition, for New York's governor, George Clinton, was dead-set against any alteration of the Articles of Confederation.

And well he should have been concerned, for under the proposed Constitution, collection of import duties would become a federal monopoly ("No State shall, without the Consent of Congress, lay any Imposts or

Duties on Imports or Exports . . . and the net Produce of all Duties and Imposts . . . shall be for the Use of the Treasury of the United States").[1] The ban on the states pocketing custom duties radically altered the status quo. Under the Articles of Confederation the national "government" never received a penny from this rich source of funds; it had no independent taxing powers and hence was utterly reliant on voluntary contributions from the several states. Every cent of custom revenues was collected and kept by the states where the ports were situated. New York having the busiest harbor on the Atlantic coast, its coffers were so filled with the receipts from "duties on imports" that New Yorkers paid no other taxes.[2] In contrast, the federal Treasury was bankrupt. In diverting import duties to "the use of the United States Treasury," the Constitution left Governor Clinton with no option but to try to defeat its ratification.

There was a personal aspect to the fight over ratification as well. Clinton and Hamilton were personal enemies. Hamilton, in a newspaper partial to him, publicly accused Clinton of "conduct . . . in office [that] confers greater attachment to his *own power* than to the *public good* and furnishes strong reason to suspect a dangerous predetermination to oppose whatever may tend to diminish the *former*, however it may promote the *latter*."[3] In response, the governor had one of his staff reply publicly in one of the pro-Clinton newspapers, accusing Hamilton of being "a superficial, self-conceited coxcomb. . . ."

To overcome the likely opposition of local political officials like Clinton, the Constitutional Convention in Philadelphia had provided that ratification of the proposed Constitution would be decided by state "conventions," not by state legislatures.

Delegates to the New York State Convention were to be elected in dozens of discrete districts scattered about the state, leaving Hamilton and Madison with the problem of how to influence scores of separate and differently circumstanced elections. Their solution, as we know, was to craft their monumental defense of the proposed Constitution and get it published (segmented into twice-weekly columns) in the local newspapers within each district. There resulted a verbal torrent that ultimately added up to 175,000 words. Complained one anti-Federalist halfway through the campaign: "Publius [the pseudonym Hamilton and Madison adopted] has already written 26 numbers, as much as would jade the brains of any poor sinner . . . so that in decency he should now rest on his arms and let the people draw their breath for a little while."[4] Publius rejected the advice.

The point is that by 1787 the freedom of newspapers to engage in robust public debate without fear of government oppression was already established. Fifty years later, Tocqueville marveled at the liberties of the American press. Moreover, he came to realize that newspapers played a still larger role than mere mouthpieces for politically partisan rivals and government critics. They performed a vital social function, enabling isolated and otherwise impotent individuals to attract like-minded persons and collaborate with them. That is, newspapers distributed moral power to ordinary persons, enabling them to act in concert without waiting for the aid—or at least for the initiative—of the state:

> [I]t frequently happens that a great number of men who wish or who want to combine cannot accomplish it because as they are very insignificant and lost amid the crowd, they cannot see and do not know where to find one another. A newspaper then takes up the notion or the feeling that had occurred simultaneously, but singly, to each of them. All are then immediately guided toward this beacon; and these wandering minds, which had long sought each other in darkness, at length meet and unite. The newspaper brought them together, and the newspaper is still necessary to keep them united.[5]

But, after asserting that newspapers were critical in augmenting the power of the individual, he uttered this caution about the increased influence of publishers and journalists in a free society: "The power of the newspaper press must therefore increase as the social conditions of men become more equal."[6]

The Arrival of Abundance

In the 1800s virtually all newspapers in America were highly partisan. There were Democratic-Republican ones and opposition ones. Such notions as "objectivity" and "being fair and balanced" would have sounded laughable. Newspapers were there to inform and motivate fellow partisans. There was no need to worry about offending readers of the other party; there were none.

But with the expansion of the Industrial Revolution after the Civil War, the nation experienced an unprecedented condition of abundance. For the first time in human history "potential supply," as historian David Potter observed, could "outrun demand."[7] Factories could produce *more* than consumers thought they needed.

As a result, the profession of advertising was born in order to heighten demand. To stimulate, even to create, consumer appetites, producers and retailers sought to buy space in newspapers to promote their goods, and publishers happily obliged—to their profit. In fact, by 1935 the advertising revenues of newspapers had grown to be twice as large as their subscriber revenues. In effect, advertising was subsidizing newsgathering, enabling publishers to lower the prices of their papers so as to expand their readership. In turn, the larger their readership, the more they could charge their advertisers.

The effect of this new emphasis on increased circulation was to incline publishers (and their editors) to be inoffensive—that is, to become less partisan. The change was marked by the introduction of new features like comic pages, extensive sports coverage, self-help columns, and daily crossword puzzles. "Objective" journalism became the new byword. Admittedly, the publisher might speak his mind and tuck away a partisan outburst on the editorial page, but the reporters of news were expected to keep their personal slants out of their stories.

That trend, however, in defining journalistic "professionalism" as lack of bias would gradually peter out. For one thing, inoffensive reporting tended to be bland and boring, creating a market niche for outspoken and partisan periodicals with an axe to grind. Over time, sufficiently large communities of like-minded readers developed to support them.

Newspapers also found themselves in competition with new media—radio and television—media that possessed two advantages over newsprint: they were "free," and they were timely, able to scoop newspapers, which by their nature were always a day late. To differentiate the print media from their electronic competition, which the Federal Communications Act (until recently amended) required to be neutral in reporting controversial matters, newspapers gradually became more opinionated.

There was a third reason why strict objectivity became a less insistent journalistic standard. Schools of journalism, which bestowed honors on what they considered professional excellence, began to celebrate reporters who rejected objectivity. Three events led to legitimating bias—the civil rights movement and its efforts in the segregated South, the engagement of American troops in the Vietnam War, and the impeachment of President Richard Nixon in his second term (1973-1974). Southern intolerance, the "wrong war" in Vietnam, and the Nixon "cover-up" became moral issues. Like slavery in the pre–Civil War era, those three matters were not in doubt, and to be fair and balanced in reporting about them was to be immoral, thereby providing a pretext for one-sided journalism. The heroes of the media were understood to be partisan crusaders, like Tom Wicker and David Halberstam of the *New York Times* (reporting on civil rights and the Vietnam War, respectively) and the *Washington Post*'s Bob Woodward and Carl Bernstein (with their revelations concerning the Nixon White House).

The Return of Partisanship

The upshot was that reporters began to throw aside the habits of neutrality. Admittedly, readership went down: after all, who wants to read something that continually offends them? But the homogeneity of the remaining readers increased. The *New York Times* led the way. In the decade between 1993 and 2004, its circulation within the thirty-one counties near New York City slipped from 758,000 to 594,000, a decline of 22 percent. However, much of that loss in local readership was offset, thanks to advances in technology, by publishing out-of-town editions in places likely to agree with its increasingly obvious bias, localities like Berkeley, California, Madison, Wisconsin, and Austin, Texas.

Paradoxically, however, despite the declining circulation in the New York area (and consequent loss of advertising revenues), the *Times*'s national influence grew. That development was due to the decreasing profitability of regional newspapers throughout the country, the Internet being the major factor. "Free" services like Craigslist provided the public an inexpensive substitute for local classified ads, which had theretofore been a substantial revenue-producer for papers like the *San Francisco Chronicle* and the *Seattle Times*. Forced to prune their reporting staffs, they increasingly relied on reprinting articles they purchased from the *New York Times*. Thus, while it was losing readers, its articles were reaching an ever greater readership. For example, the *Chronicle* provided a steady stream of *Times* news articles to its 400,000 subscribers in the San Francisco Bay area—a circulation almost equal to that of the *Times* itself in the metropolitan area it served.

Moreover, the same trend was occurring in electronic news. Radio and TV, while becoming principal channels of news, reduced their news departments and increased their reliance on the news staffs of the print media, and especially the army of reporters employed by the *New York Times*. If they needed news on Thailand or Iraq or the United Nations, or the arts or the military or the market, or even on sports, they bought it from the *Times*. When the producers of cable and network television news sat down to decide what news they should broadcast that evening, their selections were influenced by what they were reading in the *Times*. Moreover, the emerging role of bloggers further magnified the influence of the *Times* because bloggers had no news staffs and were even more dependent on *Times* journalists than TV and radio broadcasters.

All the while that its national influence was growing, the *Times* was becoming more partisan. A marker of its lost neutrality was an assessment contained in a report commissioned by the *Times* itself in 2005. Beset by a plague of serious scandals in its news department stemming from phony stories and misleadingly edited articles, the *Times* felt it needed to examine itself. It commissioned an internal review, and the resulting report turned out to be highly critical and highlighted four disturbing trends.[8] One, "columnists" were getting their one-sided punditry printed on the front page of the paper, appearing indistinguishable from news reports. Two, the *Times* was publishing so many articles on certain subjects, with each reporter using "the same assumption as a point of departure, [that it left] the impression that the paper has chosen sides."[9] Three, reporters and editors were "uncritically accept[ing] a stereotype or unfairly marginaliz[ing]" whole groups.[10] Four, reporters were being recruited from increasingly narrow and select circles, with limited worldly experience (none with military service, exposure to rural life, or deep religious conviction).[11]

All this, mind you, was what the *Times*'s own self-scrutiny revealed. Unquestionably, bias had crept in under the leadership of its publisher, Arthur Sulzberger III, who had defined his paper to be "the liberal spokesman." Little wonder that few of the changes urged by the report were put into effect.[12]

The Conservative Response

As one might expect in a robust society like America's, there was a reaction to this "liberal spokesman." Those who saw things differently created a "conservative" mainstream, the linchpin of which was the *Wall Street Journal*, with its own print circulation of twice that of the *Times*. It employed more than six hundred reporters on its global news staff and another nine hundred-plus on its Dow Jones Newswires. But it was the *Journal*'s editorial section that challenged the *Times* most directly and effectively. Those in charge of the *Journal*'s editorial pages had more than forty reporters on

their staff, who worked independently of the *Journal*'s own news department. They developed their own sources. Moreover, the editorial pages
were open to contributions by public intellectuals who adhered to conservative perspectives. The news appearing in the *Journal*'s opinion and commentary pages was then broadcast by conservative outlets like Fox News
Channel, radio pundits like Rush Limbaugh, and Internet bloggers galore.

Behind the Partisanship of the Left and the Right

These two distinct and partisan mainstreams—one liberal, one conservative—flooded the public with clashing points of view. They differed in three
important ways: the events they selected to report, the sources they turned
to for information, and the assessments they made of the information they
gathered.

By 2007 the contrast between their front pages was startling. Typically,
the front page of the *Times* was dominated by "bad news": casualties in
Iraq; the humiliation of several terrorist suspects in Iraq's Abu-Ghraib
prison by five American soldiers; foreign policy mistakes that offended
West European sensibilities; the "mess" in America's health care system;
discrimination against virtually everybody—women, African Americans,
Muslims, Hispanics, gays, terrorists; corruption in the criminal justice system; the failure of charter schools; and so on. Meanwhile, the *Wall Street
Journal* reported "good news": achievement in the Iraq war (like three successful elections with massive and peaceful turnouts, the formation of a
legitimate Iraqi government, the ratification of a constitution, Iraq's growing economy, its creation of a capital market, and eventual victory); beneficial repercussions of Saddam Hussein's overthrow (the detection of
Pakistani scientist A. Q. Khan's covert delivery of nuclear weapons technology to terrorists and rogue nations, Libya's cessation of its nuclear
weapons program, and the detection of massive fraud in the UN's Oil-for-
Food bureaucracy); foreign policy successes, especially in our relations with
China, Japan, and South Korea; doctors providing inexpensive care for
America's poor; achievements of nearly every kind of American—women,
African Americans, Muslims, Hispanics, gays (but not terrorists); success
in uncovering corruption in America's plaintiffs' bar and its misuse of the
civil tort system; the achievements of charter schools in our inner cities;
and so on.[13]

As to sources, the *Times* invariably went to its list of favorite liberal think
tanks, the *Journal* to its list of favorite conservative think tanks.

And as to implications, one example will suffice. America's success in establishing a free democracy in Muslim Iraq boded ill, said the *Times* editorialists: "The future of women's freedom is in serious question. [The new democratically elected Iraqi leaders] could be consigning Iraqi women to a life of subjugation" and secular Iraqis to a "bleak, Iran-like future."[14] The *Wall Street Journal,* in turn, scoffed at its competitor's sour grapes.

Now why these stark differences? At first glance, they would appear to result purely from political partisanship.[15] When control of the White House would change from Republican to Democratic, it was argued, the *Times* would start emphasizing the good news and the *Journal* would trumpet the bad. That was a plausible prediction, and there is some evidence of its truth, but it begs the question, Why did the publisher and editors of the *Times* become fiercely liberal, and of the other fiercely conservative? And why did it keep on hiring only like-minded reporters and editors who continually scoured the world for bad news, while those at the *Journal* became fiercely conservative, employing reporters and editors who looked for good news? Could there be a deeper reason that underlay their partisanship?

Belief Systems Have Consequences

Consider this explanation: the two organizations have different notions of newsworthiness. Each believes that "news" is what's unusual, that reporting anomalies ("man bites dog") constitutes its responsibility, and that normal events don't warrant media attention. They radically differ, however, on what is the norm from which newsworthy events depart.

The saying goes that political beliefs fall into one or the other of two camps. One view is that humanity is essentially noble but is corrupted by institutions. The other is that humankind is essentially corrupt and is ennobled by institutions. The first view is Jeffersonian and has a respectable provenance back to the secular French Enlightenment, the imagination of Jean-Jacques Rousseau, and, ironically enough, the insights of Karl Marx. Its basic premise is that humans are reasonable, and reason will enable mankind to perfect society.

The second view, of man's corruption, is Hamiltonian; its philosophical pedigree can be traced back to Judeo-Christianity and runs through the works of Englishmen Thomas Hobbes and Edmund Burke. It assumes that humans are sinful and prone to unreasoning emotions, and the harmful expressions of those tendencies must be regulated by civilization's manners. While material circumstances may improve, human nature remains the same mixture of good and evil, always susceptible to the dual temptations of desire and hatred.[16] Perfection is not for this earthly existence of ours.

These two views create different expectations. If an editor or reporter believes that persons are born angelic—the underlying premise of liberalism—it follows that when the American government and its military do something good in the world, like leading it against genuinely monstrous evils; giving aid and comfort after the war to former enemies on a scale never before seen; repelling aggression against South Korea, Kosovo, and Kuwait; protecting our allies against totalitarian Soviet communism; reunifying Germany and rehabilitating middle European countries long oppressed by the Soviet empire; and rescuing hundreds of thousands from nature's devastations in South Asia, that's normal, hence not "news." But if a few vagrant soldiers amuse themselves by humiliating some Iraqi insurgents imprisoned at Abu-Ghraib, that's newsworthy because the government and its military have not behaved perfectly.

But suppose the contrary; suppose an editor expects humans to be fundamentally flawed in their natures, forever given to cruelty and avarice—the fundamental axiom of conservatism. Then, when persons surprise with their selflessness and generosity, that's newsworthy, deserving a place on the front page. It's *not* "normal" to be decent; rather, it's something out of the ordinary, and people (the editor thinks) will want it brought to their attention and will appreciate its honorable character. When a group of doctors, or lawyers, or journalists, or governments act in defiance of such low expectations, they have transcended their inherent tendencies. And that's news to take your hat off to.

We know these two opposed views of human nature as Romantic and Skeptical. The irony is that the rosy optimism of the Romantic view that underlies liberalism is always disappointed, while the suspicious pessimism of the Skeptical view that is the foundation of conservatism is invariably pleasantly surprised.

Little wonder that these two viewpoints produce startlingly different front pages. Each newspaper perceives what it looks for—departures from its notions of normality. It is just a further instance of what we know as the paradox of perception: *believing* (or belief systems) *is seeing*.

NOTES

1. Article I, Section 10.
2. Ron Chernow, *Alexander Hamilton* (New York: Penguin, 2004), 244.
3. Ibid., 237.
4. Ibid., 261.
5. Alexis de Tocqueville, *Democracy in America,* trans. Henry Reeve (New York: Bantam 2000 [1840]), vol. II, book 2, chap. 5.
6. Ibid. Thomas Jefferson early recognized the power of newspapers. By 1787 he was saying, "Were it left to me to decide whether we should have a government without newspapers, or newspapers without a government, I should not hesitate a moment to prefer the latter." Letter to Edward Carrington, 1787. So powerful did he feel newspapers could be that when he became president in 1801, he arranged to have his own paper in Washington. According to political scientist James Sterling Young, even before being elected president, Jefferson persuaded Samuel Harrison Smith to move his printing press from Philadelphia to the new capital city, there to publish a partisan newspaper called the *National Intelligencer.* Smith and Jefferson shared "a common partisanship in the Republican cause, and . . . Smith was also selected as official reporter for the congressional debates, receiving sundry public printing contracts as well." Of course, payments from the public treasury for the "sundry public printing" jobs subsidized Smith's daily *National Intelligencer,* which routinely excoriated the Federalists and permitted Jefferson and his allies, under pseudonyms, to express administration views, scotch (or create) rumors, and repel Federalist attacks. Thus Jefferson, through his newspaper, broadcast his ideas to fellow partisans, members of Congress, and the families they brought to the new capital. James Sterling Young, *The Washington Community: 1800-1828* (New York: Columbia University Press, 1968), 173-174.
7. David M. Potter, *People of Plenty: Economic Abundance and the American Character* (Chicago: University of Chicago Press, 1954), 172.
8. The following, including quotations, is the assessment of the Credibility Group, Allan M. Siegel, chair, "Preserving Our Readers' Trust: A Report to the Executive Editor," 2005.
9. By way of illustration of this bias, the report elaborated: "The overall tone of our coverage of gay marriage . . . 'approaches cheerleading.' By consistently framing the issue as a civil rights matter—gays fighting for the right to be treated like everyone else—we failed to convey how disturbing the issue is in many corners of American social, cultural and religious life."

10. "Words like moderate or centrist inevitably incorporate a judgment about which views are sensible and which are extreme. . . . We often apply 'religious fundamentalists', another loaded term, to political activists who would describe themselves as Christian conservatives."

11. "[W]e are missing stories because our staff lacks diversity in viewpoints, intellectual grounding and individual backgrounds. We should look for all manner of diversity. We should seek talented journalists who happen to have military experience, who know rural America first hand, who are at home in different faiths."

12. For example, on January 12, 2008, the *Times,* a bitter opponent of the "Bush war against Iraq," published a long, front-page article, written by Deborah Sontag and Lizette Alvarez and headlined "Across America, Deadly Echoes of Foreign Battles," alleging that veterans of the Iraq and Afghanistan wars were responsible for 121 killings since their return from combat, creating "a cross-country trail of death and heartbreak." A "blogger" on Powerline.com, while conceding that some of these homicides may have resulted from wartime post-traumatic stress syndrome, calculated that annually 3 in every 100,000 Iraqi and Afghan veterans committed a homicide, a tiny fraction of the homicide rate for civilian eighteen- to twenty-four-year-olds, which was 27 per 100,000. The *Times,* for whatever reasons, "missed" supplying its readers that comparative (and obviously important) perspective.

13. Of course, once in a while the *Times* will become a cheerleader for the human race, and the *Wall Street Journal* will dig up some mucky business doings by some wayward corporate executive. But the overall differences are striking, and when you turn to the different editorial pages, it's like reading about two different countries.

14. *New York Times,* March 24, 2005, A-22.

15. Another explanation for the "bad news" tendencies of newspapers is the old journalistic canard, "No news is bad news, good news is dull news, and bad news makes marvelous copy," hence sells newspapers. Again, that may partially explain the gloom spread on the pages of the *Times,* but it doesn't explain why the *Journal* exhibits a happier face *and* enjoys double the circulation of the *Times.*

16. Will and Ariel Durant in their *The Lessons of History* (New York: Simon and Schuster, 1968), 51, quote the French conservative Joseph de Maistre: "I do not know what the heart of a rascal may be; I know what is in the heart of an honest man; it is horrible."

22

FREE-MARKET CAPITALISM

Commerce is naturally adverse to all the violent passions; it loves to temporize, takes delight in compromise, and studiously avoids irritation. It is patient, insinuating, flexible, and never has recourse to extreme measures until obliged by the most absolute necessity. Commerce renders men independent of one another, gives them a lofty notion of their personal importance, leads them to seek to conduct their own affairs, and teaches them how to conduct them well; it therefore prepares men for freedom, but preserves them from revolutions.

Alexis de Tocqueville, *Democracy in America* (1840)

One fundamental, but subterranean issue underlies American political life. In the best of times, it is barely discernible, submerged under a patina of full employment, elevated levels of prosperity, and exuberance. When the business cycle turns down, however, when economic recession, frustrated hopes, and stubborn fact arouse public anxieties (and periodic downturns inevitably occur), the question assumes center stage.

That recurrent political question is this: Is free-market capitalism compatible with electoral democracy? Does "big business"—Big Oil, Big Tobacco, Big Pharma, Wall Street—manipulate democratic government so as to serve its interests at the expense of the "people"? Latent in the American mind is a suspicion of large corporations and an anxiety concerning our individual dependence on the ups and downs of the free market. Hence, when euphoria gives way to despair, movements variously called populism, progressivism, communism, and Judeo-Christian socialism arise just as predictably as night follows day.

An Important Distinction

In thinking about that fundamental question, we start with an important distinction. There are two possible ways in which a society can produce and distribute the commodities and services it needs.

One way is central planning. Here government, relying on legal penalties, regulates both the production and allocation of the food, shelter, health care, tools, arts, and services essential to maintain civilization. There are many variations on this type of economy, ranging from the selective takeover of a few significant industries (as Great Britain "nationalized" the coal and steel industries in the immediate aftermath of World War II) to comprehensive control of every significant economic activity (as in the former Soviet Union and present-day Cuba). These variations all entail planning, bureaucratic expertise, and concentration of responsibility. There are two pretexts for central planning: mobilization for war on the one hand, and economic equality on the other. The word we use for centrally planned economies, in all their variations, is *socialism*. Characteristic of socialist societies are three features: the dominant value of *equality*, the pursuit of *stability,* and a vision of *community*.

The alternative to socialism is decentralization, with individuals employing reciprocal power in free markets. By exchange, private individuals determine what is produced and to whom products are distributed. *The Federalist Papers* describe such a society as a "commercial republic."[1] Today, in these post-Marxian days, it is more common to call it "free-market capitalism."

A free-market capitalist society pivots on two legal inventions. One is the technique of *contract*, which permits private parties to engage in mutual regulation of one another's conduct. Contracts are miniature pieces of legislation, proposed and ratified by the parties to whom they apply. By entering into a contract, each party gains the assurance that the other will live up to his promises—or else courts of law will compel him to do so. Contracts thereby make nonsimultaneous exchanges possible, with one party completing his end of the bargain prior to the other party delivering on his.

The other legal invention is the *corporation*. Corporate law enables the pooling of significant resources—of *capital*—by limiting the risk of each shareholder of a corporation to the amount of his investment. Limiting the liability of investors differentiates the corporation from a partnership of individuals, where each partner is liable for the indebtedness of the *entire* partnership.[2]

Free-market capitalism not only decentralizes production and distribution, but also disperses the responsibility for policing itself. Persons harmed by the neglect or indifference of a private entity—say, passengers injured in a car accident caused by a defective brake—can prosecute in a court of law: they possess *the authority to sue in tort*; that means they can bring an action for the wrongful behavior of the person or business causing the harm.[3] Thus the task of policing any misbehavior of producers or distributors is not reserved exclusively to government, but is shared with the individuals most motivated to enforce the duty of due care.

Three characteristics distinguish a commercial or free-market society from a centrally planned one—the dominant value of *liberty*, a pursuit of *innovation*,[4] and a culture of *competition*.

Capitalism and Socialism Compared

Oversimplifying a complex variety of systems, we might summarize the differences this way. Socialist societies pursue the leveling of incomes and wealth by subsidizing the needy and suppressing the accumulation of private fortunes. Capitalist societies pursue personal freedom, motivating initiative and rewarding individuals to be industrious, inventive, and self-reliant.

Socialist societies stress predictability as the key to human happiness and are wary of the downsides of change; they worry about the possible unintended consequences of technological improvements and are cautious about society's rational capacities to adapt quickly. Capitalists embrace things "new" and accept the destruction of the old as a legitimate cost of creativity; they are confident that they can improvise solutions to problems attendant to each innovation and welcome a degree of instability as a productive challenge.

Socialists envision a world where people get along, are content, and have time and leisure to "hang out" with one another. Capitalists promote lawful competition as a cure for mankind's proclivity to sloth[5] and self-satisfaction.

Hamilton and Tocqueville on "Commerce"

The authors of the U.S. Constitution chose the commercial, free-market capitalist way, with very definite expectations. In *Federalist* No. 12, Alexander Hamilton introduced into the American political debate the two great themes of Adam Smith's *Wealth of Nations* (1776): the mutual enrichment that results from the division of labor (e.g., Hamilton demonstrated how the "interests" of agriculture and commerce "are intimately blended and interwoven") and the "invisible hand" (i.e., the pursuit of self-interest energizes individuals, which produces personal wealth, which increases national wealth, which enlarges government revenues).[6] Hamilton foresaw that if the government would refrain from "arbitrary and vexatious" taxation and regulation, all Americans would prosper *and* government would obtain the funding necessary to defend itself and secure its people.

When Tocqueville arrived in the United States, he was impressed by the *economic* effects of America's free-market economy, but he found its *moral* consequences even more significant. It "prepare[d] men for freedom," he wrote. "Commerce is naturally adverse to all the violent passions; it loves to temporize, takes delight in compromise, and studiously avoids irritation. It is patient, insinuating, flexible, and never has recourse to extreme measures until obliged by the most absolute necessity. Commerce renders men independent of one another, gives them a lofty notion of their personal importance, leads them to seek to conduct their own affairs, and teaches them how to conduct them well. . . ."[7]

That is, Tocqueville perceived that free-market capitalism cultivated moral virtue: empathy, a sense of fairness, patience, self-reliance, self-improvement, self-esteem, and an entrepreneurial perspective toward other people's problems.

Moreover, Tocqueville observed that those who became engaged in commerce hated wars and were indifferent to politics of any kind, wryly commenting,

> [In America] no one is fully contented with his present fortune; all are perpetually striving, in a thousand ways, to improve it. Consider any one of them at any period of his life and he will be found engaged with some new project for the purpose of increasing what he has. Do not talk to him of the interests and the rights of mankind. This small domestic concern absorbs for the time all his thoughts and inclines him to defer political agitations to some other season. This not only prevents men from making revolutions, but deters men from desiring them.[8]

Combining the Insights of Hamilton and Tocqueville

Were we to combine Hamilton's economic expectations with Tocqueville's moral observations, we would anticipate a future in which America's commercial society would be marked by five distinctive traits: a widely shared entrepreneurial "can-do" attitude, economic abundance, a passion for innovation, an abhorrence of war, and a relative lack of interest in politics. Today these very features distinguish American life from nations with more centralized economies.

The "Can-Do" Attitude of the Entrepreneur

Anyone who has ever visited Thomas Edison's nineteenth-century lab in West Orange, New Jersey, or viewed Henry Ford's mid-twentieth-century assembly line in River Rouge, Michigan, or has driven through present-day Silicon Valley in Northern California quickly gains an appreciation of what is meant by a "can-do" perspective. Edison, Ford, and the pioneers of electronics technology found needs and filled them. The entrepreneurial genius Henry J. Kaiser put the attitude well: "A problem is nothing more than an opportunity in work clothes."

There are literally millions of American entrepreneurs today. A recent article in the *Wall Street Journal* related the story of one in absorbing detail.[9] It's the tale of a man who, in Tocqueville's words, "conduct[ed] his own affairs . . . and conduct[ed] them well":

> Augie Nieto, a once chubby teenager who opened a gym to support his way through college, liked a stationary exercise bike that recorded his heartbeat. He sold his gym, bought marketing rights for the machine, spent a year traveling 5,000 miles across the country—and sold 11 bikes. Undaunted by failure, he and the bike maker sent free "Lifecycles" to 50 big health clubs, which installed them. The exercise bikes proved popular, and soon paying customers were lining up to buy them. Seventeen years later, Nieto sold his business for $310 million.
>
> Then, misfortune struck. Nieto was diagnosed with ALS [amyotrophic lateral sclerosis, or "Lou Gehrig's disease," a degeneration of the nerve cells in the brain and spinal cord]. No treatment helped him. "Your first reaction is denial, then anger," Nieto told the journalists. "Then you get ready to fight."[10]

The *Wall Street Journal* article continued: "Taking matters into his own hands, Mr. Nieto drew up plans for an ALS foundation, Augie's Quest, that he and his wife's family put money into. To raise funds for a study, he turned to the Muscular Dystrophy Association, or MDA, a group involved in more than 40 neuromuscular diseases and one of the biggest funders of ALS research. He wanted the project to have the attributes of an entrepreneurial business—speed, efficiency and focus."

According to the *Journal* article, Nieto quickly became exasperated with the slow reaction of the nonprofit association to his initiative: "Nieto's doctor warned him that the MDA tended to organizational inertia, the kind of frustrating behavior that Nieto had encountered in selling exercise machines. He wore down MDA's resistance to move swiftly, but never got its wholehearted support ('We have defined ways of doing things,' said an MDA vice president, Sharon Hesterlee. 'Augie wants us to do things very quickly. He's blown things apart')."

Thereafter, he overcame one obstacle after another. His health continued to deteriorate, he could no longer feed himself, his illness caused troubling mood swings, his talk became slurred. Nonetheless, he transformed a dinner honoring him personally into a fund-raiser that generated a million dollars, which Nieto then used as capital to gain the cooperation of scientists, clinics, and genomics research laboratories. He found a way to circumvent government privacy regulations in order to obtain genetic data from 1,250 ALS victims, information necessary to the genetic-related research he was sponsoring. He decided to release the results of the research long before they could be published in a peer-refereed journal, a timeliness that accelerated the efforts of competing research teams at Johns Hopkins University and the National Institutes of Health. Through it all, he was simply indomitable. The *Journal* article ended with this triumphal last paragraph:

> Mr. Nieto says his mind is as sharp as ever and he isn't stopping. His latest project: to financially kick-start a new institute that focuses on cutting-edge ALS research. "The business of ALS is a blast," Mr. Nieto says. "The disease sucks."

There, in graphic detail, is what is meant by the entrepreneurial perspective: high energy, getting "things done very quickly," the drive to achieve, curiosity, optimism, relentless searching for opportunities, impatience with routines, persistence in the face of problems and obstacles, using competition to prod himself and others to work supernormally hard, a willingness to risk failure, and, above all, a desire to be useful to others in solving their problems.

Imagine Nieto and others like him—his story is not unique—confined in a centralized system, where government planners would resist his every move to break through routine; where there would be no competitor to play off against; and where his energy, his curiosity, his optimism, his work habits, and his relentless spirit would be wasted.

The extent of entrepreneurship in America astounds. There are more than six million private firms in America at the present time, each of which was originated by someone with an idea and the personal ambition to transform it into something that customers would find useful. Most of these enterprises are "small businesses" with less than five hundred employees. During the past century these "small" firms have produced many of the nation's most notable innovations, from the personal computer to soft contact lenses to double-knit fabrics. And no one is excluded from the ranks of entrepreneurship. Women, for example, own more than a million businesses and provide jobs for twenty million Americans, a workforce that outnumbers all the employees in the nation's five hundred largest companies *combined*.[11]

Not all commercial undertakings succeed. Entrepreneurs take risks and not infrequently end up losing their investments of time, energy, and money. Laws of bankruptcy encourage such risk-taking, however, permitting those who have tried and failed a "second chance" by relieving entrepreneurs of their financial indebtedness and thus enabling them to begin again. The nation's founders thought this "safety net" of such importance in spurring entrepreneurship that they expressly gave Congress the constitutional authority to "establish . . . uniform laws on the subject of bankruptcies throughout the United States."[12]

Abundance

In the last chapter we spoke of the abundance of the American economy, of how by the end of the nineteenth century potential supply began to outdistance actual demand, thereby spurring a need for the art of advertising. Today, in America's "affluent society,"[13] for instance, the average household has 1.9 cars. Even the 13 percent of Americans below the so-called poverty line have "stuff": two-thirds of them have air conditioners, the poorest households own an average of 2.1 television sets, 95 percent have refrigerators, 60 percent own computers. According to the Bureau of Labor Statistics, "More than 92% of Americans below the poverty line said they had enough food, as of 1998. Some 86% said they had no unmet need for a doctor, 89% had no roof leaks, and 87% said they had no unpaid rent or mortgage."[14]

There is, however, a disconcerting anomaly in the midst of this abundance: the tragic appearance of an underclass.[15] The underclass is distinguished by three traits: illegitimacy (out-of-wedlock births to single mothers), nonparticipation in the labor market (males who are neither in school nor seeking work), and predatory criminality.[16]

In the past half-century, the number of illegitimate children who were raised in fatherless homes soared across all ethnic lines, but most starkly among black Americans. In 1964, two in ten black children were born out of wedlock; today that number has grown to seven in ten. That has meant that in some neighborhoods, there are virtually no married fathers holding steady, secure jobs and taking their parenting responsibilities seriously.

Coincident with this explosion of illegitimacy in the black community has been an equally troubling trend in nonparticipation in the labor market. Despite tight labor markets and an abundance of job opportunities in prosperous years, a quarter of all black males, aged sixteen to twenty-four and not enrolled in school, had no job and were not seeking one (a figure aggravated whenever the economy turns down). In those crucial, youthful years, they are passing up the opportunity to master job skills, adopt good work habits, and build a steady job history. Consequently, when and if they want to get a job, they lack the necessary resources to be useful except in menial, unskilled, and insecure work.

What so many of these fatherless, jobless youth were turning to was predatory crime. While the national crime rate actually fell in the last decade, the principal cause of declining criminality was increasing rates of incarceration. In the last three decades, when penalties for crime grew in severity, the number of persons "under correctional supervision"—that is, persons in prison, on probation, or on parole—tripled from under two million to nearly six million. The number in prison quadrupled since 1980, from a half-million to two million. With countless offenders off the streets, the streets grew safer. Nevertheless, the number of persons engaged in crime, or would be but for their incapacitation behind bars, rose.

One dismal consequence of this expanding urban underclass has been that ever larger numbers of fatherless, male adolescents are growing up in neighborhoods where the only adult male visible as a model is a criminal predator notable for his irresponsible sex, irresponsible work habits, and irresponsible violence. The growth of this American underclass, unseen amidst the dazzling abundance most Americans enjoy, promises a troubled future.

The causes of this growth of an underclass of social misfits are complex and probably interactive—a belief that the solution to poverty is to increase the "dole," encouragement of welfare dependency, conditioning welfare on being a husbandless mother, illegal addictive drugs, cultural permissiveness, a culture of "victimhood," elite denigration of traditional American ways, and insidious political leadership. What is clear, however, is that free-market capitalism did *not* contribute to it. Despite the entrepreneurial opportunities and the availability of jobs that our commercial society has generated, a segment of the population has shunned the chance to improve its lot and gone down a different and corrupting path.

Sociologist Charles Murray has studied the underclass for over three decades and has uttered this sobering (and humane) cry from the heart:[17]

[T]o be a member of what we call the underclass is an awful way to live a human life. It is awful for reasons having nothing to do with food, shelter, clothing, medical care, or any of the other commodities that activist government knows how to provide. . . . We have successfully assuaged our guilt about the underclass by spending money on the commodities. Providing the other requisites of a satisfying life—family, neighborhood, safety and civility, productive work—is too tough. Thinking about how these good things come about would require us to think about how it is that families form and become nurturing centers of life; how neighborhoods form and find willing recruits to perform the functions of neighborhoods; how children grow up understanding the necessity and the dignity of productive work. . . .

[We are presently moving] toward what I have . . . called "custodial democracy," whereby the mainstream subsidizes but also walls off the underclass. In effect, custodial democracy takes as its premise that a substantial portion of the population cannot be expected to function as citizens. . . . We just increase the number of homeless shelters, restore the welfare guarantee, build more prison cells, and life for the rest of us goes on, pleasantly. At some point we will be unable to avoid recognizing that custodial democracy has arrived. This will mark a fundamental change in how we conceive of America. Will anyone mind?[18]

"Creative Destruction"

The third consequence of free-market capitalism is an avalanche of improvements. Of course, with every new and improved product there is a multitude of unsettling consequences, destabilizing the old order. Wooden buggy wheelwrights went bankrupt when Henry Ford invented an inexpensive car. The Internet destroyed the monopoly of major networks over entertainment. Few of the major corporations who comprised the original Dow Industrial Average are still in existence. "Creative destruction" is the name for this process of improvement and oblivion, a term coined by one of America's most influential economists, Joseph Schumpeter.[19]

Central planners are averse to the disruption caused by improvements. They depend on stability because their plans are founded on the conditions they know at the outset of their planning. They also feel responsible to maintain the status quo lest anyone then alive suffer disruption. They would, in Hamlet's poignant phrase, "rather bear those ills we have than fly to others that we know not of."[20] Indeed, being planners and removed from the actual production and distribution of things, they haven't a clue as to what is yet to be. To borrow from *Hamlet* once again, this time out of context but applicable as a warning to central planners, "There are more things in heaven and earth . . . than are dreamt in your philosophy."[21]

Aversion to War

The fourth consequence of capitalism is a public loathing of war. Imagine how the entrepreneur Augie Nieto would feel about war. Irritated would be too mild a word. Far from being a field of glory, a war would interrupt his relentless, single-minded pursuit of a cure for ALS. Entrepreneurs—and in a free-market capitalist society practically everyone feels himself an entrepreneur—are too busy conducting their own affairs to want to be heroic.[22]

In contrast, a war is like manna from heaven for central planners, presenting them an occasion for heroic effort.[23] Pathologically, the one purpose effectively served by central planning is winning wars.[24]

Indifference to Politics

Finally, capitalism creates an indifference to government and politics. People want to be "left alone" to do their own thing. That they don't depend on an active government has beneficial consequences for democratic politics. When government plays a marginal role in a free-market capitalist society, its relative unimportance permits electoral democracy to thrive. Since the scope of government in a commercial society is limited, the personal stake any American has in an election outcome is relatively insignificant, allowing him to be more or less indifferent as to who wins political office. He quietly accepts changes in the public administration.

If, however, individual livelihoods, family hopes, and personal dreams depended on an agent of government—on some assistant deputy secretary of commerce, for instance—Americans would care, and care so deeply about election outcomes that they would not suffer defeat calmly and tolerantly. They would take to the streets with rage and guns.

Capitalism's Power to Distort?

If free-market capitalism generates can-do perspectives, material abundance, inventiveness, peacefulness, and political tolerance of opposition, what's not to like about it?

The criticism leveled by some intellectuals is that free-market capitalism distorts political democracy, thereby inhibiting government from rectifying material inequalities. In a capitalist society large corporations become too powerful an influence in elections. Consider the allegations made by two celebrated political scientists, Robert Dahl and Charles Edward Lindblom. While they are not alone in their concerns, they are both representative of their breed and also rightly regarded as among the very best of them. Lindblom's *Politics and Markets*[25] and Dahl's *On Democracy*[26] are the most coherent of the arguments condemning free-market capitalism for the harm it does to democracy and the quest for material equality. Let's assess their three central criticisms.

Undue Moral Power

Their first concern is that big business exercises undue moral power. Lindblom charges that the "incessant, broadly targeted, and vast advertising" of commercial corporations is "a powerful instrument for indoctrination." According to Lindblom, corporate America speaks with an "authority so broad, so deep, so unconstrained as to require the emasculation of the authority of the church, labor union, fraternal association, school—even family." This omnipotent source of ideas is silent as to the "grand issues" of distributive justice—the "high degree of corporate autonomy, protection of the status quo on distribution of income and wealth, close consultation between business and government, and restriction of union demands to those consistent with business profitability."[27]

According to Lindblom, the networks are filling the air with ads that propagate pro-business ideas, and their production of coarse and violent programs diverts the viewers' attention from social inequities and elite iniquity.

But are large corporations as all-powerful as Lindblom insists? For purposes of argument, let us stipulate that the motives of the once-dominant television networks and their corporate advertisers were to silence debate on issues of injustice and corporate misbehavior. Have their efforts been successful? I'd suggest not. It sometimes looks to me like corporations are the very entities that bring Professor Lindblom's issues to the fore, and are paying their corporate critics to raise questions about their products and power. Yes, we find paid advertisements telling us about the better ideas of individual corporations like GE, Ford, and Pfizer, but I am more struck by the incessant condemnation of the bad ideas of cigarette companies, the shortcomings of American car manufacturers, and the nefarious practices of pharmaceutical companies. Corporations apparently don't speak with one voice; they are competitors. To be sure, cigarette companies don't condemn their own practices, but pharmaceuticals denounce the products of cigarette companies.

Moreover, corporate voices aren't "overwhelmingly loud" amidst the cacophony of Internet bloggers, cable television, FM radio stations, celebrated universities, and competing political parties, all of which have obliterated the monopoly of the three major television networks. If there was a problem of superior corporate amplification in 1977, the very improvements that capitalism brought about destroyed the structures that begot the problem. Any fear that George Orwell's nightmarish *1984* was in the offing looks utterly groundless today. [28]

Undue Coercive Power

The second criticism is directed at the undue coercive power of corporate America, that it exercises disproportionate weight in elections because it can better mobilize voters to threaten the defeat of any incumbent who dares to be unresponsive to its demands.

Professor Dahl contends that free-market capitalism "generat[es] inequalities in the distribution of political resources."[29] By "political resources," he refers to the means of prompting voters to change (or retain) their elected officials. Corporations and their lobbyists, he points out, provide pro-business candidates with disproportionate amounts of money, organizational skills, access to media, political skill, time, and knowledge of policies. Elections, thus, are biased in favor of the upper economic classes at the expense of the public interest.

Dahl undoubtedly is right that big businesses dependably assist candidates of their political persuasion. So, however, do unions, and so (most reliably of all) do government workers—those we used to dismiss as "the courthouse gang." It's also worth noting that organized labor and government workers (and those sympathetic to them) contribute as much money to electioneering as big business does, and they are not lacking in all the other political resources—organizational and political skills, knowledge, and access to media.

True, there are some groups in America that lack equivalent political resources: noncitizens don't vote at all, and the truly poor—the homeless, criminals imprisoned behind bars, the mentally ill, and those who for one reason or another are unable to get a job—rarely enter the electoral process. Nevertheless, their causes enjoy the well-organized and dependable support of social workers, religious organizations, legal assistance lawyers, charitable foundations, and sympathetic others who lobby and vote on their behalf.[30]

Dahl's critique, in my opinion, founders on his meaning of "inequalities" of political resources. An equal distribution of political resources is a condition that defies convincing definition and is impossible to perfectly attain so long as people have diverse talents and live in different circumstances. Not even Dahl denies that nowadays the *opportunity* to vote is available to virtually everyone, and no one that I know asserts that elected officials are responsive *only* to their "base." With respect to political resources other than the vote, yes, some groups—corporations, unions, media, Hollywood, plaintiffs' lawyers, the "rich"—may be able to contribute more money to an official's campaign fund. But, to repeat a point made earlier in Part I, others have different and offsetting resources: students may have more time than persons engaged in running a business, ministers may have more respectability among their parishioners, nonprofits may have more organizational skills, and academics may have greater in-depth knowledge of particular issues. Nonmoney resources, like time, status, political adeptness, and information, are all invaluable assets in election campaigns. Having different political resources does not mean having unequal political resources.

Undue Reciprocal Power

The third criticism is that corporations wield undue reciprocal power over government. Regarding the making of public policy, critics speak of the Iron Triangle of influence, a cabal of big corporations, bureaucracies, and elected officials.[31] The notion of an Iron Triangle emphasizes the exclusion of the public from having a say in the making of public policy.

It is Lindblom's contention that corporate America can, "over a broad range, insist that government meet their demands, even if those demands run counter to those of citizens expressed through [democratic] controls."[32]

He offers a subtle explanation for big business's undue bargaining power. Democratically elected governments, he points out, do not control the means of production. Corporations do; they provide jobs, goods, services, and economic prosperity, and they invent the solutions to problems like ill health and dirty environments. While government officials take credit for good times (and hence get elected), they get blamed (and hence get defeated) for the onset of unemployment, high commodity prices, a slowing economy, and the perpetuation of problems. In other words, their reelection depends upon the private sector being vigorous and successful. Thus their dependence on big business compels them to accede to its demands to be left alone (or to be given goodies), even if the citizenry as a whole objects. Corporations drive hard bargains because they can, figuratively speaking, blackmail elected officials into lowering taxes, lightening regulation, and tolerating exorbitant profits. In a nutshell, business can do without government, but a democratically elected government cannot do without a prosperous business sector.[33]

But is the balance of power of corporations and government really so askew as Lindblom suggests? Is the bargaining power of corporations so great that they need not compromise? The statutes passed by Congress and the state legislatures strike me as awash with compromise. Corporations did not get their way when unionization of workers was legalized; or when they were compelled to clean up the environment at their expense; or when they were required to compensate any worker injured on the job, even when the worker himself caused the harm; or when they were saddled with supporting older citizens (they provide half the revenues of Social Security); or when they were taxed at 35 percent and more on their profits.[34] There's no evidence that they are being left alone, and a lot of evidence that their efforts to drive a hard bargain don't avail them much. In fact, it may be that their very size and the extent of their assets may make them vulnerable to counterthreats, diminishing their bargaining power and causing them to deal fairly.

Capitalism and Personal Freedom

Against these problematic allegations that free-market capitalism distorts democracy by overweighting the opinions, electoral muscle, and bargaining power of large corporations, one sets its benefits.

Even to the collectivist goals of Lindblom and Dahl, free-market capitalism makes two contributions. Its inventiveness and specialized skills produce prosperity and create government revenues sufficient to meet the real needs of people. And, by offering competition to virtually every governmental undertaking, it improves government performance and bureaucratic responsiveness to the public needs.

But, more importantly, free-market capitalism requires individuals to collaborate through reciprocal power, and thereby it cultivates the habits and morals that citizens need in order to live in a free society—self-improvement, empathy, trustworthiness, and mattering to others. In this connection its superiority to collectivist socialism is striking.

No doubt, genuine socialists are driven by a compassion for the least powerful in a market-capitalist society. Karl Marx, socialism's forefather, did not scorn commerce out of hand; he conceded its great energy and creativity, but he denied the morality of free-market capitalism. As he saw it, reciprocity made human nature worse, motivating people to be greedy, callous, and mean. Socialism, he claimed, would bring out our better angels.

In this, he was dead wrong.

What turns out to be morally pernicious is not capitalism but Marx's cure for inequality, summed up in his aphorism, "From each according to his ability, to each according to his need!"[35] Socialism turns the healthy motivations of reciprocity topsy-turvy. If an individual is entitled to the resources of a society "according to his need," he has to remain needy. Unless he stays improvident, unschooled, unhealthy, and disinclined to improve himself, he loses his entitlements. Worse yet, if anyone does improve his abilities and earns an income by being useful to others, he is punished by expropriation "according to his ability." There lie the makings of a pathologically self-destructive society.

Without demeaning their good intentions, we can condemn socialists for corrupting the very traits they were trying to strengthen. Their scheme creates a horrific "moral hazard." And, in addition to interfering with the character-improving dynamic of reciprocity, it also creates a "political hazard." It leads communities back to coercion—back to the threat of force—as the exclusive means of securing cooperation.

To condemn socialism we need not claim that free-market capitalism is perfect and will run by itself. The late Pope John Paul II warned, "Capitalism without the discipline of morality turns savage." The possibility always exists that a commercial people will find their ambition turning into avarice, their anxieties into cut-throat competition, and their empathy for others' needs into exploitation of others' weaknesses. These morbid tendencies require careful pruning under the promptings of religion,[36] education, and enlightened taxation (as we shall see in the next chapter). But if it is the case that capitalism without the discipline of morality may turn barbaric, it is no less true that morality lacking the motivation of reciprocity turns flaccid and stops regenerating itself.

NOTES

1. *Federalist* No. 6.
2. To clarify: if I invest $1,000 in a partnership that goes bankrupt owing $100,000, I will not only lose my $1,000 investment, but I am also liable for the entire $100,000 owing to creditors. If I invest $1,000 in a corporation that eventually goes bankrupt owing $100,000, I will only lose my $1,000 investment.
3. In the example, the injured victims have a monetary incentive to prosecute their case against the manufacturer of the brake manufacturer *and* the car company that installed it.
4. Innovation *destabilizes* old ways of doing things.
5. *Sloth:* I have always loved the word. One of my favorite poets, Linda Pasten, wrote a poem about the vice of sloth. It goes this way: "The indolent sloth / has three toes / on each front foot, / a small mammal, slow moving / and from . . . / South America. / Since you ask, / I would tell you which country, / but I am too tired / to look it up."
6. Consider two paragraphs from *Federalist* No. 12:

    The prosperity of commerce is now perceived and acknowledged, by all enlightened statesmen, to be the most useful as well as the most productive source of national wealth; and has accordingly become a primary object of their political cares. By multiplying the means of gratification, by promoting the introduction and circulation of the precious metals [i.e., money], those darling objects of human avarice and enterprise, it serves to vivify and invigorate the channels of industry, and to make them flow with greater activity and copiousness. The assiduous merchant, the laborious husbandman, the active mechanic, and the industrious manufacturer, all orders of men look forward with eager expectation, and growing alacrity to this pleasing reward of their toils. The often agitated question, between agriculture and commerce, has from indubitable experience received a decision, which has silenced the rivalships that once subsisted between them, and has proved to the satisfaction of their friends, that their interests are intimately blended and interwoven.

> The ability of a country to pay taxes must always be proportioned, in a great degree to the quantity of money in circulation, and to the celerity with which it circulates. Commerce, contributing to both of these objects, must of necessity render the payment of taxes easier, and facilitate the requisite supplies of the treasury.

7. Alexis de Tocqueville, *Democracy in America,* trans. Henry Reeve (New York: Bantam 2000 [1840]), vol. II, book 3, chap. 21.

8. Ibid.

9. Gautam Naiik and Antonio Regalado, "A Fitness Mogul, Stricken by Illness, Hunts for Genes," *Wall Street Journal,* November 30, 2006, 1.

10. Ibid.

11. U.S. Department of Labor, Bureau of Labor Statistics; U.S. Department of Commerce, Census Bureau, "Statistics of U.S. Businesses." Roughly 120 million Americans have jobs in the private workplace. Another 20 million are employed in the civilian public sector as teachers, law enforcement officials, "bureaucrats," and the like. In addition, roughly 1.5 million are military personnel on active duty.

12. U.S. Constitution, Article I, Section 8, Paragraph 4.

13. The title, incidentally, of economist John Kenneth Galbraith's popular book, *The Affluent Society* (Boston: Houghton Mifflin, 1958).

14. Mark Trumbull, "Poverty Now Comes with a Color TV," *Christian Science Monitor;* Bureau of Labor Statistics, *Consumer Expenditure Survey Interview Data, 1992 and 2002.*

15. This discussion of the American underclass is drawn exclusively from Charles Murray's indispensable article, "The Underclass Revisited" (Washington, D.C.: American Enterprise Institute Online, 2000).

16. As to the size of the underclass, Joel Devine and James D. Wright, in *The Greatest of Evils: American Poverty and the Underclass* (Piscataway, N.J.: Aldine Transaction, 1993), 91, conclude,

> With no firm consensus on the very definition of the underclass, there can obviously be no firm estimate of its size. [T]he urban underclass, defined simply on the basis of demographic conditions, could not comprise more than about 3 or 3.5 million persons, or roughly a tenth of the total poverty population. But the demographic exclusions used to produce that number (e.g., children, the elderly, the working poor) would clearly include large numbers of urban poor living in underclass neighborhoods, who by our present definition would therefore have to be included. The earlier figure perhaps better represents the maximum size of the perpetrator subgroup, not the class as a whole.

17. Murray, "The Underclass Revisited," 17–18.

18. Ibid., Murray condemns America's then current welfare policies:

Thinking about those questions honestly, without self-indulgence, would require us to consider the possibility that a large underclass exists in the midst of the affluence and opportunities of American society only because of destructive public policies that encourage its existence. . . .

Broad swathes of American society are becoming more civil and less vulgar, more responsible and less self-indulgent. The good news is truly good, and extends beyond the qualities measured by statistics. The bad news is, perhaps, manageable. One way to interpret the nation's success in reestablishing public order is that we have learned how to cope with the current underclass. One may then argue that the size of the underclass is stabilizing, meaning that we can keep this up indefinitely. It requires only that we set aside moral considerations and accept that the huge growth of the underclass since 1960 cannot now be reversed.

19. Joseph A. Schumpeter, *Capitalism, Socialism, and Democracy*, 3rd ed. (New York: Harper and Row, 1950 [1942]).
20. William Shakespeare, *Hamlet*, Act III, Scene 1.
21. Ibid., Act I, Scene 5.
22. Census data estimate that there are 25 million small businesses in the United States. To that figure must be added the countless millions with commercial side interests (e.g., engaged in Internet auctions, garden sales, and antique collecting).
23. No one makes this point more convincingly than Walter Lippmann in *The Good Society* (New York: Grosset and Dunlap, 1956 [1937]).
24. Politically, dictators of socialized economies use wars to distract people from the stagnation and failures of their planning. See, among others, Lippmann, ibid., and Natan Sharansky, *The Case for Democracy* (New York: Perseus Books, 2004).
25. Charles E. Lindblom, *Politics and Markets: The World's Political-Economic Systems* (New York: Basic Books, 1977).
26. Robert A. Dahl, *On Democracy* (New Haven, Conn.: Yale University Press, 1989).
27. Lindblom, *Politics and Markets*, 53, 356, and 204–205.
28. As to what explains America's inattention to Lindblom's "grand issues," recall Tocqueville's description of America in 1832, when there were no big corporations equipped with mass-communication technologies: every American "will be found engaged with some new project for the purpose of increasing what he has, [which] inclines him to defer political agitations to some other season." *Democracy in America*, vol. II, book 3, chap. 21. Certainly a plausible explanation of Americans' seeming indifference to "political agitations" is their concentration on projects of their own devising and their personal responsibility for their success.
29. Dahl, *On Democracy*, 177.

30. For more on the topic of who constitutes the electorate, see Chapter 26.
31. Critics often note that government regulators leave their agencies to join the firms they had been regulating and legislators retire to become lobbyists for corporations whose causes they had championed.
32. Lindblom, *Politics and Markets*, 356.
33. "One of the great misconceptions of conventional economic theory is that businessmen are induced to perform their functions by purchase of their goods and services. What is required in addition is a set of governmentally provided inducements in the form of market and political benefits. . . . In the 18th century, for example, England established almost a thousand local road improvement authorities. . . . When railroads became feasible, special legislation—more than 600 parliamentary acts between 1844 and 1847—granted attractive benefits to railroad companies. . . . In the United States, Alexander Hamilton's *Report on Manufactures* put government in an active, supportive role for business." Ibid., 173–174.
34. The federal tax rate currently has been reduced to 35 percent, but states and local governments also tax corporations on their profits and properties.
35. Karl Marx, *Critique of the Gotha Program* (1875).
36. By "religion" I mean it in the sense of the scholar Joseph Needham's definition: "[T]he theology of a transcendent creator-deity." See Samuel P. Huntington, *Who Are We? The Challenges to America's National Identity* (New York: Simon and Schuster, 2004), 109.

23

THE MORAL EFFECTS OF TAXATION

[The Prince] ought to encourage his citizens peaceably to pursue their affairs, whether in trade, in agriculture, or in any other human activity, so that no one will hesitate to improve his possessions for fear that they will be taken from him, and no one will hesitate to open a new avenue of trade for fear of taxes.

Niccolò Machiavelli, *The Prince* (1513)

How should a free-market, capitalist society be governed? An old Chinese saying urges, "Governing a great country is like cooking a small fish: Don't overdo it." Translated, that piece of wisdom warns that when coercion is not absolutely necessary, it's absolutely necessary not to use it. To ensure safety, deter theft (in all its varieties), and provide the conditions to make reciprocity effective, government coercion is indispensable. Otherwise, leave people to do what they want.

But is that all there is to governing? Should there not be a leadership component to influence the citizenry to enlarge their ideas of what they want? And if there should be, how might political leaders go about that task in a commercial society?

Ironically, America's system of taxation has proved to be a remarkably effective instrument of moral improvement. I say "ironically" because the power to tax would appear to be like robbery ("your money or your life"). When carefully employed, however, taxation can direct actions in beneficial directions and elevate beliefs about hard work, constructive stewardship, good citizenship, charitableness, and risk-taking.

For two reasons, taxation is an effective means of inducing social change in a free society (and of securing consensus as well). It offers people choices of behavior—an offer often too good to refuse, but a choice, nonetheless. Moreover, its influence recurrently is felt by vast numbers of people—i.e., all of America's taxpayers. Therefore, attention needs to be paid to the ways the government uses its taxing powers as an instrument of social engineering.

Americans Pay a Large Amount of Taxes

But first, we need a rough idea of how much Americans pay in the way of taxes. For a general understanding, approximate figures of revenues and percentages will suffice.

The taxes collected by American governments are considerable. In each year of the first decade of the twenty-first century, tax revenues added up to $5 *trillion*, half of which were assessed by the federal government and half of which were raised by the governments of the fifty states and their countless local governing units—$2.5 trillion to Washington and $2.5 trillion for such entities as the state of Nebraska, Cook County, the city of Peoria, and the like.

Of the $2.5 trillion paid annually to the federal government, half of that (a bit more than $1.25 trillion) was raised by personal and corporate income taxes. The other $1.25 trillion came from a variety of sources—Social Security taxes (often called "payroll taxes"), gas taxes, estate taxes, excise taxes, phone taxes, import duties, airport fees, fees for services, and so on. Of the various revenue sources available to the federal government, personal and corporate income taxes were the most volatile, for they depended on the robustness of the economy. For example, once the shock of the terrorists' attacks on September 11, 2001, was absorbed, corporate income tax revenues doubled to $300 billion in the short space of two years, and personal income tax revenues rose 22 percent to a trillion dollars in that same period of renewed prosperity. Then, with the recession that followed, both sources of revenue plummeted once again.

Personal income taxes were additionally volatile because they were "progressive" in nature. That is, the more a family made, the higher the tax rate that applied to its income. A married couple with two children paid no federal income tax if their income was $35,000 or less. The same family with an income of $50,000 owed $1,500 in taxes, which meant its effective tax rate was roughly 3 percent. In contrast, wealthy families (that is, those who earned $1,200,000 or more, and hence were in the top 1 percent of taxpaying households) paid at a 30 percent–effective federal tax rate.[1] While there were 130 million or so taxpayers, this top 1 percent ended up paying roughly 40 percent of all federal personal income tax revenues; the top 25 percent paid 85 percent. When that relatively tiny group of the very rich momentarily suffered a financial setback (as it did in 2008), the government experienced a serious revenue shortfall.[2]

The Effect of Taxes on Habits of Behavior

I have simplified the discussion by not discussing the great variety of taxes assessed by state and local governments (in addition to personal and corporate income taxes, they reaped revenues from sales taxes, property taxes, and auto fees), which Americans must pay over and above their federal income tax. But by now, it may be apparent that the average American pays a lot of what he earns to government—about $1 of every $3 he makes. What are the consequences?

Recall Machiavelli's advice on how to govern well:

[The Prince] ought to encourage his citizens peaceably to pursue their affairs, whether in trade, in agriculture, or in any other human activity, so that no one will hesitate to improve his possessions for fear that they will be taken from him, and no one will hesitate to open a new avenue of trade for fear of taxes.[3]

Taxes are the archetypical coercive act. Because taxes are enforced by threat—government gets something for nothing, or at least for what might appear to be less than it gives back—Machiavelli warned that tax levies will necessarily have collateral effects; the taxpayer is likely to react by fighting or fleeing from them. If the object to which a tax attaches is either his labor or his improved property, his reaction will be to reduce the ardor with which he pursues his "trade" and the ambition that prompts him to improve his assets. Experience taught Machiavelli that the immediate consequence of raising the rates of tax—the unintended effect—is for the taxpayer to dwarf his taxable asset. High tax rates diminish the motivation to work, save, invest, purchase, or do anything else that is taxable.

History abounds with evidence bearing out Machiavelli's insight. Once upon a time French monarchs applied high taxes to salt, and soon salt disappeared as an ingredient in French cuisine. Then they taxed windows in their subjects' houses, and soon people were building their homes without windows. Likewise, in more recent times, the city of Oakland, California, attempted to tax new homes according to the number of rooms in them. Almost immediately, homes were being designed without any interior walls. (Readers might be relieved to know that the city quickly repealed the tax.)

Similarly, taxes on work, at some rate, will reduce work. There is some evidence of that effect. Recall that Americans pay on average one dollar of taxes on every three dollars they earn. Europeans pay one dollar and a half on every three dollars they earn, 50 percent more than in the United States. American per capita output—that is, the total value of goods and services produced by the American labor force divided by 150,000,000, America's civilian full-time workers—was $39,700 in 2003, almost 40 percent higher than the average of $28,700 for Europeans that year. It would appear that Americans work harder and longer than their European counterparts, and lower taxes on the fruits of their labors might have something to do with it. Machiavelli, for one, would not be surprised by that fact.

The Laffer Curve

If we were to express Machiavelli's insight graphically, we would see this: On the graph, the horizontal axis would display tax rates on income, from a low of 0 percent to a high of 100 percent, while the vertical axis would represent the government's receipts resulting from the income tax, from no revenue to, let's say, a trillion dollars. If the rate of tax on income is 0 percent, government revenues from income taxes will obviously be zero. If the rate of tax is elevated to 100 percent, government revenues will also be zero, for people will cease to work for profit if all the income stemming from their work is taken away from them.

If the tax is only 5 percent, people will probably continue to work vigorously; in fact, they may work even harder to generate more income to make up for the 5 percent they have to pay to government. If the rate is 10 percent, the same may hold true for taxpayers—they probably will continue to work, and voilà, the government will reap twice the revenues it acquired when the rate was 5 percent. Continue to raise the rate: the taxpayers may continue doggedly to work, and government revenues will continue to increase. But at some point, the citizenry's aversion to taxes will become significant. The disincentive effect of high taxes will overwhelm their motivation; they will stop working hard, productivity will decline, and the tax base on which the higher rates are applied will shrink, with the result that government revenues will start going down—to zero when the rate hits 100 percent.

Thus our graph will depict a curve, the apogee of which is indeterminate or, to put it another way, is dependent on the circumstances. One can imagine, for example, that in wartime taxpayers might feel that high taxes are being legitimately assessed and, as a result, they continue to work hard, even though a significant fraction of their incomes (say, 65 percent) is taxed away. On the other hand, were they to become convinced that many of government's activities were unnecessary, they might cut back on their workaholic habits when the tax rate approaches 50 percent and shift their energies to nonmoney activities like family, hobbies, and fun.

Consequently, changing tax rates sometimes can have a paradoxical economic result. When the government increases "[the rate of] taxes," tax revenues go down, and when it "cuts taxes"—that is, if the government lowers the rate of tax—tax revenues go up. For example, in 2004 Congress reduced the capital gains and dividend tax rates; as a result, the revenues from capital gains taxes went up 79 percent, and revenues from taxes on dividends rose 35 percent.

The economic fact represented in that hump-backed graph is called the Laffer Curve. Its name is new, but it represents an insight as old as Machiavelli: tax an activity, and you will get less of it; exempt it, and you will encourage it.

The point is, taxes have unintended effects: they can darken homes, remove salt from French cuisine, eliminate inner walls from homes, and stifle work. But can taxes be used *intentionally*, so as to engineer socially valuable consequences and enlighten the self-interest of people?

The Moral Effects of the American Tax Code

Since taxpayers will invariably strive to escape the threat of taxes, policymakers can create escape hatches—"loopholes"—and restrict access to them to those taxpayers who do something worthwhile. Instead of "rewarding" taxpayers for abstaining from salt (to revert to the French example), government can reduce the tax bills for those who improve the lives of others and increase the general welfare.

Example No. 1: Home Mortgage Interest

When Americans buy a home, they invariably take out a mortgage. They borrow from a lending institution at market rates, say, 6 percent. If the "ordinary Joe" borrows $100,000, he pays $6,000 of interest per year. That interest payment, according to the federal tax code, is "deductible"; that is, it will reduce the taxpayer's taxable income by $6,000. Since he is the average American and pays taxes at an effective rate of 33 percent, his interest deduction reduces his tax bill by $2,000. Some economists put it this way: of that $6,000 of interest payments, "ordinary Joe" pays $4,000 and the government pays $2,000.

That is a pretty good deal for the homeowner, especially when contrasted with the tax treatment of tenants, whose payments to their landlords are *not* deductible.

Why the disparate treatment of homeowners and renters? The object of the mortgage-interest loophole is to prod Americans to take a big risk and assume the responsibilities of ownership. The incentive has seemed to succeed: nearly seven in ten American families own their own homes, a rate of homeownership unmatched in the world. And with good effect, for the evidence is that homeowners pour their energies into maintaining and improving their homes ("sweat equity"); renters don't. While homeowners spend their weekends cutting their grass, tiling their bathrooms, painting their kitchens, and otherwise improving the nation's housing stock, renters tend to picnic at the beach and loll on couches gazing at television.[4]

Example No. 2: Tax-Free Treatment of Municipal Bond Interest

Loopholes, even the wisest ones, tend to invite controversy and popular condemnation. Several years ago a number of Congress members drew public attention to the fact that a dozen or so very wealthy Americans were paying no federal income taxes.[5] Typically, they were wealthy widows, ones like a hypothetical dowager we shall call "Mrs. Dodge," who lived in metropolitan Detroit.

Detroit, the one-time "auto capital of the world," has suffered several horrific setbacks in recent decades. The most devastating American urban riots of the 1960s had occurred there, and the scars still remained visible half a century later. Fearful of further violence, Detroiters were fleeing the city in droves. Once the nation's fourth most populous city, Detroit saw its population drop to 800,000, less than that of metropolitan Fresno, California. The sagging fortunes of the auto industry, Detroit's lifeblood, further contributed to its decline. Property values plummeted, and so did property tax revenues, leaving Detroit's parks, schools, streets, public health, and police and fire services neglected and decimated. If ever a city needed an infusion of money, it was Detroit.[6]

Mrs. Dodge obliged, no doubt at the urgings of her accountants. She bought $20 million worth of Detroit's municipal bonds—that is, she lent her considerable wealth to Detroit, in return for which Detroit paid her interest at a rate of 3 percent, half the percentage the private borrower would have to pay. Mrs. Dodge will earn an annual income of $600,000 from her loan to Detroit. Because the Internal Revenue Code exempts municipal bond interest from tax, however, Mrs. Dodge has no tax to pay because she had no *taxable* income.

The reader can visualize the likely newspaper headline: "RICH AMERI-CAN EXPLOITS LOOPHOLE, PAYS NO TAX." The reporter would contrast her zero tax with that of the law-abiding ordinary Joe, who had $60,000 of taxable income but would be paying $20,000 of taxes, $1 of every $3 he earns. (In fact, he would be paying less because of the progressive character of federal and state income taxes, but for illustration's purposes, we will stipulate his taxes are that high.) The editorial comment would condemn Mrs. Dodge, the embodiment of America's "haves," getting away without paying a cent to support the federal government, while the "have-nots" pay for the government that protects her.

But was there injustice? Was the hypothetical Mrs. Dodge shirking her duty to pay her fair share of the nation's burdens? The answer is no, and here is why.

Suppose, instead of buying Detroit's bonds at 3 percent, Mrs. Dodge had put her $20 million into bonds issued by a private company, say, Harrah's Gambling Casinos, which would pay her market rate interest. Remember, it was 6 percent. From that loan, she would receive annual interest payments amounting to $1,200,000. Because she is in the highest federal and state tax brackets, her effective tax rate (the sum of her federal and state taxes) is higher than the 33 percent effective rate paid by "ordinary Joe." Let's assume it's 50 percent (39 percent federal and 11 percent state income tax). That would mean she would pay a tax of $600,000, leaving her with a net income of $600,000—the exact same amount that she would have received, tax free, from investing in Detroit.

But if she's no richer from investing in Detroit's tax-free bonds, who is better off? The answer is the city of Detroit, which has been able to attract an investor with a mere 3 percent interest. The city has saved $600,000 on the money it has borrowed.

Yes, the federal and state governments have been deprived of $600,000 of tax, but their tax codes have given the city of Detroit a savings of $600,000. The headline decrying Mrs. Dodge's "unfair tax-dodge" was all wrong. It should have read, "FEDERAL AND STATE GOVERNMENTS COME TO AID OF A DESPERATE CITY." That would have been the headline had Mrs. Dodge lent her money to Harrah's and sent $600,000 in taxes to Washington (and Lansing, Michigan's state capital), which then granted that sum to Detroit.

Same result, different headlines.

In fact, however, the results would differ a bit. The $600,000 coming by way of Washington and Lansing would have been burdened by "red tape." The government grants of $600,000 would have come with a host of limitations, regulations, and accountants to audit how the funds were being used.

Notice that the purpose and result of the tax-free treatment of municipal bonds—that "loophole"—did not make Mrs. Dodge richer. Its purpose was federalism, its end result was assisting a troubled municipality, and its means avoided excessive bureaucratic entanglement.

Other Examples

Without going into details unnecessary to an understanding of the moral effects of American taxes, it's worth noting several other examples of purposeful social engineering. The deduction for charitable contributions is one.

In 2007 Americans donated $306 *billion* to charity—to the poor and the victimized—and to churches, educational institutions, hospitals, and the arts.[7] No country's citizenry comes close to giving so generously.

Now there's nothing extraordinary about the genetic makeup of Americans: they are no smarter, no more virtuous, and no freer of inclinations to greed than others of the human race. Like everyone else, most Americans are born eight pounds big, twenty-two inches long; and their DNA, allowing for insignificant individual differences, is the same as the rest of humanity's. But they live in a country whose tax code rewards personal generosity, thereby encouraging Americans privately to support great symphony orchestras, ballet companies, opera companies, and art museums;[8] the finest hospitals in the world; a vast array of energetic religious communities and extraordinary universities; vigorous charities like the Salvation Army; passionate public interest groups like the Sierra Club; and an outpouring of donations to the victims of disasters like the tsunami in

Southeast Asia (2004), Hurricane Katrina in New Orleans (2005), and earthquakes in Iran (2003), Pakistan (2005), China (2008), and Japan (2011, devastated by both earthquake and tsunami). Why?

There is a multitude of reasons, but one of them, an important one, is the charitable contributions loophole. It is a loophole that provides an incentive to be personally generous out of self-interest. Government—or rather its tax code—encourages the sharing of one's bounty with others and nurtures habits of giving.

The treatment of capital gains is another example. The rate on them is roughly half of that on ordinary income, a reward for saving and risk-taking. It reinforces the American tradition of entrepreneurship.

Sometimes a loophole designed to encourage one result produces an additional, serendipitous benefit. My favorite example has always been the oil-depletion allowance, now repealed. It provided an advantage to one of the riskiest industries, prospecting for oil.

Boring a hole into rock formations thousands of feet below the Earth's surface in a daring gamble that oil will be found is the very definition of high risk. Initial costs are astronomical, and the existence of oil in an exact location can't be assured before the well is actually drilled. To induce people to undertake such a foolhardy enterprise, Congress provided that a fraction of the revenues resulting from a successful recovery would be free of taxes.

But oil exploration is not only risky; it also requires living in barren places like bitterly cold Wyoming and the sweltering deserts of Texas. Few persons in their right mind would prefer Texas's Permian Basin, for example, to a life in Connecticut. No one, that is, except those who noticed the oil-depletion "loophole" and were willing to sacrifice "easy living" in a temperate and cultivated place in order to reduce their taxes.

There were such people. One of them was a well-educated son of a well-to-do investment banker in New York. He had been a hero in World War II, and he could have had a promising career in the financial world and enjoyed a rich cultural life. Instead, he chose Texas and did the backbreaking work of the "roughneck" in places where the summer temperatures averaged over 100 degrees Fahrenheit and cultural amenities were notable for their absence. All these challenges he willingly faced because 15 percent of his income from selling oil, providing he discovered any, would be tax-free.

That fellow's name was George Herbert Walker Bush, the forty-first president of the United States and father of the forty-third president,

George Walker Bush. He, along with a host of other ambitious men and women, arrived in Texas after the Second World War, raised their children there, and stayed to build a civilization in what was once a godforsaken land. Besides developing their oil fields, the "oil-depletion" generation poured its personal energies and earnings into building several of the world's great universities, major scientific centers, the nation's finest hospitals, extraordinary art museums, symphony orchestras, dance and theatrical companies, and major corporations like Dell Computer. It is not unreasonable to believe that none of that would have happened but for the seductiveness of the oil-depletion loophole.

Five Cautions

So much for the social benefits of particular loopholes. The tax code, which on its face seems so fearsome and coercive, is in reality a moral force for inducing Americans to be personally generous, to save and invest in the future, to maintain our housing stock, to lend money to our neediest governments at bargain-basement rates, and to settle and improve some of the most barren parts of our country. It nurtures habits that are likely to endure and grow for reasons other than merely saving taxes.

It's a smart government that provides productive loopholes. It's a government of which Machiavelli would approve.

There are limits, however, to using the tax code to good moral effect. The first is that government can make mistakes in using the social-engineering effects of taxes. Worse, "favoritism" can invite corruption of the legislative process.

Second, the tax system's incentives for good behavior only apply to taxpayers. Only the "haves" can be induced to behave well with loopholes. For the "have-nots," some other means of social engineering has to be devised. Half a loaf is better than none, but with the dispossessed, reciprocal power—the exchange of tax savings for useful behavior—has its limits.

Third, a government can overdo it. For example, it is tempting to use loopholes to induce an ever-wider variety of good behavior—to save energy, buy Toyota Priuses, or build a waterhole in one's backyard. But in that case the tax code becomes so complicated as to appear unfair.

Fourth, policymakers inclined toward egalitarianism want to use the tax code to redistribute wealth—to take from the rich and give to the poor. Pursuing such a purpose is at odds with the character-shaping function Machiavelli would wish taxes to perform.

Fifth, taxation cannot work its benign effects unless the government's public policies not only appear fair but also put the revenues to acceptable and productive purposes. Otherwise, taxpayers begin to feel that they have been victimized and start devising their own "loopholes," ones that are either illegitimate (like cheating) or unproductive (like unnecessarily complex legal arrangements).

NOTES

1. Effective tax rates differ from "tax bracket" rates (e.g., "He's in the 35 percent tax bracket") for two reasons: exemptions and credits often reduce the tax otherwise owed, and the higher tax rates are applied only to the last dollars earned. Presently, for example, the 35 percent federal tax rate applies only to any taxable dollars in excess of $90,000.
2. Interestingly, one major American tax is "regressive," causing lower-income families to pay at a *higher effective rate* than wealthier families. With Social Security taxes, employees in 2010 were assessed a 6.2 percent tax on their wages and salaries. (Their employers matched their payments.) But that flat 6.2 percent Social Security tax on the earnings of employees was applied only to the first dollars they earned. On any income they received above $94,000, there was no further tax. Thus the *effective* rate of Social Security tax on high earners turned out to be *lower* than that on employees with lesser salaries. Ironically, regressive taxes applied to first dollars turn out to be a more stable source of revenues, "unfair" as they may be.
3. Niccolò Machiavelli, *The Prince*, trans. Daniel Donno (New York: Dell, 1996 [1513]), chap. 21.
4. For a test of the different care given to residential property by owners and tenants, walk through any neighborhood and see if you can determine which homes are occupied by their owners and which by tenants. I'll bet your guesses will be 90 percent right—that the well-groomed home will be owned by its occupants and the unkempt home next door will be a rental property. As a result of the mortgage-interest loophole, America's housing stock is in excellent shape—well maintained and constantly being improved.
5. The controversy led Congress to establish the Alternative Minimum Tax to reduce the availability of "loopholes" when "rich" taxpayers didn't pay what Congress thought should be their "fair share" of the tax burden. Over time prosperity and inflation put middle-class taxpayers within the definition of

"rich," resulting in the unintended consequence of application of the Alternative Minimum Tax to a huge swath of the population.

6. See, for example, Matt Labash, "Down and Out in Detroit: The City Where the Sirens Never Stop," *Weekly Standard*, December 29, 2008, 16–32.

7. Center on Philanthropy, *Giving USA 2008* (Bloomington: Indiana University Press, 2008).

8. Other nations have world-class symphonies, museums, hospitals, and the like, but theirs are established and supported by the state; they are funded by taxes and run by government bureaucrats. The American ones are not; they are the products of personal generosity. That this should be so accords with Tocqueville's observations of America back in 1831: "Wherever at the head of some new undertaking you see the government in France, or a man of rank in England, in the United States you will be sure to find an association [of private individuals]." Alexis de Tocqueville, *Democracy in America*, trans. Henry Reeve (New York: Bantam, 2000 [1840]), vol. II, book 2, chap.5.

In Tocqueville's time, however, American government was so weak and undeveloped that individuals had to combine their private efforts if there were to be *any* new "undertakings." Today American government is no longer a paltry and inept thing, yet Tocqueville's observation remains true.

24

FEDERALISM AND FREEDOM

It is incontestable that the people frequently conduct public business very badly; but it is impossible that the lower orders should take a part in public business without extending the circle of their ideas and quitting the ordinary routine of their thoughts. The humblest individual who co-operates in the government of society . . . is canvassed by a multitude of applicants, and in seeking to deceive him in a thousand ways, they really enlighten him. He takes a part in political undertakings which he did not originate, but which give him a taste for undertakings of the kind. New improvements are daily pointed out to him in the common property and this gives him the desire of improving that property which is his own. He is perhaps neither happier nor better than those who came before him, but he is better informed and more active.

Alexis de Tocqueville, *Democracy in America* (1835)

The story goes that when Ronald Reagan won the California governorship in 1966, among the first things he did was to ask economist Bill Niskanen to assess the possibility of consolidating some of the state's numerous school districts. Reagan believed that if several small school districts could be united into a single large one, some economies of scale might be achieved.

A few months later, Niskanen reported the results of his research. "Governor, I've got some good news and some bad news," he said. "The good news is that there is nearly universal agreement among parents, teachers, and administrators about what to do. The bad news is that they all agree that consolidation is a terrible idea. Virtually everyone insists that 'smaller is better,' and they strongly oppose any move towards further consolidation. What's more, they'd like to break up what has already been consolidated." Thus ended any further speculation about economies of scale.

Consolidation in education was not a new idea. A variant of it was put into effect following the Second World War, when Harvard president and noted physicist James G. Conant proposed that American high schools be consolidated into very large ones. The purpose was not so much financial savings as educational improvement. Conant believed that with large high schools, a greater variety of courses could be offered, especially in advanced math and science. Unfortunately, his suggestions were followed. Huge high schools of four to seven thousand students replaced ones that were small in scale—four hundred to seven hundred students.

Research since has questioned the Conant Report. Yes, some advanced courses did appear in the curricula of these behemoth-like schools and became available to relatively few students. But researchers have concluded that the undesirable aspects of these enormous high schools significantly outweighed their benefits.[1] A serious problem was that large schools offered students far fewer opportunities to develop their talents than littler ones. Where ten modest-sized high schools provided ten varsity football teams, a giant institution provided only one. Likewise, there was only one newspaper, one student council, one debate team, one dramatics group, and one band, utilized only by the most precocious and aggressive among the student body. In contrast, in small high schools, shy students, late-developing students, and students lacking self-confidence were actively recruited— were literally being dragged into participation—because there was always a need for an additional debater, journalist, performer, saxophonist, and left tackle. Once recruited, these more passive boys and girls often developed otherwise undiscovered talents. Smaller indeed is better.

But how to explain the unpopularity of expanding the size of school *districts*? The answer: the more extensive the district, the less control parents felt they had over events affecting their children's education. The school board, the principals, and the officials who taxed and spent to support the schools were more distant, more mired in bigger bureaucracies, busier, less known, less trusted, and less approachable. Compared to smaller and nearby governments, large and remote ones required citizens to exhaust much more time and energy to have any effect.

What Is Federalism?

Federalism functions to combine the advantages of small scale with a society's needs for large scale. The *Federalist* essays coined the term *compound government* to explain the novel regime established by the Constitution.

Consider a great seaport like San Francisco Bay. There, ships are subject to two sovereign governments. The U.S. Coast Guard, besides setting out navigational buoys, rescuing foundering ships, interrupting smugglers, and posting weather warnings, formulates and enforces regulations that apply to all ships. At the same time, the California state government forbids freighters and passenger liners to enter or leave the Bay until a pilot trained and licensed by the state comes aboard to guide them to and away from their dockages. That kind of layering of law upon law is the result of federalism.

Without being overly technical about it, federalism is a distribution of legal authority between a central and local government—a sharing of legal power that cannot be changed by ordinary legislation. It has three essential features:

- Each government is directly connected to the individual citizens (e.g., is elected by them and can tax and regulate them).
- Each government is free to devise its own structure and procedures.
- Each government is entrusted with authority over significant matters.

The original American Constitution was largely concerned with designing a central government that was connected to the people through elections of its principal officers. As for the local (i.e., state) governments, the Constitution was largely silent as to their structure and connection to the people, except that they were required to have "a republican form." The states' jurisdiction encompassed all domestic matters within their geographical bounds; in the words of *Federalist* No. 45, their powers "extend[ed] to all the objects which, in the ordinary course of affairs, concern the lives, liberties and properties of the people, and the internal order, improvement and prosperity of the state."[2]

There were, however, four sections of the Constitution that narrowed their authority.

Article IV required each state to recognize—to give "full faith and credit to"—the legal statuses of individuals established in the other states, especially contractual arrangements, including marriage and, of course, the legal status of slavery.

Article III gave the federal judiciary the right to remove certain types of cases from the jurisdiction of state courts.

Article VI, the Supremacy Clause, declared that the Constitution and laws of the central government in those matters entrusted to it would prevail in the event of an irreconcilable conflict with state laws.

And Article I prohibited the states from meddling in foreign affairs, manipulating the money supply, granting "any title of nobility," and "impair[ing] the obligation of contracts."

But if the Constitution left the states with much of their original sovereignty, it also delegated to the central government broad powers of taxing, spending, conducting foreign affairs, and regulating the commercial life of the nation.[3]

The Advantages of Federalism

There are five advantages of federalism, but also four dangers.[4] The authors of *The Federalist* wrote of two of the advantages. One was that it reduced the likelihood of tyranny. Federalism, they wrote, would function to "controul" the despotic tendencies of government officials. Competing levels of government would check one another from abusing their police powers. Subsequent events have proved the worth of this precaution. In the twentieth century, for example, the federal government took action to stop state governments from practicing racial discrimination and manipulating their electoral systems. At the climax of the struggle for the civil rights of African Americans, the federal government actually sent in the National Guard to compel state officials to desegregate (Arkansas, 1957; Mississippi, 1962). Conversely, local governments have called federal officials to account, as was the case in a notorious instance in Massachusetts when state police were instrumental in uncovering corruption in the FBI's Boston office.[5]

Moreover, a federal system provides another safeguard against despotism: it makes political democracy more effective by providing safe havens in which to organize opposition to the incumbent officeholders. State governors enjoy an autonomy that frees them and their supporters to criticize a corrupt president or congressional majority; they can also organize within their administrations a team of competent colleagues who will be fully prepared to run the central government whenever the national electorate decides to vote the incumbent regime out. It is no coincidence that it has been former governors who have won back the White House in recent years—Texas Republican governor George W. Bush defeated Democrats in

2000, Arkansas Democrat Bill Clinton defeated Republicans in 1992, California Republican Ronald Reagan defeated Democrats in 1980, and Georgia Democrat Jimmy Carter defeated Republicans in 1976.[6] Fortunately, the executive experience of being a governor is a fitting preparation for presidents.

A second advantage anticipated in *The Federalist Papers* is that compound government is more available to the people. Citizens are provided with multiple points of political access. If government at one level fails to respond to a person's needs, other governments at a different level may see things differently and assist. Moreover, local governments are geographically closer to their citizens. Because states have broad powers—"powers [that] extend to all the objects which . . . concern the lives, liberties and properties of the people, and the internal order, improvement and prosperity of the state"—Americans don't have to travel to the nation's capital to zone their cities, develop a workable coastal conservation policy, solve the medical liability crisis, build a university system, upgrade the quality of their public schools, or fix a pothole.

Tocqueville's Insights

In and of themselves, the prevention of tyranny and the prompting of governmental responsiveness would be enough to commend federalism, but Tocqueville pointed to two other advantages to compound government. One was the enriched political education of Americans. Local governments offer ordinary citizens the opportunity to hold political office. Wrestling with significant public problems broadens an individual's vision beyond his family and commercial interests, all the while exercising his political skills in winning over opposition. In Tocqueville's words, participation in the public affairs of his community creates "the close tie that unites private to general interest."[7]

Tocqueville contrasted the stimulation that the ordinary American gains from political participation with the discouragement and resultant alienation that French citizens of his day felt from confronting their highly centralized governmental structure. "In some countries," he wrote, "the inhabitants seem unwilling to avail themselves of the political privileges which the law gives them; it would seem that they set too high a value upon their time to spend it on the interests of the community; and they shut themselves up in a narrow selfishness, marked out by four sunk fences and a quickset hedge."[8]

Tocqueville emphasized a fourth advantage: federalism enables America to mount a strong national defense, yet continue to attend to the more mundane details of domestic matters. He foresaw that America inevitably would be embroiled in international wars. It would then need to raise a formidable military to remain safe, and that could only be accomplished by a central government using the resources of the entire nation. "In wars," Tocqueville wrote, "nations desire, and frequently need, to increase the powers of the central government."[9] But while the central government would then be preoccupied with foreign affairs, local governments would have the authority and competence to discern and respond to the people's domestic concerns.

States as Public Policy Laboratories

Compound government contributes a fifth advantage, one anticipated neither by the founders nor by Tocqueville: the making of better laws. Federalism facilitates a creative process of trial and error. Local officials often are the first to advance solutions for problems and put them into practice within the bounds of their jurisdictions, where their intended and unintended consequences are publicly demonstrated. In other words, the states serve as experimental laboratories for public policy.

The examples are countless. Massachusetts pioneered in the area of no-fault automobile insurance, hoping to eliminate the human and legal costs of litigation in connection with car accidents. Its good intentions proved much more costly than anticipated when owners of dilapidated, unsellable automobiles started running them "accidentally" into telephone poles in order to recover compensation sufficient to buy themselves a better vehicle. Michigan learned from Massachusetts's flawed experiment and developed a no-fault program that controlled the abuses arising in Massachusetts. The Michigan version was then copied by a number of other states—to good effect.

Oregon legalized medical euthanasia, exempting doctors from murder charges when they assisted in the voluntary suicide of their patients. The jury is still out on the moral acceptability of euthanasia, but at least the Oregon experiment provides real outcomes to assess.

Massachusetts legalized gay marriage. The other states waited and took time to observe how Massachusetts would handle such questions as divorce, child custody, welfare entitlement, and taxation of the joint incomes of same-sex couples.

Wisconsin devised a serious welfare-to-work program, helping former welfare recipients adapt to the responsibilities of holding a job. It succeeded so well that the national government adopted parts of it.

In fact, virtually every successful national program—whether it's been collective bargaining legislation, welfare reform, farm subsidies, workers' compensation, unemployment benefits, or food and drug safety—was "tried out" in some state or another before its adoption nationwide.

It's even arguable that virtually always when national programs have been implemented before their kinks have been ironed out at state levels, the results have proved disappointing; Medicare with its unexpectedly high costs is a case in point. Federalism gives the nation a governmental structure that promotes inventiveness and provides laboratories to experiment with creative ideas that would never have seen the light of day nor been perfected in a more centralized system.

Four Potential Dangers of Federalism

Countering these considerable benefits of federalism are four possible dangers. The first is confusion in emergencies over who's in charge. In the aftermath of Hurricane Katrina and the flooding of New Orleans in 2005, for example, the Federal Emergency Management Agency (FEMA) alleged that it delayed providing assistance for a critical twenty-four hours because the Louisiana governor did not request its aid—a condition legally necessary for FEMA to take charge of the rescue operations. In turn, the governor faulted FEMA officials for failure to explain to her the extent of the disaster. And the New Orleans mayor blamed both FEMA and the governor—everybody but himself. Confusion resulted in evasion of responsibility and unnecessary harm.

A second danger is a frequent conflict of laws. Sometimes the conflicts are quite subtle. Take the matter of train lengths, for example. What happens when the federal regulations are silent as to the allowable length of freight trains, but a state, in the interest of safety, prohibits trains pulling more than seventy cars from crossing its borders? In this instance, the railroad companies asserted that the inaction of the federal government overrode the stringent limits that the state imposed. It took long and expensive litigation to resolve the issue. (The Supreme Court upheld the railroads.[10]) At other times, the legal conflict can be obvious, even dire. Throughout the civil rights movement in the 1960s, violence broke out between those who adhered to the antidiscrimination laws of the central government and those who clung to the Jim Crow laws of the local governments in the

South. In virtually every major area of public policy, one finds conflicting laws vying for dominion. Fortunately, a consensus has emerged that the federal judiciary—"the least dangerous branch"—is the proper forum to resolve these conflicts.

The third danger of federalism is cutthroat competition between local governments. Typically, one state will woo an industry to leave a rival state by giving it an especially sympathetic deal on the taxes it has to pay, creating legal inequities within states' tax systems and an "unfair" shifting of local tax burdens. The need to "win" in the short term invites this kind of fiscal irresponsibility in the long term. Competition between the states, however, can also serve beneficial purposes; it can stimulate states to make improvements—to create better universities, for example, or safer highways, or cleaner environments.

The fourth and perhaps the most worrying danger inherent in American federalism has been inequality. For example, if one state is rich and another poor, the former can offer unusual educational opportunities to its citizens that the latter can't. In the past, invidious disparities did exist when America's southern states stagnated economically. The revenues of the Mississippi government, to take the classic example, were so meager that conditions in its public schools became intolerable by any standard, whereas New York was providing its youngsters the best of educations. In recent years, however, the gap in revenues of the various states has greatly diminished. Thanks to the national government's success in rooting out legalized racial discrimination, the economies of the South have grown, and the worrisome inequalities of opportunity have begun to disappear.

Federalism and Freedom

On balance, the advantages of federalism far outweigh its dangers, particularly because a system of compound government provides the circumstances in which personal freedom thrives. Federalism narrows the central government's responsibilities and turns over the bulk of governmental tasks (along with the police powers attendant to those tasks) to small-scale governments that tend to be more accessible, responsive, and amateurish in the best sense. At the same time, federalism permits the central government to have the resources necessary to provide a national defense sufficient to keep the citizenry free from fear of hostile nations. And finally, federalism gives Americans the freedom to choose what government they want to assist them in their pursuit of happiness.[12]

* * *

This chapter concludes our examination of eight political institutions. Before turning to look at the character of American society, consider three important points about these eight establishments.

First, in each of them, its members employ the three techniques of gaining the collaboration of others—coercion, reciprocity, and moral power. Political skill within them consists of using power effectively, particularly in overcoming the resistance that coercion arouses, enlisting the willing cooperation that reciprocity induces, and quelling the anomie that moral power produces.

Second, American institutions all have a uniquely democratic character. Whether elective, as in the presidency and legislatures, or not, as in courts, media, and corporations, they exist in a socially democratic culture where all persons are deemed equal; where individualism, personal responsibility, and the pursuit of self-interest are encouraged; and where competition is understood as necessary to create and animate a robust and free society. "The people reign in the American political world as the Deity does in the universe," as Tocqueville observed. "They are the cause and the aim of all things."[11]

Third, the central issue of politics is the question raised earlier in Part I: "How do you control power?" Especially, how does a society use and restrain the employment of coercion? Whether America's political institutions perform well or ill has to be assessed, first and foremost, with respect to that question. In light of the oppression and atrocities perpetrated by despotic governments in the last century, all other measures are of secondary importance. And by such a criterion, the nation's institutions have measured up very well.

In the next part we turn to examine the free society that those institutions have nourished.

NOTES

1. Christopher R. Berry, "School District Size and Student Outcomes," in William Howell, ed., *Besieged: School Boards and the Future of Education Politics* (Washington, D.C.: Brookings, 2005), 64–65:

   One of the earliest and most influential studies of school size was the "Conant Report" [which] concluded that large "comprehensive" high schools were more cost efficient and provided higher-quality schooling through a wider range of course offerings. . . .

More recent and more rigorous studies generally have not supported Conant's argument that larger schools produce better student outcomes at lower cost. Of the seven studies of school size and student performance . . . only one . . . found increasing returns to scale; the remaining six studies found decreasing returns. . . . African American students were particularly harmed by large school size, [as were] students of low socioeconomic status. . . .

2. When the Bill of Rights was ratified in 1791, the Tenth Amendment made explicit the importance of the local governments: "The powers not delegated to the central government by the Constitution, nor prohibited by it to the States, are reserved to the States."

3. One of the great political ploys of the proponents of the Constitution during the campaign for its ratification was to commandeer the name "Federalist" for themselves. *Federalist* is a word that *appears* to emphasize the sovereignty of the states and a relatively weak central government. By appropriating the word for themselves, the "Federalists" denied the use of it by those who preferred the Articles of Confederation, with its weak central government. The opponents of the Constitution ended up calling themselves "antifederalists," a name that sounded like they were opposed to states' rights and the diffusion of power, when just the opposite was true. That misnomer was what we would call in this age of political purity a "dirty trick."

4. The founders made no claim that the "compound government" they had designed was without ambiguity and error; they saw it as a necessary compromise. *Federalist* Nos. 37 and 38 conceded its shortcomings. In *Federalist* No. 38 Madison countered the criticism directed at its possible impracticality with a memorable analogy of the doctor and his sick patient:

> A patient who finds his disorder daily growing worse; and that an efficacious remedy can no longer be delayed without extreme danger; after coolly revolving his situation, and the characters of different physicians, selects and calls in such of them as he judges most capable of administering relief, and best entitled to his confidence. The physicians attend: the case of the patient is carefully examined: a consultation is held. They are unanimously agreed that the symptoms are critical, but that the case, with proper and timely relief, is so far from being desperate, that it may be made to issue in an improvement of his constitution. They are equally unanimous in prescribing the remedy by which this happy effect is to be produced. The prescription is no sooner made known, however, than a number of persons interpose, and without denying the reality or danger of the disorder, assure the patient that the prescription will be poison to his constitution, and forbid him under pain of certain death to make use of it, might not the patient reasonably demand before he ventured to follow this advice, that the authors of it should at least agree among themselves, on some other remedy to be substituted? And if he found them differing as much from one another, as from his first counselors, would he not act prudently in trying the experiment

unanimously recommended by the latter, rather than in hearkening to those who could neither deny the necessity of a speedy remedy nor agree in proposing one? Such a patient, and in such a situation is America at this moment.

5. The incident was described in detail in a five-part series appearing in the *Boston Globe*, "Agent, Mobster Forge a Pact on Old Southie Ties," July 19–24, 1998.
6. And that's not to mention New York governor Franklin D. Roosevelt, who assumed the presidency in 1932 in the midst of America's worst economic calamity—the Great Depression.
7. Alexis de Tocqueville, *Democracy in America*, trans. Henry Reeve (New York: Bantam 2000 [1835]), vol. I, chap. 14:

   It is incontestable that the people frequently conduct public business very badly; but it is impossible that the lower orders should take a part in public business without extending the circle of their ideas and quitting the ordinary routine of their thoughts. The humblest individual who co-operates in the government of society acquires a certain degree of self-respect; and as he possesses authority, he can command the services of minds more enlightened than his own. He is canvassed by a multitude of applicants, and in seeking to deceive him in a thousand ways, they really enlighten him. He takes a part in political undertakings which he did not originate, but which give him a taste for undertakings of the kind. New improvements are daily pointed out to him in the common property and this gives him the desire of improving that property which is his own. He is perhaps neither happier nor better than those who came before him, but he is better informed and more active. I have no doubt that the democratic institutions of the United States, joined to the physical constitution of the country, are the cause (not the direct, as is so often asserted, but the indirect cause) of the prodigious commercial activity of the inhabitants. It is not created by the laws, but the people learn how to promote it by the experience derived from legislation.

8. Ibid.
9. Alexis de Tocqueville, *Democracy in America*, trans. Henry Reeve (New York: Bantam, 2000 [1840]), vol. II, book 4, chap. 4, 300.
10. *Southern Pacific Co. v. Arizona*, 325 U.S. 761 (1945).
11. Tocqueville, *Democracy in America*, vol. I, chap. 4.
12. The Fourteenth Amendment, ratified in 1868 in the aftermath of the American Civil War, imposed new and significant limits on the states' authority regarding free speech, the freedom of the press, religious practices, police behavior, court procedures, and election laws. So substantial have been the changes wrought by the Amendment's command, "No State shall . . . deprive any person of life, liberty, or property, without due process of law," that legal scholars speak of America having a second constitution. See, for example, Chapter 19, regarding the nationalization of limits on local police practices.

PART III

AMERICAN SOCIETY

25

WE THE PEOPLE

We the People of the United States, in Order to form a more perfect
Union . . . and secure the Blessings of Liberty to ourselves and our
Posterity, do ordain and establish this Constitution for the United
States of America.

Preamble, *The Constitution of the United States*

The first three words of the U.S. Constitution speak of "We the People."
But what kind of people are Americans? Do the individuals inhabiting the
fifty states share a set of traits so that it's helpful of think of them as "We,"
a distinctive community amidst the universe of mankind? If so, what might
explain how being American shapes the personalities of the inhabitants of
a nation extending the width of an entire continent? Who do we think
we are?

Americans by the Numbers

Let's begin by counting the number of people who call themselves Americans. In October 2006 the nation's population passed the 300 million
mark—a hundred times the number of Americans when Alexander Hamilton and James Madison started writing *The Federalist Papers* in 1788.[1] Four
decades later, when Alexis de Tocqueville got off his ship in New York in
1831, there had been a fourfold increase, up to 12.5 million Americans.
On the eve of the Civil War in 1861 that number had nearly tripled; 31.4

million Americans were about to be plunged into a civil struggle that would leave 600,000 American men dead. Despite that terrible carnage, over the next seven decades, up to the beginning of the Great Depression in 1930, the country's population quadrupled, to 123 million. It took only sixty years more, until 1990, before that figure doubled to 249 million. Then, within the lifetimes of freshmen entering college in the autumn of 2007, America's population grew by another 50 million.

Those 300 million brains and 600 million hands produced and exchanged $13.2 trillion of goods and services in 2006.[2] The magnitude of their productivity can only be grasped by comparing it with the gross domestic product of other nations. The next most productive economy (using 2006 figures) was Japan's at $4.3 trillion, then Germany's at $2.9 trillion.[3] To single out one illustrative instance of the nation's productivity, America's farmers grew three times as much food on one-third as many acres and a third fewer man-hours as seventy-five years ago, and they had the technological capacity to feed a population many multiples of that of America.[4]

As a result of this astounding rise in productivity, according to economist Stephen Moore, this "demographic milestone [of 300 million Americans] is not cause for alarm—as some prophets of doom would have it. Rather, it is cause for celebration. We 300 million Americans are on balance healthier and wealthier and freer than any population ever: We breathe cleaner air, drink cleaner water, earn higher incomes, have more leisure time, and live in less crowded housing. Every natural resource we depend on—water, food, copper and, yes, even oil—is far more abundant today measured by affordability than when our population was 100 million or even 30 million."[5]

America's population growth is due to three factors. One is immigration—legal and otherwise. The figures astound. According to the U.S. Census Bureau, 37.3 million of today's Americans were born in a foreign country—more than the entire American population in 1860. A new immigrant arrives here every forty-five seconds; just in the seven years from 2000 to 2007, 10.7 million immigrants came to the United States.[6]

A second factor is a stable birth rate; Americans maintain themselves with a birth rate of 2.1 babies per woman, as compared with the German fertility rate of 1.8 children per woman. Japan's fertility rate is 1.3 babies and Italy's 1.2 babies.[7] (As a result, Japan and many European nations are expected to experience a debilitating absolute decline in their populations, in some cases as much as 25 percent over the next fifty years.)

The third factor is that Americans are living longer. Life expectancy keeps climbing year after year (in 2003 it was 77.6 years).[8] Again, according to Stephen Moore, "Our population is rising mainly because early childhood death rates in the U.S. have fallen by 90% in the last century, and continue to fall: A child born today in the U.S. is *four* times more likely to live to adulthood than one born in 1950, and *twelve* times more likely than one born in 1900. And our children will live longer; life expectancy has increased by more than 30 years in the last century."

Diversity of Americans

The striking aspect of the American people is the dozens of different ancestral families from which they come. Thanks to the 2000 American census, which contained the request to "state your ancestry," it's possible to estimate just how diverse the population has become. While many Americans can claim three and four nationalities in their backgrounds and nearly 10 percent of the respondents merely answered "American," the diversity of family origin the census reveals is astonishing.[9]

There are 60 million German Americans, 50 million English Americans, 33 million Irish Americans, 9 million Polish Americans, and 7 million Scottish Americans. Mixed in with these former Europeans are 36 million African Americans, 26 million Mexican Americans, and 1.25 million Cuban Americans, not to mention 4.5 million Native Americans. Asia and the Middle East are well represented: one can find 3 million Arab Americans, half a million Iranian Americans, almost 4 million Chinese Americans, more than 1.25 million Japanese Americans, and 1.25 million Korean Americans. A million Asian Indian Americans live side by side with half a million Pakistani Americans.

Adherents to religions, once mutually hostile, live together peaceably in the United States: six million Jewish Americans and nearly six million Italian Americans (presumably Roman Catholics) are embraced within the nation's borders. Nationality groups whose ancestors murdered each other unite as Americans: most notably, Armenian Americans, the estimates of whom run between half a million and two million, mingle with approximately 150,000 Turkish Americans.

These nationality groups are scattered throughout the United States: half a million Swedish Americans, for example, reside in California alone; 300,000 Nicaraguan Americans live in Florida. Immigrants have arrived down through America's history and continue to come: most of the 1.25

million Vietnamese Americans have arrived in the United States since 1975, while the majority of the 1.25 million Greek Americans can trace their ancestors' arrival in America back a century.

Virtually every nation in the world has contributed its families, linguistic habits, senses of humor, folklore, and musical, artistic, and culinary cultures to the United States. While the new arrivals tend to converse in other languages (three-quarters of a million Russian Americans speak Russian, for example), their children speak English as their native language and, when grown, intermarry outside their own nationality groups, often over their parents' objections.[10]

Today's heterogeneous America looks very different from the America through which Tocqueville traveled in 1831–1832. Then, it was a country populated by "the British race . . . all belonging to one family, owing their origin to the same cause, and preserving the same civilization, the same language, the same religion, the same habits, the same manners, and imbued with the same opinions, propagated under the same forms."[11]

Tocqueville's America, Contemporary America

Yet anyone who ponders Tocqueville's observations of Americans as they lived nearly two centuries ago must be struck by their resonance with the American way of life today. Let's look at eight uniquely American characteristics that appeared early and have persisted to the present day.

To provide us with a view of contemporary America, I have turned to author David Brooks and his delightful but astute *On Paradise Drive*. Brooks tells us that modern Americans don't stay still: "About 120 million Americans, 46 percent of the country, moved between 1995 and 2000."[12] They weren't stick-in-the-muds in Tocqueville's day, either. Tocqueville wrote of their *mobility*, their restless and constant transplanting of themselves:

> In the United States a man builds a house in which to spend his old age, and he sells it before the roof is on; he plants a garden and lets it just as the trees are coming into bearing; he brings a field into tillage and leaves other men to gather the crops; he embraces a profession and gives it up; he settles in a place, which he soon afterwards leaves to carry his changeable longings elsewhere. If his private affairs leave him any leisure, he instantly plunges into the vortex of politics; and if at the end of a year of unremitting labor he finds he has a few days' vacation, his eager curiosity whirls him over the vast

extent of the United States, and he will travel fifteen hundred miles in a few days to shake off his happiness. Death at length overtakes him, but it is before he is weary of his bootless chase of that complete felicity which forever escapes him.[13]

Tocqueville noted a second characteristic, an *undue anxiety*: "In America I saw the freest and most enlightened men placed in the happiest circumstances that the world affords; it seemed to me as if a cloud habitually hung upon their brow, and I thought them serious and almost sad, even in their pleasures."[14]

Perhaps, then, there was reason for worry: the existence of slavery in the southern states threatened to shatter America; slavery was cause to be "sad" and anxious. Today, however, the United States is united. Slavery is gone, and numerous African Americans hold prominent places in public affairs and the corporate world and constitute an ever-growing fraction of America's middle class. The nation reigns as the world's superpower economically, culturally, and militarily. Prosperity and employment, despite the deep recession that began in 2008, are at or near historic highs. Yet two of every three Americans think the country is going in the wrong direction.[15]

Despite their worries (or perhaps because of them), Americans pour their energies into *making money* to support an "amazing" and affluent way of life. Writes Brooks: "Americans spend more than $40 billion on lawn care each year, more than the total tax revenues of the federal government in India. The average American family spends $2,000 a year on food in restaurants. According to Cotton Incorporated's magazine, *Lifestyle Monitor*, American women between the ages of sixteen and seventy have, on average, seven pairs of jeans in their wardrobes. Nearly three quarters of the new cars on the road have cruise control and power door locks."[16]

Tocqueville, too, was struck by the American passion for money and material prosperity (to which he extended a far kinder and more profound understanding than other notable Europeans, such as Charles Dickens, Matthew Arnold, Max Weber, and D. H. Lawrence). Consider his explanation: "Men living in democratic times have many passions, but most of their passions either end in the love of riches or proceed from it. The cause of this is not that their souls are narrower, but that the importance of money is really greater at such times. When all the members of a community are independent of or indifferent to each other, the co-operation of each of them can be obtained only by paying for it: this infinitely multiplies the purposes to which wealth may be applied and increases its value."[17]

Fourth, the American of 1831 was intrigued by the future and every-thing novel: new gadgets, new ideas, new laws, change seemingly for change's sake. He had a *faith in progress* that intrigued Tocqueville: "The American, taken as a chance specimen of his countrymen, must then be a man of singular warmth in his desires, enterprising, fond of adventure and, above all, of novelty. The same bent is manifest in all that he does: he introduces it into his political laws, his religious doctrines, his theories of social economy, and his domestic occupations. . . ."[18]

Likewise, Brooks is struck by a similar dreamy optimism that he expresses in the subtitle of his book, *How We Live (And Always Have) in the Future Tense*. He writes:

> Some nations are bound . . . by a common creation myth, a tale of how they came into being. Americans are bound . . . by a fruition myth. [A] Paradise Spell is the controlling ideology of American life. Just out of reach, just beyond the next ridge, just with the next home or entrepreneurial scheme or diet plan; just with the next political hero, the next credit card purchase, or the next true love; just with the right all-terrain vehicle, the right summer home, the right meditation technique, or the right motivational seminar; just with the right schools, the right community values, and the proper morality; just with the right beer and a good set of buddies; just with the next technology or after the next shopping spree, there is this spot you can get to where all tensions will melt, all time pressures are relieved, and all content-ment can be realized.[19]

The Humanity of Americans

But despite their restlessness, anxieties, materialism, and dreamy opti-mism, Americans personally are uniquely *generous* toward others:[20] recall that in 2007 Americans in huge numbers donated $306 *billion* to philan-thropic causes. Tocqueville would not have been surprised, having identi-fied that same American charitableness in 1831: "When an American asks for the co-operation of his fellow citizens, it is seldom refused; and I have often seen it afforded spontaneously, and with great goodwill. If an acci-dent happens on the highway, everybody hastens to help the sufferer; if some great and sudden calamity befalls a family, the purses of a thousand strangers are at once willingly opened and small but numerous donations pour in to relieve the distress."[21]

Much of that charitable giving and volunteer activity, Tocqueville thought, was stimulated by a sixth American characteristic, their *religiosity*, which he described this way:

> In the United States on the seventh day of every week the trading and working life of the nation seems suspended; all noises cease; a deep tranquility, say rather the solemn calm of meditation, succeeds the turmoil of the week, and the soul resumes possession and contemplation of itself. On this day the marts of traffic are deserted; every member of the community, accompanied by his children, goes to church, where he listens to strange language which would seem unsuited to his ear. He is told of the countless evils caused by pride and covetousness; he is reminded of the necessity of checking his desires, of the finer pleasures that belong to virtue alone, and of the true happiness that attends it.[22]

Brooks notes the continuation of the religious character of the modern American, remarking on their active participation in church organizations and its consequence for heightened involvement in the lives of those in need. He notes that "Americans attend religious services at rates well above those of all comparable nations. Fifty-eight percent of Americans say their belief in God is very important to their lives, compared to only 12 percent of the French and 19 percent of the British. . . . About one-third of Americans do unpaid work for religious organizations, compared to 5 percent of the French and 6 percent of the British."[23]

A seventh enduring American characteristic is the individual's *capacity for voluntary, private teamwork*. In earlier parts of the book, I spoke of the countless organizations Americans voluntarily formed to spread "truths" and to cooperate in doing good works. Brooks comments on those same habits: "Our tendency to donate time to community service and voluntary associations such as Big Brother programs is . . . unmatched. Global surveys reveal that about 80 percent of Americans belong to some sport or voluntary association, compared with only 36 percent of, say, Italians and Japanese."[24]

Likewise, in 1831 Tocqueville was deeply impressed with the skills of teamwork he observed in the New World:

> The citizen of the United States is taught from infancy to rely upon his own exertions in order to resist the evils and the difficulties of life; he looks upon the social authority with an eye of mistrust and anxiety, and he claims its

assistance only when he is unable to do without it. This habit may be traced even in the schools, where the children in their games are wont to submit to rules which they themselves have established, and to punish misdemeanors which they themselves have defined. The same spirit pervades every act of social life. If a stoppage occurs in a thoroughfare and the circulation of vehicles is hindered, the neighbors immediately form themselves into a deliberative body; and this contemporaneous assembly gives rise to an executive power which remedies the inconvenience before anybody has thought of recurring to a pre-existing authority superior to that of the persons immediately concerned.[25]

The eighth enduring characteristic is the Americans' *love of their work* and their constant efforts to improve themselves. Tocqueville found that Americans worked with an energy that astounded him. The key to these workaholic tendencies was that Americans honored work for profit, or as he writes, "[L]abor is identified with that of prosperity and improvement...; it is honored.... [N]o one is idle, for the ... population extend their activity and intelligence to every kind of employment; ... they ... work without shame.... [Each person] sells his services, but they are purchased only when they may be useful.... [T]he resources of his intelligence are astonishing, and his avidity in the pursuit of gain amounts to a species of heroism."[26]

Brooks attests to a continuation of those work habits in present-day America: "Americans remain the hardest-working people on the face of the earth. We work the longest hours and take the shortest vacations of any affluent people. Polls indicate that it is not all forced; far more than people in other lands, Americans choose to live this way.... As Seymour Martin Lipset observed in his book *American Exceptionalism,* 'The recent comparative studies of work behavior indicate that Americans are ... workaholics....' "[27]

In short, being an American appears to transform the personalities of an entire population of 300 million to live "in the future tense" (to borrow Brooks's happy phrase) so that they anticipate change, prepare themselves for it, and expect to have a better future as a result of it. Within a generation, immigrants become distinctively American, throwing off the outlooks of their ancestors and assimilating into America.[28] How come?

The major cause of their transformation is commerce. In the commercial republic that is America, everyone becomes a merchant of his services and products. In the New World, wrote Tocqueville, each person "knows that the surest means of obtaining the support of his fellow creatures is to win their favor."[29] The individual considers others as persons with needs and acts to be "useful" in filling them. He thrusts his feet into their shoes in his self-interest and, by understanding their desires and their customs, he makes them his customers. He shapes his talents to make them attractive in the marketplace. He transforms his wares and his ways to fit the American environment. He learns the language Americans speak, adopts their religious traditions, participates in their ceremonies, gives to their charities, and absorbs their standards of honor. From his customers he gains a taste for their undertakings and a desire to improve himself according to their standards. He perseveres to bridge the gap between his inherited traditions and the American way of life, not because he's coerced to do so, but because it's good business.

In America's open market, year by year, decade by decade, immigrant wave by immigrant wave, countless commercial relationships have transformed new arrivals into Americans and shaped their personalities into restless, energetic, enterprising, generous, ambitious, future-minded, self-improving, self-reliant, team-playing, anxious, hopeful, education-seeking, religious, neighborly, novelty-loving, problem-solving, workaholic suburbanites, "just like us."[30]

That's the point Tocqueville makes at the conclusion of his first volume of *Democracy in America*:

> No power on earth can shut out the immigrants from that fertile wilderness which offers resources to all industry and a refuge from all want. Future events, whatever they may be, [whether] bad laws, revolutions, [or] anarchy, [will not] be able to obliterate that love of prosperity and spirit of enterprise which seem to be the distinctive characteristics of [the British] race or extinguish altogether the knowledge that guides them on that way.[31]

The spirit of the Scottish Enlightenment—of Adam Smith, David Hume, and those who saw that the "invisible hand" of commercial reciprocity was the greatest antipoverty program ever devised—has been absorbed into the personalities of those who chose to be a part of "We the People."[32]

NOTES

1. According to the first census taken in 1790, America had grown to 3.9 million people. Compare the hundredfold increase of the American population with that of metropolitan France, the present population of which is about 60 million, only twice its population in 1780 of roughly 29 million.

2. Louis D. Johnston and Samuel H. Williamson, "What Was the U.S. GDP Then?" Measuringworth.com, 2007.

3. World Development Indicators, database, World Bank, July 1, 2007.

4. Unless otherwise acknowledged, the source of the data in this chapter is David Brooks, *On Paradise Drive: How We Live (And Always Have) in the Future Tense* (New York: Simon and Schuster, 2004).

5. Stephen Moore, "300,000,000," *Wall Street Journal,* October 22, 2006.

6. Steven A. Camarota, "Immigrants in the United States" (Washington, D.C.: Center for Immigration Studies, 2007), 1.

7. Rob Stein, "U.S. Fertility Rate Hits 35-Year High, Stabilizing Population," *Washington Post,* December 21, 2007, A11. "Experts . . . cite a complex mix of factors [for the U.S. high fertility rate], including lower levels of birth control use than in other developed countries, widely held religious values that encourage childbearing, social conditions that make it easier for women to work and have families, and a growing Hispanic population."

8. National Center for Health Statistics, "Life Expectancy Hits Record High," February 28, 2005.

9. I have supplemented the census figures with estimates made by scholars and various ethnic associations.

10. My orthodontist neighbor once laughingly described the effects of intermarriage this way: "Combine a Swedish upper jaw and an Italian lower jaw, and what you get is a lot of orthodontistry."

11. Alexis de Tocqueville, *Democracy in America,,* trans. Henry Reeve (New York: Bantam, 2000 [1835]), vol. I, chap. 18. Tocqueville, however, recognized two different species within "the British [or Anglo-American] race": the Virginian (turbulent, restless, adventurous, greedy, and without spiritual or educational aspirations) and the New Englander (educated, with intellectual and spiritual cravings, morally disciplined, accompanied by family). Ibid., vol. I, chap. 2. The American character was an amalgam of the two.

12. Brooks, *On Paradise Drive,* 75.

13. Alexis de Tocqueville, *Democracy in America,* trans. Henry Reeve (New York: Bantam, 2000 [1840]), vol. II, book 2, chap. 13.

14. Ibid.

15. The Harris Poll, February 6–10, 2008.

16. Brooks, *On Paradise Drive, 79.*

17. Tocqueville, *Democracy in America*, vol. II, book 3, chap. 17.

18. Ibid., vol. I, chap. 18.

19. Brooks, *On Paradise Drive, 268–269.*

20. Not all agree that Americans continue their high degree of personal generosity. For example, Robert D. Putnam, in his evidence-rich but single-minded effort to establish a significant decline since 1970 of "social capital"—i.e., willingness to trust one another. He asserts, "[O]ver the last four decades, Americans have become steadily more tight-fisted. . . ." *Bowling Alone: The Collapse and Revival of American Community* (New York: Simon and Schuster, 2000), 127. I find his argument intriguing but ultimately unconvincing.

21. Tocqueville, *Democracy in America*, vol. II, book 3, chap. 4.

22. Ibid., chap. 15.

23. Brooks, *On Paradise Drive, 76.*

24. Ibid., 76–77.

25. Tocqueville, *Democracy in America*, vol. I, chap. 12.

26. Ibid., chap.18.

27. Brooks, *On Paradise Drive, 232.*

28. Political scientist Samuel P. Huntington dissents: "The continuation of high levels of Mexican and Hispanic immigration plus the low rates of assimilation of these immigrants into American society and culture could eventually change America into a country of two languages, two cultures, and two peoples." *Who Are We? The Challenges to America's National Identity* (New York: Simon and Schuster, 2004), 256. His concerns are plausible, worth heeding, but (I believe) exaggerated.

29. Tocqueville, *Democracy in America*, vol. I, chap. 18.

30. See, generally, Samuel G. Freedman, *The Inheritance: How Three Families and America Moved from Roosevelt to Reagan and Beyond* (New York: Simon and Schuster, 1996).

31. Tocqueville, *Democracy in America*, vol. I, chap. 18.

32. Cf. Christopher Caldwell, *Reflections on the Revolution in Europe: Immigration, Islam, and the West* (New York: Doubleday, 2009), chap. 2, "The Immigrant Economy," which cites the generous welfare allowances of Western European nations that enable immigrants to avoid entering the labor force and integrating into the larger community.

26

THE AMERICAN ELECTORATE

*As the election draws near, . . . the whole nation glows with fever-
ish excitement; the election is the daily theme of the press, the subject of private conversation, the end of every thought and every
action, the sole interest of the present. It is true that as soon as the
choice is determined, this ardor is dispelled, calm returns, and the
river, which had nearly broken its banks, sinks to its usual level;
but who can refrain from astonishment that such a storm should
have arisen?*

Alexis de Tocqueville, *Democracy in America* (1835)

Who among the 300 million people living in the United States constitute
the American political electorate? In the 2004 presidential general election,
120 million persons voted—approximately 40 percent of every man,
woman, and child residing in the United States—a typical election turnout.[1]
Is there anything that differentiates the 40 percent who do vote from the 60
percent who do not vote? Is there a group amidst the general population—
liberals, conservatives, African Americans, Hispanic Americans, women, or
young adults, for example—whose turnout rate is significantly lower than
average, so low, in fact, as to make the electorate nonrepresentative of
America in its rich diversity? To put the question opportunistically, is there
a segment of people sitting on the sidelines and waiting to be awakened
politically so as to shift the present electoral balance? Or to express it more

direfully, are American elections in some sense illegitimate because they don't reflect the "will of the people" accurately?

In 2004 the estimate of nonvoters was 170 million. We know something about them. Obviously, kids didn't vote. Anyone who hadn't reached his or her eighteenth birthday was excluded from the electorate. If we assume that an average of 4.2 million babies were born in each of the previous eighteen years, we can multiply that figure by eighteen and find that 75 million Americans were underage in 2004. That leaves 95 million nonvoters unaccounted for.

Then there were resident noncitizens. Nearly 10 percent of America's population—roughly 30 million—were foreign-born, two-thirds of whom, or 20 million, had not yet gained citizenship.[2] If we decrease the total adult nonvoters by that 20 million, we find we have about 75 million adults who didn't cast a ballot. Who were they?

Some were ineligible to vote because they had been convicted of serious crimes. State law, for example, bars inmates and recent alumni of prisons from voting. One and a half million felons were in state and federal prisons at this time; that's one of every 250 persons.[3] But even more arresting was the figure of 5.5 million, representing the sum of those who were in prison, on parole, and on probation. Subtract those 5 million or so, and we end up with 70 million nonvoters who were otherwise eligible to vote, or 36.5 percent of the eligible population. That means that 63.5 percent of eligible Americans did vote. What groups would have had a turnout rate of less than 63.5 percent? Who were they?

The best account of who tends not to vote is the careful work of Professors Raymond Wolfinger and Steven Rosenstone.[4] Here is what they found.

Low Turnout: Little Schooling, Youth, Mobility

Low turnout is related to low formal education. Those who never graduated from high school have turnout rates of 40 percent. Graduates of high school but no college turn out 70 percent of the time. College graduates vote at a rate in the high 80 percents. And practically everyone with a graduate degree votes.

Those without a high school degree differ from other Americans: they aren't well informed about politics, aren't very interested in politics, and rarely read about politics. Education—not race, not ethnicity, not gender—explains virtually all the differences in levels of turnout. African

Americans, for example, vote in higher numbers than their white counterparts in every range of formal education.

Age is the second most important factor in determining who turns out. Eighteen- to twenty-four-year-olds have turnout rates of 50 percent, whereas oldsters, ages thirty-seven to seventy-eight, turn out half again more often, 75 percent. Young adults are disproportionately "single," without spouse and children, and no matter the age group, "singles" are 10 percent less likely to vote than someone who has a family.

In addition, young adults tend to move about a lot. Mobility hinders voting. People recently moved to a community tend to vote in lesser numbers than those who have established roots in a community. Upon moving to a new community, an individual has much to do: find a suitable home, find a good school for the children, make friends, and settle into a new job—all of which are more important than registering and rushing out to vote. Since 16 percent of Americans move each year, the number of mobile nonvoters is considerable. Once settled in a community for two years, however, newcomers start voting at roughly the same rate as that of their long-established neighbors.

In sum, the less educated, the young, the new person in town, and the "single" are underrepresented in the electorate. Everybody else votes reliably; every other group is fairly represented in the electorate.

That so many people do vote raises a puzzling question: Why do so many persons take their voting duties so seriously? After all, voting requires time to know whom and what to vote for, as well as making the effort to get to the polling station or obtain an absentee ballot. Voting is out of the ordinary. If you have a job, you have to get up early or miss supper on Election Day. If you have children, you've got to have someone sit with them while you're away. And if you travel a lot, you've got to think ahead and call for an absentee ballot. Or maybe it's difficult for other reasons: you've come down with a headache or got the sniffles.

Why do people vote?[5] The question arises because so many endure these inconveniences to vote, even though they know their individual ballot is unlikely to make any difference at all. Elections aren't usually close, and even the close ones are rarely decided by less than a thousand votes. It's hard to think of any activity equally inconvenient that has so little real-world consequence to the individual.

The paradox is compounded by the fact that the better educated and the more experienced the citizen, the more likely he or she is to vote. One might think that the savvier and worldlier one is, the clearer the futility of casting a vote ought to become. Instead, it's just the opposite.

Let's leave that question behind to mull upon. But it's an interesting question, a much more fruitful one than the one more frequently asked: Why don't Americans vote at the same high rate as folks living under despotisms in such places as Cuba ruled by the Castros or Iraq in the days of the late and unlamented Saddam Hussein?

High Turnout: Working for or in the Shadow of Government

Two population groups vote in significantly greater numbers: government employees and farmers. "The courthouse gang" pays attention to elections. That public school teachers turn out at unusually high rates should not surprise. After all, they are college-educated, but one finds equally high turnout among all government workers, irrespective of their educational attainments: clerical workers, trash collectors, and prison guards.

One explanation is that government workers spend much of their time in an environment filled with political information. Their political education outpaces their formal education. Add to this "information" explanation the "patronage factor," and it becomes clearer why public employees might vote in such large numbers. If your paycheck, promotion, and conditions of work depend on who's elected to be your boss, elections take on a special significance. Despite the fact that civil service reforms in many states effectively guarantee against the discharge of almost everyone doing government work, the courthouse gang votes "early and often," as the saying goes, because their pay and perks depend upon being so politically powerful that they can intimidate elected officials into being generous. In unreformed states, where *retaining* one's job may depend upon who the governor is (say, in Pennsylvania, where 50,000 patronage government jobs exist), not only do employees turn out in vast numbers, but so do their neighbors. Government employees make sure they organize their neighborhoods and shoo all their friends to the polls. Voting is key to their economic well-being.

Farmers constitute the other group with an above-average turnout rate. More than any other private occupation, those working in the agricultural sector are entangled in government programs. Crop subsidies and crop limitations have become a seemingly unalterable part of our public policy fabric. Government also guarantees cheap farm loans, provides water, improves farmland, and so on. Like government employees, farmers know more about government than their formal education might imply, and their standard of living is significantly affected by government and its budgetary outlays.

Doubtless, other Americans—nonfarmers and workers in the private sector—pay less attention to politics and have less at stake in the outcomes, but the rival candidates and their supporters embarrass, cajole, and even drive reluctant voters to the polls. Democratic and Republican partisans prod and motivate likely sympathizers to register and cast their ballots.[6] Like farmers and government employees, party activists have a stake in election outcomes because many of them hanker for government contracts, judgeships, and jobs as commissioners, district attorneys, advisers, ambassadors, and agency managers.

Even when the election is nonpartisan (as most municipal elections are), there is often a political pro in the background, who is highly motivated to get out the vote. Typically, such a local "boss" will represent a business clientele or public employees—firefighters, garbage collectors, school teachers, and the like. To secure his clients' zoning needs in the former case or wage demands in the latter, he will campaign for council members likely to regard their needs favorably. He will direct his clients to donate to the campaigns of the "slate" of candidates he designates—funds he controls to get out the vote (often by generously distributing "walking around money").[7] Moreover, once his candidates are elected, he can further transform his influence with them into personal enrichment.[8]

Whether one deems the conduct of the local boss ethical or not, his activities significantly elevate turnout rates. Thus, even in neighborhoods where there is no effective partisan competition, there are forces at work, motivating citizens to vote.

The Candidates

The American electorate sometimes is asked to vote not for candidates, but on specific issues. California, for example, pioneered what is called "direct democracy," where the citizenry is asked whether they wish to approve a wide variety of initiatives relating to taxes, government budgets, bond issues, zoning plans, government administration, and public policies. The downside of direct democracy is that complex issues are being decided by people who devote little time to studying the details of the proposals. The upside is that, in the case of at least some initiatives, the electorate gains political education. For example, in 1978 the California ballot contained the so-called Briggs Initiative, which would have banned homosexuals from teaching in public schools. Consequently, the topic of "gays in the classroom" was widely discussed in the newspapers, at dinner tables, and at office water coolers. Media, always looking for stories to fill space, did much to humanize the issue. People began exchanging personal stories about gays and lesbians they had known, recalling a beloved third-grade teacher who was gay and who, under the proposal, would be fired. Bad memories were discussed as well. The end result of this collective deliberation was the defeat of the initiative by more than a million votes. The public conversation provoked by the initiative may help explain the notably tolerant attitudes of Californians about homosexuality.[9]

But usually Americans vote for candidates who work tirelessly to meet the electorate in order to demonstrate their can-do spirit, knowledge, eloquence, toughness, integrity, and humanity. Their stands on issues, of course, influence a citizen's voting decisions, but their policy positions are less important than the characteristics they display in talking about them.

Who are these candidates who compete with one another, and how do they become their parties' nominees? For example, at the national level, who decides which persons will face off in the general election for the presidency?

In the early days of the nation, the elected members of Congress selected the parties' nominees. The Jeffersonian-Madisonian Democrats in the House and Senate would meet in caucus and wrangle and select their party's nominees for president and vice president. The Federalist congressmen would do likewise. The congressional caucus system for picking presidential candidates bore a resemblance to the British method by which the members of the competing parties in Parliament picked their leaders from among their membership. The party that won the majority of the seats then made its leader the prime minister—the equivalent of the American chief executive. The points of similarity with the American congressional caucus system were that legislators were the only electors, and they chose the contenders for the presidency only from among themselves and cabinet members.

In 1824 that system broke down, partly because the Federalist Party had become a virtual corpse, and without any competitor to rally them into unity, the Democratic-Republican caucus simply fell apart, incapable of consensus on any one candidate. One of the disappointed contenders, Andrew Jackson, together with his canny campaign manager, Martin Van Buren, set out to replace the congressional caucus with an institution that permitted noncongressional delegates to participate in the selection process. In 1828 these delegates met in national convention, which Jackson easily won. The anti-Jackson faction of the Democratic Party thereupon formed itself into the Whig Party and adopted a similar convention format to select its candidate at the subsequent election of 1832.[10]

The Convention System

The convention system consisted of a ladder of conventions—county conventions at the bottom, which selected delegates from its members to attend congressional district conventions transcending county lines, which selected delegates from its members to attend state conventions, which selected delegates from its members to attend the national convention, which selected the nominees. Since every delegate to the next-higher-level convention had to come from the subordinate one just below it, participation in the convention system was, in effect, limited to *county* delegates. County delegates were elected at precinct levels (precincts are voting units tending to be no larger than 10,000 voters). Precinct delegate elections were virtually invisible and, to the average voter, seemingly inconsequential. But for the professional politician—the "big city boss"—those precinct delegate elections were the basis of his power and were easily controlled. They permitted him to elect cronies and pack the county convention with them. His control of the convention of a populous county meant he could then dominate the next highest gathering, the congressional district convention (or perhaps several), which led to his dominance of the state conventions; the united front of his delegates at each stage almost invariably could defeat a more numerous but disorganized opposition. The national conventions in turn became packed with the adherents of these big-city bosses, who would then negotiate among themselves in the selection of their party's presidential nominee. The convention system thus became as exclusive as the old congressional caucus system, but with a different group in charge: the bosses, not congressional leaders, dominated the nominations.

These few political pros controlled the nomination process in both the Democratic and Republican Parties through the first half of the twentieth century. Then gradually, state by state, the idea of the popular party primary spread.

Because party primaries don't have the attraction of the general election, however, politically active partisans—the so-called party base—virtually always decide who will be the party nominees.[11] Thus, currently, voters in the general election are faced with a choice between two candidates, both of whom have won nomination in a primary election dominated by party activists. It's a process with much more extensive participation than either the congressional caucus or convention systems, but whether it's an improvement is open to debate.

The Importance of Party Identification

The discussion above centered on presidential nominations, but primary elections now largely determine who will be each party's candidate for lesser offices. In the general election, what leads an electorate to choose among the rival candidates? In the routine election (and all elections are routine until some pattern-breaking event comes along every seventy years or so), nothing is more important than the party label under which the candidate runs.

The reason is the voter's lack of time and interest. Think what the typical voter would have to do if it were otherwise: he would have to spend days boning up on what each candidate thinks about each issue. Moreover, he would have to analyze each issue to decide his own position. The voter would also have to discern which candidates had thought through each issue in sufficient depth so that they wouldn't change their minds once in office if their positions on an issue were challenged. Finally, he would have to assess the various candidates in terms of their integrity, political skill, and persuasiveness.

It's an impossible task for the normal voter. Learned Hand, one of the great judges of the twentieth century, once put it this way:

> I do not know how it is with you, but for myself I generally give up at the outset: The simplest problems which come up from day to day seem to me quite unanswerable as soon as I try to get below the surface. . . . My vote is one of the most unimportant acts of my life; if I were to acquaint myself with the matters on which it ought really to depend, if I were to try to get a judgment on which I was willing to risk affairs of even the smallest moment, I should be doing nothing else, and that seems a fatuous conclusion to a fatuous undertaking.[12]

Too much to know, especially when you consider Americans are asked to vote in national, state, and local elections every other year not only for president, but for governor, U.S. senator, state senator, congressional representative, state representative, and an uncountable number of other offices from school board to membership on the sewer commission. Not having the time to do all that research and also take care of really important matters like family, business, and community involvements, the voter needs a shortcut, and that shortcut is party. Parties represent competing values, ones we earlier labeled "conservative" and "liberal"—the former emphasizing personal freedom, the latter material equality. To the voter's way of thinking, each candidate must have had some reason to affiliate with one party or the other. The candidate has made a choice, and by the choice of party he or she has made, the voter gains a reliable signal as to the candidate's way of thinking. It is no surprise that Americans rely on party to determine whom they'll vote for. This is especially the case with the lesser offices; the less important the responsibility, the more important becomes the party label.

Currently, 35 percent, more or less, of the electorate say they are Republicans and reliably vote for Republican candidates, and 35 percent, more or less, say they are Democrats and reliably vote for Democratic candidates. The remaining 30 percent claim to be independent. Americans are proud of their individualism and believe they can think for themselves, "independently" of what others think. But if you ask those 30 percent who claim to be independent whether they lean one way or the other, one-third of them will say they lean Republican and another third will say they lean Democrat. Lo and behold, the leaners are as reliably party-line voters as those who acknowledge that they are Republicans and Democrats.[13]

That leaves 10 percent of the electorate who are "pure" independents, and they are largely nonparticipants in elections. With respect to politics, they are genuinely ignorant and apathetic: they don't know, and they don't care. Knowing nothing about politics, the issues, and the candidates, they do other things on Election Day than show up.[14]

The current American electorate thus ends up being neatly divided: 45 percent vote reliably Republican and 45 percent vote reliably Democratic. Today's parity of party support is unusual. Over the course of this nation's history the typical political pattern has been to have a majority party and a minority party. As mentioned earlier, from 1933 on to the early 1980s, the majority of voters identified themselves as Democrats. In the seventy years after the Civil War until 1933, it was otherwise; most voters identified as Republicans. And before that, from Thomas Jefferson's election in 1800 up to the Civil War, the majority of the electorate saw themselves as Democrats.

But the point is, if you know the party identification of a voter and the party affiliation of the candidate, you can predict with considerable certainty for whom that voter will cast his ballot.[15]

The Transformation of the Electorate

American elections surge with energy. It would seem as if everybody becomes like an excited spectator at a horse race on which he has placed a $2 bet. It has been this way since the nation's founding.[16]

What are the consequences of all this feverish electoral activity? First, we get, more often than not, energetic, responsive, informed officials who are fair-minded and interested in their constituents, and who don't care a whit about conquering foreign nations. In the political histories of the world, that has not been true of the bulk of kings, priests, and autocrats. More likely than not, these historical figures developed into slothful, selfish, cruel, and militarily aggressive wretches. In Lord Acton's pithy aphorism, the historical picture has been one where "power tends to corrupt, and absolute power corrupts absolutely."[17] Under conditions of competitive electoral democracy, however, those who have won power have tended to develop a broadened vision and a deeper ethical judgment. They are improved by their office.

At the same time, the American electorate has grown far more informed about the nation's political life than people in nondemocracies. And well they should, for they are deluged with data and instructed incessantly by rival candidates for public office. Like a jury listening to competing advocates, a substantial part of the electorate absorbs information regarding public matters.

A quarter of a century ago, Sidney Drell, professor of physics at Stanford University, engaged in correspondence with a celebrated Soviet dissident, the Russian physicist Andrei Sakharov, on the issue of thermonuclear war. In one letter Sakharov disputed Drell's belief that America should agree to "freeze" further production of nuclear weapons. It was Drell's contention that once the "peace-loving" people of the Soviet Union *knew* America had ceased enlarging its supply of nuclear weapons, they would demand that their government stop its production of them. Sakharov pointed out that Drell's pacifist views depended on a false assumption; he reminded Drell of the extreme political ignorance of citizenries who live in unfree societies. He made his point with a then-current illustration, saying, "[W]e don't even know how, or by whom, the [Soviet] decision to invade Afghanistan [in 1980] was made! People in our country do not have even a fraction of the information about events in the world and in their own country which the citizens of the West have at their disposal. The opportunity to criticize the policy of one's national leaders in matters of war and peace as you do freely is, in our country, entirely absent."[18]

In short, Americans, at least by international standards, are all "political junkies." Despite their general lack of sustained interest in politics, their shallow involvement in elections, their subordination of civic duty to more pressing activities, and their reliance on inherited party loyalties at the expense of conscious choice, Americans know a great deal. They listen to opinion leaders within their friendship groups—their local bartender, their shop steward, their priest, and their gossipy neighbor who watches the nightly news. Americans accept this political division of labor and let the more politically attentive among them advise them about the details they don't have time to master, given their other responsibilities. Then voters, in one way or another, go about validating the soundness of this advice before acting on it. The result is that, while most of the people are uninformed about details, the electorate as a whole ends up with considerable general knowledge. Besides, whenever a public issue develops that really matters to anyone, the door to active and informed participation is wide open.

Paradoxically, a democracy of free people is served well by this political division of labor. As political scientist Bernard Berelson and his colleagues long ago pointed out, a democratic political system has to do a number of contradictory things. Popular elections need both the passionate energies of intensely competitive advocates and also the public restraint sufficient for reconciliation after an election is over. Democracy expects citizens to think for themselves, yet it needs voters to take guidance from those who have a deeper and more nuanced knowledge of public affairs. It thrives when persons pursue their self-interest through the ballot box and, at the same time, it needs a citizenry that votes with a concern for the public good. Voters are supposed to approach the voting decision with shrewdness and logic, but also with an enlightened idealism to offset cold, unsympathetic calculation. And finally, while they expect the political system to change to meet changing conditions, they also demand that it display a high degree of stability. The mixture within the electorate of involved and indifferent voters, of individualists and conformists, of people who attend to details and those who only react to general impressions, may help the democratic political system to be animated by these contradictory characteristics simultaneously.[19] As Berelson and his coauthors put it, "[O]ur electoral system calls for apparently incompatible properties—which although they cannot all reside in each individual voter, can (and do) reside in a heterogeneous electorate."[20]

NOTES

1. In the era of the modern presidency, the average voter turnout has run between 37 percent and 40 percent of the *entire* American population. The turnout in the relatively routine election of 2004, therefore, was on the high side.
2. "The Impact of Non-Citizens on Congressional Apportionment," testimony of Steven A. Camarota, director of research, Center for Immigration Studies, before the U.S. House Subcommittee on Federalism and the Census, December 6, 2005.
3. The incarceration rate of 1:250 is more than quadruple that of 1960, a staggering demographic change.
4. Raymond E. Wolfinger and Steven J. Rosenstone, *Who Votes?* (New Haven: Yale University Press, 1980).
5. This question is raised most provocatively by Anthony Downs in his invaluable book, *An Economic Theory of Democracy* (New York: HarperCollins, 1957), especially chap. 13.
6. E. E. Schattschneider, *Party Government* (New York: Rinehart and Company, 1942), makes this point particularly forcefully.
7. "Walking around money" signifies "contributions" to neighborhood opinion leaders—particularly ministers of low-income religious congregations.
8. For example, at the local level there is nothing of greater importance than zoning decisions. Zoning is the closest thing to government totalitarianism that one is likely to experience in a free country. Typically, it is forbidden to operate a gas station in a neighborhood, develop a high-rise office or apartment building, expand a hospital, or modify a factory unless local authorities give their permission. Getting a zoning permit is ticklish work, requiring a property owner to persuade a set of elected officials—the city council or a zoning commission appointed by the city council—to confer an advantage that is denied to others.

   The difficulty of negotiating such zoning regulations provides a political boss a financial opportunity. Since his efforts, funding, and media have been responsible for the election of an effective majority of the members on the city council (or zoning board), it is likely that they will be receptive to his guidance.

That leads property owners with problematic building projects, sooner or later, to come to him and be willing to pay his "law firm" or advisory service for the benefits of his influence.

9. Initiatives voted by the electorate bypass the cautionary procedures to which legislation is subjected. Kenneth P. Miller's judicious *Direct Democracy and the Courts* (New York: Cambridge University Press, 2009) views the judiciary functioning to provide a check on direct democracy otherwise missing.

10. The history of the caucus and convention systems is graphically described in Moise Ostrogorski's indispensable *Democracy and the Organization of Political Parties*, trans. Frederick Clarke (New York: Macmillan, 1902), vol. 2.

11. The base, being more politically informed but less moderate than the remainder of the electorate, presents the candidates a dilemma—to win the primary they may have to take immoderate positions, which will alienate the general electorate. See Herbert McClosky, Paul J. Hoffman, and Rosemary O'Hara, "Issue Conflict and Consensus among Party Leaders and Followers," *American Political Science Review* 54 (June 1960): 406-427.

12. Bernard R. Berelson, Paul F. Lazarsfeld, and William N. McPhee, *Voting: A Study of Opinion Formation* (Chicago: University of Chicago Press, 1954), 312.

13. Bruce E. Keith, David B. Magleby, Candice J. Nelson, Elizabeth Orr, Mark C. Westlye, and Raymond E. Wolfinger, "The Partisan Affinities of Independent Leaners," *British Journal of Political Science* 16 (April 1986): 155-185.

14. One might argue that it's a good thing that they stay away. Would it not be terrible to have elections hang on the discernment of the politically frivolous, the least informed, and the least interested? They might vote on fears that have no basis, or on appearances that have no validity. There are some, however—notably some newspaper editorialists—who feel otherwise, and who think that an empty head is the same as an open mind, and open mindedness is key to a virtuous choice. Personally, I think they're wrong.

15. See, e.g., Nelson W. Polsby and Aaron Wildavsky, *Presidential Elections: Contemporary Strategies of American Electoral Politics*, 8th ed. (New York: Free Press, 1991), 179, Table 4.2.

16. I can't resist repeating Tocqueville's awe in observing the presidential election of 1832, the campaign in which the Whigs mounted a forceful opposition to Andrew Jackson's Democrats:

> For a long while before the appointed time has come, the election becomes the important and, so to speak, the all-engrossing topic of discussion. Factional ardor is redoubled, and all the artificial passions which the imagination can create in a happy and peaceful land are agitated and brought to light. The President, moreover, is absorbed by the cares of self-defense. He no longer governs for the interest of the state, but for that of his re-election; he does homage to the majority, and instead of checking its passions, as his duty commands, he frequently courts its worst caprices. As the election draws near, the activity of intrigue and

the agitation of the populace increase; the citizens are divided into hostile camps, each of which assumes the name of its favorite candidate; the whole nation glows with feverish excitement; the election is the daily theme of the press, the subject of private conversation, the end of every thought and every action, the sole interest of the present. It is true that as soon as the choice is determined, this ardor is dispelled, calm returns, and the river, which had nearly broken its banks, sinks to its usual level; but who can refrain from astonishment that such a storm should have arisen? [Alexis de Tocqueville, *Democracy in America*, trans. Henry Reeve [New York: Bantam, 2000 (1835), vol. I, chap. 8.]

17. Perhaps the most pungently phrased political phrase in the English language, "power tends to corrupt," appeared in a letter to Mandell Creighton, dated April 1887, in which Acton defended his criticism of the papacy as follows: "I cannot accept your canon that we are to judge Pope and King unlike other men, with a favorable presumption that they did not wrong. If there is any presumption it is the other way against holders of power, increasing as the power increases. Historic responsibility has to make up for the want of legal responsibility. All power tends to corrupt and absolute power corrupts absolutely. Great men are almost always bad men, even when they exercise influence and not authority: still more when you superadd the tendency or the certainty of corruption by authority." As an introduction to the brilliant, witty, scholarly John E. E. Dalberg Acton, the reader cannot do better than John Neville Figgis, et al., in his introduction to Acton's *The History of Freedom and Other Essays* (New York: Cosimo Classics, 2005 [1922]), ix–xxxix.

18. Andrei Sakharov, "The Danger of Thermonuclear War: An Open Letter to Dr. Sidney Drell," *Foreign Affairs* (summer 1983): 1001–1016, at 1009, 1011, and 1015.

19. In this paragraph I have borrowed generously from Berelson et al., *Voting: A Study of Opinion Formation*, 313–314.

20. Ibid., 314.

27

TOCQUEVILLE'S WARNINGS

The first of the duties that are at this time imposed upon those who direct our affairs is to educate democracy, to reawaken, if possible, its religious beliefs; to purify its morals; to mold its actions; to substitute a knowledge of statecraft for its inexperience, and an awareness of its true interest for its blind instincts, to adapt its government to time and place, and to modify it according to men and to conditions.

Alexis de Tocqueville, *Democracy in America* (1835)

Alexis de Tocqueville and his traveling companion, Gustave de Beaumont, left New York City and began their journey through America on June 29, 1831, traveling up the Hudson River to Albany and then traversing New York State to Buffalo, from where they boarded a ship to Detroit. In Detroit they boarded a large passenger steamship called the *Superior* on August 1 (it carried two hundred cabins) and traveled the Great Lakes—stopping at Sault Sainte Marie, Fort Michimilimackinac (which was then on Mackinac Island), Green Bay, and back to Detroit. From there they journeyed to Niagara Falls and Canada and then on to Boston. By this time winter was approaching, a winter that turned out to be one of the coldest recorded in the nineteenth century. Nonetheless, they were determined to journey on west and south. After visits to New York, Philadelphia, and Baltimore, they traveled to Pittsburgh by stagecoach and boarded the riverboat *Fourth of*

July down the Ohio River. She promptly struck a sandbar and sank just off of Wheeling, West Virginia.

Tocqueville and Beaumont continued west on a second riverboat, which not long after got hung up on the ice just west of Cincinnati. The two Frenchmen were thus forced to go overland to Memphis, where they boarded still another steamboat to descend the Mississippi River to New Orleans. Having to meet their departure date for France on February 20, 1832, Tocqueville and Beaumont hastened through the South for a quick visit to Washington and a final two weeks in New York City. That was their American journey—nine months of travel, to every part of the then–United States.[1]

Over the next eight years Tocqueville wrote and published volumes I and II of *Democracy in America*. The first volume, published in 1835, largely was devoted to how a democratic society governed itself. Tocqueville's enthusiasm bubbled over. In America he found that ordinary people—persons who would have been dismissed as "commoners" in France—were quite capable of governing themselves.

His key insight pertained to the moral code that bound American society. He identified a "chain of opinions," the "last link" of which was "the grand maxim": "[E]very human being [has] the degree of reason necessary to direct himself in the affairs that interest him exclusively."[2] (Emphasis added.) That belief in the universality of human empathy, aptitude, and purposefulness, according to Tocqueville, was applied to all relationships: the "father of a family applie[d] it to his children, the master to his servants," and so on. Because of those reasoning powers, "every human being" could thrive without a superior directing him or her in what to do. The belief that all persons were created alike in their capacity to conduct themselves—*moral* equality—was at the center of American culture, the foundation of its *mores*.

Once liberated to pursue their self-interest, free of the yoke of so-called superiors, the American common man and woman worked relentlessly to improve themselves and their posterity; they learned how to team up in mutual cooperation, and they regulated their short-run impulses with their dreams for the long term. The result was an unimaginably energetic, robust, self-improving, self-governing, and prosperous society, one that Tocqueville was certain would surpass any nation subjected to an authoritarianism that would waste the potential energies inherent in its people.

Habits of the Mind

In the second volume, which he published eight years after his return to Europe, Tocqueville ceased to play the cheerleader. Rather, he turned to examining the dangerous susceptibilities of free, socially egalitarian societies. The starting point of his diagnosis was the "habits of mind" generated in a democratic society, a belief that people were basically alike. The unconscious assumption Americans made was that "the constitution of man . . . is everywhere the same."[3]

Therefore, Americans took for granted that if they knew themselves, they would understand everybody else. The aspirations they had, others had as well. Others sought dignity, as they did. Others were as mortal as they were, and no less anxious. Others had imagination and creativity, as they had. Others possessed "a moral instinct" (to borrow Jefferson's phrase), just as they did. No passage in Tocqueville's work is more spiritually powerful than his summary of the American habit of mind:

> But among the thoughts which [social equality] suggests, there is always one that is full of poetry, and this is the hidden nerve which gives vigor to the whole frame.
>
> Looking at the human race as one great whole, they easily conceive that its destinies are regulated by the same design; and in the actions of every individual they are led to acknowledge a trace of that universal and eternal plan by which God rules our race. . . .
>
> I need not traverse earth and sky to discover a wondrous object, woven of contrasts, of infinite greatness and littleness, of intense gloom and amazing brightness, capable at once of exciting pity, admiration, terror, contempt. *I have only to look at myself.* Man springs out of nothing, crosses time, and disappears forever in the bosom of God; he is seen but for a moment, wandering on the verge of the two abysses, and there he is lost.[4] [Emphasis added.]

That individuals are everywhere alike, with similar aspirations and anxieties, is the central idea in the American belief system: "I have only to look at myself." Consider the core idea of President George W. Bush's second inaugural address in 2005. He expressed that exact same intellectual habit, assimilating all to all:

From the day of our Founding, we have proclaimed that every man and woman on this earth has rights, and dignity, and matchless value, because they bear the image of the Maker of Heaven and earth. Across the generations we have proclaimed the imperative of self-government, because no one is fit to be a master, and no one deserves to be a slave. Advancing these ideals is the mission that created our Nation.

When President Bush said, "It is presumptuous and insulting to suggest that a whole region of the world—or the one-fifth of humanity that is Muslim—is somehow untouched by the most basic aspirations of life for personal freedom and self-government," Americans concurred. They needed no evidence to "know" Iraqis and all other inhabitants of the Muslim world aspired to personal freedom. They had only to look at themselves.

The differentiating concept of "class" was an alien construct to the socially democratic mind of Americans. That did not mean they turned a blind eye to the differences in wealth or celebrity in a socially egalitarian society. By their denial of the existence of social class, they meant that there were no fundamental, insuperable barriers separating humankind into communities of superior and inferior human beings. According to the American mind, all persons wanted to "better . . . their condition." Since persons were created equal, no one was without "matchless value."[5]

Tocqueville brilliantly orchestrated that theme. He demonstrated how the assumption of a universal human nature explained Americans' skepticism of authority; their pragmatism in science and engineering; their focus on the subjective in poetry, literature, and drama; their coarseness of language; their historiography, with its emphasis on impersonal forces and minimization of leadership and heroic virtues; their yearning for big, general theories to simplify the task of understanding; their nonhierarchical religions; their motive for self-improvement; their impatience, and their troubling expectation of attaining perfection on Earth.

Tocqueville's assessment was that there were both good and dangerous consequences of this "habit of mind." The good consequence was the intellectual stimulation resulting from the notion that the constitution of man was "everywhere the same." The presupposition that humankind shared the same spiritual nature was a stimulating perspective in which to examine the factors that created individual variety. At the same time, the assumption nurtured sentiments of brotherhood: it was an antidote to such discordant ways of thought as cynicism (humanity divides between "smarts and dumbs"), xenophobia ("civilized and savages"), Manichaeism ("saints and villains"), and Marxism ("vanguards and proletariats").

One danger of projecting one's own "constitution" onto others was disillusionment. The reality is that significant cultural differences do exist that alter the truths humans carry around in their heads. Deemphasizing those differences can sometimes lead to very unpleasant surprises.

Habits of the Heart

But Tocqueville warned of a worse danger. A free society tended to breed a pair of troublesome "habits of the heart," which he called unenlightened "individualism" and short-sighted "materialism." By "individualism," he meant a moral detachment from others, a turning inward, a tending to one's garden exclusively, a lack of regard for the public good, and a severing of oneself from "the mass of his fellows."[6] By "materialism," he meant a failure to prepare for the long run—shortsightedness, heedlessness for the lasting consequences of one's immediate actions, and an obsessive grasping for petty comforts.

Unenlightened individualism was fostered by the prosperity that a free society produced. In a free society that honored work for profit, an unprecedented abundance of material goods was produced.[7] "Give democratic nations education and freedom and leave them alone," Tocqueville wrote. "They will improve each of the useful arts and will day by day render life more comfortable, more convenient, and more easy." As a consequence of prosperity, a majority of the people would attain the comforts of the middle class. Once their material wants were satisfied, Tocqueville warned, they would come to think that they were self-sufficient, that "their whole destiny [was] in their own hands," and that "[t]hey owe[d] nothing to any man, [and] they expect[ed] nothing of any man."[8]

Unenlightened individualism also resulted from the disappearance of the small communities that had once naturally existed on the estates of landed aristocracies. Liberated from their feudal bonds, individuals found themselves in the midst of a classless crowd; there they lacked ties to any finite, face-to-face group in which dependable fellowship was nourished. Tocqueville worried that modern times would destroy those small attachments intermediate between family and the entirety of the human race. Freedom would overwhelm the isolated individual with such questions as, "Who is my neighbor? Since I can't look out for everyone, to whom should I attend?" Confused, unable to distinguish a particular set of persons for whom and to whom he was responsible, he would end up "confin[ing] him[self] within the solitude of his own heart."[9]

Tocqueville warned that a citizenry that did not care about one another ran a political danger. A culture of human indifference would leave the individual feeling helplessly vulnerable, without anyone expected to assist him when he was overwhelmed by sudden difficulty. Isolated, he would, as a last resort, look to the ruling regime with all its apparent resources. Desperate for help, he would willingly surrender his personal freedom and submit to whatever demands the state made of him.[10]

Tocqueville's insight into detached individualism and the people's susceptibility to entrust a lone "imposing power" to care for them may explain the fervor of the German society embracing the Fascist state of Adolf Hitler when the Prussian aristocratic system of order was shattered by the First World War. In its aftermath, Germany, which had been the world's most enlightened and prosperous nation of the early twentieth century, renounced the prize of freedom and embraced total subservience to a cruel despot—the "sole and necessary support of [their] own weakness."[11]

Tocqueville's cure for unenlightened individualism was vigorous "involvement" in voluntary, face-to-face groups—local government, churches, and civic associations, and sporting, cultural, and charitable organizations. Associating in them would transform a self-centered detachment into an empathetic individualism. In these voluntary organizations the individual would have the opportunity to lend a hand and make the lives of others better and at the same time gain the assurance that he was not alone. "Nothing is more deserving of our attention," wrote Tocqueville, than "learn[ing] voluntarily to help one another."[12]

A Short-Sighted Materialism

Tocqueville cautioned against a second bad "habit of the heart," a short-sighted "materialism." As we have seen, Tocqueville didn't scorn the making of money. Quite the contrary: he found much to praise about the commercial life. What Tocqueville meant by the term *materialism* was an obsessive pursuit of the quick buck, of easy money, without toil—the day trader, "ten easy ways to become a millionaire overnight," and the get-rich-quick scheme—in contrast to the painstaking pursuit of a distant and worthwhile object. Heedless materialism offended Tocqueville because it impelled the individual to grasp after "petty"[13] comforts at the expense of bettering himself and his usefulness to others.

Tocqueville believed the cause of this impatient materialism was the precarious character of a free society. The continuous innovation and surge of improvements stimulated by social democracy changed the human environment so rapidly that the individual grew fearful that any special skill he would develop over the long term would at any moment become obsolete, the victim of "creative destruction." (For a modern example, the uncanny skills of a master auto mechanic are becoming devalued, now that the diagnosis of needed repairs can be computerized.)

Shortsighted materialism was a dysfunctional adaptation to the "universal competition"[14] for recognition in a classless world.[15] Tocqueville anticipated that where every human being contended with everyone else for the respect of society-at-large, life would become unpleasantly contentious. When people regarded all their fellow beings as competitors and not as teammates and customers, relationships would deteriorate into nothing but a series of cutthroat rivalries, where cheating and injuring were justified in the imperative of standing out above the crowd. Rather than bravely sticking to his plans to nurture his "sublimest faculties"[16]—"to know, to love," to be charitable, and to matter to others—the individual would feel he had to cut corners in order to get ahead. He would do the expedient thing instead of honing his talents and daring to take the time to build a lofty enterprise.[17]

Paradoxically, such timidity gradually would undermine an individual's sense of adventure, turning him into a fearful, nonassertive victim of fate, unwilling to take risks. In Tocqueville's eloquent words, materialism "enervate[d] the soul and noiselessly unben[t] its springs of action."[18] Personal timidity, when widespread, resulted in an overcautious society. Tocqueville lamented, "When property becomes so fluctuating and the love of property so restless and so ardent, I cannot but fear that men may arrive at such a state as to regard every new theory as a peril, every innovation as an irksome toil, every social improvement as a stepping-stone to revolution, and so refuse to move altogether for fear of being moved too far."[19]

In order to mitigate shortsighted materialism, Tocqueville recommended much the same cures he had prescribed to enlighten individualism. Religion would focus the mind on questions about the long run: "Why am I here? What is the meaning of my mortal life? What legacy will I leave behind when I shuffle off?" Likewise, involvement in local government, civic associations, and philanthropy would exercise habits of long-term thinking, like setting distant goals and sustaining the effort to reach them. Involvement would cause the citizen to contemplate what he wanted the future to be like when his grandchildren would be raising their families. Participation in public activity would restrain impulsiveness and promote an understanding of how adherence to a program of sustained improvement leads to real accomplishment.

Without the influence of religion and involvement, Tocqueville worried lest a democratic order degenerate into the nightmare of "an innumerable multitude of men, all equal and alike, incessantly endeavoring to procure the petty and paltry pleasures with which they glut their lives."[20] However—and here Tocqueville's optimism asserted itself amidst the gloom of his second volume—if a democratic society would nurture its religious and civic associations, those bad habits could be transformed into an empathetic, energetic individualism and a productive, far-sighted materialism.

Summary

The essence of social democracy is devolving power, so that all persons—rich and poor, man and woman, no matter their background, clan, or ethnicity—can dream of a better future and take "control of their own destiny." To prevent government from dominating the individual citizen, political devices like periodic elections, well-informed representative legislatures, free markets, and constitutional restraints are necessary. But these political arrangements are not sufficient to produce a healthy society in the absence of elevating moral arrangements to guide and exercise "the habits of the [democratic] heart."

Tocqueville warned that a free society was imperiled by the evils of self-centeredness, rampant greed, cheating, and the kind of moral confusion that leads individuals to reject the noble values of selflessness, sacrifice, integrity, and courage. None of these dangers is inevitable, but a democratic society must anticipate and mitigate them. With that object in mind, Tocqueville offered this advice:

> The first of the duties that are at this time imposed upon those who direct our affairs is to educate democracy, to reawaken, if possible, its religious beliefs;[21] to purify its morals; to mold its actions; to substitute a knowledge of statecraft for its inexperience, and an awareness of its true interest for its blind instincts, to adapt its government to time and place, and to modify it according to men and to conditions.[22]

NOTES

1. During the 1970s Richard Reeves retraced Tocqueville and Beaumont's American journey and wrote a splendid book about the changes and continuities they observed: *American Journey: Traveling with Tocqueville in Search of "Democracy in America"* (New York: Simon and Schuster, 1982).
2. Alexis de Tocqueville, *Democracy in America*, trans. Henry Reeve (New York: Bantam, 2000 [1835]), vol. I, chap. 18.
3. Alexis de Tocqueville, *Democracy in America*, trans. Henry Reeve (New York: Bantam, 2000 [1840]), vol. II, book 3, chap. 17.
4. Ibid., vol. II, book 1, chap. 17.
5. Ibid., vol. II, book 2, chap. 15.
6. Ibid., chaps. 2, 4.
7. Ibid., vol. I, chap. 18.
8. Ibid., vol. II, book 2, chap. 2.
9. Cf. Ibid., vol. II, book 3, chap. 5.
10. Recall (in Chapter 1) Alex Kotlowitz's poignant book, *There Are No Children Here*, about life in a low-income public housing project, where he depicted the powerless isolation of its occupants. Although there were a dozen apartments on each floor, every family was a stranger to all the others. "They don't even have telephones," Kotlowitz observed. They were certain that the only assistance they could count on had to come from the "Authority"—the Chicago Housing Authority (which never came).
11. Tocqueville, *Democracy in America* , vol. II, book 4, chap. 3.
12. Ibid., vol. II, book 2, chap. 5.
13. Ibid., chap. 17.
14. Ibid., chap. 13.
15. Think, for example, of the current competition to get into Ivy League schools, now that they have virtually eliminated the economic barriers that once barred all but the very affluent few from admission.
16. Tocqueville, *Democracy in America*, vol. II, book 2, chap. 15.
17. Ibid., vol. II, book 3, chap. 19: "I believe that ambitious men in democracies are less engrossed than any others with the interests and the judgment of posterity; the present moment alone engages and absorbs them. They are more apt to complete a number of undertakings with rapidity than to raise lasting monuments of their achievements, and they care much more for success than for fame."
18. Ibid., vol. II, book 2, chap. 11.
19. Ibid., vol. II, book 3, chap. 21.

20. Ibid., vol. II, book 2, chap. 13.
21. In Robert D. Putnam and David E. Campbell's richly informative survey of religious Americans, *American Grace: How Religion Divides and Unites Us* (New York: Simon and Schuster, 2010), 492, the authors ask, "Was Tocqueville right that religion contributes to American democracy?" They conclude he was: "Religious Americans are generally better neighbors and more active citizens, though they are less staunch supporters of civil liberties than secular citizens. Moreover, religious Americans are more satisfied with their lives. As we have seen, however, theology and piety have very little to do with this religious edge in neighborliness and happiness. Instead it is religion's network of morally freighted personal connections, coupled with an inclination toward altruism, that explains both the good neighborliness and the life satisfaction of religious Americans."
22. Tocqueville, *Democracy in America,* vol. I, Introduction.

28

EQUALITY

There is, in fact, a manly and lawful passion for equality that incites men to wish all to be powerful and honored. This passion tends to elevate the humble to the rank of the great; but there exists also in the human heart a depraved taste for equality, which impels the weak to attempt to lower the powerful to their own level and reduces men to prefer equality in slavery to inequality with freedom. Not that those nations whose social condition is democratic naturally despise liberty; on the contrary, they have an instinctive love of it. But liberty is not the chief and constant object of their desires; equality is their idol; they make rapid and sudden efforts to obtain liberty and, if they miss their aim, resign themselves to their disappointment; but nothing can satisfy them without equality, and they would rather perish than lose it.

Alexis de Tocqueville, *Democracy in America* (1835)

The American Constitution that was ratified in 1788 made no mention of "equality" of condition.[1] Its silence in that respect stood in marked contrast to the motto of the French Revolution in 1789: "liberty, equality, brotherhood."[2]

In the aftermath of the American Civil War, the Constitution was amended to provide former slaves (and persons similarly situated) "the equal protection of the laws." But with that one exception regarding legal justice, the supreme law of the United States to this day remains devoid of

any mention of equality. Rather, it proclaims the paramount importance
of personal freedom. In its Preamble, the founders made their purpose
clear that they were establishing the Constitution to "secure the Blessings
of Liberty to ourselves and our posterity." Moreover, the Fifth and Fourteenth Amendments forbid both Congress and the states from depriving
any persons of their "liberty or property, without due process of law." The
United States was conceived and dedicated to be a land of the free, not of
the leveler.

In *Federalist* No. 10, James Madison emphasized the point. Uniquely,
Americans should be free to use their "faculties of acquiring property" and
to strive for "different degrees" of wealth and income. Indeed, "the protection of these faculties," he asserted, "is the first object of government."
History had demonstrated to him that "over-bearing" and envious demagogues invariably arose to urge the less wealthy to "trampl[e]" on these
protections. He condemned "theoretic politicians" who aspired to render
the citizenry "perfectly equalized . . . in their possessions" and denounced
any plan "for an equal division of property" as a "wicked project."[3]

Madison admired the new Constitution because it made economic class
warfare less likely to succeed—first, by filtering popular passions through
representative government; and second, by enabling the nation to grow
geographically, thereby making it more difficult to organize a majority
coalition bent on economic leveling.

The Pursuit of Equality

If liberty was their object and economic inequality their expectation, the
founders correctly foresaw America's future. Consider the present economic disparity between a wealthy American family and an ordinary one.
According to the survey of U.S. family incomes conducted by the Federal
Reserve Board in 2004,[4] the average, middle-aged American family had an
income of $55,000 and a net worth of $105,000.[5] To be sure, that family
was much better off than it had ever been. Compared with its counterpart
in 1990, the average middle-aged family had more "stuff." For example, its
house was 12 percent larger; it went out for dinner 12 percent more often;
its income (in dollars adjusted for inflation) was 12 percent greater; and its
net worth (also in adjusted dollars) was 16 percent greater.

Compared to the wealthiest middle-aged families, however, its financial
situation appeared quite ordinary. The median income of the wealthiest 10
percent of middle-aged families was $184,000—more than three times the

earnings of the average American family—and its net worth was a whopping $1,430,000. Even more striking was how much this average wealthy family had prospered since 1990. Compared to its counterpart back then, in 2004 its earnings and net worth were 85 percent and 72 percent greater, respectively. In other words, at least when measured in dollars, American society was characterized by considerable economic inequality, and the equality gap separating the rich from other Americans, instead of narrowing, had grown despite the increase in general prosperity.[6]

In 1840 Tocqueville warned that economic disparities might destabilize democratic societies. Freedom would bring prosperity, but unevenly. Conspicuous economic differences would develop; they would arouse popular resentment. Popularly elected governments would respond with public policies designed to equalize economic conditions. Such policies would fail because individuals were born with different talents, some more useful to the larger society than others. To motivate the development and sharing of those talents, society would have to bestow greater rewards on the exceptional few who had such desirable aptitudes. Thus economic realities would frustrate the political goal of egalitarianism; frustration would lead to further, intensified political efforts to equalize wealth and earnings; an accelerating vicious cycle of resistance and force would be set in motion; and the end result would be the eradication of society's most valued contributors.

In Tocqueville's own words, "But men will never establish any equality with which they can be contented. Whatever efforts a people may make, they will never succeed in reducing all the conditions of society to a perfect level; and even if they unhappily attained that absolute and complete equality of position, the inequality of minds would still remain, which, coming directly from the hand of God, will forever escape the laws of man."[7]

Tocqueville was advancing an insight that has been called "the revolution of rising expectations." He expressed that insight with a memorable metaphor. He had his readers imagine the prominence of a single hill elevated above a level prairie. He continued:

However democratic . . . the social state and the political constitution of a people may be, it is certain that every member of the community will always find out several points about him which overlook his own position; and we may foresee that his looks will be doggedly faced in that direction. When inequality of conditions is the common law of society, the most marked inequalities do not strike the eye; when everything is nearly on the same level, then the slightest are marked enough to hurt it. Hence, the desire of equality always becomes more insatiable in proportion as equality is more complete.

That is, a society animated by materially egalitarian ideas would end up causing nearly all its members to be discontent with their invidiously low "position." By reminding them that what matters is the amount of their wealth, the idea of equality would goad them to reduce anyone who had risen above them back to their level. To put it simply, egalitarian beliefs would end up diverting the people's energies from the constructive task of self-improvement to the destructive act of tearing down any and all those who had reached conspicuous heights.

Alternatively, Tocqueville noted, "It is possible to conceive of men arrived at a degree of freedom that should completely content them; they would then enjoy their independence without anxiety and without impatience." In other words, in a society where the guiding principle was personal freedom the energies of its members would be focused on creating their personal paths through life. They would look backwards to appreciate how far they had progressed and look ahead toward achieving an honorable destination of their own devising. Instead of envying the wealthiest, each wayfarer would consider others, rich and poor alike, as possible sources of assistance in making his way.

Whither American Society?

By what measure do contemporary Americans assess their lives? Do they envy the most wealthy by glancing upward and noting the disparity of income and wealth in their society, or do they value the effort they have made to better their own lives? A remarkable study by Robert Lane sheds light on this question.[8]

Lane, a political scientist but trained to listen to others with a psychotherapist's "third ear," spent long hours with each of fifteen white, working-class American men who labored, among other things, as a roofer, building custodian, maintenance man, policeman, truck driver, shoe salesman, bookkeeper, clerk, and factory worker. None owned a business; all depended on weekly (not monthly) paychecks; nearly half held down two jobs. They were good citizens, steady churchgoers, and responsible husbands and fathers. They were beset by the usual worries, especially about their health, knowing that if an accident or sickness kept them from working every day, they could provide no safety net to protect their families. They lived hard, demanding, and sometimes frustrating lives.

Feelings toward the Wealthy

But they were not envious of those who had more. They were not angry at their wealthy bosses except when they were given no respect. They regarded their employers as the source of payment, and earning a paycheck made them proud. They identified with their companies and embraced their companies' goals so long as they felt they were being regarded as spiritual and moral equals.

For example, addressing the issue of social class and the equality gap that existed between him and those he considered wealthy, the shoe salesman expressed the sentiments of the group:

> I think a lot of people place a lot of stress on the importance of social classes, [but] I feel that I have a job to do, I have my own little unit to take care of. If I can do it to the best of my ability that is instilled in me at birth or progress through the years, I feel that I rightly deserve the highest classification you can get. I don't particularly like the headings, "upper, middle, working, and lower."[9]

Because in America education was available to all, Lane's "common men" embraced the belief that the educated should earn more, save more, and be taxed fairly and not exorbitantly. If their social status was different from that of their bosses, they preferred it that way; they felt relieved that they did not have to keep up appearances, entertain their bosses in their homes, or discuss matters that didn't interest them. In short, they felt they were as happy as, if not happier than, those who had wealth but who also bore more responsibility and had more worries, more "headaches,"[10] and less time to enjoy themselves. A typical expression of this sentiment was the mechanic's:

> Well, even though this rich man can go places and do things that others can't afford, there's only certain things in life that I think make people happy. For instance, having children, and having a place to live—no matter where it is, it's your home . . . the majority of these big men—I don't think they devote as much time and get a thrill out of the little things in life that the average guy gets, which I think is a lot of thrills.[11]

Possibility, Not Equality

Within their status group, they saw that they had bettered themselves (or at least had had the opportunity to do so). They had developed comfortable relations with their colleagues at work; their work was acknowledged and rewarded with praise, small raises, and added responsibility; and because they had improved their skills, they performed their jobs more dexterously and effectively. In other words, they were proud of the personal progress they had made. Yes, they worried about the future, but, provided they stayed healthy, it was a future they probably could shape to their purposes.

They saw disparity of income motivating them to make the effort to keep on trying and to discipline them against lapsing back into "their hedonistic inclinations."[12] "Every one of the clients with whom I spent evenings for seven months," Lane reported, "believed that equality of income would deprive men of their incentive to work, achieve, and develop their skills."[13] That is, they valued the possibility that they could better their lot by improving themselves, and they were proud of their achievements.[14]

Summary

Note how these ordinary Americans adapted the lesson of Tocqueville's metaphor. They did not look upward at the wealthy, but gazed behind them to gauge how far they had progressed along the path they had chosen to tread. They had selected objectives of their own devising and were laying down paths toward them. While they might compare their progress against that of others, they did so only with those who were proceeding along the same trail as they.[15]

In other words, material equality—distributive justice—was not something these Americans cared much about; what mattered to them was the hopeful possibility of proceeding to achieve manageable goals.[16] So long as they believed that others—their employers, their friends, the culture—respected them for doing the best with what they had, they had no gripes about economic disparities, no hankering to level the rich and famous.

The idea of freedom dignified them.[17] Their belief systems, pivoting as they did on notions of free will and personal responsibility, gave them credit for their accomplishments, made them feel worthwhile, and assured them that they were morally equal to any of their fellows, including their wealthy bosses. To borrow Tocqueville's words, their "manly . . . passion for equality elevate[d] [them] to the rank of the great."[18]

NOTES

1. The Constitution employs the words *equal* or *equally* four times, all in connection with purely political matters, such as the apportionment of congressional seats to the several states, but never with reference to economic equality.

2. This same motto has been incorporated into the present French Constitution.

3. To be fair to the totality of Madison's views, one should note his reflections four years after composing *Federalist* No. 10. In Chapter 12, you will recall, Madison attributed the extreme partisanship of the post-Constitution decade to the economic gap separating rich from poor and warned of the need to remedy it: "The great object should be to combat the evil [of extreme partisanship]: 1. By establishing a political equality among all. 2. By withholding *unnecessary* opportunities from a few, to increase the inequality of property, by an immoderate, and especially an unmerited, accumulation of riches. 3. By the silent operation of laws, which without violating the rights of property, *reduce extreme wealth towards a state of mediocrity, and raise extreme indigence towards a state of comfort.*" (Emphasis added.) William T. Hutchinson, ed., *The Papers of James Madison* (Chicago: University of Chicago Press, 1962), vol. 1, chap. 15.

4. Brian K. Bucks, Arthur B. Kennickell, and Kevin B. Moore, "Recent Changes in U.S. Family Finances: Evidence from the 2001 and 2004 Survey of Consumer Finances" (Washington, D.C.: Board of Governors of the Federal Reserve, 2005).

5. Four definitions of terms used in this section: (1) Middle-age describes adults aged thirty-five to fifty-five years old; in 2004 this generation was born between 1949 and 1969 and had made lifetime commitments as to careers and lifestyles: they had bought a home, had had children, were at the peak of their earning powers, had sufficient time to recover from any financial mistakes, still worried about being a "success," and were not yet resigned to their lot. They were also a generation raised in a legal environment free of racial segregation. (2) Net worth does not include values arising from post-retirement benefits such as Social Security and pensions. (3) The average, or median, American family is that family whose earnings exceed 50 percent of other middle-aged American families and is exceeded by the other 50 percent. (4) The average or median wealthy middle-aged family has earnings that exceed 95 percent of all middle-aged families and are exceeded by 5 percent of those families.

6. There is a sizeable fraction of the population that is incapable of work—the mentally and physically ill and those whom we earlier labeled "the underclass," the 6 percent who appear unable to cope in a commercial society.

7. Alexis de Tocqueville, *Democracy in America,* trans. Henry Reeve (New York: Bantam, 2000 [1840]), vol. II, book 2, chap. 13.

8. Robert E. Lane, *Political Ideology: Why the American Common Man Believes What He Does* (New York: Free Press, 1962). While almost fifty years old, Lane's findings hold up well under contemporary scrutiny. Cf. Alan Wolfe, *One Nation, After All: What Middle-Class Americans Really Think about God, Country, Family, Racism, Welfare, Immigration, Homosexuality, Work, the Right, the Left, and Each Other* (New York: Penguin Putnam, 1998), 320–321:

> Although I cannot speak with certainty about all Americans, I am persuaded from the results of this study that there is little truth to the charge that middle-class Americans, divided by a culture war, have split into two hostile camps. Middle-class Americans, in their heart of hearts, are desperate that we once again become one nation. From a middle-class point of view, the ideal society would be one in which everyone—immigrants, minorities, the poor—would uphold middle-class values so that someday they might obtain middle-class incomes. That is another way of saying that their solution to class inequality is to insist on moral equality. One of the reasons the left has had trouble sinking deep roots into American culture is that it has persistently denied this moral ideal of one nation. The left's approach to welfare, for example, implicitly accepted the idea that there would exist a permanent class of dependent people—a nation within the nation, if you will—of individuals whose fortunes would not be under their own control.

9. Lane, *Political Ideology,* 63.

10. Ibid., 78.

11. Ibid., 65.

12. Ibid., 77.

13. Ibid., 76.

14. For an eloquent testimony to the feeling of pride that results from achievement in a free society, see the fine novel by Ha Jin, *A Free Life* (New York: Vintage, 2007).

15. Lane describes their state of mind as "the fear of equality." He might well have called it "the paradox of equality"—*people hang out with others with whom they can be mutually useful.*

16. Samuel P. Huntington reports: "Americans have not only worked more than other peoples, but they have found satisfaction in and identified themselves with their work more than others have. In a 1990 international values survey of ten countries, 87 percent of Americans reported that they took a great deal of pride in their work. In most countries, less than 30 percent of workers expressed that view." *Who Are We? The Challenges to America's Identity* (New York: Simon and Schuster, 2004), 72.

17. Cf. Will and Ariel Durant, *The Lessons of History* (New York: Simon and Schuster, 1968), 20:

Inequality is not only natural and inborn, it grows with the complexity of civilization. Hereditary inequalities breed social and artificial inequalities; every invention or discovery is made or seized by the exceptional individual, and makes the strong stronger, the weak relatively weaker, than before. Economic development specializes functions, differentiates abilities, and makes men unequally valuable to their group. If we knew our fellow men thoroughly we could select thirty per cent of them whose combined ability would equal that of all the rest. Life and history do precisely that, with a sublime injustice reminiscent of Calvin's God.

Nature smiles at the union of freedom and equality in our utopias. For freedom and equality are sworn and everlasting enemies, and when one prevails the other dies . . . the best that the amiable philosopher can hope for is an approximate equality of legal justice and educational opportunity.

18. Alexis de Tocqueville, *Democracy in America*, trans. Henry Reeve (New York: Bantam, 2000 [1835]), vol. I, chap. 3.

29

RACIAL EQUALITY

*The stream that the Indians had distinguished by the name of
Ohio, or the Beautiful River, waters one of the most magnificent
valleys which have ever been made the abode of man. Undulating
lands extend upon both shores of the Ohio, whose soil affords inex-
haustible treasures to the laborer; on either bank the air is equally
wholesome and the climate mild; and each of them forms the
extreme frontier of a vast state; that which follows the numerous
wanderings of the Ohio upon the left is called Kentucky; that upon
the right bears the name of the river. These two states differ only in
a single respect: Kentucky has admitted slavery, and the state of
Ohio has prohibited the existence of slaves within its borders. Thus
the traveler who floats down the current of the Ohio to the spot
where that river falls into the Mississippi may be said to sail
between liberty and servitude; and a transient inspection of
surrounding objects will convince him which of the two is most
favorable to humanity.*

Alexis de Tocqueville, *Democracy in America* (1835)

In December 1831 Alexis de Tocqueville departed Pittsburgh down the
Ohio River. His destination was the former French colony of New Orleans
in Louisiana. By the time his steamboat reached Louisville, Kentucky, however, the river had frozen over, making it impassable. Forced to alter his

plans, Tocqueville took a stagecoach, spending a full week to traverse the four hundred miles between Louisville and Memphis, Tennessee. Traveling overland was strenuous and time-consuming (causing him to compress the duration of his stay in New Orleans), but it also led to unplanned encounters that deepened his insight into the American South and the territories west of the Appalachian Mountains. Most important was his first-hand exposure to black slavery. Seeing the difference "between liberty and servitude"[1] left him convinced more than ever of the transformative power of personal freedom.

Before his ship foundered on the ice, he had enjoyed a stopover in Cincinnati, Ohio, where he had witnessed the economic growth, ceaseless improvements, and prodigious outpourings of entrepreneurial energy of the city. Experiencing the "wealth and contentment which is the reward of . . . labor for profit [that] is honored" made a deep impression on him.

The people's industry in Ohio would provide a marked contrast with life in Kentucky and elsewhere in the South, where he found idleness and an indifference to progress. His southern journey was to convince him that the laws of slavery caused the indolence of the region. White southerners, small farmers and large-plantation owners alike, believed that hard work was shameful, something to be done only by slaves. Their outlook reminded Tocqueville of the way French aristocrats thought, but with this difference. In the American South, "the whole race of whites formed an aristocratic body," in which many "were poor, but none who would work; its members preferred want to labor." The South had developed two distinct classes, one white and the other black, with impermeable and isolating barriers separating them.

As for the slaves, Tocqueville realized that they often exhibited considerable native intelligence and skills. Nevertheless, living in fear and helplessness, they had absorbed the belief that they were naturally inferior. Slavery, lamented Tocqueville, thanks to time and habit, had attained "a kind of moral power."

Constitutional Concessions

Most of those who framed the Constitution in 1787 understood the horrors resulting from the laws of slavery and their insidious effects on master and slave alike. But no one knew how to rid the new nation of it. Northerners were certain that immediate emancipation of a population that had been denied education promised unimaginable social chaos. And southerners feared that gradual easing of the oppressiveness of the slave system would inspire a devastating outbreak of slave revolts.[2] (As for the possibility of exporting the slaves back to Africa, the labors of Sisyphus would have paled by comparison.)

With their region's survival at stake, then, the southern delegates to the Constitutional Convention demanded compromise on issues of slavery as the price of union. Delegates from the northern states, fearful that the new nation would be defenseless against foreign powers without union and a strong central government, sought compromise as well, and agreed to two important concessions regarding slavery.

The first was to provide the South a twenty-year grace period in which Congress would be prohibited from putting a stop to the *international* importation of slaves.[3] This concession had two effects: one was to accelerate the shipping of slaves into the South between 1788 and 1808, and the second, paradoxically, was to better the treatment of American slaves; this was because absent a further supply from Africa, the only renewable source of slave labor was the fertility of healthy domestic slaves.[4]

The North's second concession was in the makeup of Congress. According to the Constitution, membership in the House of Representatives was to be apportioned to the states "according to their respective numbers."[5] The issue was whether slaves should count in a state's "numbers" or be treated as nonpersons and therefore excluded. Inclusion would vastly increase the number of southern representatives; more importantly, it would add to the South's representation in the body that selected the nation's president, the Electoral College, since the number of a state's electors equaled the total of its U.S. senators and representatives.[6] Compromise resolved the issue, with the North conceding that each slave would count as three-fifths of a person for purposes of apportioning seats in the House of Representatives. The partial inclusion of slaves in the states' numbers thereby heightened the influence of the South in presidential elections. (In fact, without these additional electors from the slave states, the antislavery New Englander, John Adams, would have defeated the southerner, Thomas Jefferson, in the presidential election of 1800.) With its numbers augmented, the South maintained a virtual lock on the presidency from 1800 through the election of 1856.[7] And since presidents nominated justices to the Supreme Court, the Court's makeup tended to be disproportionately southern and proslavery.[8]

The *Dred Scott* Case

During those first decades under the Constitution, sectional positions on the slavery issue hardened. Forces in the North were determined to keep the territories west of the Mississippi River free of slavery. Meanwhile, white southerners were growing ever more fearful of slave revolts as the size of the slave population swelled. Southern judges institutionalized increasingly severe practices, like legitimating the infliction of cruel punishments as "lawful chastisement" and sanctioning a lawless process by which fugitive slaves could be seized and returned to their owners.

In the course of time, the premise justifying the slave laws changed as well. At the Constitutional Convention in 1787, perpetuating slavery was considered an unfortunate necessity (i.e., freeing millions of slaves whom white society left uneducated and illiterate would wreak social havoc). In the 1830s, southern spokespersons were characterizing the slaves as racially different—congenitally uneducable and unfit for freedom.

The original equilibrium between free and slave states had prevented the U.S. Senate from taking any steps toward abolishing slavery. By 1850 the imminent admission of states from the western territories, especially from the Nebraska territory (which included the future states of Kansas and Nebraska), threatened to break the political deadlock in the U.S. Senate. Most of the new states would be opposed to slavery and would add their votes in the Senate to the antislavery coalition there. The southern way of life was in deep danger.

In 1857 the Supreme Court, dominated by a majority of justices born and raised in the South, took matters into its own hands in an attempt to protect southern interests. In *Dred Scott v. Sandford*,[9] the Court held that Congress had no power to abolish slavery anywhere, nullifying two national laws that had up to then prohibited involuntary servitude within the western parts of the country.[10] Chief Justice Roger Taney's opinion even went so far as to assert that *every state* (other than the original thirteen) also lacked the authority to exclude slavery. (One of those states was Illinois, where a young, ambitious lawyer named Abraham Lincoln lived.)

Moreover, Taney's opinion denied slaves (and even their descendants *and* previously emancipated slaves) access to federal courts, thereby leaving legal issues involving slavery to be decided in state courts (which would be largely southern and proslavery). Africans, Taney declared, had long been considered "beings of an inferior order, and altogether unfit to associate with the white race, either in social or political relations, and so far inferior that they had no rights which the white man was bound to respect."[11]

Abraham Lincoln's Response

Abraham Lincoln, then campaigning as a Republican in Illinois for the U.S. Senate, denounced the decision:

> The difference of opinion [between those opposed to *Dred Scott* and those who support it], reduced to its lowest terms, is no other than the difference between the men who think slavery is wrong and those who do not think it wrong. The Republican party think it wrong and [because] we think it as a wrong, we propose a policy that shall deal with it as a wrong, in so far as we can prevent its growing any larger, and so deal with it in the run of time when there may be some promise of an end to it.[12]

In 1861 that same Abraham Lincoln, now the newly elected president of the United States, entered the White House. Almost immediately, hostilities between North and South broke out, and the Civil War began—"a terrible war"[13] that lasted four years and took the lives of more than 600,000 Americans.

In 1863, just as the war was turning in the North's favor, Lincoln spoke at Gettysburg, Pennsylvania, the site of one of the war's deadliest battles. His address lasted only two minutes, but it continues to resound decades after. In his conclusion, Lincoln pledged "that this nation, under God, shall have a new birth of freedom."[14]

That "new birth of freedom," at least for African Americans, was to be delayed a century. The South, defeated in war, ruthlessly resisted the liberation of what Taney had dismissed as "the negro African race." Through terror, political cunning, and control of the states' police power, it kept African Americans from integrating into southern society, forbidding racial intermarriage and any intermingling in schools, places of recreation, and commercial life.[15] Of equal importance, lawyers sympathetic to the South, along with its scholars and artists, spread to every corner of the nation the racist ideas expressed in *Dred Scott*, notably that African Americans "were beings of an inferior order." *Dred Scott* lived on.[16]

Social Anomie and the Black Community

What the law did, the law conceivably could undo. And so in 1954 Chief Justice Earl Warren, writing for a unanimous Supreme Court, declared in *Brown v. Board of Education*[17] that race-based segregation of public schools violated the Constitution's Fourteenth Amendment guaranteeing the equal protection of the laws. While it took nearly two more decades before the final vestiges of legal discrimination were vetted from the policies of the southern states, Warren's opinion immediately entered constitutional law textbooks, there to be read and discussed by the million or so lawyers-to-be that were passing through the nation's hundreds of law schools over the next half-century. Thanks to their legal training, they absorbed the ideas expressed in *Brown*, that legally sanctioned separation of the races was wrong, that it bred "a sense of inferiority" among African Americans and unfairly impeded them from "succeed[ing] in life." Warren's opinion powerfully affected the largely white legal profession, animating attorneys in their communities to spread the Court's outlook. Lawyers tended to interpret *Brown* as an indictment of white Americans that spread a sense of guilt in the white community.[18] After a period of significant, sometimes violent, resistance, the white community grew to accept the ideas underlying *Brown*.

But what of the once separate African American community? How was it affected by Chief Justice Warren's opinion?[19]

Here, it is useful to think back to Chapter 10 and the depiction of social anomie by Robert Penn Warren in *All the King's Men*. Recall Willie Stark telling the impoverished, upstate small farmers that they should reject the claims of the rich and powerful to "superiority," that "hicks" had no less "stuff and character" than the plutocracy that ran the state, that the poverty they were enduring was the result of being "wronged," and that they should stand up "on [their] hind legs" and claim the respect and the treatment they deserved. Recollect the confusing effect of Stark's ideas and how they undermined the "common sense" of the "hick" community. Those small farmers found that Stark's challenge to them unsettled those deeply ingrained notions of the good life that gave meaning to the daily deeds of their hardscrabble lives. In short, Stark's words created a moral and intellectual chaos that took time to resolve.

Brown had a similarly unsettling effect within the black society. It shook its moral foundations. Why? In the century following the Civil War, millions of former slaves and their descendants formed and inhabited socially isolated communities within a white society. Within those bounds, they had constructed a social order with its own distinctive mode of self-regulation. Black Christian clergy, by virtue of their education, eloquence, and independence of white employers, tended to rise to leadership. They "legislated" the three great Christian values—to aid the poorest and unluckiest among them, to be personally responsible to try, and to forgive human failings (even those of the white class that refused them integration). They bestowed their approval on anyone who did their best to conform to these values; and their Gospel message provided consolation to their congregations for the indignities suffered at the hands of white people.[20]

Black churches celebrated laypersons who became doctors, teachers, merchants, and useful contributors to black society and conferred respect on them. Those who worked hard at their jobs, got married, made sure their children went to school, and avoided breaking the law were lauded as role models.

The Unexpected Effects of *Brown*

Just as Willie Stark's brand of populism destabilized the beliefs and relationships of the impoverished farmers, so *Brown* turned the moral world of these self-sufficient black communities topsy-turvy. For in the perspective advanced by Chief Justice Warren's opinion that whites had victimized blacks, had created a false consciousness of black inferiority, and kept them from succeeding, the black clergy and their adherents appeared gullible and cowardly, and the values they advanced—"trying," usefulness, and forgiveness—seemed to be the products of that false consciousness.

With traditional values shaken, some African Americans—and particularly the young—stopped looking up to the respected men and women of the community. They scoffed at those who had counseled patience in the face of white bigotry, disparaging them as "Uncle Tom's."[21]

Amidst the uncertainty created by the disruption of the traditional social order, those who were once considered social pariahs—people who, according to the Christian ethic, had behaved shamefully—seized the moment. Largely, they were young men, and they claimed they were now the real community leaders. They redefined manliness as defying the law, disrupting the larger society, and being a "stud"—that is, someone who fathered children and then abandoned them and their mothers. They said that such behavior was a matter of "black pride."[22] The message of these former outcasts was anarchic: hate your white oppressors, treat them as enemies, mistrust their every move, and (where possible) separate from them.

White media made things worse by turning these militants—some of them former violent felons—into heroes. Public officials, out of confusion and guilt, often ended up endorsing their claims to leadership as well.

The upshot of this abrupt break in the black community's common sense was social turmoil: crime within the community soared, school classrooms became unruly, children were raised without fathers in unfathomable numbers, and men lived off crime and the welfare checks of their women.[23]

The Resilience of the Black Churches

But such was not the case in all parts of the black community. The black churches persevered, continuing to expound on the old values and the traditional ideas about manhood and womanhood. Some church leaders, like Martin Luther King Jr., Fred Shuttlesworth, and Joseph Lowery, preached integration and envisioned the removal of racial class barriers. They became nationally prominent role models with their messages of nonviolent engagement with the white society. Black clergy often had organizational skills, and they put them to use, assuming leadership in many of the signal events of the civil rights era—the boycott of the segregated buses in Montgomery, Alabama, in 1955; the march in Birmingham, Alabama, that evoked the barbaric reaction of the city's police, which was photographed for the whole world to see in 1963; the march on Washington, which was climaxed by King's soaring "I Have a Dream" speech at the Lincoln Memorial, also in 1963; and the march across the state of Alabama that was viciously dispersed by state police outside the city of Selma in 1965.[24]

Through their words and actions, the leaders of the black churches demonstrated the civil way to change, as well as adjust to, a white society into which they sought integration. Most African Americans subscribed to their point of view, behaving with great courage, forgiveness, and the willingness to seek change through established American institutions.[25]

I know no story that better illustrates the effect of the black churches than one told by the child psychiatrist Robert Coles of a six-year-old girl named Ruby Bridges.[26]

The year was 1959, the city New Orleans. Under the protection of federal marshals, Ruby Bridges was one of the first black children to attempt to enter a formerly all-white elementary school in New Orleans under an order of federal judges that the public schools be integrated. Each day when she walked to school, she endured the threats of a mob of furious white men and women in front of the school building. The parents of the white students had boycotted the school, resolved to keep their children out until Ruby (and her protective federal marshals) ceased coming. Ruby thus was the only child in school. When the school day was over, she emerged and endured more threats and curses.

Coles interviewed her throughout the year, anticipating that Ruby would eventually suffer extreme social stress. He puzzled, however, because Ruby appeared happy. She slept well and showed no sign of stress. Her parents, while illiterate, struck Coles as insightful and sensitive to Ruby's state of mind; they told Coles that Ruby wasn't upset.

Then, one day, one of Ruby's teachers told Coles she had seen Ruby talking to various individuals in the mob. Coles was curious and asked Ruby about it.

"I wasn't talking to them," Ruby responded. "I was just saying a prayer for them." When Coles probed as to why she prayed for them, she replied, "Because they need praying for." She even told him that she had made a list of some of those who taunted her and prayed for each of them every night before getting into bed. She also told him about the minister at her parents' Baptist church, who also prayed for the people mistreating Ruby. Publicly. Every Sunday.

Befuddled, Coles waited several weeks and then asked Ruby once again why she thought she should pray for those who persecuted her each day. Ruby answered, "Because if you're going through what they're doing to you, you're the one who should be praying for them." She told Coles that the minister said Jesus went through a lot of trouble and that Jesus said about the people who were causing the trouble, "Forgive them, because they don't know what they're doing."[27]

In time, the anomie resulting from the intellectual and moral conflict that had so destabilized the social order of the black community would abate, and the Christian values of the churches would prevail. Partly, their victory was by way of default. The militant and violent worldview failed: it fueled hatred, produced destruction, and foreclosed opportunities. But the more pertinent explanation was that the religious community was organized to endure. It had a coherent text (the Bible), a designated body of ministers to interpret and apply that text to everyday life, preachers to teach the text's significance slowly and patiently to their congregations, and (finally) mutual respect between the ministers and their followers. As the church had proved its vitality and value in times of slavery, so this moral institution survived the social anomie that another moral institution, the law, had produced in the first place.[28]

There is never a sudden, obvious end to a social revolution of the magnitude of the one that brought racial equality to America. Instead, it was studded with highly visible and recordable landmark events. Then almost imperceptibly, the revolution disappeared into history, to be replaced by new preoccupations. But one landmark of the racial equality revolution in America was the election of an African American president in 2008. The admiration paid him and his family, the acknowledgment of his considerable intelligence, and the respect for his religious faith represented a complete break from the times when the dominant attitude in America was that persons of African heritage were less worthy—"unfit to associate with the white race," in the stark words of *Dred Scott*.

In his inaugural address, President Barack Obama sought to dispel the moral confusion that had bedeviled the black community and the guilt that had troubled white Americans throughout the half-century since *Brown*. Consider how he defined the very behavior that *all* Americans— black or white, Christian or Muslim—should expect of their fellow citizens:

> It is the kindness to take in a stranger when the levees break [and] the self-lessness of workers who would rather cut their hours than see a friend lose their job which see us through our darkest hours. It is the firefighter's courage to storm a stairway filled with smoke, but also a parent's willingness to nurture a child, that finally decides our fate. . . . [T]hose values upon which our success depends—honesty and hard work, courage and fair play, tolerance and curiosity, loyalty and patriotism—these things are old. These things are true. They have been the quiet force of progress throughout our history. What is demanded, then, is a return to these truths. What is required of us now is a new era of responsibility.[29]

It was truly an extraordinary moment in the history of race in America.

Notes

1. All quotes in the first section of the chapter, unless otherwise noted, come from Alexis de Tocqueville, *Democracy in America*, trans. Henry Reeve (New York: Bantam, 2000 [1835]), vol. I, chap. 18.
2. Herbert Aptheker, in his *Negro Slave Revolts in the United States, 1526–1860* (New York: International Publishers, 1939), substantiated a minimum of 250 slave revolts.
3. U.S. Constitution, Article I, Section 9.

4. The North, however, did *not* concede Congress's or the states' power to prohibit domestic slavery altogether. Consequently, the southern states needed to maintain a balance with the northern ones so as to create equilibrium in the U.S. Senate; there the South could create deadlock over the slave issue. The threat that the southern states might become outnumbered if new, antislavery states were admitted from the western territories precipitated the Civil War in 1861.

5. U.S. Constitution, Article I, Section 3.

6. "Each state shall appoint . . . a number of electors, equal to the whole number of senators and representatives to which the state may be entitled in the congress." U.S. Constitution, Article II, Section 1.

7. From 1800 until 1860, when the South's proslavery electorate split its vote among three candidates, no candidate with antislavery views would win the Electoral College. John Quincy Adams (the one seeming exception) won the presidency in 1824 only because no candidate won a majority in the Electoral College that year, whereupon the House of Representatives chose who would be president.

8. In *Federalist* No. 85 Hamilton lamented that these concessions to slavery had been necessary. The Constitution "is the best which our political situation . . . will admit." But with a realism born of hard experience, he cautioned, "I never expect to see a perfect work from imperfect man."

9. *Dred Scott v. Sandford,* 60 U.S. 393 (1857).

10. Ibid.

11. 60 U.S. 393, at 407. Taney went on to describe the danger of slave revolt:

> More especially, it cannot be believed that the large slaveholding States regarded [Africans] as included in the word citizens, or would have consented to a Constitution which might compel them to receive them in that character from another State. For if they were so received, and entitled to the privileges and immunities of citizens, it would exempt them from the operation of the special laws and from the police regulations which they considered to be necessary *for their own safety*. It would give to persons of the negro race, who were recognised as citizens in any one State of the Union, the right to enter every other State whenever they pleased, singly or in companies, without pass or passport, and without obstruction, to sojourn there as long as they pleased, to go where they pleased at every hour of the day or night without molestation, unless they committed some violation of law for which a white man would be punished; and it would give them the full liberty of speech in public and in private upon all subjects upon which its own citizens might speak; to hold public meetings upon political affairs, and *to keep and carry arms* wherever they went. And all of this would be done in the face of the subject race of the same color, both free and slaves, inevitably producing discontent and insubordination among them, and endangering the peace and safety of the State. [60 U.S. 393, at 416-417; emphasis added.]

12. Sixth debate with Sen. Stephen Douglas at Quincy, Illinois, October 15, 1858.

13. Lincoln's second inaugural address, 1865.

14. His remarks in their entirety consisted of 272 words and were as follows:

> Four score and seven years ago our fathers brought forth on this continent, a new nation, conceived in Liberty, and dedicated to the proposition that all men are created equal.
>
> Now we are engaged in a great civil war, testing whether that nation, or any nation so conceived and so dedicated, can long endure. We are met on a great battlefield of that war. We have come to dedicate a portion of that field, as a final resting place for those who here gave their lives that that nation might live. It is altogether fitting and proper that we should do this.
>
> But, in a larger sense, we cannot dedicate—we cannot consecrate—we cannot hallow—this ground. The brave men, living and dead, who struggled here, have consecrated it, far above our poor power to add or detract. The world will little note, nor long remember what we say here, but it can never forget what they did here. It is for us the living, rather, to be dedicated here to the unfinished work which they who fought here have thus far so nobly advanced. It is rather for us to be here dedicated to the great task remaining before us—that from these honored dead we take increased devotion to that cause for which they gave the last full measure of devotion—that we here highly resolve that these dead shall not have died in vain—that this nation, under God, shall have a new birth of freedom—and that government of the people, by the people, for the people, shall not perish from the earth.

15. V. O. Key Jr., assisted by Alexander Heard, *Southern Politics in State and Nation* (New York: Knopf, 1950), a book I consider the finest, most significant piece of American social science in the first half of the twentieth century, describes how white leaders in the southern states perverted the democratic process by eliminating competitive political parties.

16. Racial inferiority was the basis of the Supreme Court's opinion in *Plessy v. Ferguson*, 163 U.S. 537 (1896), endorsing the doctrine of "separate but equal."

17. *Brown v. Board of Education,* 347 U.S. 483 (1954). See Richard Kluger's splendid account of this landmark decision, *Simple Justice: The History of Brown v. Board of Education and Black America's Struggle for Equality* (New York: Alfred A. Knopf, 1976).

18. African American scholar Shelby Steele makes that point, especially in two powerfully argued books, *The Content of Our Character: A New Vision of Race in America* (New York: HarperCollins, 1990) and *White Guilt: How Blacks and Whites Together Destroyed the Promise of the Civil Rights Era* (New York: HarperCollins, 2006).

19. In the following discussion, generalizations abound—which, while necessary and helpful to insight, vastly oversimplify a much more complex reality.

20. For a comparable event involving an isolated and politically impotent minority living in the midst of a hostile society, see David Liss, *The Coffee Trader: A Novel* (New York: Random House, 2003), for his account of the religious regulation of Portuguese Jews in Holland during the early seventeenth century.

21. Sociologist Charles Murray in his book *Losing Ground: American Social Policy, 1950-1980* (New York: Basic Books, 1984), 189, recounts a conversation with a black journalist friend who recalled returning in the 1980s to his Newark, New Jersey, high school to present the Honor Society reward—"an occasion which in the early 1960s had been a major event for the school." He found that the ceremony was now held in the evening, with only the honorees attending—because "a school-wide assembly could not be held without the student body jeering the proceedings to a halt."

22. Former Black Panther leader Eldridge Cleaver was an African American, eighteen years old and just convicted of rape, who was locked up in Soledad (California) State Prison a month before *Brown* was announced. In his story, *Soul on Ice* (New York: McGraw-Hill/Ramparts, 1968), 3-6, he describes the effect *Brown* made on him and his fellow inmates:

> Of course I'd always known that I was black, but I'd never really stopped to take stock of what I was involved in. I met life as an individual and took my chances. Prior to 1954, wc lived in an atmosphere of novocain. Negroes found it necessary, in order to maintain whatever sanity they could, to remain somewhat aloof and detached from "the problem." We accepted indignities and the mechanics of the apparatus of oppression without reacting by sitting-in or holding mass demonstrations. Nurtured by the fires of the controversy over segregation, I was soon aflame with indignation over my newly discovered social status, and inwardly I turned away from America with horror, disgust and outrage.
>
> In Soledad state prison, I fell in with a group of young blacks who, like myself, were in vociferous rebellion against what we perceived as a continuation of slavery on a higher plane. We cursed everything American—including baseball and hot dogs. All respect we may have had for politicians, preachers, lawyers, governors, Presidents, senators, congressmen was utterly destroyed as we watched them temporizing and compromising over right and wrong, over legality and illegality, over constitutionality and unconstitutionality. We knew that in the end what they were clashing over was what to do with the blacks, and whether or not to start treating us as human beings. I despised all of them. . . .
>
> While all this was going on, our group was espousing atheism. Unsophisticated and not based on any philosophical rationale, our atheism was pragmatic. I had come to believe that there is no God; if there is, men do not know anything about him. Therefore, all religions were phony—which made all preachers and priests, in our eyes, fakers, including the ones scurrying around the prison who, curiously, could put in a good word for you with the Almighty Creator of the universe but could not get anything down with the warden or parole board—they could usher you through the Pearly Gates *after you were dead,* but not through the prison gate *while you were still alive and kicking.* Besides, men of the cloth who work in prison have an ineradicable stigma attached to them in the eyes of convicts because they escort condemned men into the gas chamber. Such men of God are powerful arguments in favor of atheism. Our atheism was a source of

enormous pride to me. Later on, I bolstered our arguments by reading Thomas Paine and his devastating critique of Christianity in particular and organized religion in general.

23. Such is the argument of Murray, *Losing Ground*. There are thoughtful scholars, such as Thomas J. Sugrue, *Sweet Land of Liberty: The Forgotten Struggle for Civil Rights in the North* (New York: Random House, 2008), 515, who challenge this explanation of social turmoil in the black community as overly simplistic. Sugrue suggests the greater importance of factors like the declining economies in America's inner cities, "the travails of the education system, and the persistence of segregation." One might respond, however, with a question: What caused the economies and school conditions of the cities to deteriorate in the first place? I would suggest that social anomie was the "root cause."

24. See the compelling account of Taylor Branch, *Parting the Waters: America in the King Years 1954-63* (New York: Simon and Schuster, 1988).

25. E.g., Eldridge Cleaver, a key member in the militant Black Panther Party in the 1960s and early 1970s and author of *Soul on Ice*, above, converted to Christianity later in his life.

26. Robert Coles, "The Inexplicable Prayers of Ruby Bridges," in Kelly Monroe, *Finding God at Harvard: Spiritual Journeys of Thinking Christians* (Grand Rapids, Mich.: Zondervan, 1996), 33–40.

27. A news article describing the ordeal of Ruby Bridges inspired artist Norman Rockwell's iconic painting "The Problem We All Live With," which first appeared as an illustration on the cover of *Look* magazine on January 14, 1964. The painting is now exhibited in the Norman Rockwell Museum in Stockbridge, Massachusetts.

28. The Supreme Court, for all its success in transforming white attitudes and knocking down a seemingly impenetrable social class barrier, disturbed the underpinnings of the social order it sought to transform. The events illustrate the paradox of social order: *social order abhors change, even when change is necessary to preserve it.*

29. President Barack Obama, inaugural address, Washington, D.C., January 20, 2009. The Rev. Joseph Lowery, who had been one of Martin Luther King's confidants, concluded the inaugural ceremonies with a celebratory prayer, including this line: "And now, Lord, . . . help us to make choices on the side of love, not hate; on the side of inclusion, not exclusion; tolerance, not intolerance. And as we leave this mountaintop, help us to hold on to the spirit of fellowship and the oneness of our family. Let us take that power back to our homes, our workplaces, our churches, our temples, our mosques or wherever we seek your will."

30

AMERICANS AND FOREIGN RELATIONS

[T]he energy of the executive is the bulwark of the national security. . . .

Alexander Hamilton, *Federalist* No. 70 (1788)

The foresight of Alexis de Tocqueville frequently astounds. He seemed to wield a divining rod, sensitive to forces then underground that would come to shape the United States over the next two centuries. So many of his prophecies came true: the "workaholic" habits of Americans;[1] their "restless" mobility;[2] their faith in competition;[3] their personal generosity;[4] their "habit of mind" to universalize;[5] their mundane ambitions;[6] their obsession with improvement, innovation, comfort, and wealth;[7] their respect for law;[8] the universal influence of lawyers;[9] the inefficiencies of their amateur local governments;[10] their patriotism;[11] their adherence to religion in the face of scientists' skepticism and intellectuals' ridicule;[12] the inevitability of an American civil war arising over slavery;[13] the future confrontation with Russia for world domination;[14] and a free citizenry's ability to defeat despotism.[15]

As the cause of these unique features, Tocqueville pointed to the transformative power of personal freedom and moral equality. Americans were blessed with the common sense that all persons possessed an ability to govern themselves. To repeat Tocqueville's central insight, the "grand maxim upon which civil and political society rests in the United States" was that "Providence has given to every human being the degree of reason necessary to direct himself in the affairs that interest him exclusively."[16] That revolutionary idea released prodigious amounts of human energy into the nation.

Amidst these happy portents, Tocqueville made one notably gloomy prophecy, however. Curiously, it has not yet proved accurate, and therefore it warrants inquiry into what features of the American democracy he may have overlooked.

Inconstant Policies

Tocqueville predicted that America would prove incompetent in managing its foreign affairs:

> Foreign politics demand scarcely any of those qualities which are peculiar to a democracy; they require, on the contrary, the perfect use of almost all those in which it is deficient. Democracy is favorable to the increase of the internal resources of a state; it diffuses wealth and comfort, promotes public spirit, and fortifies the respect for law in all classes of society: all these are advantages which have only an indirect influence over the relations which one people bears to another. But a democracy can only with great difficulty regulate the details of an important undertaking, persevere in a fixed design, and work out its execution in spite of serious obstacles. It cannot combine its measures with secrecy or await their consequences with patience. These are qualities which more especially belong to an individual or an aristocracy; and they are precisely the qualities by which a nation, like an individual, attains a dominant position.[17]

In other words, American foreign policy, Tocqueville thought, was likely to be imprudent, inconstant, and short-sighted. Because "the people reign in the American political world,"[18] foreign policy would reflect the habits— the bad habits—of the people. Their possible pursuit of "materialism" would focus America's government only on the proximate consequences of its plans and render it blind to more remote effects. The people's tendency toward unenlightened individualism would incline their leaders to detach America from a concern for other nations. Their commercial habits would create a popular aversion to war, tempting their elected officials to appease aggressors, not resist them. Their intellectual attraction to simple ideas would cause them to deny the paradoxes inherent in a lawless world. Their practical way of thinking would lead them to think all problems could be readily and quickly solved. And their simple disregard of the difference between political and private ethics would lead them to condemn all forms of governmental secrecy. While Americans would be wise in "homely" and "practical" matters, perceptive and measured as to subjects with which they were familiar, their policies as to other nations would be shallow and mutable, naively hopeful at the outset of an undertaking and subsequently chastened by the hard slogging entailed in realizing those hopes.

Doubtless, examples of imprudence, inconstancy, and impatience can be found in America's diplomatic history. The most frequently cited example would be America's reversion to isolationism immediately after the First World War, when in 1920 the U.S. Senate refused to ratify the centerpiece of President Woodrow Wilson's internationalist policies, the League of Nations. There are other examples of inconstancy. One was opening the door to Chinese immigration in the nineteenth century, followed in the next decade by a policy of Chinese exclusion; another was promoting free trade in the 1920s, followed by the imposition of tariff barriers in 1930—a folly that contributed significantly to the Great Depression. Tocqueville himself witnessed the cruel consequence of an impulsive reversal of policy: the Andrew Jackson presidency of the 1830s renounced an earlier decision to locate the Choctaw Indian nation on their homeland and then proceeded to expel them, a "great evil" Tocqueville described with great poignancy.[19] Each of these failures to pursue a "fixed design" had cruel consequences. Such rapid alterations of policy give credence to Tocqueville's concern that American foreign policy would be impulsive and erratic.

A Steadfast Foreign Policy

But, with these exceptions, U.S. foreign policy has not proved inept, impatient, and inconstant; quite the contrary, it has been conducted with a surprising constancy. In its first century and a half, America consistently adhered to a fixed design in its foreign relations, a steady policy of neutrality toward other nations. In 1793 President George Washington proclaimed a foreign policy that the United States would pursue well into the twentieth century. America, he warned, ought not to entangle itself in wars between European nations, but rather should adhere to "our true policy to steer clear of permanent alliances with any portion of the foreign world."[20]

President Woodrow Wilson would depart from this policy of impartiality when Germany began attacking American ships in 1916 in the midst of

World War I, but once the war had ended, American foreign policy reverted back to President Washington's fixed design. Not until a second attack—that of airborne Japanese bombers on the nation's Pacific fleet in Pearl Harbor, Hawaii, in 1941—did it become clear that President Washington's policy of nonentanglement was no longer effective in a modern world.

An even more convincing proof of American steadiness and skill in foreign relations was the nation's diplomatic prowess in the last half of the twentieth century. Since the end of World War II in 1945, the United States has demonstrated a steadiness of purpose, a constancy of execution, and a patient overcoming of "serious obstacles." For more than six decades, it has persevered in an "interventionist" foreign policy of protecting free nations from any aggression.

"Containment" of the Soviet Union

In 1947 a career foreign service officer named George Kennan, who had a deep knowledge of the Soviet Union, wrote a memo outlining a "containment" policy to oppose the imperialist designs of the Soviet Union. Here, in part, is what he wrote:[21]

> [The] political action [of the Soviet Union] is a fluid stream which moves constantly, wherever it is permitted to move, toward a given goal. Its main concern is to make sure that it has filled every nook and cranny available to it in the basin of world power. But if it finds unassailable barriers in its path, it accepts them philosophically and accommodates itself to them. The main thing is that there should always be pressure, unceasing constant pressure, toward the desired goal. There is no trace of any feeling in Soviet psychology that that goal must be reached at any given time.

Predicting that the Soviet Union would act patiently, persistently, but cautiously in its pursuit of world power, Kennan urged that America's response should be watchful, measured, but steadfast in countering every Soviet action with "contrary force":[22]

> In these circumstances it is clear that the main element of any United States policy toward the Soviet Union must be that of long-term, patient but firm and vigilant containment of Russian expansive tendencies. It is important to note, however, that such a policy has nothing to do with outward histrionics: with threats or blustering or superfluous gestures of outward "toughness."

While the Kremlin is basically flexible in its reaction to political realities, it is by no means unamenable to considerations of prestige. Like almost any other government, it can be placed by tactless and threatening gestures in a position where it cannot afford to yield even though this might be dictated by its sense of realism. The Russian leaders are keen judges of human psychology, and as such they are highly conscious that loss of temper and of self-control is never a source of strength in political affairs. They are quick to exploit such evidences of weakness. For these reasons it is a *sine qua non* of successful dealing with Russia that the foreign government in question should remain at all times cool and collected and that its demands on Russian policy should be put forward in such a manner as to leave the way open for a compliance not too detrimental to Russian prestige.

He recommended "a policy of firm containment, designed to confront the Russians with unalterable counter-force at every point where they show signs of encroaching upon the interests of a peaceful and stable world."

That strategy of containment successfully resulted more than four decades later in the Soviet Union's collapse; the liberation of East Germany, Poland, the Baltic states, Hungary, Czechoslovakia, Bulgaria, and Romania; and the elimination of the Soviet threat to invade Western Europe. The details of that American policy included, among other things, the establishment of the World Bank, the International Monetary Fund, the Marshall Plan to rebuild a Western Europe that had been devastated by five years of war, and NATO (the North Atlantic Treaty Organization to integrate American and European troops), and the disruption of the alliance between the Soviet Union and Communist China.

In pursuing this subtle and long-range internationalist policy, the American government had to patiently overcome numerous "obstacles" if success were to be achieved. The military and economic strength of America's allies—of England, France, West Germany, and Japan—had to be revived. The Soviet Union's violation of the Yalta Agreement—its refusal to withdraw back to its prewar borders—needed patience and subtlety to undo. The Soviets' lawless blockade of Berlin, which lasted fifteen months in 1948 and 1949, required Americans to fly 277,000 flights into West Berlin, where they delivered more than two million tons of food, coal, and other necessities until the Soviets backed down. Later, when the Soviets walled off East Berlin from the rest of the city in 1961, America had to erode Soviet resolve by constant pressure for more than a quarter-century until the communists tore the wall down themselves in 1989. The threat to place

Soviet nuclear weapons on Cuban soil had to be rebuffed in 1962. In every corner of the globe the Soviets probed for any weakness in America's resolve—in Angola, Greece, Afghanistan, Southeast Asia, and Nicaragua. Virtually every American effort provoked a steady barrage of Soviet disinformation and anti-American hostility from nonaligned powers in the United Nations. Finally, the "containment policy" had to survive the recurrent peril of the American electoral cycle, which enabled aspirants for national office constantly to question its wisdom.[23]

What explained this remarkable perseverance in foreign affairs? Why had America's fundamental policies, first of neutrality and then of "interventionism," been so steadfast and its diplomacy so skillful?

I have asked this question of a number of scholars of foreign affairs, and their answers point in two directions. One is the foreign policy structure that has been institutionalized within the American executive to keep its eye trained on long-term consequences. The other is the very sovereignty of the people that so worried Tocqueville.

A Unitary Executive

As to the first factor, Tocqueville underestimated how a *presidential* form of democratic government might differ from a parliamentary form. As noted before, in *Federalist* Nos. 70 through 73, Alexander Hamilton had argued for a presidency of a guaranteed duration and with adequate support. He explained that the founders opposed the idea of a plural executive (such as the UN Security Council or a cabinet in a parliamentary system) because it would produce a "perpetual struggle" over policy. Moreover, an indeterminate duration in office would render the president overly dependent on the transient and impulsive approval of the people, leading him to be overcautious and disinclined to expose himself to resentment against unpopular but necessary policies. Furthermore, without a staff that was loyal to his policies, the president would be ill-informed and uncertain.

Since Hamilton's time the presidency has developed substantial mechanisms to inform and guide its actions abroad. We have already spoken of the importance of the National Security Council, but there is more to the system than that. In the State Department alone, numerous foreign service officers man the "desks" dedicated to understanding the affairs of particular countries—there is a China desk, a Brazil desk, and so on. These desks develop an understanding of the actions, outlooks, and grievances of their respective nations. In addition, there are regional bureaus whose purpose is to comprehend distinctive regions, like Western Europe and Southeast Asia. Moreover, there are units to develop and carry out foreign policy initiatives.[24]

Most of the people involved in this foreign policy structure are careerists who carry over from administration to administration, and their fixed views of the world beyond the United States supply a wholesome inertia, stabilizing and educating successive presidents' views on foreign policy and resisting sudden vacillations.

Moreover, the president has an increased capacity to teach American people from his bully pulpit and to enlighten their parochial self-interest. With the advent of radio, television, the airplane, and the Internet, the president can broadcast information and ideas far more effectively than Tocqueville could ever have imagined, constantly reminding people of the nation's long-range objectives and encouraging persistent pursuit of them.

The Anchor of Public Opinion

There is a second explanation for the constancy of American foreign policy. The "sovereignty of the people" has anchored rather than disturbed a steady American foreign policy. I think there are at least four reasons why the people have proven so resolute and (at least for the past seven decades) so concerned for the well-being of other nations.

The first is immigration. America is a nation of immigrants. Every American (other than Native Americans) has either come to America from somewhere else, or his forebears did. Tocqueville observed, but little noted, the dual sentiments of Americans—their pride in their new country and, at the same time, their special attachment to their old one. In a section where Tocqueville noted the direct influence of religion on politics, he told this story:[25]

> I happened to be staying in one of the largest cities in the Union when I was invited to attend a public meeting in favor of the Poles and of sending them supplies of arms and money. I found two or three thousand persons collected in a vast hall which had been prepared to receive them. In a short time a priest in his ecclesiastical robes advanced to the front of the platform. The spectators rose and stood uncovered in silence while he spoke in the following terms:
>
> "Almighty god! The God of armies! Thou who didst strengthen the hearts and guide the arms of our fathers when they were fighting for the sacred

rights of their national independence. Thou who didst make them triumph over a hateful oppression, and hast granted to our people the benefits of liberty and peace! Turn, O Lord, a favorable eye upon the other hemisphere, pitifully look down upon an heroic nation which is even now struggling as we did in the former time, and for the same rights. Thou, who didst create man in the same image, let not tyranny mar thy work and establish inequality upon the earth. Almighty God! do thou watch over the destiny of the Poles, and make them worthy to be free. May thy wisdom direct their councils, may thy strength sustain their arms! Shed forth thy terror over their enemies; scatter the powers which take counsel against them; and permit not the injustice which the world has witnessed for fifty years to be consummated in our time. O Lord, who holdest alike the hearts of nations and of men in thy powerful hand, raise up allies to the sacred cause of right; arouse the French nation from the apathy to which its rulers retain it, that it may go forth again to fight for the liberties of the world.

"Lord, turn not thy face from us, and grant that we may always be the most religious, as well as the freest people of the earth. Almighty God, hear our supplications this day. Save the Poles, we beseech thee, in the name of thy well-beloved Son, our Lord Jesus Christ, who died upon the cross for the salvation of all men. Amen."

The whole meeting responded: "Amen!" with devotion.

A nation of immigrants is likely to remain attached to the "other hemisphere[s]." Like the Polish Americans of Tocqueville's day, many citizens are determined to maintain a favorable American policy toward their old countries. Deep attachments, like other strongly felt moral ideas, fervently resist change.

The second explanation for the stable character of public opinion regarding American foreign policy is the formation of civil associations to sustain support for it. Hyphenated Americans, with their dual feelings of affection toward their new and their old countries, are routinely forming "moral institutions" to shape favorable popular attitudes toward their former countrymen. Here a group of Jewish Americans has formed AIPAC, the American Israel Public Affairs Committee, to justify the special relationship between America and Israel. There a group of Anglo-Americans has organized the English-Speaking Union to spread the word about America's special relationship with the United Kingdom. Yonder is the Japanese American Citizens League, promoting Japan's special relationship with the

United States. And so on. Moreover, there are innumerable groups engaging Americans in foreign affairs: the eighty-five local units of the World Affairs Council; the Council of Foreign Affairs, with its highly regarded periodical, *Foreign Affairs*; the United Nations Association (among its activities, it sponsors the Model UN, which functions to influence American youth to regard the United Nations favorably); and, of course, the Veterans of Foreign Wars. Each of these associations (along with several others) has built a dedicated membership actively engaged in teaching ordinary people its ideas about America's responsibilities in the world arena.

Higher education is a third factor that explains the public's steadfast "interventionist" outlook. As an ever-increasing fraction of each generation goes to college, knowledge of America's diplomatic and military history has spread, compelling students to reflect on the long-term consequences of past foreign policy measures. On balance, a college education makes a difference, likely to further an individual's interest in foreign affairs.

The fourth and final explanation for an enlightened public opinion on foreign matters is the effect of free-market capitalism. The spread of American commerce through what is now called "globalization" has dispersed Americans into every corner of the world. Hundreds of thousands of American salespersons, engineers, and financiers have worked with citizens of other nations, have encountered foreign cultures, and have sought to understand the problems of their foreign customers. Globalization has led to an expansion of empathy and been an antidote to parochialism. It has connected people to the fate of humankind in ways unimaginable in Tocqueville's time.

Those four factors—immigration, ethnic and international interest groups, higher education, and globalization—all have converged to strengthen popular support for an interventionist foreign policy.[26]

The stability of American support for interventionism has to be counted as a remarkable feat because modern international affairs are exceedingly complex. The American people have been asked to untangle this complexity, and especially three realities.

The first is the military reality, stemming from the coercive paradox of dispossession. While a plentiful arsenal of weapons and a superbly disciplined military will deter other strong nations from aggression, they are much less effective against "failed" states and stateless barbarians who have nothing to lose. (As noted earlier, this paradox creates the problem of the "asymmetrical relationship.") The suicide bomber, by virtue of his human detachment and irrationality, won't be deterred by a fearsome military. This military reality is a puzzling and frustrating fact for Americans to stomach as their effort to protect others endures setbacks and results in American casualties.

Second is the economic reality, stemming from the reciprocal paradox of abundance: *the more resourceful one's competitor, the worse, but the more resourceful one's customer, the better.* Whenever American efforts (such as the Marshall Plan in the aftermath of World War II and the North American Free Trade Agreement—NAFTA—currently) succeed in stimulating the economies of other nations, the United States benefits as a whole. Nevertheless, distinct sectors that compete with their flourishing counterparts abroad are threatened. That is, the prosperity of nations elsewhere creates beneficial customers for some Americans, but trade-war adversaries for others.

Third is the human rights reality, stemming from the three paradoxes of moral power—of perception, responsibility, and social order. As Americans have grown more sensitive to human rights abuses around the world and feel a growing responsibility to remedy them, they have had to understand that America's intervention is likely to be resented because it demoralizes established cultures. American ideas of individualism and personal freedom undermine the predictive, dignifying, and social functions of older, aristocratic ways of thought; tampering with them, even those that restrict freedom and cause poverty, lead to some degree of social anomie abroad. Confusion and resistance result.

None of these three realities is easy for the most skillful of governments to manage, for they involve compromise, economic adjustments, and patient diplomacy. And they require considerable sophistication of thought on the part of a democratic people.

I am certain that Tocqueville would be pleasantly surprised that history has proven his gloomy prediction wrong. He no doubt would also appreciate the reasons why his dire prophecy of a naive, short-sighted, impatient, and erratic foreign policy did not come to pass. Moreover, he would be pleased to discover that America, in which he had invested so much hope, would have become a center of world power and that its leaders had pursued, in the face of great difficulty, a far-sighted and generous foreign policy, one that transcended the confines of a narrow national interest and spread the idea of personal freedom abroad.

NOTES

1. Alexis de Tocqueville, *Democracy in America*, trans. Henry Reeve (New York: Bantam, 2000 [1840]), vol. II, book 2, chap.18.
2. Ibid., vol. II, book 3, chap. 14.
3. Ibid., vol. II, book 1, chap. 17.
4. Ibid., vol. II, book 2, chap. 18.
5. Ibid., vol. II, book 1, chap. 17.
6. Ibid., vol. II, book 3, chap. 19.
7. Ibid., vol. II, book 2, chap. 11.
8. Alexis de Tocqueville, *Democracy in America*, trans. Henry Reeve (New York: Bantam, 2000 [1835], vol. I, chap. 17.
9. Ibid., chap. 16.
10. Ibid., chap. 13.
11. Ibid., chap. 13.
12. Ibid., chap. 17.
13. Ibid., chap. 18.
14. Ibid.
15. Ibid., vol. II, book 3, chap. 24.
16. Ibid., vol. I, chap. 18.
17. Ibid., chap. 13.
18. Ibid., chap. 4.
19. Ibid., chap. 18:

   > At the end of the year 1831, while I was on the left bank of the Mississippi at a place named by Europeans Memphis, there arrived a numerous band of Choctaws. . . . These savages had left their country and were endeavoring to gain the right bank of the Mississippi, where they hoped to find an asylum. . . . The Indians had their families with them, and they brought in their train the wounded and the sick, with children newly born and old men on the verge of death. They possessed neither tents nor wagons, but only their arms and some provisions. I saw them embark to pass the mighty river, and never will that solemn spectacle fade from my remembrance. . . . The Indians had all stepped into the bark that was to carry them across, but their dogs remained upon the bank. As soon as these animals perceived their masters were finally leaving the shore, they set up a dismal howl and, plunging all together into the icy waters of the Mississippi, swam after the boat.

20. George Washington, Farewell Address (1796):

   > Against the insidious wiles of foreign influence (I conjure you to believe me, fellow-citizens) the jealousy of a free people ought to be constantly awake, since history and experience prove that foreign influence is one of the most baneful

foes of republican government. But that jealousy to be useful must be impartial; else it becomes the instrument of the very influence to be avoided, instead of a defense against it. Excessive partiality for one foreign nation and excessive dislike of another cause those whom they actuate to see danger only on one side, and serve to veil and even second the arts of influence on the other. Real patriots who may resist the intrigues of the favorite are liable to become suspected and odious, while its tools and dupes usurp the applause and confidence of the people, to surrender their interests.

21. George F. Kennan ("X"), "The Sources of Soviet Conduct," *Foreign Affairs* (July 1947).

22. "These considerations make Soviet diplomacy at once easier and more difficult to deal with than the diplomacy of individual aggressive leaders like Napoleon and Hitler. On the one hand it is more sensitive to contrary force, more ready to yield on individual sectors of the diplomatic front when that force is felt to be too strong, and thus more rational in the logic and rhetoric of power. On the other hand it cannot be easily defeated or discouraged by a single victory on the part of its opponents. And the patient persistence by which it is animated means that *it can be effectively countered not by sporadic acts which represent the momentary whims of democratic opinion* but only by intelligent long-range policies on the part of Russia's adversaries—policies no less steady in their purpose, and no less variegated and resourceful in their application, than those of the Soviet Union itself." (Emphasis added.)

23. Tocqueville ruefully noted that frequent elections exposed democracies to a "perpetual mutability" that would prevent "any steady and consistent policy." *Democracy in America*, vol. I, chap. 13.

24. The National Security Council and the Department of State are part of an enduring foreign affairs apparatus, which embraces, as well, the Defense Department, the Commerce Department, the Trade Representative's Office, the Treasury Department, and the Central Intelligence Agency.

25. Tocqueville, *Democracy in America*, vol. I, chap. 17.

26. While Tocqueville expressed concern about the possible impatience of Americans in pursuing a steady course, he acknowledged a contrary feature of American opinion: "What struck me in the United States was the difficulty of shaking the majority in an opinion once conceived." *Democracy in America*, vol. II, book 3, chap. 21.

31

THE DEMOCRATIC VISION

I often think of something a British writer said in the magazine
The Economist. "In America they call waiters sir." Yes, we do.
This is the fairest place there ever was, it's wide open, and no one
has cause for bitterness.

Peggy Noonan, *What I Saw at the Revolution* (1990)[1]

There is presently a belief with wide currency that America is the cause of much that is wrong in the world. A version of that belief goes, "We are hated in the Middle East because . . .," and out will trot the list of usual suspects: American arrogance, a president's swagger, America's failure to sign some treaty or other, its stubborn protection of Israel, its exploitation of Arab oil, and so on.

Nonsense, says the foremost English-language scholar of the Arab world, Bernard Lewis. In his recent book, *The Crisis of Islam,* he asks: "For a long time, remarkably little was known about America in the lands of Islam. . . . [Then] suddenly, or so it seemed, America had become the arch-enemy, the incarnation of evil, the diabolic opponent of all that is good and, specifically for Muslims, of Islam. Why?"[2]

Professor Lewis goes on to explain: "A key figure in the development of these new attitudes was Sayyid Qutb, an Egyptian who became a leading ideologue of Muslim radical fundamentalism and an active member of the organization known as the Muslim Brothers. . . . In [his capacity as an official in the Egyptian Ministry of Education,] he was sent on a special study mission to the United States, where he stayed from November 1948 to August 1950. His radical activism and writing began very soon after his return from America to Egypt."

Lewis recounts that Qutb was shocked by America's "sinfulness." And what was the sin? The mingling of the sexes, and the freedom and equality of rights enjoyed by women. He was repulsed by church mixers where priests permitted men and women to dance together.[3]

Lewis reports that Qutb's most powerful accusation was "the degeneracy and debauchery of the American way of life, and the threat that it offers to Islam. This threat, classically formulated by [him], became a regular part of the vocabulary and ideology of radical Islamic fundamentalists, and most notably, in the language of the Iranian Revolution. This is what is meant by the term the Great Satan, applied to the United States by the late Ayatollah Khomeini. Satan as depicted in the Qur'an is neither an imperialist nor an exploiter. He is a seducer, 'the insidious tempter who whispers in the hearts of men.'"

It might seem bizarre to think that men and women dancing together would be the cause of hatred of America. But if dancing in church basements symbolizes giving women equal status to men, Qutb's reaction becomes more understandable. The American principles of personal freedom and social equality amount to an assault on the aristocratic foundations of puritanical Islamic culture, a system of belief wherein certain men are deemed superior by virtue of their gender and knowledge of the Qur'an and are owed deference by those with an inferior understanding. American culture, with its celebration of the equal moral worth of every person, threatens those beliefs.

America's Mission

The point is that Americans and certain militant Islamic fundamentalists have competing visions of what constitutes a good society. These radical fundamentalists do not want the outcome of that rivalry to be decided in a free marketplace of ideas; they want dominance to depend on who can use threats the best.

Just because America's free society discomfits the aristocracies of the world is no reason to apologize for the values it cherishes. To blame America for the ailments caused by other nations' oppressive systems of class distinction is both self-absorbed and simple-minded. It leads to a faulty diagnosis of the world's problems and what should be done about them.[4]

What the existence of America actually causes to happen is not blameworthy, but revolutionary and exciting, although uncertain in result. People of every nation—men and women, rich and poor—are being touched by the democratic vision: democratic, not in the *political* sense of majority rule, but in the *social* sense that Alexis de Tocqueville intended. Because the information age has made our planet small, no longer does any culture survive in a sanctuary free from the penetration of this vision. The principles of personal freedom and equality infect and weaken older traditions. Just as the democratic vision disrupted Western Europe two centuries ago, it is having the same unsettling consequences elsewhere today.[5]

Think of the effect of the "self-evident truth" that all persons are created equal, meaning (as Thomas Jefferson insisted) that there are no inherently superior persons entitled to ride on the backs of the common people and direct them to do what their superiors tell them to. Recall how that belief menaced the plutocracy of Willie Stark's Louisiana, the dominance of the Youngstown Mafia dons, the tyranny of Sheriff Dial and his Mississippi posse, and the conceit of Judge Turner in frontier Marysville, each of whom claimed superiority and depended upon acquiescence to it. Their aristocratic vision of privilege and entitlement based on differences of moral worth is presently under siege by the idea of moral equality.

It is not imperialism that spreads America's vision of a good society, one where every man and woman is trusted in their pursuit of happiness because of their inherent faculties for empathy and useful accomplishment.[6] The democratic vision spreads simply because it makes sense to "hicks," women, untouchables, infidels, underdogs, and "hoi polloi" everywhere. Animated by the prospect of being masters of their own destiny, they see that they can transform their innate potential into talents that will be useful to others—their families, neighborhoods, professions, and nations. The institutions of freedom offer them the possibility to matter, and that makes all the difference.[7]

Recall a passage earlier quoted where Tocqueville foresaw the inevitability of the democratic vision. It warrants repeating:[8]

The nations of our time cannot prevent the conditions of men from becoming equal, but it depends upon themselves whether the principle of equality is to lead them to servitude or freedom, to knowledge or barbarism, to prosperity or wretchedness.

Today the democratic impulse of human equality and personal freedom throbs throughout Asia, the Middle East, Africa, and Latin America. It is in

America's interest, and to its credit, that it should attempt to relieve the social anomie inevitably resulting from this revolutionary idea.[9] America's proper mission is to teach these once aristocratic societies about the reasons for freedom and explain the political and economic forms that can channel democracy's prodigious human energies into real peace, prosperity, and forgiveness. It is a mission America should perform with conviction, with humility, and with empathy.

Objections

Intelligent and reasonable voices have been raised to object to America's involvement in the affairs of other nations as they try to adapt to "the principle of equality." The criticisms boil down to two: the first is that such an adaptation will prove *impossible* to accomplish; the second is that it is *unnecessary* because the adaptation is already underway and does not need America's intervention.

The principle proponent of the objection that adaptation is impossible is political scientist Samuel Huntington. In his *The Clash of Civilizations*[10] and, more particularly, in his recent book *Who Are We?*,[11] he asserts that America's values of freedom, social equality, enlightened individualism, and rule of law are uniquely American and are embedded in what he calls America's "Dissenting Protestantism."[12] The American creed of individual conscience and personal responsibility, he writes, "is Protestantism without God."[13] America, unlike any other country, is "a nation with the soul of a church."[14] Its traditions—ones emphasizing limits on government and clerical authority and recognizing a higher, "natural" law that confers rights of liberty and the pursuit of happiness on individuals—are incompatible with the "indigenous traditions" of much of the rest of the world.[15] Professor Huntington does not elaborate on what those indigenous traditions are, but presumably their common principle is the aristocratic claim that certain persons or classes of persons are superior to ordinary people and are entitled to impose their will by force or threat of condemnation. American efforts to encourage freedom in defiance of these aristocratic traditions will only provoke resistance and stimulate anti-American hatred. Huntington counsels: perfect our own culture rather than practice "imperialism" in nations we deem backward.[16] In subtle and not so subtle terms, Huntington is urging a return to America's erstwhile foreign policy of non-involvement because the aristocratic cultures of others are not amenable to successful change.

The other school of thought, expressed most eloquently by the scholarly journalist Fareed Zakaria in his *The Post-American World,* suggests that American intervention is unnecessary because emerging nations are already "going America's way,"[17] thanks to economic globalization. "As long as we keep the forces of modernization, global interaction, and trade growing," he writes, "good governance, human rights, and democracy all move forward." Good economics trumps bad politics. Trade will infect America's trading partners with American values. As a general rule, "[C]apitalism leads to democracy [and] countries that marketize and modernize begin changing politically around the time that they achieve middle-income status";[18] Zakaria defines middle-income status to be that point where the median personal income of a country lies "somewhere between $5,000 and $10,000." His advice: be patient, ignore criticisms from human rights advocates, stop "hectoring"[19] these other countries, and keep on assisting them to prosper by advancing their technologies. Traditional cultures will change as they adapt to domestic prosperity and the new economic realities that enable it. (Historian Arthur Herman characterizes Zakaria's advice a bit tendentiously, but with a ring of truth to it: America should become "the world's self-effacing social worker."[20])

My brief summary of Zakaria's and Huntington's thinking may have omitted important subtleties, for which I apologize. But it appears to me that despite the fact that their assessments of the mutability of aristocratic cultures are mutually contradictory, they arrive at much the same conclusion: America should leave well enough alone; it should tone down its efforts to cultivate personal freedom in countries that presently deny it.

What is wrong with such advice? First, both Zakaria and Huntington seem to be in a state of denial that America and its allies throughout the world have been attacked by freedom-oppressing nations (or nonstate entities within those nations). The al-Qaeda terrorist network, for instance, in defense of the old ways (subjection of women, hatred of the infidel, the binding force of *fatwas* issued by a theological aristocracy, the spread of Islam by force), has bombed England, Scotland, Israel, Germany, Spain, Indonesia, and the Philippines, along with America's embassies, naval ships, and financial and political capitals. It is morally and politically irresponsible for America's government not to try to change the thinking that fathered such violent attacks. To turn the other cheek, responding to unprovoked aggression with good deeds (as Zakaria would advise) or by studied ignorance (as Huntington seems to imply), has rarely, if ever, succeeded in halting international aggression.

Second, despite Huntington's claim to the contrary, "imperialism" is not the mission of America. Imperialism—the occupation of another's national territory—may have succeeded in democratizing Germany and Japan after their unconditional surrender at the end of World War II, but invariably a long occupation corrupts both the occupier and the occupied. Notwithstanding the best of intentions, territorial imperialism inevitably degenerates into exploitation, arrogance, and civil animosities. Over the last half of the twentieth century, America has eschewed foreign occupations, even giving back former territories like the Philippines, the Panama Canal, and numerous islands in the Pacific, and withdrawing its occupation of Germany, Japan, Iraq, and (prospectively) Afghanistan as soon as their governments have become capable of providing safety for their own people.

Third, as for Zakaria's views, America's mission—explicit and in practice—has not been to Westernize other cultures, with all that "Westernization" implies—"the classical legacy [of enlightened individualism and personal responsibility], Christianity, the separation of church and state, the rule of law."[21] Rather, America's mission and practices have been minimalist, to help nations discover their own ways "to control power." American policy has been to offer our model as one example of a free regime. When it has intervened in the decades since World War II, it has not done so to "Westernize," but for national security and humanitarian reasons.

In a world made small by modern forms of transportation, communication, and armaments, neither noninvolvement nor studied ignorance of the intentions of America's enemies to do violence is feasible. Huntington is correct when he warns that tyrants will always resist efforts to liberate their subjects from their tyranny. Equally useful is his caution concerning the social anomie that invariably accompanies the transformation of an aristocratic society into a democratic one. Moreover, there is evidence to support Zakaria's optimism that some nations are capable of forging their own means of controlling power. And both Huntington and Zakaria make sense when they warn America not to appear (much less to be) arrogant in its foreign relations.

But none of these considerations warrants America ceasing to protect itself and its allies against aggression. If freedom increases the chances of real peace, it is politically imprudent to withhold assistance to peoples desiring to liberate themselves from the tyrannical and repressive conditions of their pasts.

The Social Values of Freedom

Any nation that enables its people to be personally free will benefit in three ways. First, free societies need less government. Free, self-reliant individuals team up with one another and accomplish privately what governments have to do (or insist on doing) in repressive countries. That frees governments to do what they, and only they, can do: to defend their people from foreign aggression and domestic disorder.

Second, freedom makes good people. In a free society the primary means by which individuals manage to collaborate is reciprocal power, and reciprocity disciplines individuals to be virtuous and energetic. Moreover, in free association with one another, persons produce mutually useful goods and services. Motivated by self-interest, they experiment and innovate in every field, submitting their results to the tests of reality, and they thereby advance knowledge, from which the entire nation benefits. The astonishing variety of collaborative enterprise in a free society constitutes (in the words of the British essayist John Stuart Mill) countless "independent centres of improvement."[22]

Third, free societies generate patriots, whose loyalty is dependable. Free persons conform to the norm of reciprocity and voluntarily feel they "owe" the nation loyalty in return for their protection.

Four Questions

At the end, we return to the four questions with which the book began, the first of which was, *What is personal freedom?* It is more than being left alone. Humans are social animals, dependent on relationships with one another for protection and assistance. Personal freedom is the possession of power by the individual sufficient to enlist the collaboration of others in his or her pursuit of personal goals.

The second question was, *What are the circumstances under which personal freedom can thrive?* There must be a dependable source of safety to protect the individual from the abusive, coercive power of others. There must be free markets, in which individuals can get their way by using reciprocal power. There must be means by which individuals can exercise moral power, particularly the availability of education and the existence of effective restraints on governmental and social censorship. There must be a rule of law to enforce contracts and property rights.

And there must be political democracy. I say this in spite of the historic example of the Roman Empire of two thousand years ago, where Romans enjoyed a considerable measure of personal freedom despite their lack of the franchise. But the survival of freedom there was the exception that tests the current truth that elective democracy has proven to be the most reliable means to preserve freedom. Elective democracy is not perfect, by any means; what human institution is? But at least when checked by safeguards to protect minorities, it has proved to be the best servant of personal freedom. Winston Churchill's memorable quip was just right: "Many forms of Government have been tried, and will be tried in this world of sin and woe. No one pretends that democracy is perfect or all-wise. Indeed, it has been said that democracy is the worst form of Government except all those other forms that have been tried from time to time."[23]

The third question was, *What are the dangers inherent in a personally free society?* One is demagoguery: that is, the appearance of individuals or groups with such unusual moral power that they create a condition of social anomie that undermines faith in personal freedom and adherence to the norm of reciprocity. A second is short-sighted materialism: that is, an impatient eagerness for reciprocal power that leads individuals to steal and otherwise betray the norm of reciprocity. The third is a loss of compassion: that is, a callous detachment from the hardships of others that leads individuals to forget that "No man is an Island" (to borrow John Donne's magnificent phrase).[24]

And finally, we come to the fourth—and crucial—question, *Is American civilization, founded as it is on personal freedom, worth fighting for?* Yes, indeed, it is—but not because of its material abundance, though freedom produces abundance. Nor is it because it advances knowledge, though it is an unsurpassed mechanism of self-correction.[25] Nor is it because it is a key to peace, though free nations don't war against one another.

What makes America's free society worth defending is this. A civilization that values personal freedom is superior because all persons (and not just a tiny elite) have the chance to satisfy the universal yearning for spiritual fulfillment. By "spiritual fulfillment" I mean the certainty that one has usefully exercised the gifts that "Nature's God" has given him. Nothing more, but also nothing less. Spiritual fulfillment: that is what Jefferson intended when he declared Americans' right to "the pursuit of happiness"—the pursuit of their personal dream.

In 1927, in the case of *Whitney v. California*,[26] Supreme Court Justice Louis Brandeis wrote, "Those who won our independence believed that *the final end of the state was to make men free to develop their faculties, and that in* its government the deliberative forces should prevail over the arbitrary. They valued liberty both as an end and as a means. They believed liberty to be the secret of happiness and courage to be the secret of liberty."[27] (Emphasis added.)

"[T]he final end of the state [is] to make men free to develop their faculties. . . ." It could not be better said.

NOTES

1. Peggy Noonan, *What I Saw at the Revolution: A Political Life in the Reagan Era* (New York: Random House, 1990).
2. Bernard Lewis, *The Crisis of Islam: Holy War and Unholy Terror* (New York: Modern Library, 2003), 64–81.
3. In Qutb's own words, "The dance is inflamed by the notes of the gramophone; the dance hall becomes a whirl of heels and thighs, arms enfold hips, lips and breasts meet, and the air is full of lust." Quoted in Lewis, *The Crisis of Islam.*
4. Whenever someone expresses this notion of national guilt, I think of Babe Ruth's legendary misdiagnosis. Just before a game he wolfed down half a dozen hot dogs, two boxes of Crackerjack, three pint bottles of Nehi soda pop, piles of sauerkraut, several Polish sausages—and an apple. In the ninth inning, he collapsed with a horrendous stomach ache. As he was being carried off the field, he turned to the doctor and said, "I shouldn't have ate that apple."
5. In the words of former secretary of state George Shultz, "I think this is the most promising moment, almost, in the history of the world—a time when the information age has made it clear to people what it takes for them to get ahead in their lives and succeed, to have prosperity, to have growth, and it's a critical matter not to have that great opportunity aborted by a wave of radically inspired terrorists. So we have to confront this, and we have to do it on a sustainable basis because it's going to take a long time." Daniel Henninger, "The Weekend Interview with George Shultz," *Wall Street Journal,* April 29, 2006, A8.
6. "From the day of our Founding, we have proclaimed that every man and woman on this earth has rights, and dignity, and matchless value, because they bear the image of the Maker of Heaven and earth. Across the generations we have proclaimed the imperative of self-government, because no one is fit to be a master, and no one deserves to be a slave. Advancing these ideals is the mission that created our Nation." George W. Bush, second inaugural address, 2005.

7. However, Americans since Jefferson's time have seen the United States as "a light to the world that mankind was capable of self-government." Gordon S. Wood, *Empire of Liberty: A History of the Early Republic, 1789-1815* (New York: Oxford University Press, 2009), 737.

8. Alexis de Tocqueville, *Democracy in America*, trans. Henry Reeve (New York: Bantam, 2000 [1840]), vol. II, book 4, chap. 8.

9. Cf. Amy Chua, *World on Fire: How Exporting Free Market Democracy Breeds Ethnic Hatred and Global Instability* (New York: Random House/Doubleday, 2003).

10. Samuel B. Huntington, *The Clash of Civilizations and the Remaking of World Order* (New York: Simon and Schuster, 1996).

11. Samuel B. Huntington, *Who Are We? The Challenges to America's National Identity* (New York: Simon and Schuster, 2004).

12. Ibid., 68.

13. Ibid., 69.

14. Ibid., 106.

15. Ibid., 364.

16. Ibid. Huntington's proposal would circumvent what in the preceding chapter was called the "human rights reality"—that change, even for the better, demoralizes established cultures and leads to some degree of social anomie.

17. Fareed Zakaria, *The Post-American World* (New York: W. W. Norton, 2008), 218.

18. Ibid., 100.

19. Ibid., 128.

20. Arthur Herman, "The Return of Carterism?" *Commentary* 127, no. 1 (January 2009): 19.

21. Zakaria, *The Post-American World*, 74.

22. John Stuart Mill, *On Liberty* (1859), chap. III, "Of Individuality, as One of the Elements of Well-Being": ". . . the only unfailing and permanent source of improvement is liberty, since by it there are as many possible independent centres of improvement as there are individuals."

23. Winston Churchill, speech, House of Commons, November 11, 1947, in *Winston S. Churchill: His Complete Speeches, 1897-1963*, vol. 7, ed. Robert Rhodes James (London: Chelsea House, 1974), 7566.

24. "No man is an Iland, intire of it selfe; every man is a peece of the Continent, a part of the maine; if a Clod bee washed away by the Sea, Europe is the lese, as well as if a Promontorie were, as well as if a Mannor of thy friends or of thine owne were; any mans death diminishes me, because I am involved in Mankinde; And therefore never send to know for whom the bell tolls; It tolls for thee." John Donne, *Devotions Upon Emergent Occasions* XVII.

25. John Stuart Mill's *On Liberty* rests its justification of liberty on this coldly intellectual ground, which renders his eloquent essay ultimately unconvincing.

26. *Whitney v. California*, 274 U.S. 357, at 375 (1927). Justice Brandeis intentionally echoed the funeral oration given by the Athenian leader Pericles in 430 B.C., perhaps the first (and certainly the most articulate) justification of a free society in human history. See Thucydides, *History of the Peloponnesian War*, book II, "Pericles' Funeral Oration."

27. Another Supreme Court justice, Thurgood Marshall, the first African American to sit on the nation's highest court, put it plainly: a free society gives each member the chance to "d[o] the best he could with what he had." Lisa C. Jones, "The Legacy of Thurgood Marshall," *Ebony*, March 1993.

EPILOGUE

Consider this anecdote, related to me by the Honorable K. Shankar Bajpai, former Indian ambassador to both the People's Republic of China (PRC) and the United States.

Contrasting the Communist PRC with America, Ambassador Bajpai began,

You know, an ambassador is nothing more than a lobbyist on behalf of his nation. When I was a diplomat in China and I needed to lobby the Red [i.e., Communist] Chinese for some favorable policy or another, I went to visit five men—the Premier, the Foreign Minister, the Finance Minister, the military's Commander-in-Chief, and the Chairman of the Communist Party. When I had concluded those meetings, I had done my job. They were the five people whom I needed to lobby; they had all the authority; they were the only ones who made the decisions affecting my country.

When I came to the United States, however, I found I had to talk with the President and the Vice President, of course. Next, I had to talk with the chairs and vice chairs of all the relevant Congressional committees and subcommittees and also speak with the heads of important federal agencies—independent agencies like the Federal Reserve Board as well as ones more accountable to the President, like the International Trade Representative and the Secretaries of the Departments of Commerce and Treasury. Then I needed to visit governors and city mayors in their various states. There, I would go on to talk with a host of newspaper editorialists.

At this point, my job had just begun. I traveled the country to talk in union halls and at meetings of business and professional groups and outdoors to environmental groups and indoors at churches. Finally, [and a weary smile would cross Ambassador Bajpai's face] I would end up throwing a cultural festival in Flatbush.

Flatbush, as readers know, is a part of Brooklyn, New York—the very symbol of "Nowheresville," significant only because ordinary Americans live there. "Throwing a cultural festival in Flatbush" was Bajpai's delightful way of saying that it is essential for a foreign diplomat to convince the American people that India is a country that they should care about because of its decency, reliability, and common heritage.

Think about that. Consider how widely power is dispersed in this country—so widely, in fact, that an important official from India had to spend energies on a *public* relations campaign to educate the people of the United States because they had the last word, the final authority, the franchise with which they preserve "the Blessings of Liberty."

APPENDIX A.
THE ELEVEN PARADOXES
OF POLITICS

The Paradox of Dispossession: the fewer assets one has, the less vulnerable one is to another's threats; the more assets, the more vulnerable.

The Paradox of Detachment: the less the victim cares about preserving something, the less the victimizer cares about taking it hostage.

The Paradox of Face: the more ruthless one's reputation, the less ruthless one has to be.

The Paradox of Irrationality: the more delirious the threatener, the more serious the threat; the more delirious the victim, the less serious the threat.

The Paradox of Scarcity: the scarcer the supply, the higher the price; the higher the price, the more is supplied.

The Paradox of Abundance: the more resourceful one's competitor, the worse; the more resourceful one's customer, the better.

The Paradox of Equality: people hang out with others with whom they can be mutually useful.

The Paradox of Liberty: liberty requires limits.

The Paradox of Perception: beliefs enable seeing.

The Paradox of Responsibility: the more irrevocable the deed, the more irreversible the idea that sired it.

The Paradox of Social Order: social order abhors change, even when change is necessary to preserve it.

APPENDIX B.
THE CONSTITUTION OF THE UNITED STATES

The U.S. Constitution was written at a convention that Congress called on February 21, 1787, for the purpose of recommending amendments to the Articles of Confederation. Every state but Rhode Island sent delegates to Philadelphia, where the convention met that summer. The delegates decided to write an entirely new constitution, completing their labors on September 17. Nine states (the number the Constitution itself stipulated as sufficient) ratified it by June 21, 1788.

We the People of the United States, in Order to form a more perfect Union, establish Justice, insure domestic Tranquility, provide for the common defence, promote the general Welfare, and secure the Blessings of Liberty to ourselves and our Posterity, do ordain and establish this Constitution for the United States of America.

ARTICLE I

Section 1. All legislative Powers herein granted shall be vested in a Congress of the United States, which shall consist of a Senate and House of Representatives.

Section 2. The House of Representatives shall be composed of Members chosen every second Year by the People of the several States, and the Electors in each State shall have the Qualifications requisite for Electors of the most numerous Branch of the State Legislature.

No Person shall be a Representative who shall not have attained to the age of twenty five Years, and been seven Years a Citizen of the United States, and who shall not, when elected, be an Inhabitant of that State in which he shall be chosen.

[Representatives and direct Taxes shall be apportioned among the several States which may be included within this Union, according to their respective Numbers, which shall be determined by adding to the whole Number of free Persons, including those bound to Service for a Term of Years, and excluding Indians not taxed, three fifths of all other Persons.][1] The actual Enumeration shall be made within three Years after the first Meeting of the Congress of the United States, and within every subsequent Term of ten Years, in such Manner as they shall by Law direct. The Number of Representatives shall not exceed one for every thirty Thousand, but each State shall have at Least one Representative; and until such enumeration shall be made, the State of New Hampshire shall be entitled to chuse three, Massachusetts eight, Rhode-Island and Providence Plantations one, Connecticut five, New-York six, New Jersey four, Pennsylvania eight, Delaware one, Maryland six, Virginia ten, North Carolina five, South Carolina five, and Georgia three.

When vacancies happen in the Representation from any State, the Executive Authority thereof shall issue Writs of Election to fill such Vacancies.

The House of Representatives shall chuse their Speaker and other Officers; and shall have the sole Power of Impeachment.

Section 3. The Senate of the United States shall be composed of two Senators from each State, [chosen by the Legislature thereof,][2] for six Years; and each Senator shall have one Vote.

Immediately after they shall be assembled in Consequence of the first Election, they shall be divided as equally as may be into three Classes. The Seats of the Senators of the first Class shall be vacated at the Expiration of the second Year, of the second Class at the Expiration of the fourth Year, and of the third Class at the Expiration of the sixth Year, so that one third may be chosen every second Year; [and if Vacancies happen by Resignation, or otherwise, during the Recess of the Legislature of any State, the Executive thereof may make temporary Appointments until the next Meeting of the Legislature, which shall then fill such Vacancies.][3]

No Person shall be a Senator who shall not have attained to the Age of thirty Years, and been nine Years a Citizen of the United States, and who shall not, when elected, be an Inhabitant of that State for which he shall be chosen.

The Vice President of the United States shall be President of the Senate, but shall have no Vote, unless they be equally divided.

The Senate shall chuse their other Officers, and also a President pro tempore, in the Absence of the Vice President, or when he shall exercise the Office of President of the United States.

The Senate shall have the sole Power to try all Impeachments. When sitting for that Purpose, they shall be on Oath or Affirmation. When the President of the United States is tried, the Chief Justice shall preside: And no Person shall be convicted without the Concurrence of two thirds of the Members present.

Judgment in Cases of Impeachment shall not extend further than to removal from Office, and disqualification to hold and enjoy any Office of honor, Trust or Profit under the United States: but the Party convicted shall nevertheless be liable and subject to Indictment, Trial, Judgment and Punishment, according to Law.

Section 4. The Times, Places and Manner of holding Elections for Senators and Representatives, shall be prescribed in each State by the Legislature thereof; but the Congress may at any time by Law make or alter such Regulations, except as to the Places of chusing Senators.

The Congress shall assemble at least once in every Year, and such Meeting shall [be on the first Monday in December],⁴ unless they shall by Law appoint a different Day.

Section 5. Each House shall be the Judge of the Elections, Returns and Qualifications of its own Members, and a Majority of each shall constitute a Quorum to do Business; but a smaller Number may adjourn from day to day, and may be authorized to compel the Attendance of absent Members, in such Manner, and under such Penalties as each House may provide.

Each House may determine the Rules of its Proceedings, punish its Members for disorderly Behaviour, and, with the Concurrence of two thirds, expel a Member.

Each House shall keep a Journal of its Proceedings, and from time to time publish the same, excepting such Parts as may in their Judgment require Secrecy; and the Yeas and Nays of the Members of either House on any question shall, at the Desire of one fifth of those Present, be entered on the Journal.

Neither House, during the Session of Congress, shall, without the Consent of the other, adjourn for more than three days, nor to any other Place than that in which the two Houses shall be sitting.

Section 6. The Senators and Representatives shall receive a Compensation for their Services, to be ascertained by Law, and paid out of the Treasury of the United States. They shall in all Cases, except Treason, Felony and Breach of the Peace, be privileged from Arrest during their Attendance at the Session of their respective Houses, and in going to and returning from the same; and for any Speech or Debate in either House, they shall not be questioned in any other Place.

No Senator or Representative shall, during the Time for which he was elected, be appointed to any civil Office under the Authority of the United States, which shall have been created, or the Emoluments whereof shall have been encreased during such time; and no Person holding any Office under the United States, shall be a Member of either House during his Continuance in Office.

Section 7. All Bills for raising Revenue shall originate in the House of Representatives; but the Senate may propose or concur with Amendments as on other Bills.

Every Bill which shall have passed the House of Representatives and the Senate, shall, before it becomes a Law, be presented to the President of the United States; If he approves he shall sign it, but if not he shall return it, with his Objections to that House in which it shall have originated, who shall enter the Objections at large on their Journal, and proceed to reconsider it. If after such Reconsideration two thirds of that House shall agree to pass the Bill, it shall be sent, together with the Objections, to the other House, by which it shall likewise be reconsidered, and if approved by two thirds of that House, it shall become a Law. But in all such Cases the Votes of both Houses shall be determined by yeas and Nays, and the Names of the Persons voting for and against the Bill shall be entered on the Journal of each House respectively. If any Bill shall not be returned by the President within ten Days (Sundays excepted) after it shall have been presented to him, the Same shall be a Law, in like Manner as if he had signed it, unless the Congress by their Adjournment prevent its Return, in which Case it shall not be a Law.

Every Order, Resolution, or Vote to which the Concurrence of the Senate and House of Representatives may be necessary (except on a question of Adjournment) shall be presented to the President of the United States; and before the Same shall take Effect, shall be approved by him, or being disapproved by him, shall be repassed by two thirds of the Senate and House of

Representatives, according to the Rules and Limitations prescribed in the Case of a Bill.

Section 8.

The Congress shall have Power To lay and collect Taxes, Duties, Imposts and Excises, to pay the Debts and provide for the common Defence and general Welfare of the United States; but all Duties, Imposts and Excises shall be uniform throughout the United States;

To borrow Money on the credit of the United States;

To regulate Commerce with foreign Nations, and among the several States, and with the Indian Tribes;

To establish an uniform Rule of Naturalization, and uniform Laws on the subject of Bankruptcies throughout the United States;

To coin Money, regulate the Value thereof, and of foreign Coin, and fix the Standard of Weights and Measures;

To provide for the Punishment of counterfeiting the Securities and current Coin of the United States;

To establish Post Offices and post Roads;

To promote the Progress of Science and useful Arts, by securing for limited Times to Authors and Inventors the exclusive Right to their respective Writings and Discoveries;

To constitute Tribunals inferior to the supreme Court;

To define and punish Piracies and Felonies committed on the high Seas, and Offences against the Law of Nations;

To declare War, grant Letters of Marque and Reprisal, and make Rules concerning Captures on Land and Water;

To raise and support Armies, but no Appropriation of Money to that Use shall be for a longer Term than two Years;

To provide and maintain a Navy;

To make Rules for the Government and Regulation of the land and naval Forces;

To provide for calling forth the Militia to execute the Laws of the Union, suppress Insurrections and repel Invasions;

To provide for organizing, arming, and disciplining, the Militia, and for governing such Part of them as may be employed in the Service of the United States, reserving to the States respectively, the Appointment of the Officers, and the Authority of training the Militia according to the discipline prescribed by Congress;

To exercise exclusive Legislation in all Cases whatsoever, over such District (not exceeding ten Miles square) as may, by Cession of particular States, and the Acceptance of Congress, become the Seat of the Government of the United States, and to exercise like Authority over all Places purchased by the Consent of the Legislature of the State in which the Same shall be, for the Erection of Forts, Magazines, Arsenals, dock-Yards, and other needful Buildings;—And

To make all Laws which shall be necessary and proper for carrying into Execution the foregoing Powers, and all other Powers vested by this Constitution in the Government of the United States, or in any Department or Officer thereof.

Section 9. The Migration or Importation of such Persons as any of the States now existing shall think proper to admit, shall not be prohibited by the Congress prior to the Year one thousand eight hundred and eight, but a Tax or duty may be imposed on such Importation, not exceeding ten dollars for each Person.

The Privilege of the Writ of Habeas Corpus shall not be suspended, unless when in Cases of Rebellion or Invasion the public Safety may require it.

No Bill of Attainder or ex post facto Law shall be passed.

No Capitation, or other direct, Tax shall be laid, unless in Proportion to the Census or Enumeration herein before directed to be taken.[5]

No Tax or Duty shall be laid on Articles exported from any State.

No Preference shall be given by any Regulation of Commerce or Revenue to the Ports of one State over those of another; nor shall Vessels bound to, or from, one State, be obliged to enter, clear, or pay Duties in another.

No Money shall be drawn from the Treasury, but in Consequence of Appropriations made by Law; and a regular Statement and Account of the Receipts and Expenditures of all public Money shall be published from time to time.

No Title of Nobility shall be granted by the United States: And no Person holding any Office of Profit or Trust under them, shall, without the Consent of the Congress, accept of any present, Emolument, Office, or Title, of any kind whatever, from any King, Prince, or foreign State.

Section 10. No State shall enter into any Treaty, Alliance, or Confederation; grant Letters of Marque and Reprisal; coin Money; emit Bills of Credit;

make any Thing but gold and silver Coin a Tender in Payment of Debts; pass any Bill of Attainder, ex post facto Law, or Law impairing the Obligation of Contracts, or grant any Title of Nobility.

No State shall, without the Consent of the Congress, lay any Imposts or Duties on Imports or Exports, except what may be absolutely necessary for executing its inspection Laws: and the net Produce of all Duties and Imposts, laid by any State on Imports or Exports, shall be for the Use of the Treasury of the United States; and all such Laws shall be subject to the Revision and Controul of the Congress.

No State shall, without the Consent of Congress, lay any Duty of Tonnage, keep Troops, or Ships of War in time of Peace, enter into any Agreement or Compact with another State, or with a foreign Power, or engage in War, unless actually invaded, or in such imminent Danger as will not admit of delay.

ARTICLE II

Section 1. The executive Power shall be vested in a President of the United States of America. He shall hold his Office during the Term of four Years, and, together with the Vice President, chosen for the same Term, be elected, as follows:

Each State shall appoint, in such Manner as the Legislature thereof may direct, a Number of Electors, equal to the whole Number of Senators and Representatives to which the State may be entitled in the Congress: but no Senator or Representative, or Person holding an Office of Trust or Profit under the United States, shall be appointed an Elector.

[The Electors shall meet in their respective States, and vote by Ballot for two Persons, of whom one at least shall not be an Inhabitant of the same State with themselves. And they shall make a List of all the Persons voted for, and of the Number of Votes for each; which List they shall sign and certify, and transmit sealed to the Seat of the Government of the United States, directed to the President of the Senate. The President of the Senate shall, in the Presence of the Senate and House of Representatives, open all the Certificates, and the Votes shall then be counted. The Person having the greatest Number of Votes shall be the President, if such Number be a Majority of the whole Number of Electors appointed; and if there be more than one who have such Majority, and have an equal Number of Votes, then the House of Representatives shall immediately chuse by Ballot one of them for President; and if no Person have a Majority, then from the five highest on the list the said House shall in like Manner chuse the President. But in chusing the President, the Votes shall be taken by States, the Representation from each State having one Vote; A quorum for this Purpose shall consist of a Member or Members from two thirds of the States, and a Majority of all the States shall be necessary to a Choice. In every Case, after the Choice of the President, the Person having the greatest Number of Votes of the Electors shall be the Vice President. But if there should remain two or more who have equal Votes, the Senate shall chuse from them by Ballot the Vice President.][6]

The Congress may determine the Time of chusing the Electors, and the Day on which they shall give their Votes; which Day shall be the same throughout the United States.

No Person except a natural born Citizen, or a Citizen of the United States, at the time of the Adoption of this Constitution, shall be eligible to the Office of President; neither shall any Person be eligible to that Office who shall not have attained to the Age of thirty five Years, and been fourteen Years a Resident within the United States.

In Case of the Removal of the President from Office, or of his Death, Resignation, or Inability to discharge the Powers and Duties of the said Office,[7] the Same shall devolve on the Vice President, and the Congress may by Law provide for the Case of Removal, Death, Resignation or Inability, both of the President and Vice President, declaring what Officer shall then act as President, and such Officer shall act accordingly, until the Disability be removed, or a President shall be elected.

The President shall, at stated Times, receive for his Services, a Compensation, which shall neither be encreased nor diminished during the Period for which he shall have been elected, and he shall not receive within that Period any other Emolument from the United States, or any of them.

Before he enter on the Execution of his Office, he shall take the following Oath or Affirmation:—"I do solemnly swear (or affirm) that I will faithfully execute the Office of President of the United States, and will to the best of my Ability, preserve, protect and defend the Constitution of the United States."

Section 2. The President shall be Commander in Chief of the Army and Navy of the United States, and of the Militia of the several States, when called into the actual Service of the United States; he may require the Opinion, in writing, of the principal Officer in each of the executive Departments, upon any Subject relating to the Duties of their respective Offices, and he shall have Power to grant Reprieves and Pardons for Offences against the United States, except in Cases of Impeachment.

He shall have Power, by and with the Advice and Consent of the Senate, to make Treaties, provided two thirds of the Senators present concur; and he shall nominate, and by and with the Advice and Consent of the Senate, shall appoint Ambassadors, other public Ministers and Consuls, Judges of the supreme Court, and all other Officers of the United States, whose Appointments are not herein otherwise provided for, and which shall be established by Law: but the Congress may by Law vest the Appointment of such inferior Officers, as they think proper, in the President alone, in the Courts of Law, or in the Heads of Departments.

The President shall have Power to fill up all Vacancies that may happen during the Recess of the Senate, by granting Commissions which shall expire at the End of their next Session.

Section 3. He shall from time to time give to the Congress Information of the State of the Union, and recommend to their Consideration such Measures as he shall judge necessary and expedient; he may, on extraordinary Occasions, convene both Houses, or either of them, and in Case of Disagreement between them, with Respect to the Time of Adjournment, he may adjourn them to such Time as he shall think proper; he shall receive Ambassadors and other public Ministers; he shall take Care that the Laws be faithfully executed, and shall Commission all the Officers of the United States.

Section 4. The President, Vice President and all civil Officers of the United States, shall be removed from Office on Impeachment for, and Conviction of, Treason, Bribery, or other high Crimes and Misdemeanors.

ARTICLE III

Section 1. The judicial Power of the United States, shall be vested in one supreme Court, and in such inferior Courts as the Congress may from time to time ordain and establish. The Judges, both of the supreme and inferior Courts, shall hold their Offices during good Behaviour, and shall, at stated Times, receive for their Services, a Compensation, which shall not be diminished during their Continuance in Office.

Section 2. The judicial Power shall extend to all Cases, in Law and Equity, arising under this Constitution, the Laws of the United States, and Treaties made, or which shall be made, under their Authority; —to all Cases affecting Ambassadors, other public Ministers and Consuls; —to all Cases of admiralty and maritime Jurisdiction; —to Controversies to which the United States shall be a Party; —to Controversies between two or more States; —between a State and Citizens of another State; —between Citizens of different States; —between Citizens of the same State claiming Lands under Grants of different States, and between a State, or the Citizens thereof, and foreign States, Citizens or Subjects.[8]

In all Cases affecting Ambassadors, other public Ministers and Consuls, and those in which a State shall be Party, the supreme Court shall have original Jurisdiction. In all the other Cases before mentioned, the supreme Court shall have appellate Jurisdiction, both as to Law and Fact, with such Exceptions, and under such Regulations as the Congress shall make.

The Trial of all Crimes, except in Cases of Impeachment, shall be by Jury; and such Trial shall be held in the State where the said Crimes shall have been committed; but when not committed within any State, the Trial shall be at such Place or Places as the Congress may by Law have directed.

Section 3. Treason against the United States, shall consist only in levying War against them, or in adhering to their Enemies, giving them Aid and Comfort. No Person shall be convicted of Treason unless on the Testimony of two Witnesses to the same overt Act, or on Confession in open Court.

The Congress shall have Power to declare the Punishment of Treason, but no Attainder of Treason shall work Corruption of Blood, or Forfeiture except during the Life of the Person attainted.

ARTICLE IV

Section 1. Full Faith and Credit shall be given in each State to the public Acts, Records, and judicial Proceedings of every other State. And the Congress may by general Laws prescribe the Manner in which such Acts, Records and Proceedings shall be proved, and the Effect thereof.

Section 2. The Citizens of each State shall be entitled to all Privileges and Immunities of Citizens in the several States.

A Person charged in any State with Treason, Felony, or other Crime, who shall flee from Justice, and be found in another State, shall on Demand of the executive Authority of the State from which he fled, be delivered up, to be removed to the State having Jurisdiction of the Crime.

[No Person held to Service or Labour in one State, under the Laws thereof, escaping into another, shall, in Consequence of any Law or Regulation therein, be discharged from such Service or Labour, but shall be delivered up on Claim of the Party to whom such Service or Labour may be due.]⁹

Section 3. New States may be admitted by the Congress into this Union; but no new State shall be formed or erected within the Jurisdiction of any other State; nor any State be formed by the Junction of two or more States, or Parts of States, without the Consent of the Legislatures of the States concerned as well as of the Congress.

The Congress shall have Power to dispose of and make all needful Rules and Regulations respecting the Territory or other Property belonging to the United States; and nothing in this Constitution shall be so construed as to Prejudice any Claims of the United States, or of any particular State.

Section 4. The United States shall guarantee to every State in this Union a Republican Form of Government, and shall protect each of them against Invasion; and on Application of the Legislature, or of the Executive (when the Legislature cannot be convened) against domestic Violence.

ARTICLE V

The Congress, whenever two thirds of both Houses shall deem it necessary, shall propose Amendments to this Constitution, or, on the Application of the Legislatures of two thirds of the several States, shall call a Convention for proposing Amendments, which, in either Case, shall be valid to all Intents and Purposes, as Part of this Constitution, when ratified by the Legislatures of three fourths of the several States, or by Conventions in three fourths thereof, as the one or the other Mode of Ratification may be proposed by the Congress; Provided [that no Amendment which may be made prior to the Year One thousand eight hundred and eight shall in any Manner affect the first and fourth Clauses in the Ninth Section of the first Article; and]¹⁰ that no State, without its Consent, shall be deprived of its equal Suffrage in the Senate.

ARTICLE VI

All Debts contracted and Engagements entered into, before the Adoption of this Constitution, shall be as valid against the United States under this Constitution, as under the Confederation.

This Constitution, and the Laws of the United States which shall be made in Pursuance thereof; and all Treaties made, or which shall be made, under the Authority of the United States, shall be the supreme Law of the Land; and the Judges in every State shall be bound thereby, any Thing in the Constitution or Laws of any State to the Contrary notwithstanding.

The Senators and Representatives before mentioned, and the Members of the several State Legislatures, and all executive and judicial Officers, both of the United States and of the several States, shall be bound by Oath or Affirmation, to support this Constitution; but no religious Test shall ever be required as a Qualification to any Office or public Trust under the United States.

ARTICLE VII

The Ratification of the Conventions of nine States, shall be sufficient for the Establishment of this Constitution between the States so ratifying the Same.

Done in Convention by the Unanimous Consent of the States present the Seventeenth Day of September in the Year of our Lord one thousand seven hundred and Eighty seven and of the Independence of the United States of America the Twelfth. IN WITNESS whereof We have hereunto subscribed our Names,

George Washington, President and deputy from Virginia, and thirty-eight other delegates.

[The language of the original Constitution, not including the Amendments, was adopted by a convention of the states on September 17, 1787, and was subsequently ratified by the states on the following dates: Delaware, December 7, 1787; Pennsylvania, December 12, 1787; New Jersey, December 18, 1787; Georgia, January 2, 1788; Connecticut, January 9, 1788; Massachusetts, February 6, 1788; Maryland, April 28, 1788; South Carolina, May 23, 1788; New Hampshire, June 21, 1788.

Ratification was completed on June 21, 1788.

The Constitution subsequently was ratified by Virginia, June 25, 1788; New York, July 26, 1788; North Carolina, November 21, 1789; Rhode Island, May 29, 1790; and Vermont, January 10, 1791.]

Amendments

Amendment I

(First ten amendments ratified December 15, 1791.)

Congress shall make no law respecting an establishment of religion, or prohibiting the free exercise thereof; or abridging the freedom of speech, or of the press; or the right of the people peaceably to assemble, and to petition the Government for a redress of grievances.

Amendment II

A well regulated Militia, being necessary to the security of a free State, the right of the people to keep and bear Arms, shall not be infringed.

Amendment III

No Soldier shall, in time of peace be quartered in any house, without the consent of the Owner, nor in time of war, but in a manner to be prescribed by law.

Amendment IV

The right of the people to be secure in their persons, houses, papers, and effects, against unreasonable searches and seizures, shall not be violated, and no Warrants shall issue, but upon probable cause, supported by Oath or affirmation, and particularly describing the place to be searched, and the persons or things to be seized.

Amendment V

No person shall be held to answer for a capital, or otherwise infamous crime, unless on a presentment or indictment of a Grand Jury, except in cases arising in the land or naval forces, or in the Militia, when in actual service in time of War or public danger; nor shall any person be subject for the same offence to be twice put in jeopardy of life or limb; nor shall be compelled in any criminal case to be a witness against himself, nor be deprived of life, liberty, or property, without due process of law; nor shall private property be taken for public use, without just compensation.

Amendment VI

In all criminal prosecutions, the accused shall enjoy the right to a speedy and public trial, by an impartial jury of the State and district wherein the crime shall have been committed, which district shall have been previously ascertained by law, and to be informed of the nature and cause of the accusation; to be confronted with the witnesses against him;

to have compulsory process for obtaining witnesses in his favor, and to have the Assistance of Counsel for his defence.

Amendment VII

In Suits at common law, where the value in controversy shall exceed twenty dollars, the right of trial by jury shall be preserved, and no fact tried by a jury, shall be otherwise re-examined in any Court of the United States, than according to the rules of the common law.

Amendment VIII

Excessive bail shall not be required, nor excessive fines imposed, nor cruel and unusual punishments inflicted.

Amendment IX

The enumeration in the Constitution, of certain rights, shall not be construed to deny or disparage others retained by the people.

Amendment X

The powers not delegated to the United States by the Constitution, nor prohibited by it to the States, are reserved to the States respectively, or to the people.

Amendment XI *(Ratified February 7, 1795)*

The Judicial power of the United States shall not be construed to extend to any suit in law or equity, commenced or prosecuted against one of the United States by Citizens of another State, or by Citizens or Subjects of any Foreign State.

Amendment XII *(Ratified June 15, 1804)*

The Electors shall meet in their respective states and vote by ballot for President and Vice-President, one of whom, at least, shall not be an inhabitant of the same state with themselves; they shall name in their ballots the person voted for as President, and in distinct ballots the person voted for as Vice-President, and they shall make distinct lists of all persons voted for as President, and of all persons voted for as Vice-President, and of the number of votes for each, which lists they shall sign and certify, and transmit sealed to the seat of the government of the United States, directed to the President of the Senate; —The President of the Senate shall, in the presence of the Senate and House of Representatives, open all the certificates and the votes shall then be counted; —The person having the greatest number of votes for President, shall be the President, if such number be a majority of the whole number of Electors appointed; and if no person have such majority, then from the persons having the highest numbers not exceeding three on the list of those voted for as President, the House of Representatives shall choose immediately, by ballot, the President. But in choosing the President, the votes shall be taken by states, the representation from each state having one vote; a quorum for this purpose shall consist of a member or members from two-thirds of the states, and a majority of all the states shall be necessary to a choice. [And if the House of Representatives shall not choose a President whenever the right of choice shall devolve upon them, before the fourth day of March next following, then the Vice-President shall act as President, as in the case of the death or other constitutional disability of the President. —][11] The person having the greatest number of votes as Vice-President, shall be the Vice-President, if such number be a majority of the whole number of Electors appointed, and if no person have a majority, then from the two highest numbers on the list, the Senate shall choose the Vice-President; a quorum for the purpose shall consist of two-thirds of the whole number of Senators, and a majority of the whole number shall be necessary to a choice. But no person constitutionally ineligible to the office of President shall be eligible to that of Vice-President of the United States.

Amendment XIII *(Ratified December 6, 1865)*

Section 1. Neither slavery nor involuntary servitude, except as a punishment for crime whereof the party shall have been duly convicted, shall exist within the United States, or any place subject to their jurisdiction.

Section 2. Congress shall have power to enforce this article by appropriate legislation.

Amendment XIV *(Ratified July 9, 1868)*

Section 1. All persons born or naturalized in the United States, and subject to the jurisdiction thereof, are citizens of the United States and of the State wherein they reside. No State shall make or enforce any law which shall abridge the privileges or immunities of citizens of the United States; nor shall any State deprive any person of life, liberty, or property, without due process of law; nor deny to any person within its jurisdiction the equal protection of the laws.

Section 2. Representatives shall be apportioned among the several States according to their respective numbers, counting the whole number of persons in each State, excluding Indians not taxed. But when the right to vote at any election for the choice of electors for President and Vice President of the United States, Representatives in Congress, the Executive and Judicial officers of a State, or the members of the Legislature thereof, is denied to any of the male inhabitants of such State, being twenty-one years of age,[12] and citizens of the United States, or in any way abridged, except for participation in rebellion, or other crime, the basis of representation therein shall be reduced in the proportion which the number of such male citizens shall bear to the whole number of male citizens twenty-one years of age in such State.

Section 3. No person shall be a Senator or Representative in Congress, or elector of President and Vice President, or hold any Office, civil or military, under the United States, or under any State, who, having previously taken an oath, as a member of Congress, or as an officer of the United States, or as a member of any State legislature, or as an executive or judicial officer of any State, to support the Constitution of the United States, shall have engaged in insurrection or rebellion against the same, or given aid or comfort to the enemies thereof. But Congress may by a vote of two-thirds of each House, remove such disability.

Section 4. The validity of the public debt of the United States, authorized by law, including debts incurred for payment of pensions and bounties for services in suppressing insurrection or rebellion, shall not be questioned. But neither the United States nor any State shall assume or pay any debt or obligation incurred in aid of insurrection or rebellion against the United States, or any claim for the loss or emancipation of any slave; but all such debts, obligations and claims shall be held illegal and void.

Section 5. The Congress shall have power to enforce, by appropriate legislation, the provisions of this article.

Amendment XV *(Ratified February 3, 1870)*

Section 1. The right of citizens of the United States to vote shall not be denied or abridged by the United States or by any State on account of race, color, or previous condition of servitude.

Section 2. The Congress shall have power to enforce this article by appropriate legislation.

Amendment XVI *(Ratified February 3, 1913)*

The Congress shall have power to lay and collect taxes on incomes, from whatever source derived, without apportionment among the several States, and without regard to any census or enumeration.

Amendment XVII *(Ratified April 8, 1913)*

The Senate of the United States shall be composed of two Senators from each State, elected by the people thereof, for six years; and each Senator shall have one vote. The electors in each State shall have the qualifications requisite for electors of the most numerous branch of the State legislatures.

When vacancies happen in the representation of any State in the Senate, the executive authority of such State shall issue writs of election to fill such vacancies: *Provided,* That the legislature of any State may empower the executive thereof to make temporary appointments until the people fill the vacancies by election as the legislature may direct.

This amendment shall not be so construed as to affect the election or term of any Senator chosen before it becomes valid as part of the Constitution.

Amendment XVIII *(Ratified January 16, 1919)*

Section 1. After one year from the ratification of this article the manufacture, sale, or transportation of intoxicating liquors within, the importation thereof into, or the exportation thereof from the United States and all territory subject to the jurisdiction thereof for beverage purposes is hereby prohibited.

Section 2. The Congress and the several States shall have concurrent power to enforce this article by appropriate legislation.

Section 3. This article shall be inoperative unless it shall have been ratified as an amendment to the Constitution by the legislatures of the several States, as provided in the Constitution, within seven years from the date of the submission hereof to the States by the Congress.[13]

Amendment XIX *(Ratified August 18, 1920)*

The right of citizens of the United States to vote shall not be denied or abridged by the United States or by any State on account of sex.

Congress shall have power to enforce this article by appropriate legislation.

Amendment XX *(Ratified January 23, 1933)*

Section 1. The terms of the President and Vice President shall end at noon on the 20th day of January, and the terms of Senators and Representatives at noon on the 3d day of January, of the years in which such terms would have ended if this article had not been ratified; and the terms of their successors shall then begin.

Section 2. The Congress shall assemble at least once in every year, and such meeting shall begin at noon on the 3d day of January, unless they shall by law appoint a different day.

Section 3.[14] If, at the time fixed for the beginning of the term of the President, the President elect shall have died, the Vice President elect shall become President. If a President shall not have been chosen before the time fixed for the beginning of his term, or if the President elect shall have failed to qualify, then the Vice President elect shall act as President until a President shall have qualified; and the Congress may by law provide for the case wherein neither a President elect nor a Vice President elect shall have qualified, declaring who shall then act as President, or the manner in which one who is to act shall be selected, and such person shall act accordingly until a President or Vice President shall have qualified.

Section 4. The Congress may by law provide for the case of the death of any of the persons from whom the House of Representatives may choose a President whenever the right of choice shall have devolved upon them, and for the case of the death of any of the persons from whom the Senate may choose a Vice President whenever the right of choice shall have devolved upon them.

Section 5. Sections 1 and 2 shall take effect on the 15th day of October following the ratification of this article.

Section 6. This article shall be inoperative unless it shall have been ratified as an amendment to the Constitution by the legislatures of three-fourths of the several States within seven years from the date of its submission.

Amendment XXI *(Ratified December 5, 1933)*

Section 1. The eighteenth article of amendment to the Constitution of the United States is hereby repealed.

Section 2. The transportation or importation into any State, Territory, or possession of the United States for delivery or use therein of intoxicating liquors, in violation of the laws thereof, is hereby prohibited.

Section 3. This article shall be inoperative unless it shall have been ratified as an amendment to the Constitution by conventions in the several States, as provided in the Constitution, within seven years from the date of the submission hereof to the States by the Congress.

Amendment XXII *(Ratified February 27, 1951)*

Section 1. No person shall be elected to the office of the President more than twice, and no person who has held the office of President, or acted as President, for more than two years of a term to which some other person was elected President shall be elected to the office of the President more than once. But this Article shall not apply to any person holding the office of President when this Article was proposed by the Congress, and shall not prevent any person who may be holding the office of President, or acting as President, during the term within which this Article becomes operative from holding the office of President or acting as President during the remainder of such term.

Section 2. This article shall be inoperative unless it shall have been ratified as an amendment to the Constitution by the legislatures of three-fourths of the several States within seven years from the date of its submission to the States by the Congress.

Amendment XXIII *(Ratified March 29, 1961)*

Section 1. The District constituting the seat of Government of the United States shall appoint in such manner as the Congress may direct:

A number of electors of President and Vice President equal to the whole number of Senators and Representatives in Congress to which the District would be entitled if it were a State, but in no event more than the least populous State; they shall be in addition to those appointed by the States, but they shall be considered, for the purposes of the election of President and Vice President, to be electors appointed by a State; and they shall meet in the District and perform such duties as provided by the twelfth article of amendment.

Section 2. The Congress shall have power to enforce this article by appropriate legislation.

Amendment XXIV *(Ratified January 23, 1964)*

Section 1. The right of citizens of the United States to vote in any primary or other election for President or Vice President, for electors for President or Vice President, or for Senator or Representative in Congress, shall not be denied or abridged by the United States or any State by reason of failure to pay any poll tax or other tax.

Section 2. The Congress shall have power to enforce this article by appropriate legislation.

Amendment XXV *(Ratified February 10, 1967)*

Section 1. In case of the removal of the President from office or of his death or resignation, the Vice President shall become President.

Section 2. Whenever there is a vacancy in the office of the Vice President, the President shall nominate a Vice President who shall take office upon confirmation by a majority vote of both Houses of Congress.

Section 3. Whenever the President transmits to the President pro tempore of the Senate and the Speaker of the House of Representatives his written declaration that he is unable to discharge the powers and duties of his office, and until he transmits to them a written declaration to the contrary, such powers and duties shall be discharged by the Vice President as Acting President.

Section 4. Whenever the Vice President and a majority of either the principal officers of the executive departments or of such other body as Congress may by law provide, transmit to the President pro tempore of the Senate and the Speaker of the House of Representatives their written declaration that the President is unable to discharge the powers and duties of his office, the Vice President shall immediately assume the powers and duties of the office as Acting President.

Thereafter, when the President transmits to the President pro tempore of the Senate and the Speaker of the House of Representatives his written declaration that no inability exists, he shall resume the powers and duties of his office unless the Vice President and a majority of either the principal officers of the executive departments or of such other body as Congress may by law provide, transmit within four days to the President pro tempore of the Senate and the Speaker of the House of Representatives their written declaration that the President is unable to discharge the powers and duties of his office. Thereupon Congress shall decide the issue, assembling within forty-eight hours for that purpose if not in session. If the Congress, within twenty-one days after receipt of the latter written declaration, or, if Congress is not in session, within twenty-one days after Congress is required to assemble, determines by two-thirds vote of both Houses that the President is unable to discharge the powers and duties of his office, the Vice President shall continue to discharge the same as Acting President; otherwise, the President shall resume the powers and duties of his office.

Amendment XXVI *(Ratified July 1, 1971)*

Section 1. The right of citizens of the United States, who are eighteen years of age or older, to vote shall not be denied or abridged by the United States or by any State on account of age.

Section 2. The Congress shall have power to enforce this article by appropriate legislation.

Amendment XXVII *(Ratified May 7, 1992)*

No law varying the compensation for the services of the Senators and Representatives shall take effect, until an election of Representatives shall have intervened.

Notes

1. The part in brackets was changed by section 2 of the Fourteenth Amendment.
2. The part in brackets was changed by the first paragraph of the Seventeenth Amendment.
3. The part in brackets was changed by the second paragraph of the Seventeenth Amendment.
4. The part in brackets was changed by section 2 of the Twentieth Amendment.
5. The Sixteenth Amendment gave Congress the power to tax incomes.
6. The material in brackets was superseded by the Twelfth Amendment.
7. This provision was affected by the Twenty-fifth Amendment.
8. These clauses were affected by the Eleventh Amendment.
9. This paragraph was superseded by the Thirteenth Amendment.
10. Obsolete.
11. The part in brackets was superseded by section 3 of the Twentieth Amendment.
12. See the Nineteenth and Twenty-sixth Amendments.
13. This amendment was repealed by section 1 of the Twenty-first Amendment.
14. See the Twenty-fifth Amendment.

APPENDIX C.
FEDERALIST NOS. 10, 51, AND 70

Federalist No. 10

The Same Subject Continued: The Union as a Safeguard Against Domestic Faction and Insurrection.

From the New York Packet
Friday, November 23, 1787.

Author: James Madison

To the People of the State of New York:

Among the numerous advantages promised by a well-constructed Union, none deserves to be more accurately developed than its tendency to break and control the violence of faction. The friend of popular governments never finds himself so much alarmed for their character and fate, as when he contemplates their propensity to this dangerous vice. He will not fail, therefore, to set a due value on any plan which, without violating the principles to which he is attached, provides a proper cure for it. The instability, injustice, and confusion introduced into the public councils, have, in truth, been the mortal diseases under which popular governments have everywhere perished; as they continue to be the favorite and fruitful topics from which the adversaries to liberty derive their most specious declamations. The valuable improvements made by the American constitutions on the popular models, both ancient and modern, cannot certainly be too much admired; but it would be an unwarrantable partiality, to contend that they have as effectually obviated the danger on this side, as was wished and expected. Complaints are everywhere heard from our most considerate and virtuous citizens, equally the friends of public and private faith, and of public and personal liberty, that our governments are too unstable, that the public good is disregarded in the conflicts of rival parties, and that measures are too often decided, not according to the rules of justice and the rights of the minor party, but by the superior force of an interested and overbearing majority. However anxiously we may wish that these complaints had no foundation, the evidence, of known facts will not permit us to deny that they are in some degree true. It will be found, indeed, on a candid review of our situation, that some of the distresses under which we labor have been erroneously charged on the operation of our governments; but it will be found, at the same time, that other causes will not alone account for many of our heaviest misfortunes; and, particularly, for that prevailing and increasing distrust of public engagements, and alarm for private rights, which are echoed from one end of the continent to the other. These must be chiefly, if not wholly, effects of the unsteadiness and injustice with which a factious spirit has tainted our public administrations.

By a faction, I understand a number of citizens, whether amounting to a majority or a minority of the whole, who are united and actuated by some common impulse of passion, or of interest, adversed to the rights of other citizens, or to the permanent and aggregate interests of the community.

There are two methods of curing the mischiefs of faction: the one, by removing its causes; the other, by controlling its effects.

There are again two methods of removing the causes of faction: the one, by destroying the liberty which is essential to its existence; the other, by giving to every citizen the same opinions, the same passions, and the same interests.

It could never be more truly said than of the first remedy, that it was worse than the disease. Liberty is to faction what air is to fire, an aliment without which it instantly expires. But it could not be less folly to abolish liberty, which is essential to political life, because it nourishes faction, than it would be to wish the annihilation of air, which is essential to animal life, because it imparts to fire its destructive agency.

The second expedient is as impracticable as the first would be unwise. As long as the reason of man continues fallible, and he is at liberty to exercise it, different opinions will be formed. As long as the connection subsists between his reason and his self-love, his opinions and his passions will have a reciprocal influence on each other; and the former will be objects to which the latter will attach themselves. The diversity in the faculties of men, from which the rights of property originate, is not less an insuperable obstacle to a uniformity of interests. The protection of these faculties is the first object of government. From the protection of different and unequal faculties of acquiring property, the possession of different degrees and kinds of property immediately results; and from the influence of these on the sentiments and views of the respective proprietors, ensues a division of the society into different interests and parties.

The latent causes of faction are thus sown in the nature of man; and we see them everywhere brought into different degrees of activity, according to the different circumstances of civil society. A zeal for different opinions concerning religion, concerning government, and many other points, as well of speculation as of practice; an attachment to different leaders ambitiously contending for pre-eminence and power; or to persons of other descriptions whose fortunes have been interesting to the human passions, have, in turn, divided mankind into parties, inflamed them with mutual animosity, and rendered them much more disposed to vex and oppress each other than to co-operate for their common good. So strong is this propensity of mankind to fall into mutual animosities, that where no substantial occasion presents itself, the most frivolous and fanciful distinctions have been sufficient to kindle their unfriendly passions and excite their most violent conflicts. But the most common and durable source of factions has been the various and unequal distribution of property. Those who hold and those who are without property have ever formed distinct interests in society. Those who are creditors, and those who are debtors, fall under a like discrimination. A landed interest, a manufacturing interest, a mercantile interest, a moneyed interest, with many lesser interests, grow up of necessity in civilized nations, and divide them into different classes, actuated by different sentiments and views. The regulation of these various and interfering interests forms the principal task of modern legislation, and involves the spirit of party and faction in the necessary and ordinary operations of the government.

No man is allowed to be a judge in his own cause, because his interest would certainly bias his judgment, and, not improbably, corrupt his integrity. With equal, nay with greater reason, a body of men are unfit to be both judges and parties at the same time; yet what are many of the most important acts of legislation, but so many judicial determinations, not indeed concerning the rights of single persons, but concerning the rights of large bodies of citizens? And what are the different classes of legislators but advocates and parties to the causes which they determine? Is a law proposed concerning private debts? It is a question to which the creditors are parties on one side and the debtors on the other. Justice ought to hold the balance between them. Yet the parties are, and must be, themselves the judges; and the most numerous party, or, in other words, the most powerful faction must be expected to prevail. Shall domestic manufactures be encouraged, and in what degree, by restrictions on foreign manufactures? are questions which would be differently decided by the landed and the manufacturing classes, and probably by neither with a sole regard to justice and the public good. The apportionment of taxes on the various descriptions of property is an act which seems to require the most exact impartiality; yet there is, perhaps, no legislative act in which greater opportunity and temptation are given to a predominant party to trample on the rules of justice. Every shilling with which they overburden the inferior number, is a shilling saved to their own pockets.

It is in vain to say that enlightened statesmen will be able to adjust these clashing interests, and render them all subservient to the public good. Enlightened statesmen will not always be at the helm. Nor, in many cases, can such an adjustment be made at all without taking into view indirect and remote considerations, which will rarely prevail over the immediate interest which one party may find in disregarding the rights of another or the good of the whole.

The inference to which we are brought is, that the CAUSES of faction cannot be removed, and that relief is only to be sought in the means of controlling its EFFECTS.

If a faction consists of less than a majority, relief is supplied by the republican principle, which enables the majority to defeat its sinister views by regular vote. It may clog the administration, it may convulse the society; but it will be unable to execute and mask its violence under the forms of the Constitution. When a majority is included in a faction, the form of popular government, on the other hand, enables it to sacrifice to its ruling passion or interest both the public good and the rights of other citizens. To secure the public good and private rights against the danger of such a faction, and at the same time to preserve the spirit and the form of popular government, is then the great object to which our inquiries are directed. Let me add that it is the great desideratum by which this form of government can be rescued from the opprobrium under which it has so long labored, and be recommended to the esteem and adoption of mankind.

By what means is this object attainable? Evidently by one of two only. Either the existence of the same passion or interest in a majority at the same time must be prevented, or the majority, having such coexistent passion or interest, must be rendered, by their number and local situation, unable to concert and carry into effect schemes of oppression. If the impulse and the opportunity be suffered to coincide, we well know that neither moral nor religious motives can be relied on as an adequate control. They are not found to be such on the injustice and violence of individuals, and lose their efficacy in proportion to the number combined together, that is, in proportion as their efficacy becomes needful.

From this view of the subject it may be concluded that a pure democracy, by which I mean a society consisting of a small number of citizens, who assemble and administer the government in person, can admit of no cure for the mischiefs of faction. A common passion or interest will, in almost every case, be felt by a majority of the whole; a communication and concert result from the form of government itself; and there is nothing to check the inducements to sacrifice the weaker party or an obnoxious individual. Hence it is that such democracies have ever been spectacles of turbulence and contention; have ever been found incompatible with personal security or the rights of property; and have in general been as short in their lives as they have been violent in their deaths. Theoretic politicians, who have patronized this species of government, have erroneously supposed that by reducing mankind to a perfect equality in their political rights, they would, at the same time, be perfectly equalized and assimilated in their possessions, their opinions, and their passions.

A republic, by which I mean a government in which the scheme of representation takes place, opens a different prospect, and promises the cure for which we are seeking. Let us examine the points in which it varies from pure democracy, and we shall comprehend both the nature of the cure and the efficacy which it must derive from the Union.

The two great points of difference between a democracy and a republic are: first, the delegation of the government, in the latter, to a small number of citizens elected by the rest; secondly, the greater number of citizens, and greater sphere of country, over which the latter may be extended.

The effect of the first difference is, on the one hand, to refine and enlarge the public views, by passing them through the medium of a chosen body of citizens, whose wisdom may best discern the true interest of their country, and whose patriotism and love of justice will be least likely to sacrifice it to temporary or partial considerations. Under such a regulation, it may well happen that the public voice, pronounced by the representatives of the people, will be more consonant to the public good than if pronounced by the people themselves, convened for the purpose. On the other hand, the effect may be inverted. Men of factious tempers, of local prejudices, or of sinister designs, may, by intrigue, by corruption, or by other means, first obtain the suffrages, and then betray the interests, of the people. The question resulting is, whether small or extensive republics are more favorable to the election of proper guardians of the public weal; and it is clearly decided in favor of the latter by two obvious considerations:

In the first place, it is to be remarked that, however small the republic may be, the representatives must be raised to a certain number, in order to guard against the cabals of a few; and that, however large it may be, they must be limited to a certain number, in order to guard against the confusion of a multitude. Hence, the number of representatives in the two cases not being in proportion to that of the two constituents, and being proportionally greater in the small republic, it follows that, if the proportion of fit characters be not less in the large than in the small republic, the former will present a greater option, and consequently a greater probability of a fit choice.

In the next place, as each representative will be chosen by a greater number of citizens in the large than in the small republic, it will be more difficult for unworthy candidates to practice with success the vicious arts by which elections are too often carried; and the suffrages of the people being more free, will be more likely to centre in men who possess the most attractive merit and the most diffusive and established characters.

It must be confessed that in this, as in most other cases, there is a mean, on both sides of which inconveniences will be found to lie. By enlarging too much the number of electors, you render the representatives too little acquainted with all their local circumstances and lesser interests; as by reducing it too much, you render him unduly attached to these, and too little fit to comprehend and pursue great and national objects. The federal Constitution forms a happy combination in this respect; the great and aggregate interests being referred to the national, the local and particular to the State legislatures.

The other point of difference is, the greater number of citizens and extent of territory which may be brought within the compass of republican than of democratic government; and it is this circumstance principally which renders factious combinations less to be dreaded in the former than in the latter. The smaller the society, the fewer probably will be the distinct parties and interests composing it; the fewer the distinct parties and interests, the more frequently will a majority be found of the same party; and the smaller the number of individuals composing a majority, and the smaller the compass within which they are placed, the more easily will they concert and execute their plans of oppression. Extend the sphere, and you take in a greater variety of parties and interests; you make it less probable that a majority of the whole will have a common motive to invade the rights of other citizens; or if such a common motive exists, it will be more difficult for all who feel it to discover their own strength, and to act in unison with each other. Besides other impediments, it may be remarked that, where there is a consciousness of unjust or dishonorable purposes, communication is always checked by distrust in proportion to the number whose concurrence is necessary.

Hence, it clearly appears, that the same advantage which a republic has over a democracy, in controlling the effects of faction, is enjoyed by a large over a small republic,—is enjoyed by the Union over the States composing it. Does the advantage consist in the substitution of representatives whose enlightened views and virtuous sentiments render them superior to local prejudices and schemes of injustice? It will not be denied that the representation of the Union will be most likely to possess these requisite endowments. Does it consist in the greater security afforded by a greater variety of parties, against the event of any one party being able to outnumber and oppress the rest? In an equal degree does the increased variety of parties comprised within the Union, increase this security. Does it, in fine, consist in the greater obstacles opposed to the concert and accomplishment of the secret wishes of an unjust and interested majority? Here, again, the extent of the Union gives it the most palpable advantage.

The influence of factious leaders may kindle a flame within their particular States, but will be unable to spread a general conflagration through the other States. A religious sect may degenerate into a political faction in a part of the Confederacy; but the variety of sects dispersed over the entire face of it must secure the national councils against any danger from that source. A rage for paper money, for an abolition of debts, for an equal division of property, or for any other improper or wicked project, will be less apt to pervade the whole body of the Union than a particular member of it; in the same proportion as such a malady is more likely to taint a particular county or district, than an entire State.

In the extent and proper structure of the Union, therefore, we behold a republican remedy for the diseases most incident to republican government. And according to the degree of pleasure and pride we feel in being republicans, ought to be our zeal in cherishing the spirit and supporting the character of Federalists.

PUBLIUS.

Federalist No. 51

The Structure of the Government Must Furnish the Proper Checks and Balances Between the Different Departments

From the New York Packet.
Friday, February 8, 1788.
Author: James Madison

To the People of the State of New York:
To what expedient, then, shall we finally resort, for maintaining in practice the necessary partition of power among the several departments, as laid down in the Constitution? The only answer that can be given is, that as all these exterior provisions are found to be inadequate, the defect must be supplied, by so contriving the interior structure of the government as that its several constituent parts may, by their mutual relations, be the means of keeping each other in their proper places. Without presuming to undertake a full development of this important idea, I will hazard a few general observations, which may perhaps place it in a clearer light, and enable us to form a more correct judgment of the principles and structure of the government planned by the convention.

In order to lay a due foundation for that separate and distinct exercise of the different powers of government, which to a certain extent is admitted on all hands to be essential to the preservation of liberty, it is evident that each department should have a will of its own; and consequently should be so constituted that the members of each should have as little agency as possible in the appointment of the members of the others. Were this principle rigorously adhered to, it would require that all the appointments for the supreme executive, legislative, and judiciary magistracies should be drawn from the same fountain of authority, the people, through channels having no communication whatever with one another. Perhaps such a plan of constructing the several departments would be less difficult in practice than it may in contemplation appear. Some difficulties, however, and some additional expense would attend the execution of it. Some deviations, therefore, from the principle must be admitted. In the constitution of the judiciary department in particular, it might be inexpedient to insist rigorously on the principle: first, because peculiar qualifications being essential in the members, the primary consideration ought to be to select that mode of choice which best secures these qualifications; secondly, because the permanent tenure by which the appointments are held in that department, must soon destroy all sense of dependence on the authority conferring them.

It is equally evident, that the members of each department should be as little dependent as possible on those of the others, for the emoluments annexed to their offices. Were the executive magistrate, or the judges, not independent of the legislature in this particular, their independence in every other would be merely nominal. But the great security against a gradual concentration of the several powers in the same department, consists in giving to those who administer each department the necessary constitutional means and personal motives to resist encroachments of the others. The provision for defense must in this, as in all other cases, be made commensurate to the danger of attack. Ambition must be made to counteract ambition. The interest of the man must be connected with the constitutional rights of the place. It may be a reflection on human nature, that such devices should be necessary to control the abuses of government. But what is government itself, but the greatest of all reflections on human nature? If men were angels, no government would be necessary. If angels were to govern men, neither external nor internal controls on government would be necessary. In framing a government which is to be administered by men over men, the great difficulty lies in this: you must first enable the government to control the governed; and in the next place oblige it to control itself.

A dependence on the people is, no doubt, the primary control on the government; but experience has taught mankind the necessity of auxiliary precautions. This policy of supplying, by opposite and rival interests, the defect of better motives, might be traced through the whole system of human affairs, private as well as public. We see it particularly displayed in all the subordinate distributions of power, where the constant aim is to divide and arrange the several offices in such a manner as that each may be a check on the other that the private interest of every individual may be a sentinel over the public rights. These inventions of prudence cannot be less requisite in the distribution of the supreme powers of the State. But it is not possible to give to each department an equal power of self-defense. In republican government, the legislative authority necessarily predominates. The remedy for this inconveniency is to divide the legislature into different branches; and to render them, by different modes of election and different principles of action, as little connected with each other as the nature of their common functions and their common dependence on the society will admit. It may even be necessary to guard against dangerous encroachments by still further precautions. As the weight of the legislative authority requires that it should be thus divided, the weakness of the executive may require, on the other hand, that it should be fortified.

An absolute negative on the legislature appears, at first view, to be the natural defense with which the executive magistrate should be armed. But perhaps it would be neither altogether safe nor alone sufficient. On ordinary occasions it might not be exerted with the requisite firmness, and on extraordinary occasions it might be perfidiously abused. May not this defect of an absolute negative be supplied by some qualified connection between this weaker department and the weaker branch of the stronger department, by which the latter may be led to support the constitutional rights of the former, without being too much detached from the rights of its own department? If the principles on which these observations are founded be just, as I persuade myself they are, and they be applied as a criterion to the several State constitutions, and to the federal Constitution it will be found that if the latter does not perfectly correspond with them, the former are infinitely less able to bear such a test.

There are, moreover, two considerations particularly applicable to the federal system of America, which place that system in a very interesting point of view. First. In a single republic, all the power surrendered by the people is submitted to the administration of a single government; and the usurpations are guarded against by a division of the government into distinct and separate departments. In the compound republic of America, the power surrendered by the people is first divided between two distinct governments, and then the portion allotted to each subdivided among distinct and separate departments. Hence a double security arises to the rights of the people. The different governments will control each other, at the same time that each will be controlled by itself. Second. It is of great importance in a republic not only to guard the society against the oppression of its rulers, but to guard one part of the society against the injustice of the other part. Different interests necessarily exist in different classes of citizens. If a majority be united by a common interest, the rights of the minority will be insecure.

There are but two methods of providing against this evil: the one by creating a will in the community independent of the majority that is, of the society itself; the other, by comprehending in the society so many separate descriptions of citizens as will render an unjust combination of a majority of the whole very improbable, if not impracticable. The first method prevails in all governments possessing an hereditary or self-appointed authority. This, at best, is but a precarious security; because a power independent of the society may as well espouse the unjust views of the major, as the rightful interests of the minor party, and may possibly be turned against both parties. The second method will be exemplified in the federal republic of the United States. Whilst all authority in it will be derived from and dependent on the society, the society itself will be broken into so many parts, interests, and classes of citizens, that the rights of individuals, or of the minority, will be in little danger from interested combinations of the majority.

In a free government the security for civil rights must be the same as that for religious rights. It consists in the one case in the multiplicity of interests, and in the other in the multiplicity of sects. The degree of security in both cases will depend on the number of interests and sects; and this may be presumed to depend on the extent of country and number of people comprehended under the same government. This view of the subject must particularly recommend a proper federal system to all the sincere and considerate friends of republican government, since it shows that in exact proportion as the territory of the Union may be formed into more circumscribed Confederacies, or States oppressive combinations of a majority will be facilitated: the best security, under the republican forms, for the rights of every class of citizens, will be diminished: and consequently the stability and independence of some member of the government, the only other security, must be proportionately increased. Justice is the end of government. It is the end of civil society. It ever has been and ever will be pursued until it be obtained, or until liberty be lost in the pursuit. In a society under the forms of which the stronger faction can readily unite and oppress the weaker, anarchy may as truly be said to reign as in a state of nature, where the weaker individual is not secured against the violence of the stronger; and as, in the latter state, even the stronger individuals are prompted, by the uncertainty of their condition, to submit to a government which may protect the weak as well as themselves; so, in the former state, will the more powerful factions or parties be gradually induced, by a like motive, to wish for a government which will protect all parties, the weaker as well as the more powerful.

It can be little doubted that if the State of Rhode Island was separated from the Confederacy and left to itself, the insecurity of rights under the popular form of government within such narrow limits would be displayed by such reiterated oppressions of factious majorities that some power altogether independent of the people would soon be called for by the voice of the very factions whose misrule had proved the necessity of it. In the extended republic of the United States, and among the great variety of interests, parties, and sects which it embraces, a coalition of a majority of the whole society could seldom take place on any other principles than those of justice and the general good; whilst there being thus less danger to a minor from the will of a major party, there must be less pretext, also, to provide for the security of the former, by introducing into the government a will not dependent on the latter, or, in other words, a will independent of the society itself. It is no less certain than it is important, notwithstanding the contrary opinions which have been entertained, that the larger the society, provided it lie within a practical sphere, the more duly capable it will be of self-government. And happily for the REPUBLICAN CAUSE, the practicable sphere may be carried to a very great extent, by a judicious modification and mixture of the FEDERAL PRINCIPLE.

PUBLIUS.

Federalist No. 70

The Executive Department Further Considered

Saturday, March 15, 1788
Author: Alexander Hamilton

There is an idea, which is not without its advocates, that a vigorous executive is inconsistent with the genius of republican government. The enlightened well-wishers to this species of government must at least hope that the supposition is destitute of foundation; since they can never admit its truth, without at the same time admitting the condemnation of their own principles. Energy in the executive is a leading character in the definition of good government. It is essential to the protection of the community against foreign attacks; it is not less essential to the steady administration of the laws; to the protection of property against those irregular and high-handed combinations which sometimes interrupt the ordinary course of justice; to the security of liberty against the enterprises and assaults of ambition, of faction, and of anarchy. Every man the least conversant in Roman history knows how often that republic was obliged to take refuge in the absolute power of a single man, under the formidable title of dictator, as well against the intrigues of ambitious individuals who aspired to the tyranny, and the seditions of whole classes of the community whose conduct threatened the existence of all government, as against the invasions of external enemies who menaced the conquest and destruction of Rome.

There can be no need, however, to multiply arguments or examples on this head. A feeble executive implies a feeble execution of the government. A feeble execution is but another phrase for a bad execution; and a government ill executed, whatever it may be in theory, must be, in practice, a bad government.

Taking it for granted, therefore, that all men of sense will agree in the necessity of an energetic executive; it will only remain to inquire, what are the ingredients which constitute this energy? How far can they be combined with those other ingredients which constitute safety in the republican sense? And how far does this combination characterize the plan which has been reported by the convention?

The ingredients which constitute energy in the executive are unity; duration; an adequate provision for its support; and competent powers.

The ingredients which constitute safety in the republican sense are a due dependence on the people, secondly a due responsibility.

Those politicians and statesmen who have been the most celebrated for the soundness of their principles and for the justness of their views have declared in favor of a single executive and a numerous legislature. They have with great propriety, considered energy as the most necessary qualification of the former, and have regarded this as most applicable to power in a single hand; while they have, with equal propriety, considered the latter as best adapted to deliberation and wisdom, and best calculated to conciliate the confidence of the people and to secure their privileges and interests.

That unity is conducive to energy will not be disputed. Decision, activity, secrecy, and dispatch will generally characterize the proceedings of one man in a much more eminent degree than the proceedings of any greater number; and in proportion as the number is increased, these qualities will be diminished.

This unity may be destroyed in two ways: either by vesting the power in two or more magistrates of equal dignity and authority, or by vesting it ostensibly in one man, subject in whole or in part to the control and co-operation of others, in the capacity of counselors to him. Of the first, the two consuls of Rome may serve as an example; of the last, we shall find examples in the constitutions of several of the States. New York and New Jersey, if I recollect right, are the only States which have entrusted the executive authority wholly to single men. Both these methods of destroying the unity of the executive have their partisans; but the votaries of an executive council are the most numerous. They are both liable, if not to equal, to similar objections, and may in most lights be examined in conjunction.

The experience of other nations will afford little instruction on this head. As far, however, as it teaches anything, it teaches us not to be enamored of plurality in the executive. We have seen that the Achaeans on an experiment of two Praetors, were induced to abolish one. The Roman history records many instances of mischiefs to the republic from the dissentions between the consuls, and between the military tribunes, who were at times substituted to the consuls. But it gives us no specimens of any peculiar advantages derived to the state from the circumstance of the plurality of those magistrates. That the dissentions between them were not more frequent or more fatal is matter of astonishment, until we advert to the singular position in which the republic was almost continually placed and to the prudent policy pointed out by the circumstances of the state, and pursued by the consuls, of making a division of the government between them. The patricians engaged in a perpetual struggle with the plebeians for the preservation of their ancient authorities and dignities; the consuls, who were generally chosen out of the former body, were commonly united by the personal interest they had in the defense of the privileges of their order. In addition to this motive of union, after the arms of the republic had considerably expanded the bounds of its empire, it became an established custom with the consuls to divide the administration between themselves by one of them remaining at Rome to govern the city and its environs; the other taking the command in the more distant provinces. This expedient must no doubt have had great influence in preventing those collisions and rivalships which might otherwise have embroiled the peace of the republic.

But quitting the dim light of historical research, and attaching ourselves purely to the dictates of reason and good sense, we shall discover much greater cause to reject than to approve the idea of plurality in the executive, under any modification whatever.

Wherever two or more persons are engaged in any common enterprise or pursuit, there is always danger of difference of opinion. If it be a public trust or office in which they are clothed with equal dignity and authority, there is peculiar danger of personal emulation and even animosity. From either, and especially from all these causes, the most bitter dissentions are apt to spring. Whenever these happen, they lessen the respectability, weaken the authority, and distract the plans and operations of those whom they divide. If they should unfortunately assail the supreme executive magistracy of a country, consisting of a plurality of persons, they might impede or frustrate the most important measures of the government in the most critical emergencies of the state. And what is still worse, they might split the community into the most violent and irreconcilable factions, adhering differently to the different individuals who composed the magistracy.

Men often oppose a thing merely because they have had no agency in planning it, or because it may have been planned by those whom they dislike. But if they have been consulted, and have happened to disapprove, opposition then becomes, in their estimation an indispensable duty of self-love. They seem to think themselves bound in honor, and by all the motives of personal infallibility, to defeat the success of what has been resolved upon, contrary to their sentiments. Men of upright, benevolent tempers have too many opportunities of remarking, with horror, to what desperate lengths this disposition is sometimes carried, and how often the great interests of society are sacrificed to the vanity, to the conceit, and to the obstinacy of individuals, who have credit enough to make their passions and their caprices interesting to mankind. Perhaps the question now before the public may, in its consequences, afford melancholy proofs of the effects of this despicable frailty, or rather detestable vice, in the human character.

Upon the principles of a free government, inconveniences from the source just mentioned must necessarily be submitted to in the formation of the legislature; but it is unnecessary, and therefore unwise, to introduce them into the constitution of the executive. It is here too that they may be most pernicious. In the legislature, promptitude of decision is oftener an evil than a benefit. The differences of opinion, and the jarrings of parties in that department of the government, though they may sometimes obstruct salutary plans, yet often promote deliberation and circumspection, and serve to check excesses in the majority. When a resolution too is once taken, the opposition must be at an end. That resolution is a law, and resistance to it punishable. But no favorable circumstances palliate or atone for the disadvantages of dissention in the executive department. Here they are pure and unmixed. There is no point at which they cease to operate. They serve to embarrass and weaken the execution of the plan or measure to which they relate, from the first step to the final conclusion of it. They constantly counteract those qualities in the executive which are the most necessary ingredients in its composition, vigor and expedition, and this without any counterbalancing good. In the conduct of war, in which the energy of the executive is the bulwark of the national security, everything would be to be apprehended from its plurality.

It must be confessed that these observations apply with principal weight to the first case supposed, that is, to a plurality of magistrates of equal dignity and authority, a scheme, the advocates for which are not likely to form a numerous sect; but they apply, though not with equal yet with considerable weight to the project of a council, whose concurrence is made constitutionally necessary to the operations of the ostensible executive. An artful cabal in that council would be able to distract and to enervate the whole system of administration. If no such cabal should exist, the mere diversity of views and opinions would alone be sufficient to tincture the exercise of the executive authority with a spirit of habitual feebleness and dilatoriness.

But one of the weightiest objections to a plurality in the executive, and which lies as much against the last as the first plan is that it tends to conceal faults and destroy responsibility. Responsibility is of two kinds to censure and to punishment. The first is the most important of the two, especially in an elective office. Men in public trust will much oftener act in such a manner as to render them unworthy of being any longer trusted, than in such a manner as to make him obnoxious to legal punishment. But the multiplication of the executive adds to the difficulty of detection in either case. It often becomes impossible, amidst mutual accusations, to determine on whom the blame or the punishment of a pernicious measure, or series of pernicious measures, ought really to fall. It is shifted from one to another with so much dexterity, and under such plausible appearances, that the public opinion is left in suspense about the real author. The circumstances which may have led to any national miscarriage or misfortune are sometimes so complicated that where there are a number of actors who may have had different degrees and kinds of agency, though we may clearly see upon the whole that there has been mismanagement, yet it may be impracticable to pronounce to whose account the evil which may have been incurred is truly chargeable.

"I was overruled by my council. The council were so divided in their opinions that it was impossible to obtain any better resolution on the point." These and similar pretexts are constantly at hand, whether true or false. And who is there that will either take the trouble or incur the odium of a strict scrutiny into the secret springs of the transaction? Should there be found a citizen zealous enough to undertake the unpromising task, if there happened to be a collusion between the parties concerned, how easy is it to cloth the circumstances with so much ambiguity as to render it uncertain what was the precise conduct of any of those parties?

In the single instance in which the governor of this state is coupled with a council, that is, in the appointment to offices, we have seen the mischiefs of it in the view now under consideration. Scandalous appointments to important offices have been made. Some cases indeed have been so flagrant that ALL PARTIES have agreed in the impropriety of the thing. When inquiry has been made, the blame has been laid by the governor on the members of the council; who on their part have charged it upon his nomination; while the people remain altogether at a loss to determine by whose influence their interests have been committed to hands so unqualified and so manifestly improper. In tenderness to individuals, I forbear to descend to particulars.

It is evident from these considerations that the plurality of the executive tends to deprive the people of the two greatest securities they can have for the faithful exercise of any delegated power, *first*, the restraints of public opinion, which lose their efficacy as well on account of the division of the censure attendant on bad measures among a number as on account of the uncertainty on whom it ought to fall; and, *second*, the opportunity of discovering with facility and clearness the misconduct of the persons they trust, in order either to their removal from office or to their actual punishment in cases which admit of it.

In England, the king is a perpetual magistrate; and it is a maxim which has obtained for the sake of the public peace that he is unaccountable for his administration, and his person sacred. Nothing, therefore, can be wiser in that kingdom than to annex to the king a constitutional council, who may be responsible to the nation for the advice they give. Without this, there would be no responsibility whatever in the executive department, an idea inadmissible in a free government. But even there the king is not bound by the resolutions of his council, though they are answerable for the advice they give. He is the absolute master of his own conduct in the exercise of his office and may observe or disregard the council given to him at his sole discretion.

But in a republic where every magistrate ought to be personally responsible for his behavior in office, the reason which in the British Constitution dictates the propriety of a council not only ceases to apply, but turns against the institution. In the monarchy of Great Britain, it furnishes a substitute for the prohibited responsibility of the Chief Magistrate, which serves in some degree as a hostage to the national justice for his good behavior. In the American republic, it would serve to destroy, or would greatly diminish, the intended and necessary responsibility of the Chief Magistrate himself.

The idea of a council to the executive, which has so generally obtained in the State constitutions, has been derived from that maxim of republican jealousy which considers power as safer in the hands of a number of men than of a single man. If the maxim should be admitted to be applicable to the case, I should contend that the advantage on that side would not counterbalance the numerous disadvantages on the opposite side. But I do not think the rule at all applicable to the executive power. I clearly concur in opinion, in this particular, with a writer whom the celebrated Junius pronounces to be "deep, solid and ingenious," that "the executive power is more easily confined when it is one"; that it is far more safe there should be a single object for the jealousy and watchfulness of the people; and, in a word, that all multiplication of the executive is rather dangerous than friendly to liberty.

A little consideration will satisfy us that the species of security sought for in the multiplication of the executive is unattainable. Numbers must be so great as to render combination difficult, or they are rather a source of danger than of security. The united credit and influence of several individuals must be more formidable to liberty than the credit and influence of either of them separately. When power, therefore, is placed in the hands of so small a number of men as to admit of their interests and views being easily combined in a common enterprise, by an artful leader, it becomes more liable to abuse and more dangerous when abused, than if it be lodged in the hands of one man, who, from the very circumstance of his being alone, will be more narrowly watched and more readily suspected, and who cannot unite so great a mass of influence as when he is associated with others. The decemvirs of Rome, whose name denotes their number, were more to be dreaded in their usurpation than any ONE of them would have been. No person would think of proposing an executive much more numerous than that body; from six to a dozen have been suggested for the number of the council. The extreme of these numbers is not too great for an easy combination; and from such a combination America would have more to fear than from the ambition of any single individual. A council to a magistrate, who is himself responsible for what he does, are generally nothing better than a clog upon his good intentions, are often the instruments and accomplices of his bad, and are almost always a cloak to his faults.

I forbear to dwell upon the subject of expense; though it be evident that if the council should be numerous enough to answer the principal end aimed at by the institution, the salaries of the members, who must be drawn from their homes to reside at the seat of government, would form an item in the catalogue of public expenditures too serious to be incurred for an object of equivocal utility.

I will only add that, prior to the appearance of the Constitution, I rarely met with an intelligent man from any of the States who did not admit, as the result of experience, that the UNITY of the executive of this State was one of the best of the distinguishing features of our Constitution.

PUBLIUS.

INDEX